BOUNDARIES OF SELF AND REALITY ONLINE

BOUNDARIES OF SELF AND REALITY ONLINE
Implications of Digitally Constructed Realities

Edited by

JAYNE GACKENBACH
Department of Psychology
MacEwan University
Canada

JOHNATHAN BOWN
Edmonton North Primary Care Network
Canada

ACADEMIC PRESS

An imprint of Elsevier
elsevier.com

Notices

Knowledge and best practice in this field are constantly changing. As new research and
experience broaden our understanding, changes in research methods, professional practices,
or medical treatment may become necessary.

Practitioners and researchers must always rely on their own experience and knowledge in
evaluating and using any information, methods, compounds, or experiments described
herein. In using such information or methods they should be mindful of their own safety
and the safety of others, including parties for whom they have a professional responsibility.

To the fullest extent of the law, neither the Publisher nor the authors, contributors, or
editors, assume any liability for any injury and/or damage to persons or property as a
matter of products liability, negligence or otherwise, or from any use or operation of any
methods, products, instructions, or ideas contained in the material herein.

Library of Congress Cataloging-in-Publication Data
A catalog record for this book is available from the Library of Congress

British Library Cataloguing-in-Publication Data
A catalogue record for this book is available from the British Library

ISBN: 978-0-12-804157-4

For information on all Academic Press publications
visit our website at https://www.elsevier.com/books-and-journals

www.elsevier.com • www.bookaid.org

Publisher: Nikki Levy
Acquisition Editor: Emily Ekle
Senior Editorial Project Manager: Barbara Makinster
Production Project Manager: Priya Kumaraguruparan
Designer: Matthew Limbert

CONTENTS

8. The Shadow of Technology: Psyche, Self, and Life Online   **141**
Michael A. Beier

Section B: Simulation or Reality?

9. The Video Gaming Frontier   **161**
Jayne Gackenbach, Dylan Wijeyaratnam and Carson Flockhart

10. The Incarnated Gamer: The Theophoric Quality of Games, Gaming, and Gamers   **187**
Frank G. Bosman

LIST OF CONTRIBUTORS

Thomas H. Apperley
The University of New South Wales, Kensington, NSW, Australia

Michael A. Beier
Psychotherapist in Private Practice, Basalt, CO, United States

Akshya Boopalan
MacEwan University, Edmonton, AB, Canada

Frank G. Bosman
Tilburg University, Tilburg, The Netherlands

Johnathan Bown
Edmonton North Primary Care Network, Edmonton, AB, Canada

Thomas Campbell
University of Virginia, Southeast Region, United States

Wu Chen
Key Laboratory of Adolescent Cyberpsychology and Behavior (CCNU), Ministry of Education, Wuhan, China; School of Psychology, Central China Normal University, Wuhan, China

Justin Clemens
The University of Melbourne, Parkville, VIC, Australia

Denise Doyle
University of Wolverhampton, Wolverhampton, United Kingdom

Carson Flockhart
MacEwan University, Edmonton, AB, Canada

Jayne Gackenbach
MacEwan University, Edmonton, AB, Canada

Mark D. Griffiths
Nottingham Trent University, Nottingham, United Kingdom

Michael R. Heim
Mount Saint Mary's University, Los Angeles, CA, United States

Qing-qi Liu
Key Laboratory of Adolescent Cyberpsychology and Behavior (CCNU), Ministry of Education, Wuhan, China; School of Psychology, Central China Normal University, Wuhan, China

Geng-feng Niu
Key Laboratory of Adolescent Cyberpsychology and Behavior (CCNU), Ministry of Education, Wuhan, China; School of Psychology, Central China Normal University, Wuhan, China

Angelica B. Ortiz de Gortari
University of Liège, Liège, Belgium; University of Bergen, Bergen, Norway; University of Hertfordshire, Hatfield, United Kingdom

J.F. Pagel
University of Colorado School of Medicine, Pueblo, CO, United States

Joan M. Preston
Brock University, St. Catharines, ON, Canada

Tony D. Sampson
University of East London, London, United Kingdom

John Suler
Rider University, Lawrenceville, NJ, United States

Elisa White
MacEwan University, Edmonton, AB, Canada

Dylan Wijeyaratnam
MacEwan University, Edmonton, AB, Canada

Gino Yu
Hong Kong Polytechnic University, Hung Hom, Hong Kong

Zong-kui Zhou
Key Laboratory of Adolescent Cyberpsychology and Behavior (CCNU), Ministry of Education, Wuhan, China; School of Psychology, Central China Normal University, Wuhan, China

AUTHOR BIOGRAPHIES

THOMAS H. APPERLEY

Thomas H. Apperley, PhD, is an ethnographer who specializes in researching digital media technologies. He is currently a Senior Lecturer at the University of New South Wales, Australia. His open-access print-on-demand book, *Gaming Rhythms: Play and Counterplay from the Situated to the Global*, was published by The Institute of Network Cultures in 2010.

MICHAEL A. BEIER

Michael A. Beier, PhD, is a depth-oriented (Jungian) psychotherapist and executive coach in private practice near Aspen, Colorado, with almost 10 years of clinical experience in various areas of mental health counseling. Dr. Beier holds an MA in counseling from Pacifica Graduate Institute, Santa Barbara, CA, US, and a PhD in Jungian Studies from Saybrook University in San Francisco, CA, US, in addition to several European degrees. In addition, Dr. Beier is the co-founder and COO for the London-based non-profit, Centre for Technology Awareness, an organization whose mission is to build awareness about how technology affects our world and how we can use it to shape a better future.

AKSHYA BOOPALAN

Akshya Boopalan is a recently graduated student with a Bachelor's degree majoring in psychology and minoring in anthropology. Her main goal is to continue her education through a master's and PhD so she can continue working directly in the field of psychology. She hopes to incorporate dream research (presence, cognition, self-reflection, types, and themes), as well as cross-cultural psychological research in the counseling area.

FRANK G. BOSMAN

Dr. Frank G. Bosman is a cultural theologian and senior researcher at Tilburg Cobbenhagen Center, Tilburg University, the Netherlands. Bosman is specialized in the field of theological and religious game studies. He is a member of the editorial board of ONLINE, the Heidelberg Journal of Religion on the Internet (Heidelberg University, Germany).

JOHNATHAN BOWN

Johnathan Bown recently finished his M.Ed. in counseling psychology at the University of Lethbridge, Lethbridge, Canada. He has been working with Dr. Gackenbach on various projects over the last 7 years and has coauthored several papers, presentations, and a book chapter. His goal is to pursue his PhD in clinical applications of digital media. He works at Edmonton North Primary Care Network.

THOMAS CAMPBELL

Thomas Campbell, a lifelong professional applied physicist, began a parallel career in the early 1970s, researching altered states of consciousness with Bob Monroe (author of: *Journeys out Of the Body*, *Far Journeys*, and *The Ultimate Journey*) at Monroe Laboratories, where he and a few others were instrumental in getting Monroe's laboratory for the study of consciousness up and running. Campbell continued his research into the nature of consciousness and reality, and in February of 2003, published the My Big TOE trilogy (MBT), which represents the results and conclusions of over 30 years of scientific exploration into the nature of existence. This overarching model of reality, mind, and consciousness explains the paranormal as well as the normal, places spirituality within a scientific context, solves a host of scientific paradoxes, and provides direction for those wishing to personally experience an expanded awareness of All That Is. The MBT reality model explains metaphysics, spirituality, love, and human purpose at the most fundamental level, provides a complete theory of consciousness, and delivers a more advanced physics that derives both relativity and quantum mechanics from first principles, something traditional physics cannot yet do. As a logic-based work of science, My Big TOE has no basis in belief, dogma, or any unusual assumptions.

WU CHEN

Wu Chen is a doctoral student at the School of Psychology, Central China Normal University. Research interests include Internet adolescent cyberpsychology and behavior.

JUSTIN CLEMENS

Justin Clemens is an Associate Professor in the School of Culture and Communication at the University of Melbourne. His recent publications include *Lacan Deleuze Badiou* (Edinburgh UP 2014), with Dr. A.J. Bartlett and Dr. Jon Roffe, and *Psychoanalysis is an Antiphilosophy* (Edinburgh UP, 2013).

DENISE DOYLE

Denise Doyle has a background in fine art painting and digital media. She is an Artist–Researcher, Senior Lecturer in Digital Media at the University of Wolverhampton, UK, and Adjunct Professor in Virtual Worlds and Digital Practice, Ontario College of Art and Design University, Toronto, Canada. Denise has published widely on the subject of the virtual and the imaginary, the experience of the avatar body in virtual worlds and game spaces, and the use of virtual worlds for creative practice. Denise is Editor-in-Chief of the newly launched *Journal of Virtual Creativity* (Intellect, formally *Metaverse Creativity*). She sits on two other editorial boards: *International Journal of Performance Arts and Digital Media* (Routledge) and *Journal of Gaming and Virtual Worlds* (Intellect). She recently edited *New Opportunities for Artistic Practice in Virtual Worlds* (IGI Global, 2015), bringing together artists, practitioners, and theorists to consider the significance of virtual worlds and avatar-based interaction for artistic practice. Her research interests include: virtual worlds, art–science dialogues, interactive film, philosophies of the imagination, practice-based research methods, and digital narratives. She is currently developing a series of projects exploring digital embodiment in art and technology.

CARSON FLOCKHART

Carson Flockhart graduated with a BA in Psychology from MacEwan University in Edmonton Alberta. Currently, he is working in the mental health field as a child and youth care worker, as well as a support worker for adults with mental disabilities. Carson plans to attend a graduate school in Edmonton in either social work or counseling. He has worked in Dr. Gackenbach's laboratory and has several publications and conference presentations about that work.

JAYNE GACKENBACH

Jayne Gackenbach is an Associate Professor of Psychology at MacEwan University, Alberta, Canada, who is in the process of retiring. She is the editor of several books on the psychology of the Internet, including one connecting video game play to consciousness. She has been doing research into the dreams of video game players for about 20 years, with numerous book chapters and publications on the topic.

MARK D. GRIFFITHS

Dr. Mark D. Griffiths is a chartered psychologist and Professor of Behavioural Addiction at the Nottingham Trent University and Director of the International Gaming Research Unit. He has spent almost 30 years in the field and is internationally known for his work in gaming and gambling. He has published over 600 refereed research papers, 5 books, 140+ book chapters, and over 1000 other articles. He has won 16 national and international awards for his work, including the John Rosecrance Prize (1994), Joseph Lister Prize (2004), and the US National Council on Problem Gambling Lifetime Research Award (2013). He also does a lot of freelance journalism and has appeared on over 3000 radio and television programs.

MICHAEL R. HEIM

Michael R. Heim is the author of *Electric Language: A Philosophical Study of Word Processing* (Yale UP, 1987), *The Metaphysics of Virtual Reality* (Oxford UP, 1993), and *Virtual Realism* (Oxford UP, 1998). He currently teaches on the graduate faculty of Mount St. Mary's University in Los Angeles, CA, US. His legacy work can be found at www.mheim.com.

QING-QI LIU

Qing-qi Liu is a doctoral student of School of Psychology, Central China Normal University. Research interests: Internet use and adolescent self-development.

GENG-FENG NIU

Geng-feng Niu is a doctoral student at the School of Psychology, Central China Normal University. Research interests include SNS use, social and personality development.

ANGELICA B. ORTIZ DE GORTARI

Dr. Angelica B. Ortiz de Gortari is a Marie Curie COFUND postdoc research fellow in psychology at the University of Liege, Belgium. Her area of expertise is Game Transfer Phenomenon (GTP), which examines the psychosocial effects of nonvolitional phenomena, such as hearing or seeing video game elements after stopping playing. Her research on GTP has been awarded, and she has published academically and presented at several conferences. Also, her research has been featured in a large variety of media, including the TV series CSI: Cyber. She is interested in maximizing the psychological and social benefits of interactive technologies while reducing the risks it can present to some individuals.

J.F. PAGEL

Dr. J.F. Pagel is an Associate Clinical Professor at the University of Colorado School of Medicine and Director of Rocky Mt. Sleep. He is the coeditor of one of the major sleep medicine texts: *Primary Care Sleep Medicine* (Humana, 2007) (2nd Edition, Springer, 2014). Over the last 35 years, his clinical and research work, primarily focused on the cognitive state of dreaming, has resulted in more than 170 publications. These include work on the effects of dreaming on waking behavior, dreams and disasters, dream and nightmare use in creative process and filmmaking, parasomnias, machine dreaming, narcolepsy, pediatric sleep, and nondreaming, as well as the effects of insomnia, sleep apnea, PTSD, and medications on dreaming and nightmares. His books include: *The Limits of Dream: A Scientific Exploration of the Mind/Brain Interface* (Academic Press, Elsevier, 2007), *Dreaming and Nightmares* (Ed.) (Saunders, 2010), and *Dream Science: Exploring the Forms of Consciousness* (Academic Press, 2014).

JOAN M. PRESTON

Joan M. Preston, PhD, is Emeritus Professor of Psychology at Brock University, Ontario, Canada. She attended the Ontario College of Art and the University of Western Ontario. Her background in art, film, and photography informs her media psychology research, which spans the range of visual media from pictures, TV, film, music videos, and video games to virtual reality. She has contributed several book chapters about the effects of digital media on consciousness.

TONY D. SAMPSON

Tony D. Sampson is Reader in Digital Culture and Communications at the University of East London. He studied computer technology and cultural theory before receiving a PhD in sociology from the University of Essex. His publications include *The Spam Book*, coedited with Jussi Parikka (Hampton Press, 2009), *Virality: Contagion Theory in the Age of Networks* (University of Minnesota Press, 2012), and numerous journal articles and book chapters. Tony's next book, *The Assemblage Brain: Sense Making in Neuroculture* (University of Minnesota Press), will be published early in 2017. He is a co-founder of Club Critical Theory and Director of the EmotionUX Lab at the University of East London. He occasionally blogs at https://viralcontagion.wordpress.com/.

JOHN SULER

John Suler is a clinical psychologist and Professor of Psychology in the Rider University Science and Technology Center, Lawrenceville, NJ, US. His integrative research and publications have explored East/West psychology, the psychology of cyberspace, and photographic psychology. He is Honorary Professor at the Royal College of Surgeons in Ireland, as well as recipient of the Rider University Distinguished Teaching Award and the Indie Next Generation First Novel Award for *Madman: Strange Adventures of a Psychology Intern*. His academic books include *Contemporary Psychoanalysis and Eastern Thought* (SUNY Press), *Psychology of the Digital Age: Humans Become Electric* (Cambridge University Press, 2016), and the coauthored textbook with Richard Zakia, *Perception and Imaging: Photography as a Way of Seeing* (Focal Press, 2017). He authored several online publications, including The Psychology of Cyberspace, Teaching Clinical Psychology, Photographic Psychology, and Zen Stories to Tell Your Neighbors. His work has been cited in the New York Times, The Wall Street Journal, BBC, CNN, MSNBC, NPR, and The Washington Post.

ELISA WHITE

Elisa White has completed her BA at MacEwan University, where she worked with Dr. Gackenbach in an effort to further understand how the virtual world affects dream states and consciousness. She is currently a graduate student at the University of Northern British Columbia, Canada. Elisa intends to pursue a PhD after completing her graduate studies.

DYLAN WIJEYARATNAM

Dylan Wijeyaratnam recently graduated from MacEwan University with an Honors Psychology degree. While there, he completed his honors thesis on the effects of combat and companionship in video game play on subsequent nighttime dreams, which is currently being written up for publication. He plans to complete his MA and PhD in Counseling Psychology, and hopes to work in the field of marriage and family counseling.

GINO YU

Dr. Gino Yu has taught and established multimedia programs and initiatives at institutions including the University of Southern California, the Hong Kong University of Science and Technology, and the Hong Kong Polytechnic University (PolyU). He is currently an Associate Professor and Director of Digital Entertainment and Game Development in the School of Design at PolyU, where he serves as the program leader for the Masters in Multimedia and Entertainment Technology program that he founded. In 2000, he founded the Hong Kong Digital Entertainment Association. He also founded the Asia Consciousness Festival and hosted the 2009 and 2017 edition of the Toward a Science of Consciousness Conference. His main area of research focuses on the application of media technologies to cultivate creativity and promote enlightened consciousness. He has spoken at events including Technology, Entertainment and Design (TED) Talks, the Creative Leadership Summit, the World Knowledge Forum, the International Music Summit, the Cannes Lyon Festival, Burning Man, and Further Future. Dr. Gino Yu received his BS and PhD at the University of California at Berkeley in 1987 and 1993, respectively, and has over 100 conference and journal publications.

ZONG-KUI ZHOU

Dr. Zong-kui Zhou is a professor at the Central China Normal University, where he is Dean of the School of Psychology. He serves as the Director of the Key Laboratory of Adolescent Cyberpsychology and Behavior affiliated with the National Ministry of Education, China. He has collaborated with Dr. Gackenbach on previous research and has spearheaded having her book, *Psychology and the Internet*, translated into Chinese. His research interests are in cyberpsychology and behavior, and social and personality development.

PREFACE

Following the publication of two editions of *Psychology and the Internet*, with the last in 2007, the publisher approached me with a proposition that I do a third edition. I was not interested initially in just rehashing the same material, but my reading, prompted in part by two former students, Johnathan Bown and Sarkis Hakopdjanian, led me to think about a new and more speculative version of that original book. I have always been fascinated by consciousness and especially the impact of technology on our consciousness. I've pursued this inquiry by examining the dreams of video game players over the last decade. But clearly, other provocative ideas about consciousness and technology were afoot. These led me to the conceptual framework of this book, *Boundaries of Self and Reality Online*. I pitched this altered version to Emily Ekle, Senior Acquisitions Editor in Psychology for Elsevier/Academic Press. She liked the idea, and the two former students and I went on to write a full book proposal. It was accepted with some adjustments, and we were off and running. While Mr. Hakopdjanian unfortunately dropped out of the project, Johnathan Bown continued as a co-editor. His help has been instrumental in my being able to pull off such a conceptually forward book, as I am also in the process of retiring. We have created a book which is truly international, with five chapters from the US, two from China, one from Australia, three from the UK, three from Canada, and one from the Netherlands. It is also interdisciplinary, with most chapters coming from a psychological perspective. But there are also three from digital design, one from communication studies, two from humanities, one from medicine, and one from physics.

We would like to thank MacEwan University for providing the infrastructure for us to accomplish this task. I would also like to thank my family and friends for their support. Johnathan Bown would like to give thanks for the enthusiasm and support he received from Dawn and Gilly since the initial proposal for the book project, as well as the abounding encouragement from his parents, Bob and Robin. His family's warmth makes the publication of this book even more meaningful to him. Also, he would like to give thanks to the University of Lethbridge for their outstanding counselor education program, as well as Insight Psychological in Edmonton for being an excellent place to experience applied psychology. We would both like to also give a special thanks to Sarkis Hakopdjanian for his conceptual input into the formation of the book, as well as his insight into challenging ideas and advice on some practical matters around producing a book.

Jayne Gackenbach and Johnathan Bown
Edmonton, Alberta, Canada
September 27, 2016

INTRODUCTION

The evolution of our species seems to be transforming from biological to technological. As we continue to develop interesting and exotic technologies, we are not only influencing society and ourselves, but are also glimpsing into the very nature of reality. While our waking reality influences our lives the most, never before has such a large part of the population been so widely affected by a constructed reality, specifically, our technologically-constructed digital reality. Our interaction with technology is also evolving. We are no longer content to simply observe and respond to technology on a screen in front of us. As a result, we are inventing ways to *enter* technology by creating a virtually simulated environment or a virtual reality (VR). This new VR technology will not only revolutionize the industries of video gaming and entertainment, but also education, healthcare, business, and even society at large. As we are immersing ourselves in, and enjoying, these augmented realities, it is becoming increasingly likely that our mental functions are being altered.

This edited book explores the idea that technological advances are moving us in multiple domains toward various "edges." These edges range from self to society, relationships, and even to the very nature of reality. As more people are spending more time in various forms of digital worlds, this raises concerns about potential addictions, but, more importantly, we are encountering new aspects of self or losing self online, as we increasingly meet and trust strangers with our deepest secrets. We are sometimes more invested in leveling up in an online game than getting to work on time. Our language is now peppered with acronyms drawn from brief digital correspondence, and entirely new languages are evolving. Our sense of community and connection to other is at once deeper and more distant as we experience ourselves flaming a boss in an email or falling in love with a celebrity. Social action and journalism are being redefined with increasing input and participation by anyone with or on a computer. Basically, boundaries are dissolving as we all move ever closer to the edges of self, other, and community. Because of this dance at the edge, we are all redefining self, other, and relationships in a cursory manner and also more deeply and all at once.

At its most theoretical, this edited book explores the idea that technological advances are allowing us to break the frame of multiple realities. This exploration starts at the micro level, with considerations of self online, and moves to a more macro level, with considerations of relationship. Finally, at the ultimate macro level, the new conceptualizations of reality, emerging from digital physics, will be offered. Holistically, we will proceed from the concrete toward the abstract by organizing chapters in the order of: self/ relationship to consciousness/reality.

We humans often refer to ourselves as individuals, but there are at least two inaccuracies in this label. As it turns out, we can be divided further, but, more egregiously, this concept of self automatically leads us to believe that we are somehow separate from the environment around us. Perhaps we feel this way because our sensory perceptions are wired only to the edges of our bodies, or perhaps because it is a simple way to understand our experiences and it works well enough for most purposes. However, philosophers and psychologists (and mathematicians) have argued how the apparent division between self and other is, relatively speaking, an illusion. Consider that in theories of cognitive science, the accumulation of symbols in the mind inevitably leads to self-references, paradoxes that imply that "self" is an independent system existing in or around something else (e.g., the environment). Kurt Gödel proved mathematically that no set can completely define itself, that is, any system of logic (e.g., consciousness) must contain references to itself. To take it one step further, it could mean that a person's ego cannot completely understand itself and cannot exist independently, so far as we conceptualize it. Indeed, the ego is part of the environment, which is part of the whole universe. The boundaries between self and other are perhaps only illusions, and this is the idea at the heart of this book. As technology has aided humans to transcend the limit of their physical bodies, the Internet, digital media, and VR technologies are already chipping away at the illusions of individuality and self.

The following chapters are organized in such a way to draw the reader inward from the surface of this idea toward what the world may look like behind the veils we cast. It begins with a chapter by John Suler, who provides a powerful lens through which to consider cyberspace. As it turns out, cyberspace is a psychological space, and it can be mapped. Suler proposes a theory of cyberpsychology architecture: eight dimensions that shape the total experience of a person online. As the eight dimensions shift from one instance to another, so does reality for the user. The framing of cyberpsychology architecture lays the foundation for a deeper examination of the boundaries, which may or may not exist, between a person and technology-mediated reality.

In the chapters that follow, some offer deeply personal perspectives on the impact the Internet has had on our lives and how we collectively engage in behaviors we perhaps never thought possible, while others provide expert presentations on how some key modern technologies shape our world. This first section of the book presents new ideas about how people develop themselves in a digital environment, and why. What part of the human psyche is driving this development? Is there something more authentic about it? This section is lead by a chapter by Gino Yu, from Hong Kong, exploring how one can learn about self in digitally constructed realms. An exploration of avatars by Tom Apperley and Justin Clemens, communication studies researchers from Australia, reveals that something absolutely profound is occurring as people obfuscate and blur the concept of identity through unhindered and anonymous self-representation. From within a different disciple, design, Denise Doyle of the University of Wolverhampton argues that access to the experience of digitally constructed realities enables people to reflect on how their own private realities are created, which further weakens the division between self and other. Readers will also be introduced to the concept of Game Transfer Phenomena, presented by Angelica Ortiz de Gortari and Mark Griffiths, which is when elements of a video game intrude, unbeckoned, into the daily lives of gamers, an example of reciprocity in the self–other dichotomy (or, in simpler terms, as these writers suggest, a reflection of the unity of self and other). This section ends with a chapter written by Anders Beier, who provides a sobering argument against the overuse of technology. Materialism and addictions can stem from excessive reliance on technology, which ultimately draws out the dark side of human life and prevents self-actualization. This closing chapter gives the reader a somber warning about technology and online realms before we proceed to the second section of the book, an exploration of external and internal realms of consciousness.

The use of connective technologies has spread throughout the world, enhancing interpersonal communication to incredible heights. As more people participate in online communities, the divisions between people break down. Zong-kui Zhou, Geng-feng Niu, and Wu Chen provide an overview of Internet use in China, the largest population of online users. To many westerners, the Chinese Internet may be largely unknown, as it exists behind a national firewall, effectively isolating the population from the rest of the world. However, behind this Great Firewall of China, the Internet thrives. This provides researchers with the unique opportunity to analyze how new software, hardware, and user interactions develop outside the dominating influence of worldwide systems like Facebook and Google. New Chinese research details the statistics and factors of self-development in a digital age. Children, adolescents, and adults are deeply impacted by the Internet, but many intricacies of their experience determine if they will be helped or harmed by it. As places like China have massive numbers of people interacting online, the politics of user experience become a point of critical importance.

In another chapter, Tony Sampson, of the University of East London, introduces this concept in discussion of the self–other topology of the Internet. Drawing on work about power and control over groups of people, Sampson explores how shared online experiences create new commodities to be controlled, and he challenges the conventional, yet problematic, split between the psychological experience of self and the shared social self. Finally, the middle section of the book concludes with a contribution from Jayne Gackenbach, Dylan Wijeyaratnam, and Carson Flockhart of MacEwan University in Canada. These authors present the latest research on the psychological factors related to video game play, as well as some examination of the current state of the industry. They also briefly mention research out of the video game lab at MacEwan University.

The last section of the book delves into more ambiguous topics on or around the nature of reality. However, an understanding of VR technologies must be established first, which is presented by Johnathan Bown, Elisa White, and Akshya Boopalan of MacEwan University. These authors provide an overview of the history and evolution of VR technologies, interpreted through the scope of our quest for the Ultimate Display. Next, Michael Heim of Mount St. Mary's College argues how VR technology can catalyze transcendent experiences through acts of lucid living and immersion. In his chapter, he describes an example of an immersion log and how this can add a spiritual dimension to VR technology.

On the heels of the suggestion that a person can have a spiritual experience from digital media, Joan Preston of Brock University introduces the critically important dimension of videogames: absorption. The chapter examines how transpersonal experiences can occur through the use of digital media, and what factors of games can amplify consciousness. The chapter that follows, by J.F. Pagel of the University of Colorado School of Medicine, shifts the scope on the question of consciousness to encompass the entire Internet. He argues that there is strong evidence to support that the web demonstrates some aspects of consciousness. Interestingly, he argues that the web even has dreams.

The final two chapters of the book explore ideas that transcend individual reality. First, Frank Bosman of the University of the Netherlands presents his concept of the theophoric quality of video games. He argues that the act of playing video games transforms the player into the bearer of the image of God as seen in the Christian tradition. He offers in-depth discussion and analysis of the theophoric quality of four specific video games as examples. The final chapter of the book, by Thomas Campbell, a physicist writing from Virginia, presents a treatise on digital physics, that is, an overarching theory of consciousness of what subsumes physics, metaphysics, philosophy, and theology. This chapter is offered as a necessarily speculative piece, providing an explanation and prescription for the development of consciousness in our digital reality.

Our hope is that readers will enjoy the transition through the chapters of this book, each provided by experts in their own fields, and their imaginations will be moved. Beginning with new research on the impact and influence of digital technologies and moving all the way to presenting how our own reality may be digital, the chapters in this book point to much more going on below the surface of our media. As we build richer worlds and enhance the connectivity of this planet, we are pushing forward the evolution of mankind.

Johnathan Bown and Jayne Gackenbach
Edmonton, Alberta, Canada
September 28, 2016

CHAPTER 1

The Dimensions of Cyberpsychology Architecture

John Suler
Rider University, Lawrenceville, NJ, United States

Cyberspace is psychological space, a projection of the individual and collective human mind, which is why the term "cyberspace" itself is valuable. Both consciously and unconsciously we perceive this realm on the other side of our screen portals as an extension of our psyches, a territory that reflects our personalities, beliefs, and lifestyles. Early psychological studies identified how this online world entails a blurring of the boundary between mind-space and machine-space (Suler, 1996; Turkle, 1995). We experience ourselves as existing within an intermediate zone between self and other. From the perspective of traditional psychological theories, this space can be conceptualized as an intersubjective or interpersonal field (Atwood & Stolorow, 1984; Stern, 2015; Sullivan, 1953), a transitional or transformational space (Bollas, 1986; Winnicott, 1971), a territory that is part me, part other, and that provides a venue for self expression, interpersonal discovery, play, creativity, and, unfortunately, the acting out of psychopathology. In the context of such traditional theories, the digital world is a unique psychological space because it is mediated by computers that provide unprecedented speed in the processing of information, resulting in a wide variety of experiences and levels of interactivity not possible in conventional media. The design of different computer-generated spaces shapes the projected manifestation and interaction of self and other, hence determining the psychological impact of those spaces.

Cyberpsychology is then an inherently interdisciplinary or even transdisciplinary field, combining an appreciation of the technical aspects of online environments with an appreciation of the psyche. This holistic understanding of humans in the digital age can be founded on a theory that elucidates the unique features or "architecture" of each online environment (Suler, 2016). This cyberpsychology architecture consists of eight interlocking

Boundaries of Self and Reality Online
ISBN 978-0-12-804157-4
http://dx.doi.org/10.1016/B978-0-12-804157-4.00001-3

1

dimensions that regulate our experience of different digital spaces. Each dimension reflects computer-generated aspects of how a particular online environment operates, how the human psyche manifests itself there, as well as how the mind itself works. Different environments—such as social media, video-conferencing, games, avatar worlds, and email—combine the eight dimensions with varying emphasis. The essential questions concerning any particular environment are what dimensions it emphasizes, what dimensions it does not, and in what specific ways. The psychological power of the digital world comes from its versatility in developing, combining, and minimizing or maximizing these eight dimensions for outcomes that are practical, creative, and sometimes unpredictable.

THE IDENTITY DIMENSION: WHO AM I?

Identity, the sense of self, constitutes the first dimension of cyberpsychology architecture, just as it has been a fundamental concept in traditional psychological, sociological, and philosophical discourse. From the perspective of cyberpsychology, all of the other dimensions of the architecture are tributaries that feed into identity.

The identity dimension of an online domain is determined by the options it provides people for establishing who they are, what they express about themselves, what they hide, and how they transform themselves—transformations often based on idealized self-concepts, what Walther (1996) called the *hyperpersonal self*. The digital world allows individuals to narrowly or fully depict aspects of their "real" identities from their in-person lifestyles, to establish their online selves de novo as fantasy creations, or to construct something in between as a mixture of a genuine and imagined self. The many different types of online environments can lead to a decentered, dissociated, and multiplied expression of self (Turkle, 1995), while also offering opportunities for discovering previously unconscious aspects of identity, which can lead to a more individuated, cohesive sense of self. The Internet even offers the possibility of negating identity by adopting varying degrees of anonymity and invisibility. The identity dimension includes all the software vehicles for self-presentation provided by a particular online environment, including how people consciously and unconsciously use or avoid them, as well as the healthy or pathological aspects of their identities that manifest in that environment.

Usernames, biography profiles, photographs of oneself, and avatars are all commonly employed tools for establishing identity when people first enter a new online environment. Once they begin participating in it, they must grapple with the different alternatives for defining themselves: communicating via long or short text posts; uploading pictures or video that show how they look, sound, and behave, or that reveal their home, work, and social places; reposting other people's content serves the function of *self-expression by proxy* (Suler, 2016). The social norms of an online community might encourage people to portray themselves in a way that accurately reflects their real-world selves, as in traditional social media like Facebook. The norms might encourage them to adopt imaginary identities, as in games. Or the norms might create an identity dimension that mixes reality and fantasy.

Personal identity becomes compromised when people strive to maintain an ongoing symbiotic connection to others online in order to receive constant acknowledgment of their thoughts and feelings, a need that can inadvertently backfire: by forgetting how to self-reflect while being alone, one loses track of the intrapsychic boundaries that define an individuated, separated identity (Turkle, 2012). A related problem is the tendency for people to allow their self-expression in social media to become dictated by the dependency need for attaining affirmation from their online audience. Social tokens such as "likes" serve as a form of applause that selectively reinforces the expression of identity. People post items about themselves that they think others will reward with a "buttonized" reaction. They become what others seem to want them to be.

The identity dimension includes the intersection between one's online and offline selves, how the two parallel each other, differ from each other, and can be unified if there are discrepancies, as suggested by the integration principle that calls for the carry-over of online behaviors into the offline world, and vice versa (Suler, 2016). It is the balance and combination of online and offline identity that maximizes wellbeing. Understanding the dynamics of this unified, balanced sense of self will be a critical tool in the attempts of cyberpsychologists to address what has become a very problematic byproduct of our technological age: the various types of Internet compulsions, including cybersex, gaming, gambling, day trading, shopping, and social media addiction (Greenfield, 1999; Suler, 1999; Young, 1998). For all the different forms of healthy and pathological expressions of identity in cyberspace, the person–situation interaction of character type with the qualities of the online environment plays an important role. People chose a particular environment according to their personality dynamics, but the environment in turn influences their expression and development of self, often in ways unconscious to the person.

THE SOCIAL DIMENSION: WHO ARE WE?

The social dimension pertains to all interpersonal aspects of cyberspace, including relationships that are one-to-one, one-to-many, many-to-one, strong and intimate, and weak or loose ties. It entails the assessment of how many people a person interacts with, who those people are, the purpose of those social activities, and the interpersonal strategies employed. Any tools an online environment provides its members to locate, gather, and communicate publicly or privately with others are features of its social dimension. Although the social dimension intertwines intimately with the identity dimension due to the synergistic interaction between interpersonal relationships and individual identity, cyberspace does provide options for a robust expression of identity with a minimally developed social dimension, as with people in social media who operate in a performing or "expressive" mode by posting regularly but without responding to others who might react to their posts. By contrast, people who operate in a "receptive" mode view other people's online behavior while participating very little themselves (Suler, 2016).

When online, people can communicate with dozens, hundreds, thousands, and even millions of people from all walks of life. They can juggle many relationships in a short period of time or even at the same time, as in text messaging, without other people necessarily being aware of their social multitasking. By posting to social networks they create their own personal audience consisting of people who share even the most esoteric of interests. Using a search engine they can scan the vast online world to focus their attention onto particular types of people. Over time online environments have become increasingly more powerful in their tools for searching, filtering, and contacting almost any kind of person or group, which is an important feature of their social dimension.

People make conscious decisions in selecting others who share similar interests and backgrounds, or whose personalities are compatible with their own. However, the ability to sift through so many possibilities for developing online contacts also opens the door to unconscious influences stemming from past relationships, such as transference reactions and other parataxic distortions. In addition to conscious preferences, people online act on unconscious expectations and needs when selecting colleagues, friends, lovers, and enemies. As an experienced online user once said to me, "Everywhere I go in cyberspace, I keep running into the same kinds of people!" This unconscious filtering process can be sensitive, powerful, and totally misleading. A common example involves twinship transferences (Kohut, 1977) in which people with shared interests join forces online as they grow convinced of their deeply meaningful bond, only later to witness their relationships dissolve or explode in conflict when they discover their supposed alter-egos have needs that are incompatible with their own. Misunderstandings and conflicts in online relationships and groups, especially when communication entails only typed text, are common due to interpersonal misperceptions arising from transference reactions. When machine intelligence suggests possible contacts to a user based on the user's past choices, an important question is whether these suggestions contribute to an unproductive restriction in the person's interpersonal sphere.

Online romances are a particularly powerful example of how relationships in cyberspace can be enriching or simply turn into an outlet for problematic transference reactions. In online dating sites people often play with love, sexuality, and the presentation of themselves as the quintessential romantic partner (Whitty & Carr, 2006). They might unrealistically glorify themselves or their companions. The degree to which people engage such playing-at-love varies, most likely depending on the person's susceptibility to idealizing and twinship transferences (Kohut, 1977). Understanding how the acceleration and amplification of transference in cyberspace affects communication with lovers, family, friends, colleagues, and strangers is an important tool in assessing the social dimension of a person's online lifestyle.

In this social dimension of cyberpsychology architecture, people who do not establish presence in the environment are as important as the people who do. Self-selected membership and degree of participation will shape the interpersonal culture. People bring their mental sets with them, ways of thinking that are very different from others who cannot enter the environment, have no desire to do so, or who belong but rarely contribute. As long as the digital divide persists, the social dimension of the Internet as a whole will be determined directly by the people who access it, and indirectly by those who do not.

THE INTERACTIVE DIMENSION: HOW DO I DO THIS?

The interactive dimension entails how well people can understand, navigate, control, and modify an online environment. Here enters the discipline of human–computer interaction (HCI), as first described by Card, Moran, and Newell (1983), which involves the design of a computer interface that is more user-friendly because it parallels how humans intuitively perceive, think, and behave. The more readily people can immerse themselves into an online domain, the more quickly it becomes a transitional space, an extension of their minds. The more customizable it is, the more they can express their identity, shape their experiences, and feel emotionally invested and present in that environment. As the interactive power of a device increases, so does its intrapsychic power as a self-object that sustains one's sense of identity (Kohut, 1977). A purely informational website has minimal interactive qualities. Sophisticated avatar worlds possess high interactivity in the many opportunities people have to create visual representations of themselves, to venture into a variety of locations within the world, to construct their own objects and dwellings, and to form relationships with others. A highly interactive environment tends to be more complicated, requiring a steeper learning curve and greater skill, which becomes a challenging task when people undergo *media transitions* (Suler, 2016). For complicated environments, an effective human–computer interface is critical.

No matter how sophisticated electronic tools become, there will always be moments when they fail, when the machine does not work properly, or when noise intrudes into the experience. Under these conditions interactivity declines, often unexpectedly and precipitously. The exasperation, depression, and even primitive rage people experience in reaction to these technical breakdowns points to the psychological power of the machine in gratifying then frustrating the need for control and symbiotic attachment. An unexplained lack of response from the machine—the *black hole experience*—opens the door for projecting anxieties onto the machine or the people with whom one expects to communicate but cannot (Suler, 2016).

The interactive dimension includes not just how users relate to the machine, but also how the machine relates to them, including such factors as how it prompts people with notifications about their online habitats; how it offers suggestions about what they can do based on its ability to recognize their preferences; and how much machine intelligence forces itself on users as opposed to allowing them to decide what level and type of interaction they desire. The interactive power of an environment increases when it steers people toward higher, more enjoyable, and more easily controlled participation, either because it gave them an uncomplicated opportunity to tell it what they like, or due to its ability to effectively but transparently analyze their past behaviors with the best of intentions for their wellbeing.

As the machine becomes more interactive, people tend to anthropomorphize the device by consciously or unconsciously projecting human qualities into it. Advances in artificial intelligence that deliberately attempt to build human qualities into the machine will escalate these tendencies to the point where people cannot always distinguish a computer program from a human, as illustrated by the Turing Test (Turing, 1950). Unconscious reactions to computer-generated beings include the curious phenomenon of the *uncanny valley* (Mori, 2012) in which people feel comfortable anthropomorphizing such beings up to the point where the machine comes very close to appearing human, but not quite, resulting in a precipitous drop in the person's comfort level along with feelings of eeriness, anxiety, and fear. This phenomenon points to the strangely ambiguous differentiation between self and other, as well as to the intangible experience of the unconscious that Freud (1919) noted in his paper about the uncanny aspects of automaton creatures in literature. In addition to presenting challenges in the design of artificially intelligent "beings," the uncanny valley might also affect the interactive dimension of virtual environments with ambient intelligence (e.g., Riva, Loreti, Lunghi, Vatalaro, & Davide, 2003), when users imagine an eerie presence operating behind an environment that feels "alive" in its ability to anticipate and respond to the user.

THE TEXT DIMENSION: WHAT IS THE WORD?

In the early days of cyberspace everyone talked via typed text. Although this changed dramatically with the rise of visual and audio features, text still prevails as one of the most important tools for communicating, as it has throughout modern history. It appears in a variety of long and short forms: websites, blogs, email, social media posts, texting, and short messaging systems. Some researchers refer to it as *text speak* or *computer-mediated communication*, while I prefer the term *text talk* because it implies both an individual's attempt to communicate as well as conversation among people.

Drawing on different cognitive skills than speaking and listening, typing one's thoughts and reading those of another is a unique strategy for expressing one's identity, understanding others, and establishing interpersonal relationships. As an internalized, self-reflective dialogue, writing facilitates insight into oneself, while experiencing another person's text facilitates insights into that person as well as oneself as the reader. The verbal systems of the left cerebral cortex tend to involve thinking that is more conceptual, logical, factual, linear, and consciously controlled. For this reason, "putting it into words" during text talk gives people the opportunity to identify, shape, and master otherwise intangible experiences, a fact that gave rise to writing therapy (Pennebaker, 2004). Individual differences in preference for writing may reflect varying degrees of skill in taming unconscious experience through the power of the word. Some people express themselves better in writing rather than talking, as well as understand others better by reading their text rather than listening to them speak. They enjoy that opportunity for writing as self-reflection, as a way to sort through ideas and emotions, which is one reason why personal blogs became so popular as a modern, much more public version of the traditional diary or journal. Strong advocates of text relationships even claim that it is the most powerful method to intimately merge their minds with their online companions.

Text communication does pose problems, even for people who are skilled at it. Lacking sounds and visuals, it is not a rich sensory encounter. People cannot see others' faces or hear them speak. All the important cues provided by voice, body language, and physical appearance disappear. Without them it is easier to misunderstand the other person, which amplifies interpersonal misperceptions and transference. For some people, the lack of physical presence generated by voice and appearance reduces the sense of intimacy, trust, and commitment in the relationship. Typed text can feel formal, distant, unemotional, and lacking an empathic tone. Without a sensory connection one can never be absolutely certain about the other's identity. This absence of face-to-face cues, which adds a small dose of anonymity and invisibility, encourages other people to regress or act out inappropriately in what has been called *the online disinhibition effect* (Suler, 2004). Even though some people respond to the lack of face-to-face cues in text communication as an opportunity to be intimately expressive, which can be the benign version of the disinhibition effect, that expressiveness sometimes progresses too quickly into self-disclosures that one later regrets or that causes the online companion discomfort.

As social media blossomed, text talk began to dwindle in length, frequency, and richness. People relied more on sharing photographs as a means to communicate. When photo-sharing became ubiquitous via mobile devices, as in the very popular Instagram, text talk fell to the bare minimum. Pictures did most of the talking. The designers of social media offered smaller, harder to access boxes for typing, with fewer tools for formatting text. The domination of text by photos does speak to the power of images, but as a double-edged sword it also contributes to the superficial quality of social media when people do not talk in depth with each other. Although photographs can be powerful condensations of meaning, the development of relationships in cyberspace requires verbal, usually text, communication.

THE SENSORY DIMENSION: HOW AM I AWARE?

The sensory dimension of an online environment entails how much it activates the five senses: hearing, seeing, feeling, smelling, and tasting. The appearance of multimedia gaming and social environments, video conferencing, podcasting, and Internet-mediated phone calls lifted online activities into a more heightened sensory experience than text alone, which dominated cyberspace in its beginnings. Researchers pioneering the development of virtual realities attempt to invent environments that come as close as possible in mimicking the complex sensory experiences of the physical world. Although great progress has been made in the realms of seeing, hearing, and even the transmission of tactile sensations using haptic technology, the senses of smelling, tasting, and feeling with the whole body stand as significant, if not impossible, barriers to cross in the attempt to fabricate robust, integrated sensory experiences in cyberspace. The Matrix, the Star Trek holodeck, or similarly sophisticated virtual environments are still science fiction.

When interacting with other people, the multiple sensory cues of visual appearance, voice dynamics, bodily contact, and in very intimate situations, smell and taste, provide a bountiful encounter with a person, with different cues affirming, supplementing, and at times contradicting each other, as when a person's body language does not match what that person says. In many scenarios, such full sensory experiences generate a heightened sense of presence, stimulate more emotions, enhance the impact of self-objects, and encourage a stronger psychological commitment to the situation. A rich sensory environment provides more immediate clarity about where you are, who you are, what you are doing, and what specific meanings you find in that situation, as compared to the usually more ambiguous text environment. It tends to magnify presence, immersion, and the elusive but powerful sense of truly "being here." Research on the virtual pit, in which subjects attempt to cross a plank stretched across a deep hole, demonstrates how relatively simple sensory situations can trick the instinctual areas of the brain into perceiving danger even when the rational mind knows better (Blascovich & Bailenson, 2012).

The power to generate a specific experience through complex sensory stimulation might prove to be a drawback when the goal is to encourage a subjective interpretation of a scenario, when the expectation is that people will participate in the creation of the experience by projecting meaning into it, rather than having it provided to them in a prepackaged sensory form. As a reader might about a book without illustrations, "I'm glad there were no pictures. I wanted to see the story for myself."

Even if virtual realities containing complex stimulation are someday possible, we should not overlook the usefulness of cyberspace for isolating, eliminating, and combining the five senses in unique ways for the purpose of better understanding sensation, perception, and such cognitive phenomena as repression, dissociation, sensory deprivation, and sensory overstimulation. Research can examine the psychological aspects of a particular sensory modality isolated from other modalities, as well as unique combinations of the senses. Such research might lead to methods of enhancing particular pathways of perception, or for insights into novel and useful integrations of different senses.

Given their proliferation in cyberspace, images play an especially powerful role in the sensory dimension. Online photo-sharing in particular has become an important feature of social media. Images enable the communication of experiences that are not easily captured by words, or that might be distorted by conscious attempts to verbalize them. As vehicles of primary process thinking, they contain modes of experience—often personal, symbolic, and driven by fantasy—that reveal the unconscious mind. Like dreams, they can be highly creative constructions that condense a wide range of emotions, memories, needs, and wishes, making them an effective method for depicting one's identity. A photograph or any visual creation serves as a concrete external representation of what people are, want to be, or fear. The explosion in the popularity of "selfies" points to this psychological power of the image as a tool for visual rather than simply verbal self-expression—a power evident in the person's ability to create an idealized version of the self, in the enhanced sense of presence generated by the visual self, and in the visual expression of unconscious aspects of identity, such as in body language. To understand how personal photographs might promote psychological growth, as opposed to simply reinforcing shallow narcissism, we can draw on insights into the transformative role of images in psychotherapy, therapeutic photography, and phototherapy (Suler, 1989; Weiser, 1993).

THE TEMPORAL DIMENSION: WHAT TIME IS IT?

The use and experience of time in cyberspace constitutes its temporal dimension. Often it differs significantly from in-person encounters. Each environment tends to have its own particular brand of temporality, which is determined by the technical design of its communication channels as well as the social norms for their use. The many possibilities for altering the experience of time in cyberspace reflect how the mind interprets temporality. Even though rational conscious thinking entertains a fixed forward march of seconds, the unconscious blends past, present, and future, suspends time, and even transcends it. Elements of the temporal dimension include synchronous versus asynchronous communication, the acceleration of time, frozen time, ephemeral time, and the intersection of cyberspace time into real-world time.

The distinction between synchronous and asynchronous encounters plays an important role in the temporal dimension. The "live" synergy of synchronous communication tends to encourage spontaneity, resulting in more uncensored, ad hoc, quickly paced, and revealing dialogues. By contrast, people tend to be more careful about what they say to each other during asynchronous exchanges, with the interaction feeling composed or even studied. Presence tends to be enhanced during synchronous meetings, in part due to the increased feeling of spontaneity that imitates in-person situations, but also because people sense their mutual coexistence in the moment. The absence of temporal cues in asynchronous communication can prove to be a disadvantage because pauses in the conversation, coming late to a meeting, and no-shows often convey important psychological meanings. On the other hand, asynchronous dialogues have the advantage of slowing down or even freezing the pace of interaction, which provides the convenience of replying whenever one wants, along with a zone for reflection in which people can contemplate, carefully construct, and appropriately censor what they say. It is important to remember that a strict dichotomy does not exist between synchronous and asynchronous communication, but rather a continuum where the sense of mutual presence in the moment can become a subjective and at times uncertain feeling, as during texting when people are not sure another person is continuously "with" them in the same temporal space because the pause before that person replies feels too long.

Time in cyberspace can feel accelerated, in part due to the fact that online environments and their populations change more quickly than in the physical world. Because cyberspace greatly facilitates communication, it can also speed up the cycle of social processes, including the forming and dissolving of work relationships, friendships, romances, and social or political movements. During addictive, highly immersive, and what Voiskounsky (2008) described as *flow* activities, time seems to move so quickly that it feels transcended. Experiences in cyberspace can also be suspended in time, remaining exactly as they are, similar to memories in the unconscious. In environments mediated by recorded video or animation, events can be paused for as long as desired, while almost everything one does online can be preserved. Whenever people want, they can go back to re-examine those events from the past.

Some forms of social media grew in popularity because they blocked the ability to freeze time by deliberately making communication ephemeral, as exemplified in the phone application Snapchat. By enabling the transmission of text and images to someone that lasted on the screen for only a few seconds, the application became the perfect tool for playful communication in the fleeting moment. It was popular for surreptitious flirting and sexual teasing. Such environments illustrate how exaggerating one dimension of cyberpsychology architecture, in this case the temporal dimension, can dramatically shape the psychological impact of the experience.

Cyberspace time intersects the real time of our everyday schedules. People vary in when they go online: morning, afternoon, or night. They vary in how often they go online: a few times a day, every hour, every few minutes, or almost continuously all day long. They vary in the amount of time they spend in the digital world. The temporal dimension of cyberspace architecture entails when these moments of online time cross over into the flow of everyday living, as well as how that crossover affects the experience of time in both realms.

THE REALITY DIMENSION: IS THIS FOR REAL?

We define reality according to what we consensually experience throughout our lives in the physical world, which some online environments attempt to recreate. A video closely resembles the visual qualities of an actual situation, while a voice transmission sounds like how that person actually talks. As long as text communications seem to be based on reason and rationality, we accept them as valid references to reality. Other online environments intentionally generate much more imaginary scenarios, deviating either slightly or dramatically from the world as we know it. It does not matter whether the environment is created in a virtual reality filled with rich state-of-the-art sensory stimulation, or simply via plain text. Flights of fantasy can be as elaborate in text role-playing games as they are in highly imaginative avatar worlds replete with sights, sounds, and kinesthetic action.

When assessing the reality dimension of an online environment, we ask how much it creates experiences based on fantasy and how much it is grounded in the everyday world. Many games in cyberspace inspire make-believe, while social media usually encourage people to represent themselves as they actually are, without deception. Other environments, such as traditional chat rooms, can be more ambiguous. With no visual references or rules specifically steering people toward reality or fantasy, the location becomes what people make of it. In fact, social norms can modify the reality dimension intentionally built into an environment, as evident by how some people in social media do alter their identity, while people playing online fantasy games try to become acquainted with the players behind the imaginary characters. In all contemporary media, the distinction between reality and fantasy has progressively blurred, as evident in "reality shows" and supposedly real-life videos on YouTube that actually turned out to be contrived in some way. The proliferation of transference reactions in cyberspace also points to this infusion of fantasy into perception. Depending on their developmental history of object relations, their capacity for reality testing, and the qualities of the environment, some people online fare much better than others in distinguishing what is real and what is not. Some researchers might argue that self-delusion exists to a certain extent for everyone online, in part due to the strong social norms in social media to "brand" oneself rather than be oneself.

The potentially creative blurring of reality into fantasy arises from unconscious mental functions, especially the illogical, symbolic, personal, imagistic, loose, and emotional thinking of primary process (Suler, 1980). The intrapsychic world operates along a polarity between reality and fantasy, between primary process and the more reality-oriented, practical thinking of secondary process. We need grounding in the familiar, in what we have always known to be real—and yet, seemingly by its intrinsic nature, the human mind also seeks out imaginative states of perception and self-expression. As evident in dreams, we need these experimentations at the border between reality and fantasy, between reason and instinct, in order to express unconscious forces while also discovering adaptive opportunities for psychological development. Cyberspace as a dream world provides a realm for these experimentations.

In addition to clarifying the powerful impact of the sensory dimension, research on the virtual pit demonstrates how the instinctual human mind cannot tell the difference between reality and virtual reality even when the rational mind knows better. When asked to cross the plank stretched across a deep and dark hole, some subjects freeze with paralyzing anxiety. The researchers chose well when using the virtual pit as their paradigm. The fear of heights is inborn for many species. In the case of humans, it is also a powerful symbol of the unknown, the helpless fall into sin, and the dark regions of the unconscious. Online and offline, reality is determined not just by our rational perceptions of the everyday world, but also by archetypal patterns and unconscious ideation. As Morpheus said in the movie *The Matrix*, "your mind makes it real"—an idea that the reality dimension of cyberpsychology architecture invites us to explore.

THE PHYSICAL DIMENSION: HOW IS THIS TANGIBLE?

The physical dimension of an online environment entails its impact on the physical world and body, including physical sensations and movement, or the lack thereof. In the early days of the Internet, people sat motionless at their computers while venturing around the online world. Cyberspace was disembodied space. Physical posture and movements served little purpose within this space other than keeping one's attention focused on the screen. One of the biggest errors in the cultural preoccupation with computerized devices is the belief that we can use them for hours on end without their having a detrimental physical effect. At this point in the history of technology it comes as no surprise that our devices lead to health problems, such as excessive sedentariness, computer vision syndrome, and repetitive stress disorders.

The dissociation of the mind-in-cyberspace from the corporeal body can be conceptualized as a type of mind/body duality, a dichotomy that plays out in the many science fiction tales of a human's consciousness being uploaded into cyberspace, as well as among computer scientists who believe that the human mind can be recreated via artificial intelligence. Here evolutionary psychology must intervene with the reminder that humans are intrinsically embodied beings, that mental and physical experiences are two sides of the same coin, inseparably intertwined. Even when we sit passively in our chairs as we pursue a wide variety of online adventures, the psychological energies of those adventures still register in the body.

The physical dimension of cyberpsychology architecture draws a distinction between the dissociated and integrated physicality of online environments (Suler, 2016). The dissociated type, which includes bodily activity that has very little to do with the online activity, can pose significant problems, as evident when people attempt to cross the street while staring into their phones. Physics tells us that two objects cannot occupy the same space at the same time. Now cyberpsychology shows us how one mind cannot occupy a physical and online space simultaneously, at least not effectively or safely, despite the claims of those who strongly advocate for the power of multitasking. Although dissociated physicality poses problems, this aspect of cyberpsychological experience does provide the opportunity to study ruptures between mind and body, as in dissociative disorders.

In integrated physicality, one's bodily movements and sensations are more connected to the activity in cyberspace. Examples of integrated physicality include games of sport that involve the mimicry of real-world movements; walking around an environment to take photos that are then uploaded; haptic technology that creates tactile stimulation via cyberspace; and any virtual reality scenario that changes in response to head and body motion. In all these cases, physical movements and kinesthetic sensations become an integral part of the online experience, rather than being mostly irrelevant to it.

The physical dimension also entails the psychological impact of how portals into cyberspace appear in the physical world and become part of our physical bodies. While using mobile devices people move through different environments as they interact online. Even if they are not reporting on the changes in their physical locations to their cyberspace companions, the characteristics of their surroundings consciously or unconsciously affect how they are communicating. Texting while in bed or on a crowded subway are different situations. As suggested by the concept of the *Internet of things*, all types of appliances, machinery, cameras, and sensors have become arms of cyberspace that extend into the physical world. At this stage in the evolution of the Internet, we are just beginning to understand what might be called environmental cyberpsychology: the study of how behavior, cognition, and emotion are influenced by physical spaces overtly or covertly infused with cyberspace devices that transmit to and from the environment. With the introduction of mobile devices and wearable computers that people carry with them all day long, humans have taken one step closer to being cyborgs who are part body, part machine, part corporeal individual, part symbiotically merged with cyberspace consciousness.

APPLYING THE DIMENSIONS IN THE ASSESSMENT OF AN INDIVIDUAL

The dimensions of cyberpsychology architecture serve as a useful model in comprehensively assessing an individual's digital lifestyle, analyzing the psychological impact of different digital environments, and exploring critical concepts in research. These applications reveal the distinct but intertwining aspects of the dimensions.

When examining a person's digital lifestyle, the identity dimension lies at the core of the assessment with all the other dimensions converging on it. Key questions revolve around what they reveal and hide about themselves in their different online environments; how they might create idealized versions of themselves; and how they present themselves online as compared to in-person. Some questions might lead into anxiety-provoking areas, such as inquiring about when someone chooses to be anonymous or invisible, and if the person does things online that he or she does not typically do in the "real" world. Unconscious expressions of identity might be inferred from online behavior as revealed in the assessment of the other seven dimensions.

Because perceptions of self and other affect each other, the social dimension interacts synergistically with the identity dimension. Assessment inquiries would reflect this fact, such as why individuals choose to communicate with some people or participate in some groups, but not others; what roles they play and what statuses they have in these online relationships and groups; and how these relationships and groups affect them. A person might have difficulty verbalizing answers to some questions, such as during inquiries about susceptibilities to misperceiving others online. However, most people can report at least one or two examples of how they failed to accurately interpret someone's emotions or intentions, possibly resulting in interpersonal conflicts that provide a glimpse into unconscious interpersonal distortions.

An assessment of the interactive dimension reveals the effectiveness of the interface design, but more importantly the psychology of the individual. Understanding the person's technical skills and knowledge according to HCI research will help clarify the person's behavior in this dimension, especially cognitive abilities. Other assessment questions provide insight into personality style, including how people customize their devices and react to the challenge of mastering new environments; how much they feel they control their devices and how much their devices seem to control them; and how they react when their applications are not doing what they want. Replies to such inquiries might indicate how a person tends to anthropomorphize the machine, which indicates transference tendencies.

Questions about the text and sensory dimensions can be integrated with each other. The assessment would focus on the types of text communication a person likes or dislikes, including preferences for long and/or short forms.

Here an assessment of reading and writing skills, along with the person's attitudes about these activities, will help clarify behavior in the text dimension. Such inquiries can be juxtaposed with assessments of sensory stimulation, such as how a person reacts to visuals, sounds, and physical/tactile sensations created by devices; when the person prefers to eliminate sensory stimulation, as in deciding to text rather than talk on the phone, talk rather than use video communication, or use video rather than meet in-person; and how the person pays attention to the visual formatting of text, including creative keyboarding techniques and visual supplements to text, such as emojis. Borrowing techniques from phototherapy (Weiser, 1993), one might inquire about the kinds of images the individual likes as an indication of lifestyle and personality, especially the photos and "selfies" typically uploaded by the person. In assessing the text and sensory dimension of the individual's online experience, the difference in cognitive style between people who rely primarily on language (verbalizers) and those who prefer images (visualizers) might be relevant (Richardson, 1969).

For the temporal dimension, inquire about the person's preferences for synchronous versus asynchronous communication, which indicate such traits as spontaneity versus self-control. To pinpoint the kinds of digital experiences that activate intrapsychic hotspots, ask about when time seems to go fast, especially activities that result in "flow." Concerning the person's attempt to freeze or transcend time, inquire into why he or she deliberately saves some content accessed from cyberspace, but not others. Asking about when during the day, how often, and for how long the person enters the digital realm will clarify the temporal intertwining of in-person and online living, as well as addictive tendencies.

Assessing the person's reaction to the reality dimension is particularly helpful in understanding their predilection for practical, rational thinking and/or flights of fantasy. Inquire into how people react to places that are imaginary versus realistic, in addition to how they distinguish fact from fiction while online. Such assessments reveal a person's abilities for reality testing, creativity, and imagination, with preferences for certain types of fantasies indicating unconscious dynamics the person might not be able to verbalize.

Finally, for the physical dimension, the assessment focuses on the interaction between cyberspace and the physicality of the person's body and environment, including occurrences of dissociated and integrated physicality, medical problems stemming from device use, where and how the person uses mobile technology, how the person employs the Internet in navigating and interpreting the environment, and how portals to and from cyberspace affect the person's habitats, other people who are present there, and the person.

In my course on cyberpsychology, students undertake an exercise in which they use the eight dimensions to assess their digital lifestyles. One consistent outcome of this activity is their discovering how big an impact cyberspace has on their lives—"more than I even realized," as one student commented. The assessment process helps elevate subconscious experience to conscious awareness. This finding was particularly true concerning the identity and physical dimensions. Students had not fully comprehended the ways in which they construct their online identity or how that identity differs from who they are in the real world. Nor did they understand how chronic device use has detrimental effects on their physical health, or the fact that their phones allow them to be tracked in the physical world.

APPLYING THE DIMENSIONS IN THE ANALYSIS OF AN ONLINE ENVIRONMENT

As an example of applying the model in an analysis of an online environment, consider the phone application Yik Yak. At first glance it seems like a traditional chat room that relies primarily on the text rather than sensory dimension for communication, which leads to the unique psychological atmosphere created by text talk, such as the social ambiguity of missing face-to-face cues, the potential for self-reflective expression, and a tendency toward transference reactions along with the online disinhibition effect. In the sensory dimension, users do employ emojis, but they rarely take advantage of the feature for sharing photos. Similar to the social dimension of other online environments, users can rate each other's posts with "up" and "down" votes, which tends to increase the pressure in such buttonized cultures to construct a persona that will increase one's social status, as indicated in Yik Yak by one's overall "Yakarma" rating.

Unlike most chat rooms, instant messaging systems, and discussion boards that have a similar cyberpsychology architecture, Yik Yak only allows users to communicate with people within a few mile radius, a unique design feature in the physical dimension of its architecture. Invented by two college students, the application was intended for students to talk to each other within the vicinity of the campus, which is why the application was quickly adopted by students around the world, filling the void created by Facebook when it no longer catered just to college students. In the social dimension, students once again had their own territory to cultivate according to their needs in their particular geographical and cultural environment, without the distraction of parents and relatives who had moved into Facebook. Yik Yak did include the ability to "peek" into discussions at other locations, but not the ability to participate. Later, Yik Yak modified its interactive dimension by adding the "my herd" feature that allowed students to continue communicating even when they were not on campus, a change that also affected its temporal dimension by improving the continuity of the group over time, particularly during the summer, visits home, and other off-campus activities. Young people in towns, cities, high school, and middle school also use Yik Yak, but mostly college students consider it their domain. The very distinct physical and social dimensions of campus life fortify the cyberpsychology architecture of Yik Yak as a collegiate experience. The fact that the interactive dimension of the application involved a clean, simple, and easy-to-use interface also made it a popular substitute for the increasingly complex environment of Facebook.

The effects of the unique manipulation of the physical dimension in Yik Yak reverberate throughout its cyberpsychology architecture. In the social dimension, discussions revolve almost entirely around campus events and the concerns of college-age students, with a culture clash sometimes developing between the college group and any high school students from the nearby community who enter the conversation. In the reality dimension, flights of fantasy are rare or grounded in the facts of everyday life on campus. In the temporal dimension, many conversations pertain to events at the college that day or at that moment, including pressing situations such as warning each other that dorm residents are making their rounds. This tendency toward communicating recent news is encouraged by the fact that only posts within the past hour or so are visible in the public discussion. The temporal preservation of the culture via recorded interactions is therefore minimal.

The most intriguing implications of physical proximity in Yik Yak are in its identity and social dimensions. Many people do not create a username, which adds to the invisibility and anonymity of text communication that fuels the hostility of toxic disinhibition as well as the intimate self-disclosures of benign disinhibition. Common posts include sexual humor, emotional confessions about love relationships, and heartfelt sympathy or advice, along with offensively critical, lewd, and hostile comments, which all combined leads to a starkly contrasted emotional climate. Although such phenomena due to the invisibility of identity occur in other forms of text-driven social media, the Yik Yak experience is infused with the knowledge that everyone in the conversation is a fellow student, within walking distance, perhaps in the room down the hall or at the other table in the library. As a result, the identity dimension becomes an arena for speculating about who others might be, a guessing game that encourages playful fun, frustrating teases, or paranoid anxiety. A nearby secret admirer might flatter the person who is adored, but posting a vitriolic ad hominem attack about loud music in another dorm room can make the music listener speculate with anger about the identity of the irate Yakker. In some middle and high schools, Yik Yak was banned using geofencing technology because cyberbullying turned pernicious when victims knew that the unknown aggressor was nearby and aware of one's actions. The reason why Yakkers rarely take advantage of the sensory dimension option to post photos might be due to the fact that a photo could easily "blow one's cover."

APPLYING THE DIMENSIONS TO EXPLORE RESEARCH CONCEPTS

As an example of how the architecture model can be applied in research, consider the fundamental concept of "presence" in an online environment. A series of valuable exploratory questions emerge from the model, revealing the psychological complexity of presence when examined from the different perspectives of the eight dimensions. In the identity dimension, we would need to inquire about how revealing, hiding, and transforming various characteristics of the user affects that person's psychological experience of "being here" as well as "being here with others." If we speculate that even a simple blinking cursor in a purely text environment is an elemental form of presence, as some theorists do, we might then also speculate that living in an elaborate virtual world with an avatar closely resembling one's psychological self would be a very sophisticated and enhanced form of presence. In the social dimension, we would explore the factors that make other people feel present to the user, including the number of people, the kinds of people, the types of social activities, the culture, the qualities of the environment, and the propensity for transference reactions and other interpersonal distortions that complicate social perceptions.

When considering the interactive dimension, a critical issue is preventing the interface from disrupting the sense of "being here." Software tools that are difficult to master draw attention to themselves rather than to the experience of the digital environment, which is why Steve Jobs always encouraged his Apple designers to simplify, simplify, simplify.

In the sensory dimension we would ask what combinations of visual, auditory, tactile, and olfactory stimulation enhance the type of presence necessary for a particular objective, as well as when reduced sensory stimulation is needed to allow users to project their own unique sense of presence into a digital experience, similar to the person who might say, "I'm glad this book had no pictures because I wanted to see the story for myself." In the text dimension, there will be wide individual differences in reading and writing abilities that determine how well the written word serves as a vehicle for feeling and expressing presence in a digital environment. Long versus short forms, the lack of face-to-face social cues, and the tendency toward transference and online disinhibition are other features of the sensory dimension that will influence presence. Generally speaking, more information and more correctly perceived information about a person's identity make that person more present as a unique individual.

A series of interesting issues emerge concerning the role of the temporal dimension in creating presence. Synchronous communication can enhance the feeling of "being with" others because people share the same real-time spontaneous space. So too the zone for reflecting and composing in asynchronous communication might enhance the feeling of presence by enabling people to better understand and express themselves. Change often adds to the sense of presence, because the actual world is always changing, but if online environments change too quickly over time, that temporal acceleration might facilitate or diminish presence. By contrast, freezing time might create an unnatural state of suspended presence or allow for a close contemplation of experience that enriches it. We might wonder what factors contribute to or detract from "flow" in cyberspace, when people experience a transcending of time because they are intensely immersed in an activity. Researchers might also investigate how the intersection of digital time with real-world time affects presence—for example, the effect of circadian rhythms on presence in digital realms, or how often during the day people immerse themselves into an environment and for how long.

In the reality dimension we might safely assume an environment that realistically mimics the physical world would enhance the sensation of actually being in that place. We also should not overlook how imaginative novelty piques attention, curiosity, the urge to explore, and hence feeling present. Unusual environments that arouse unconscious fantasies and archetypal experiences do generate emotional reactions, even in defiance of realistic thinking, as subjects standing above the virtual pit demonstrate. If the mind intrinsically needs dream states to maintain its healthy functioning, then dream-like virtual environments might engender an important and unique type of presence, not unlike lucid dreaming.

Finally, in the physical dimension we arrive at the intriguing, perhaps paradoxical conclusion that integrated physicality facilitates presence via kinesthetic engagement, while intense dissociated physicality indicates magnified presence, as when people passively sit transfixed at their computers because they are so immersed in their online experience. This begs the question as to when physicality is needed for presence and when the mind alone suffices, a debate related to the distinction between body-immersion and brain-stimulated virtual realities (Suler, 2016). The presence of cyberspace portals that transmit data to and from the physical world around us during our everyday activities leads us to another important issue. When is augmented reality a valuable type of presence—an intertwined, enhanced existence between cyberspace and physical space that enriches awareness in both realms—and when does the switching back-and-forth multitasking of attention between these spaces simply detract from the feeling of fully "being here" in either of them? Such a divided presence could very well turn into a jack-of-all-trades mode of being, but a master of none.

REFERENCES

Atwood, G. E., & Stolorow, R. D. (1984). *Structures of subjectivity: Explorations in psychoanalytic phenomenology*. London: Routledge.

Blascovich, J., & Bailenson, J. (2012). *Infinite reality: The hidden blueprint of our virtual lives*. New York: William Morrow.

Bollas, C. (1986). The transformational object. In G. Kohon (Ed.), *The British school of psychoanalysis: The independent tradition* (pp. 83–100). New Haven: Yale University Press.

Card, S., Moran, T. P., & Newell, A. (1983). *The psychology of human computer interaction*. Mahwah, NJ: Lawrence Erlbaum Associates.

Freud, S. (1919). The uncanny. In J. Strachey (Ed. & Trans.), *The standard edition of the complete psychological works of Sigmund Freud* (Vol. 17, pp. 219–256). London: Hogarth Press.

Greenfield, D. (1999). *Virtual addiction: Help for Netheads, Cyberfreaks, and those who love them*. Oakland, CA: New Harbinger Publications.

Kohut, H. (1977). *The restoration of the self*. Madison, CT: International Universities Press.

Mori, M. (June 2012). The uncanny valley. *IEEE Robotics and Informatics*, (2).

Pennebaker, J. W. (2004). *Writing to heal: A guided journal for recovering from trauma and emotional upheaval*. Oakland, CA: New Harbinger.

Richardson, A. (1969). *Mental imagery*. London, UK: Springer.

Riva, G., Loreti, P., Lunghi, M., Vatalaro, F., & Davide, F. (2003). Presence 2010: The emergence of ambient intelligence. *Emerging Communication*, 5(1), 59–84.

Stern, D. (2015). *Relational freedom: Emergent properties of the interpersonal field*. London: Routledge.

Suler, J. (1980). Primary process thinking and creativity. *Psychological Bulletin*, 88, 144–165.

Suler, J. (1989). Mental imagery in psychoanalytic treatment. *Psychoanalytic Psychology*, 6, 343–366.

Suler, J. (1996). *The psychology of cyberspace*. Retrieved from truecenterpublishing.com/psycyber/psycyber.html.

Suler, J. (1999). To get what you need: Healthy and pathological internet use. *CyberPsychology and Behavior, 2*, 385–394.

Suler, J. (2004). The online disinhibition effect. *CyberPsychology and Behavior, 7*, 321–326.

Suler, J. (2016). *Psychology of the digital age: Humans become electric*. New York: Cambridge University Press.

Sullivan, H. S. (1953). *The interpersonal theory of psychiatry*. New York: Norton.

Turing, A. (1950). Computing machinery and intelligence. *Mind, 59*, 433–460.

Turkle, S. (1995). *Life on the screen: Identity in the age of the internet*. Cambridge, MA: The MIT Press.

Turkle, S. (2012). *Alone together: Why we expect more from technology and less from each other*. New York: Basic Books.

Voiskounsky, A. (2008). Flow experience in cyberspace: Current studies and perspectives. In A. Barak (Ed.), *Psychological aspects of cyberspace: Theory, research, applications* (pp. 70–101). New York, NY: Cambridge University Press.

Walther, J. B. (1996). Computer-mediated communication: Impersonal, interpersonal, and hyperpersonal interaction. *Communication Research, 23*, 3–43.

Weiser, J. (1993). *Phototherapy techniques*. San Francisco, CA: Jossey-Bass.

Whitty, M., & Carr, A. (2006). *Cyberspace romance: The psychology of online relationships*. Hampshire, England: Palgrave Macmillan.

Winnicott, D. (1971). *Playing and reality*. New York: Penguin.

Young, K. (1998). *Caught in the net*. New York: Wiley.

SECTION A

Self Online

CHAPTER 2

Understanding the Self Through the Use of Digitally Constructed Realities

Gino Yu

Hong Kong Polytechnic University, Hung Hom, Hong Kong

Today's advancements in computer performance enable artificial intelligence that exceeds the cognitive abilities of most humans (Ferrucci et al., 2013; Silver et al., 2016). These recent feats have rekindled discussions of computer-based human–like intelligence first proposed by Alan Turing (1950), the notion of artificial consciousness (Buttazzo, 2001) and the possibility of "uploading" one's mind to a computer substrate (Kurtzweil, 2000). Developing computing systems that are capable of interactions that are indistinguishable from humans requires defining compatible models of self and reality. However, how does one model and objectively quantify a "self" or "personality"?

American philosopher and psychologist William James tackled this question in his theory of self (James, 1910, 1950). In his theory, the self can be viewed as the subject of thought (i.e., the "I" or "pure ego" that is outside of and underlies every mode of experience) or as an object of thought (i.e., the empirical "me"). As an object of thought, the self is further decomposed to the "material self" (e.g., the body, possessions, etc.), the "social self" (e.g., personas), and the "spiritual self" (e.g., personality, character, values, etc.). This chapter focuses on the "spiritual self" and "social self" from the perspective of behavior (Schneider & Morris, 1987) and its relationship to the "material self," specifically the development of the body through the process of experience. Although one's underlying motivations for an action are unique and ultimately unknowable, the mechanisms of action are physiologically based and, hence, objectively measurable. Correlating psychologically motivated intentions with objectively measurable physiological processes allows researchers, such as behavioral biologists, to develop a testable philosophy of mind.

Boundaries of Self and Reality Online
ISBN 978-0-12-804157-4
http://dx.doi.org/10.1016/B978-0-12-804157-4.00002-5

Interactive digital media experiences provide a unique interface between the realm of the biologically based processes of psychology and the silicon-based processes of today's computing machines. Computers create experiences that engage a user's psychology and motivate a response. With today's latest virtual reality technologies, it is now possible for designers to create real-world situations in a digital environment and trigger behavioral responses that mirror their real-world responses. In fact, the application of virtual reality exposure therapies has been shown to be effective in the treatment of anxiety and specific phobias (Botella et al., 2004). These therapies work because the virtual reality presentation provides perceptual cues similar to the real-world experiences that trigger the physiological stress response. Sufferers learn to overcome their anxiety and phobia by carefully designing the virtual experience, varying the severity of the stimuli, and entraining interventions to reduce sympathetic nervous system activation.

While these forms of virtual reality therapy are based upon activating subconscious physiological responses, these same mechanisms are involved in conscious responses where decisions are made based upon symbolic interpretation. Video games engage players and evoke emotional responses by manipulating symbols. Unlike passive media, video games give the player a sense of agency. In a video game, the decisions made by the player will impact their game character (i.e., avatar). The degree of engagement, emotional response, and conscious decisions is based upon their interpretation of the symbols and context within the virtual experience. Thus, the conscious decisions made by a player in a video game environment provide an encapsulated representation of their "self."

In order to develop a theoretical framework for understanding behavior it is important to first establish some foundational assumptions. These assumptions bound the scope of the framework and provide a contextualization for designing experiments and interpreting results. The foundational assumptions are as follows:

1. *There is a physiological basis for consciousness that is embodied*—While it is widely agreed that consciousness has a physical basis, science has not yet been able to explain why and how it so arises (Chalmers, 1995). We do not yet know how our memories are stored or recollected, though there is evidence that the hippocampus is involved in the process (Eichenbaum & Cohen, 1993). The premise of this foundational assumption is that although we do not know how a person's experience of the moment, beliefs, and processes for thinking are implemented, the perceptions,

encodings, and processes are ultimately physiologically based. Our phenomenological experience of the moment is directly related to the biochemistry and neural activity of the brain. As evidence for this, psychedelic drugs such as lysergic acid diethylamide (LSD) and N,N-dimethyltryptamine (DMT) alter cognition and perception (Fadiman et al., 2003).

2. *Focus on symbolic representation*—To developmental psychology pioneer Jean Piaget, one of the most important accomplishments for an infant to attain is the understanding that objects continue to exist even when they cannot be observed (Piaget, 1954). From Piaget's work, object permanence develops during the "sensorimotor" stage of development by the age of two, although subsequent research indicates the development as early as 3 months (Baillargeon, 1987). It is from object permanence that babies begin to develop cognitive models of the world (i.e., schemata) first from objects and then from symbols (Wadsworth, 2004). Digitally constructed realities are inherently symbolic and experiences are presented as symbols and symbolic relationships.

3. *Interactive experience*—Digitally constructed realities may be passive (e.g., animation) or interactive (e.g., video game). Because the focus of our framework is toward developing a behavior-based understanding of self, the digital experience must be interactive. An intentional response that can be quantified is necessary to measure behavior. For example, interactive role-playing games in which the player is represented by an avatar provide a sense of agency in the digital environment. Their interactions in the game provide a signature that encapsulates their interpretation of the experience.

4. *No action (or stillness) as baseline*—In designing digital interactive experiences, no action (or user input) correlates to stillness. The premise is that any action by the user is directly based upon their subjective interpretation of the symbols and relationships presented by the experience. Hence any action represents a conceptually motivated intention. Although in some interactive situations, a user may intend no action, such intentions are indistinguishable from the baseline. Hence, no action = no intention.

A model that represents a user's engagement of interactive digital experiences will be developed from these foundational assumptions. The model will help designers create experiences that shed insight into an understanding of how experiences motivate behavior to reveal the nature of self.

EMERGENCE OF A SELF FROM PRESYMBOLIC CONSCIOUSNESS

All animals, from single-cell protozoa to the blue whale, must respond and adapt to the environment that they live in. Behavior, either innate (e.g., the sucking display when a newborn baby is presented with a nipple or nipple-like surface near their mouth) or learned, alters the relationship between an organism and its adaptation to the environment. Innate behaviors are deter-mined by the "hard wiring" of the nervous system and the biochemical processes encoded in the genetics. The leading theory from an evolutionary biology perspective is that our "physiologically programmed" innate instincts evolved to nurture growth (e.g., sucking) or keep us physically safe (e.g., hand grasping).

In Piaget's model for human development (Piaget, 1954), infants are not born with the ability to represent information or reason. New exter-nal stimuli and sensations from internal processes influence the equilib-rium between the physiology and its surroundings. New knowledge is acquired by actively exploring the environment to interpret the world and their relationship with it. In Piaget terms, new schema build upon and supplant the innate schemata that we are born with. Learned behav-iors are adapted to maintain homeostasis within the physiology to sup-port metabolic processes and to maintain equilibrium with the immediate environment. External stimuli alter behavior patterns as demonstrated by early experiments in classical (e.g., Watson & Rayner, 1920) and operant conditioning (e.g., Skinner). Conditioning uses the mechanisms underly-ing instincts for physical safety (fear) and nurturing growth (desire) that, in simple terms, trigger the activation of the sympathetic nervous system (fear) and the regulation of neurotransmitters such as dopamine and serotonin (desire).

At some point after conception or during the sensorimotor stage of development, the embryo or baby develops a sense of a self that is separate from its environment (Rochat, Broesch, & Jayne, 2012). Before this event, with limited perception and motor skills, they were simply aware of experi-ence (i.e., awareness) and the actions driven by the genetically programmed innate behaviors and biochemistry of the mother (Fig. 2.1). After this event the embryo or baby develops a sense of agency and a sense of a separate self (i.e., self-awareness). Symbolic knowledge and a mental worldview (i.e., the collective sum of all schemata) emerges from this sense of a separate self that consciously acts on its surroundings. As one develops a symbolic worldview,

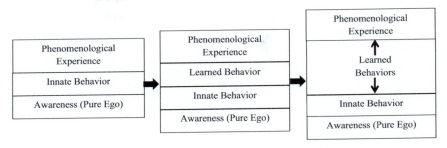

Figure 2.1 Development of learned behaviors from experiences in awareness.

factors that drive behavior become less about responding to the immediate physical surroundings (innate behaviors), and more about expanding their worldview and learned behaviors.

SYMBOLIC CONSCIOUSNESS AND THE BODY

Testing and exploring the boundaries of a mental worldview leads to new experiences and its expansion. Each new experience serves to expand and refine one's conceptual worldview. From Piaget's schemata model, this is driven by a process of adaptation to the world and happens through assimilation, accommodation, and equilibration and forms the basis of constructivism (Wadsworth, 2004). Actions and their intentions are motivated by physiological processes of emotional projections (such as joy, fear, need, and desire for example) that are triggered by the phenomenological experience of the moment processed by the cognitive framing (i.e., context and narrative). The underlying neurological structure of the brain is altered as behaviors and their expected outcomes are reinforced with repetition. Thus, experiences at earlier stages of development influence subsequent development and behavior. Attachment theory is based upon the idea that the quality of one's earliest relationship (with the primary caretaker) influences social development and subsequent relationships (Prior & Glaser, 2006).

Although we still do not know the underlying physiological mechanisms of memory or mental activity, it is experience that binds symbolic knowledge in the mental realm to the embodied somatic processes. Since symbolic knowledge is coupled to physiological processes, recalling the symbolic knowledge will trigger a corresponding physiologically based emotional response. For example, thinking about a stressful situation may activate the sympathetic nervous system. Since each person has a unique genetic composition and developmental history of experiences, that binding is unique to each person.

Paul Rozin theorizes that feelings such as "disgust" arise from the born response associated with the taste of bad things that, from an evolutionary perspective, evolved to prevent the body from ingesting harmful or poisonous substances (Rozin & Haidt, 2013). Feelings toward objects are an extension of the emotions that have evolved from the innate behaviors that keep the organism safe and healthy. In this way, learned knowledge in the symbolic realm uses the same underlying physiological mechanisms that evolved to keep us physically safe. Antonio Damasio in his work also argues that even rational decisions have an emotional (and hence, physiological) basis and underpinning (Damasio, 2008).

Perceiving the external world through phenomenological experience, emotions and feelings are triggered and intentions are developed and acted upon through the physiology in engagement with the external world (Fig. 2.2).

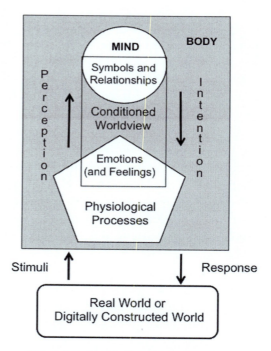

Figure 2.2 A unified model for experience.

The perceived consequences of these actions serve to refine and expand one's learned behaviors and worldview. At the level of symbolic cognition, whether this external world is the "real world" or a "digitally constructed world," the underlying mechanisms are similar.

SYMBOLS AND PSYCHE

Carl Jung developed a theory of the psyche and the relationship between the conscious and the unconscious mind linked by symbolic archetypes (Jung et al., 1964). Archetypes are components of the "collective unconscious" that serve to organize, direct, and inform thought and behavior. Mythologist Joseph Campbell extended Jung's work this by directly relating the conscious to the unconscious (Fig. 2.3). The conscious mind ("ego") comes to understand the nature of the unconscious (i.e., anima, animus, self, shadow) by way of projection to objects and symbols in the material world (Campbell, 1972).

Campbell's projection of unconscious processes onto the objects and symbols of the material world is consistent with the "binding" of physiological processes of the body (the unconscious) with the symbolic representations accessible to the conscious mind (ego) by experience. Past experiences encoded in the physiological processes of the body implement the unconscious processes that motivate behavior. The "forces" driving conscious action and behavior are the physiological mechanisms underlying emotion.

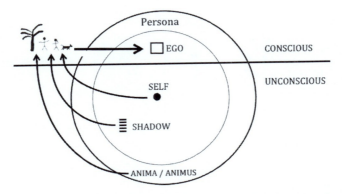

Figure 2.3 Jung/Campbell model of the psyche (Campbell, 1996).

USER ACTION IN A DIGITALLY CONSTRUCTED REALITY

In a digitally constructed reality, engagement is mediated between a user and a program though a digital interface. The presentation of a digitally constructed reality is delivered through an interface (i.e., primarily visual, auditory, and haptic). The engagement is through the presentation and manipulation of symbols. Computer algorithms define the mechanics including the presentation, relationships, scope of behaviors, and narrative of the reality. The situations and context change based upon the user's response.

Users' responses in a digitally constructed reality are based upon their interpretation of the symbolic relationships presented, their perceived role within the reality and their conditioned behavior (Fig. 2.4). Symbols in themselves are inert. It is the emotions that one projects upon the symbols that constitute meaning. And the meanings that one places upon symbols are a result of their prior experiences and associations with the symbol and the related thoughts and ideas that are triggered by the symbol and the context in which they are presented. These relationships and behaviors are somehow encoded within one's physiology as a "binding" between the conceptual knowledge in the mind and underlying physiological processes that encode that knowledge.

The presentation of experience in a digitally constructed reality may simulate and mirror aspects of the real world, or may be complete abstractions. The user will have some role to play within the projected symbolic environment. Their intentions are typically expressed through a haptic device such as a joystick or touch screen. Mediated through a

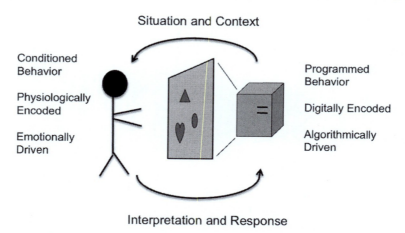

Figure 2.4 Relationship between player and computer in a computer-mediated experience.

digitally symbolic realm, there are no physical stimuli. The response of a user to a digitally constructed reality is entirely driven by their subjective interpretation of the symbolic experience. The baseline is the underlying awareness and innate behaviors that keep us physically safe at birth (e.g., how would a newborn baby that lacks symbolic consciousness respond to this experience?). Thus, the actions that they take represent the knowledge that is physiologically encoded in their being, their learned behavior. A user's behavior is thus quantified by their actions as defined by their responses to the situations and contexts delivered through the interface.

A "sense of self" is projected into the digitally constructed reality (often times in the form of an avatar). The symbolic presentation and relationships (i.e., stimulus) engage cognition and evoke a response. Every user action represents an intention. The psychophysiological mechanisms that trigger the emotional response (e.g., autonomic nervous system, dopamine release, etc.) are similar to those that motivate intention in the real world. They are also similar to those that underlie media, language, and even the placebo effect. Somehow the thoughts and stories of the mind are able to regulate the physiological processes underlying affect, for without an emotion, there is no intention, no action. Video games are known to cause frustration, amusement, surprise, and other emotions (Frome, 2007).

Further evidence that digitally constructed realities share the same underlying physiological processes that drive our daily life is in their ability to entrance users into a state of "flow" (Ben Cowley et al., 2008; Csikszentmihalyi, 1990). Four aspects of this transported state include the lost sense of bodily awareness, lost awareness of the environment, suspension of reality testing, and experience of real emotions in relation to character and story (Holland, 2009).

MODELING BEHAVIOR FROM USER ACTION

A person's history of learning is embodied in automatic and habitual behaviors, which are more predictive of behavior than conscious, seemingly rational analysis. Much of a person's behaviors throughout the day are driven by an implicit cognition that occurs without conscious awareness (Bargh & Chartrand, 1999). Engagement within digitally constructed realities more closely matches real-world engagement and provides a more accurate measure of behavior in comparison with questionnaires that engage the language faculties and deliberation.

A user's cognitive, affective, and behavioral patterns may be identified and classified by analysis of their inputs to a video game (Bakkes et al., 2012; Charles et al., 2004; Lankveld et al., 2011; Spronck et al., 2012; Yannakakis et al., 2013). Current approaches use existing commercial games supported by observational studies, real-time biometric data (e.g., affect response), and surveys. There have been many attempts to represent player personality and motivations based upon playing style (Stewart, 2012). The objective of this work is to provide game designers with a better understanding of their audience in order to create more compelling experiences. Real-time in-game profiling enables games to customize the experience to individual players (Houlette, 2003).

Our interest is in understanding the self through the use of digitally constructed realities. The user interface (i.e., inputs and outputs) provides an objective and quantified representation of user behavior (i.e., stimuli and response). Can analysis of the stimuli and response lead to a better understanding of self?

The use of digitally constructed realities provides an ideal platform for testing and validating conceptual theories proposed in psychology and personal development. By carefully designing immersive experiences that directly engage the user, digitally constructed realities may be used to help the conscious mind better understand the physiologically encoded responses that motivate behavior.

The Jung/Campbell theory provides designers of digitally constructed realities with insight into the construction of meaningful experiences. The design of symbols should conform to the "volkergedanken" or "folk ideas" of the culture (Bastian, 1860) and also imbue archetypal characteristics. It is only when the archetypes of the experience connect with the unconscious of the player that deep engagement happens. Joseph Campbell defines a symbol as an energy-evoking and –directing agent that functions on three simultaneous levels, the corporeal of waking consciousness, the spiritual of dream, and the ineffable of the absolute unknowable (Campbell, 2002). Utilizing the archetypal symbols of the collective unconscious, understanding of self transcends the personal behaviors of corporeal waking consciousness to the spiritual realm of dream and the ineffable of the absolute unknowable.

CHARACTER STRUCTURE

Wilhelm Reich developed a theory of five key types of individual personality groups that arise as a result of perceived trauma during different stages of early childhood development, from pregnancy until 5 years of age (Reich, 1933). Perceived trauma induces prolonged activation of the autonomic nervous system. The coping strategies become learned behavior patterns that influence neurological development of the brain and physiological development of the body. The body shape, function of the organs, and muscle development are all affected by suppressed feelings. Thus, each of the five key types (i.e., schizoid, oral, masochist, psychopath, rigid) correlates body structure to a personality with specific emotional and mental defenses. As the child develops into adulthood, these defense strategies are applied in times of stress.

Reich's theory of development is consistent with the formulation of our framework that learned behaviors are a consequence of adapting to our environment. The description of each character type and coping strategy is well defined and testable with digitally constructed realities by crafting experiences that evoke a stress response and offer a variety of coping strategies. The behavior in the digitally constructed reality should mirror real-world behavior.

IDENTIFYING LEVEL OF DEVELOPMENT

Inspired by the works of Jean Piaget and Abraham Maslow (Maslow, 1943), Clare Graves developed the Emergent Cyclic Levels of Existence Theory (Graves, 1970). The premise is that as a person's worldview continues to develop with new experiences, their motivation system, nature of existence, and problems of existence change. His approach combines four different disciplines of biology (neuroscience), psychology (personality), sociology (anthropology), and systems theory. The theory lays out a series of eight "levels" that correspond to behavioral states; each outlines a specific worldview with corresponding motivations, ethics and values, learning system, and belief system. The theory, with its clearly defined stages, provides a model for classifying the development stage of a person based upon how they frame and engage in an experience.

Although no custom experience has been developed to conduct an assessment based upon this theory, analysis of in-game player data has demonstrated a correlation between in-game behavior with a commercial massively multiplayer online game and real-life behavior as modeled by Clare Graves' Emergent Cyclic Levels of Existence Theory (Wang & Yu, 2016).

CONCLUSIONS

At some point after your conception, a "self" emerged the moment that you became aware that you are independent of your direct experience. All of the experiences that you have had, from that moment to this moment of your reading this sentence, shape your understanding of this writing. These experiences are encoded in your physiology and form the basis of your attitudes and behaviors. Your perception of these symbols in relation to your conditioning influences your physiology to regulate your feelings about what you've read. New thoughts and ideas may emerge, triggered by memories and implications.

Technology has advanced considerably since the advent of print media. Digitally constructed realities also communicate symbolically but offer a much richer medium of expression to create more visceral experiences. Their interactive and immersive nature supplants one's perception of the physical world. Engagement represents the interplay between the physiologically encoded worldview of the user and the algorithmically encoded reality of the designer mediated through the digital interface. Observing the user's responses to stimuli reveals qualities of their worldview. The developmental psychology theories and theoretical models of the psyche form the basis for design and analysis.

It is our hope that interdisciplinary teams of game designers, psychologists, and biologists will apply our proposed framework to create digitally constructed realities that provide users with experiences that promote greater self knowledge (Yu, Martin, & Chai, 2012).

REFERENCES

Baillargeon, R. (1987). Object permanence in 3½-and 4½-Month-old infants. *Developmental Psychology, 23*(5), 655.
Bakkes, S., et al. (2012). Player behavioural modelling for video games. *Entertainment Computing, 3*(3), 71–79.
Bargh, J. A., & Chartrand, T. L. (1999). The unbearable automaticity of being. *American Psychologist, 54*, 462–479.
Bastian, A. P. W. (1860). *Der Mensch in der Geschichte (Man in history)*. Berlin, Germany: University of Berlin.
Ben Cowley, B., et al. (2008). Toward an understanding of flow in video games. *Computers in Entertainment, 6*(2), 20:1–20:27.
Botella, C., et al. (2004). Virtual reality and psychotherapy. *Studies in Health Technology and Informatics, 99*, 37–54.
Buttazzo, G. (2001). Artificial consciousness: Utopia or real-possibility? *IEEE Computer, 34*(7), 24–30.
Campbell, J. (1972). *Myths to live by*. New York: Penguin Books.
Campbell, J. (1996). *Mythos I: Psyche and symbols*. Joseph Campbell Foundation.
Campbell, J. (2002). *Flight of the wild gander: The symbol without meaning*. California: New World Library.
Chalmers, D. (1995). Facing up to the problem of consciousness. *Journal of Consciousness Studies, 2*(3), 200–219.
Charles, D., et al. (2004). Dynamic player modelling: A framework for player-centric digital games. In *Proceedings of the International Conference on computer games: Artificial intelligence, design and education*.

Csikszentmihalyi, M. (1990). *Flow: The psychology of optimal experience* (1st ed.). New York: Harper & Row.

Damasio, A. (2008). *Descartes' error: Emotion, reason and the human brain*. London: Vintage Digital.

Eichenbaum, H., & Cohen, N. J. (1993). *Memory, amnesia, and the hippocampal system*. Cambridge, MA: MIT Press.

Fadiman, J., Grob, C., Bravo, G., Agar, A., & Walsh, R. (2003). Psychedelic research revisited. *The Journal of Transpersonal Psychology, 35*(2), 111–125.

Ferrucci, D., et al. (2013). Watson: Beyond Jeopardy!. *Artificial Intelligence, 199*, 93–105.

Frome, J. (2007). Eight ways videogames generate emotion. In *Presented at the DiGRA*. Retrieved from http://homes.lmc.gatech.edu/~cpearce3/DiGRA07/Proceedings/111.pdf.

Graves, C. (1970). Levels of existence: An open system theory of values. *Journal of Humanistic Psychology, 10*(2), 131–155 Fall, 1970.

Holland, N. (2009). *Literature and the brain*. Gainesville, FL: The PsyArt Foundation.

Houlette, R. (2003). Player modelling for adaptive games. In *AI game programming wisdom II* (pp. 557–566). Hingham, MA: Charles River Media.

James, W. (1910). *Psychology: Briefer course*. New York: Henry Holt.

James, W. (1950). *The principles of psychology* (Vol. 4). New York: Dover.

Jung, C., et al. (1964). *Man and his symbols*. London: Aldus Books.

Kurzweil, R. (2000). Live forever–uploading the human brain... closer than you think. *Psychology Today*.

Lankveld, G. v, et al. (2011). Games as personality profiling tools. In *2011 IEEE Conference on computational intelligence in games, International Conference (CIG'11)*.

Maslow, A. H. (1943). A theory of human motivation. *Psychological Review, 50*(4), 370–396.

Piaget, J. (1954). *The construction of reality in the child*. New York: Basic Books.

Prior, V., & Glaser, D. (2006). *Understanding attachment and attachment disorders: Theory, evidence and practice*. London, UK & Philadelphia, USA: Jessica Kingsley Publishers.

Reich, W. (1933). *Character-analysis*. New York: Orgone Institute Press.

Rochat, P., Broesch, T., & Jayne, K. (2012). Social awareness and early self-recognition. *Consciousness and Cognition, 21*(3), 1491–1497.

Rozin, P., & Haidt, J. (2013). The domains of disgust and their origins: Contrasting biological and cultural evolutionary accounts. *Trends in Cognitive Science, 17*, 367–368.

Schneider, S., & Morris, E. (1987). A history of the term radical behaviorism: From Watson to skinner. *The Behavior Analyst, 10*(1), 36.

Silver, D., et al. (2016). Mastering the game of go with deep neural networks and tree search. *Nature, 529*(7587), 484–489.

Spronck, P., Balemans, I., & van Lankveld, G. (2012). Player profiling with fallout 3. In *Artificial intelligence and interactive digital entertainment Conference*.

Stewart, B. (2012). *Personality and playstyles: A unified model*. Gamasutra.

Turing, A. (1950). Computing machinery and intelligence. *Mind, 59*(236), 433–460.

Wadsworth, B. J. (2004). *Piaget's theory of cognitive and affective development* (5th ed.). New York: Longman.

Wang, C., & Yu, G. (2016). The value system characteristics of Chinese online game players. *Entertainment Computing, 17*, 1–8.

Watson, J. B., & Rayner, R. (1920). Conditioned emotional reactions. *Journal of Experimental Psychology, 3*, 1–14.

Yannakakis, G. N., et al. (2013). Player modeling. In *Dagstuhl seminar on artificial and computational intelligence in games*.

Yu, G., Martin, J. A., & Chai, P. (2012). Shifting world-view using video game technologies. In J. Gakenbach (Ed.), *Video game play and consciousness*. Nova Science Publishers.

CHAPTER 3

Flipping Out: Avatars and Identity

Thomas H. Apperley[1], Justin Clemens[2]
[1]The University of New South Wales, Kensington, NSW, Australia; [2]The University of Melbourne, Parkville, VIC, Australia

In July 2016, the world was suddenly abuzz with news of *Pokémon GO*. It seemed almost impossible to find anything in social media news feeds that wasn't directly related to the Android/iPhone app. Real life was the same; everywhere, there were people wandering through schools, parks, and public spaces, caught up in the capture of virtual menageries. From Tokyo to Tacoma, there was a palpable transformation in the behavior in vast numbers of otherwise totally unrelated peoples, who, armed with mobile phones, swept through such spaces, scoping and swiping as they went. Everywhere, stories of assaults, thefts, and accidents assailed us from social media, as the Pokémon swarm stormed through the world, following the virtual summonses issuing from millions of tiny screens. Whatever one's opinion of the game, its players, and its consequences, there seems no question that *Pokémon GO* constitutes an event in the transformation of both publics and public spaces by video games.

Pokémon GO is the latest project by Niantic Labs, a company that emerged from the aftermath of the 2015 reorganization of Google. Niantic has a track record of making games and apps for mobile devices, which are based on real-world maps. The precursor game by Niantic, *Ingress* (2013), had involved crowdsourcing a gigantic database of playable locations that eventually became the database on which *Pokémon GO* operates today. If *Pokémon GO* is merely the most recent and most successful augmented reality game that has been developed so far, it expressly builds on hardware and software networks that have been in development for some time.

What is particularly notable for our discussion here is the central role that the avatar has in the smooth operation of *Pokémon GO* and how a particular deployment of the avatar concept facilitates this mass shift in behavior. While *Pokémon GO* is indeed just one augmented reality game among others in a genre that has a long history (Moore, 2015a,b), *Pokémon GO* focuses on the avatar as the mediating device between real and virtual

Boundaries of Self and Reality Online
ISBN 978-0-12-804157-4
http://dx.doi.org/10.1016/B978-0-12-804157-4.00003-7

41

spaces. Traditionally, augmented reality games seek to blend the digital world with the material, using real-world environments as a part of the backdrop for digital gaming. In *Pokémon GO*, by contrast, the avatar itself becomes the key element through which this interplay is organized and experienced. In doing so, it also transforms the status of established realities by inducing its private users to remake public spaces according to the contingent exigencies of a video game globally connected in real time.

Like all apps, the first step is the download. When the app is opened for the first time, it invites the player to customize a manga-esque avatar by choosing a gender, hairstyle, and the color of the avatar's pants, shoes, jacket, hat, and backpack. Only once these decisions are made can play begin, whereupon the avatar appears on a location-based map, which has richly detailed roads and streets, but lacks buildings. These have been replaced by "PokéStops" and "Gyms." The newly created avatar sits at the center of the map, marking the player's own location in the detailed network of roads and pathways displayed on the screen. The game then delivers the instruction to "walk to move your avatar," which is elaborated in the Niantic support website:

> To move your avatar on the map, you need to change your location by walking in the real world. Your avatar represents your location, and as you move, you'll see your location move on your screen. Once you start moving in the real world, you'll be able to find Pokémon, PokéStops, and Gyms.
>
> **Niantic Labs (2016).**

Let us underline the astonishing reversal that these instructions at once presuppose and effect. The avatar is no longer simply an index for locating us in virtual space, but has become the technology that organizes our relationship between spaces, which are simultaneously "real" and "virtual." It is crucial to emphasize that this new use extends traditional understandings of what an avatar is and does. An avatar is usually understood as the graphical representation of the real user in a virtual space, if for some scholars the avatar concept also extends to describing the user's alter ego or character in the sense of how someone may self-represent online may be different from their "actual" selves (Coleman, 2011; Miller, 2011). Graphic or visual avatars may take either a 3-D form, as in digital games like *Assassin's Creed*, virtual worlds like *Second Life*, or a 2-D form as an icon in Internet forums and other online communities. One such example is the social media platform Twitter, where the picture that appears beside a tweet is called the user's "avatar."

Simply put, avatars are now almost everywhere, not least because in this time of ubiquitous computing, pervasive media, and the so-called "Internet of things," an unprecedented amount of everyday life is now spent connecting with computers and smart phones. This means that the impact of technology on every level of existence goes far beyond any one individual's experience and, for that matter, powers of analysis.

As the German media philosopher Gernot Böhme notes: "Technology has become a sort of infrastructure of human life itself, a medium of human life. What it is to travel in our contemporary lifeworld, what communication is, what work is, what perception is, can no longer be determined independently of technical structures" (Böhme, 2012, p. 18). One of the primary consequences of such a development is that what we could broadly denominate the phenomenological domain, that is, any individual's experiences of the world, from perception to psychology and beyond, now becomes misleading and incomprehensible without an attention to the *imperceptible* restructuring of the conditions of life itself by technics. Along these lines, Böhme speaks of "invasive technification," thereby emphasizing the disruptive violence of contemporary globally integrated technological civilization into the daily lives of individuals, cultures, and societies.

For his part, the French thinker Bernard Stiegler speaks of "technologies of the spirit" under "hyperindustrial capitalism," whereby:

> *By taking control of processes of adoption at all levels, and, in the first place, at the levels of the primary and secondary processes of identification that constitute psychic individuals, hyperindustrial capitalism brings about the destruction of processes of individuation at both the psychic, as well as collective levels. Through the employment of contemporary forms of hypomnémata, which, as information and communication technologies, are technologies of control, and not of individuation, service capitalism generalizes a process of proletarianization in which the producers have lost their savoir-faire to the same extent that consumers have lost their savoir-vivire.*
> **Stiegler (2014, pp. 33–34).**

As Stiegler further suggests, "the stakes" for our new era of technology therefore "concern the constitution of a new milieu of psychic and collective individuation." Insofar as contemporary technologies "change the *telos*, that is, the rule of ends," they accordingly "require a new libidinal economy" (Stiegler, 2009, p. 35). For Stiegler, the technologies of our time are, without any real countervailing intervention from established political systems, and often with their covert imprimatur, directing asocial processes of dissociation (including desocialization, de-symbolization, and desublimation), in turn inspiring what are essentially plagues of anxiety, depression, and other affective disorders.

Whatever one makes of such analyses and rhetoric, it is noteworthy how little the accounts make of the key role that avatars play in this radical extension or expansion of technical operations into the everyday. To take a handful of immediate instances of this phenomenon, neither Böhme nor Stiegler note the various and intense modalities under which avatars operate, thereby de facto taking for granted the dissemination and uptake of the new technologies. Significantly, and whatever the general pertinence of his claims, Stiegler himself lays aside the question of the avatar in favor of a catalog of technical developments including WiFi and Bluetooth systems, and a phenomenological description of, inter alia, mobile telephony. To give a single further example: in a series of recent interviews with some of the most influential discussants of contemporary technology, including Johanna Drucker, Ulrik Ekman, N. Katherine Hayles, Stiegler, and others, there is not a single mention of the role played by avatars (Simanowski, 2016). Yet it would prima facie seem that, whatever we would want to say about the incontrovertible determining centrality of communications technology in everyday life, something like the avatar—for almost all users, the first and most effective point of contact with the new technologies—would have to be at stake. Both hardware and software designers are well aware that the success or failure of applications, platforms, devices, and techniques are significantly determined by the appeal and ease of use of the interface.

In such a context, the avatar serves a range of indispensable multiple functions: it is a vector of the user's agency within a particular platform, an in-world representative of the user that facilitates access and action between on- and offline spaces, and a mode of identification. This means that the avatar is not just an interface in a neutral or descriptive sense, but a crucial modality of human integration into the nonhuman circuitry of new technology. As such, the avatar directly addresses what the Italian philosopher Paulo Virno calls "human generic characteristics," that is, a certain underdetermination by nature, which requires supplementation by technical and cultural inventions, and is coterminous with the essentially sign-oriented environments that humans build. For Virno, one of the consequences of the current situation is that "today's industry — based on neoteny, the language faculty, potentiality — is the externalized, empirical, pragmatic image of the human psyche, of its invariant and metahistorical characteristics. Today's industry therefore constitutes the only dependable textbook for the philosophy of mind" (Virno, 2009, p. 145). What we wish to do here, then, is to examine how avatars are at once designed to exploit human biological underdetermination for hyperspecialized tasks (e.g., the "swipe" touch screen, the new relation between the opposable thumb and perception enabled by games consoles, etc.) while also forcing a constant turnover of skills and ongoing reeducation for each individual. What "identity" is, in the sense of a sense of self, a project or a community, necessarily becomes more obscure and abstract in the age of avatars.

As we have already noted, the current ubiquity, the "pervasiveness" of networked digital media, including mobile phones, tablets, and laptop computers, among much else, entails a concomitant proliferation and dispersion of avatars of all kinds. Now if many of the more "culturalist" commentators seem to avoid any dedicated discussion of the role of the avatar, it is nonetheless the case that while many aspects of the avatar have received intensive attention from the technology industries and new media scholars, the focus of the work to date has tended to be on the technical efficiency of the interface, rather than understanding the full social implications of its use.

Scholarship in game studies has often approached the avatar in this technical sense, regarding it as a device that allows the player to act in and upon the game world. For example, the avatar is discussed as a "cursor" that marks the location of the player in virtual space (Fuller & Jenkins, 1995, pp. 57–72) and as a vehicle for moving through virtual space (Newman, 2002). Other work seeks to balance the technical understanding of the avatar with a more sociocultural analysis of the way that the avatar is represented, both in terms of character (Frow, 2012, pp. 360–80) and in relation to the depiction of race and gender (Fordyce, Neale, & Apperley, 2016; Shaw, 2015). Certainly, the avatar concept is used in many different types of digital games from mobile apps like *Pokémon GO* to big-budget blockbusters like *Fallout 4*, and includes both avatars that are fully customizable down to the minutest detail, such as in *Dragon Age: Inquisition*, and those that are noncustomizable, as in games that include iconic multimedia characters like Sonic the Hedgehog or Kirby.

In accordance with the well-known tendency whereby digital media begin to affect already existing conceptions of human social interaction (e.g., the common parlance in which the human brain is spoken of as if a "computer"), the contemporary conceptualization of the avatar has recently shifted outside of "purely" digital games to include how we understand social media more generally. Daniel Miller uses the term "avatar" in his ethnography of Facebook to understand the difference between the private individual and the public performance of their persona as mediated through social media. For him, the avatar is a performance of the self to a public audience, which creates a sense of "co-presence," but that is separate from the private self (Miller, 2011, p. 66). Similarly, for Coleman, the "avatar provides a shorthand for the experience of the networked subject," a subject in which identity, behaviors, and community are impacted by the global adoption of networked communication technologies, a subject for whom the notion of the "unmediated encounter" is no longer possible (Coleman, 2012, pp. 79–98). She argues that avatars include many modes of representation used to facilitate "a continuum of exchanges between virtual and real spaces" (Coleman, 2011). Coleman's expanded definition seems entirely appropriate for *Pokémon GO*, and in the remainder of this chapter, we will explore the concept of avatar in this broader sense.

In drawing upon such studies of the phenomenological, psychological, anthropological, sociological, and even ontological consequences of avatars, we would like to suggest here that there are three inseparable aspects of the avatar that require further thought. The first crucial aspect we wish to note is that avatars should not be defined or cataloged according to the range of *forms* that they assume, but as an indissociable fusion of (technical) *function* and (user) *action*. Although "avatar" is the name today loosely given in popular culture to the custom altered creatures familiar from video gaming, in its strictest acceptation, an avatar is any interface technique that serves to bind computing hardware to an extra computer body; hence, whatever *focuses attention*, *signals location*, and enables the *elaboration of intentions* within a screen environment should also be considered an avatar.

The avatar is therefore not only an in-world representation of a user and a functional operator, but a programmer or re-programmer of its user too; that is, an avatar is essentially a pedagogical device working through interactive, granular modulations or dosing of affect. In this second aspect, it is absolutely vital to see how the operations of the virtual–actual avatar–user interface entail real-world behavioral modifications as well. If an avatar is designed to function simultaneously as a vector of the user's agency within a particular platform, as well as an in-world representative of the user and as a mode of identification, avatars are also designed to exploit human cognitive plasticity (or biological underdetermination) in order to refocus them for hyperspecialized tasks (e.g., via touchscreens, forging new relations between the opposable thumb, perception, and reaction, etc.) while also forcing a constant turnover of skills and ongoing reeducation for each individual user.

In this sense, we believe, thirdly, that the psychological consequences of such modifications for the users cannot be understood outside of the affordances (and, so to speak, the unaffordances) mandated by the avatar's relation to the "real world," on the one hand, and the "technical world" of the software/hardware nexus, on the other. In a word, what we are seeking to do in this chapter is to negotiate between the broad-brush discussions of the implications of the new technologies for any "ontology of the present" and the technical discussions of the production and role of avatars. As we will argue here, without appropriate modes of user integration into these circuits, the uptake and deployment of such technologies would remain partial, a fact not lost on the great media and software companies themselves. It is with respect to this ideal integration of user and technology that the avatar has been developed, if not perfected.

Digital games are the logical starting point for an examination of the operations and implications of the avatar. Precisely because games have a certain "nonnecessity" to their consumption—very simply, while we need our word processors for work, it is a rare workplace that will pay for its employees to play *Candy Crush Saga* (King, 2012)—part of their appeal depends on the effectiveness with which they can continue to motivate users to play and thus maintain their own integration with the game. Moreover, digital games are the technologies through which the avatar was introduced into our everyday media use and the first pedagogies of the management and integration of exchanges between virtual and real spaces took place.

To this end, we will begin by outlining a general methodology for our approach: the FLIP complex, illustrating the account with detailed examples from several games, including *Pokemon GO*, *Resident Evil 4*, and *Crossy Road*. Our approach, FLIP, stands for Focalization–Localization–Integration–Programming. FLIP is a key operational complex that can take on a truly staggering multiplicity of forms, both within the screen environment and in the real world, too. For purposes of the current chapter, we would like to sketch out, in a preliminary and rather abstract fashion, some current limits and tendencies of the FLIP complex (see Apperley & Clemens, 2016, pp. 110–124).

The FLIP model maintains that avatars are the central interface element for contemporary communication technologies (i.e., there is no interface that does not contain, however minimally, an "avatar function"). However, while avatars can take an extremely wide variety of forms and affordances (as we have briefly outlined above), that variegation does not vitiate the fact that avatars perform an essential cluster of functions (i.e., not necessarily the usual idea of a representational in-world figure). In fact, these variations are, in almost every case, determined by a relation between the hardware and software, and between projected functions and users (i.e., a double determination, first, at the level of the software–hardware nexus, and second, at the level of the device–user nexus). This double relation is itself reflexively targeted by design as the crucial instrument for the incitement and integration of *user affect* as a melding of cognitive intentionalization and identification (i.e., to hook users into certain modes of attention to the virtual space of the game, to enforce certain call-and-response movements on the user's part, and to encourage the continuation of this stasis). The production of this particular bond of cognition–affect–action then enables further behavioral modifications that may not have very much to do with the provisions of the game itself through the de facto continuance of these cognitive and practical actions into other zones (i.e., through the articulation of different platforms that deploy comparable sets of attentiveness and movements).

Let us pause momentarily to see how this works with respect to a single example, drawn from the work of Angela Ndalianis. If we began this chapter by invoking the mass public swarms of *Pokémon Go* users, we now turn to what seems, on the face of it, a more established, solitary, and private experience of the avatar. In the course of a phenomenological description of playing *Resident Evil 4*, Ndalianis writes:

> *While video gaming shares this haptic visuality with the cinema through the player's sensory and affective connection to the fictional world, it also involves a literal haptic connection through the player's interaction with the controller and, in turn, in the way command of the controller translates onto the body of the avatar who then participates in a haptic experience of the virtual space that surrounds it….the actual act of the union of player and her avatar.*
>
> **Ndalianis (2012, p. 44).**

Let us first underline the *postconvergent* aspects of digital gaming, that is, its inherently multimedia references. For Ndalianis, who is here concentrating on a particular *genre* of game, that of "horror," which, if given a cinematic allusion here, itself has a much older (in this case, literary) history; this transmediatic genre is part of the appeal of the game in the first place. Yet the genre is now refashioned in and for an entirely new set of technologies, for Ndalianis is using a Wii console, which works according to a fiction of a "whole body" integration with the technology. As Ndalianis elaborates, the game console is "what facilitates the unraveling of action onscreen but it also serves the role of umbilical cord, connecting the body of the player to the body of the game space and to its affective potential" (Ndalianis, 2012, p. 48), so Ndalianis also speaks here, given the generic horror context that is the object of her study, of the affect of the "moral occult," which serves to bind extra-generic intensities (e.g., sudden percepts) to specific generic expectations (e.g., narrative suspense). This is surely one of the core strengths of such games, which indiscriminate expectation, perception, and movement in their productions of affect. As Ndalianis is at pains to emphasize, the forging of a human–tech *union* is what is at stake and is dependent here on the success of the merging of the moving image of the avatar with the body of the gamer (Apperley, 2013).

With the Wii console in particular, "my arms and body now have a central role to play as my movements in real space are translated across the body of my avatar" (Ndalianis, 2012, p. 50). This last point requires further discussion. The Wii, which seems precisely to enable the direct translation of "real" corporeal action into the game world, has a further paradoxical effect. Rather than simply injecting the body of the gamer into the world of the game, the game world itself extrudes virtual pseudopodia (what Ndalianis, mobilizing a symptomatically maternal metaphor, calls "the umbilical cord") to engulf the gamer's body in a form of virtual phagocyt- ism. The player's body thereby becomes not simply the master of an avatar, but *an avatar of itself*. An avatar is a digital phagocyte. This is essential to the logic of the FLIP complex: the becoming avatar of the real body itself, even in supposedly "real-world" situations, whereby real movements of the body themselves become accommodations with the demands of the avatar.

On the basis of our brief exegeses of *Pokémon GO* and Ndalianis's account of *Resident Evil 4*, we can now further detail that the problem of avatar function and design involves the following linked rubrics:

1. "User-friendly": that is, large infant gestures, simple color-coded controls, etc. Much technology is now a priori targeted for maximum ease of learning and use across maximum diversity of populations.
2. Despite the familiar rhetoric of "proprioception" and "synaesthesia," tar- geting, affecting and rearticulating the eye–hand nexus is the crucial operator of control, even when the entire human body comes to be integrated à la the Wii or even *Pokémon Go*.
3. The avatar is placed in an arbitrary but absolute (algorithmic) relation between the "controls" and the "two worlds" thereby coupled (the design space of the game with the body of the user in real space).
4. A "game world" is itself a total design space (that is, tends toward being *algorithmically complete*) that seeks to transform the "real world" in accor- dance with its requirements.

5. Each user must enter each new game world in a graded fashion (the avatar is here a *probability threshold modulator*).
6. Each world grade engages new sets of user retraining through repetition of basic movements (including serial dosing of affect in a graded hierarchy of internally ratified accomplishment).
7. Every world, if it seeks to provide a kind of immersive totality, also marks itself as necessarily partial (there are many other worlds) and interruptible (for a variety of physical reasons, from the call of nature to the demands of other worlds, such as work schedules).
8. Every user movement is, de facto and de jure, tracked, recorded, and harvested (big data), in order that the data generated is reinvested in the design and production of the avatar itself.

If these propositions can indeed hold for games as otherwise different as *Pokémon GO* and *Resident Evil 4*, let us now attempt to triangulate our approach by examining the structuring of avatars in an entirely different game from either of these, Crossy Road (2014), developed by the indie Australian game design team of Hipster Whale. The game can be played on phone, tablet, and associated devices with touchscreen technology. The game's name alludes to the title of another famous game *Flappy Bird* (dotGEARS, 2013), which caused an international incident when it was pulled from App Store and Google Play in early 2014 by its own developer, Dong Nguyen. *Flappy Bird* is a notoriously difficult game in which the user attempts to negotiate a deliberately retro "8-bit" avatar.

As the name *Crossy Road* alludes to *Flappy Bird* and thus also overtly alerts prospective users to what they might come to expect in terms of an "endless runner" game with retro graphics and minimal transformations in action, it also adverts to the history of gaming. Its prime precursor is the old arcade game *Frogger* (Konami, 1981) in which the player uses a four-directional joystick to control the movements of a frog across a busy road and a log-swept river. The semantics of the title *Crossy Road* thereby propose a knowingly "infantile" sensibility with a highly nourished set of semiotic references to the history and contemporaneity of video gaming. Although one need know absolutely nothing of this history in order to play the game, which is openly designed to appeal to "all ages," it is nonetheless significant that this net of allusions enables further sets of connections to be made with other games, both internally and externally to *Crossy Road* itself. The various avatars prove crucial to making these links; at the time of writing, the game has the capacity for no less than 155 different avatars. These include: the "Hipster Whale," a blocky whale which shares its name with the company that produces the game, sports a goatee, cap, and black-rimmed glasses, and carries a coffee cup in one flipper and a camera in the other; "Daddy," a blue-suited dude with a black quiff; the Easter Bunny; and so on. There are additionally all sorts of frogs, fowl, cats and dogs, and fabulous creatures and characters from the North, South, West, and East. Cute, funny, culturally diverse, and intriguing, these avatars can be acquired by random variable in-game rewards by express purchase (mostly 99 cents each from the app store) or unlocked by secret in-game operations.

As with many other games, these avatars are crucial to its monetization; if you don't want to spend real money, you can watch targeted in-games ads for other games, which provide credits that can be used to purchase most (but not all) of the avatars. "Gotta catch them all!" is one of the tags for *Pokémon Go*, and such acquisitive exhaustiveness is also one of the behaviors that *Crossy Road* attempts to induce in its players. There are also opportunities for real-world merchandising, including T-shirts and plush stuffed versions of some avatars available. Other avatars are straight out of contemporary pop culture, such as Doge, a Shiba Inu breed accompanied by subgrammatical phrases such as "Wow!" "So Amaze!" "Very respect!" Another avatar is Pew Die Pug, which refers to the massively successful YouTube Swedish gamer Felix Arvid Ulf Kjellberg, whose online handle is PewDiePie, itself allegedly formed by the sound made by in-game sci-fi guns ("Pew!"), and whose own favorite dog is the pug. This set of avatars is open (indefinitely more can always be added), diversified (insofar as each appeals to a dense global network of forms, characters, and themes that exceed any traditional language, culture, and nation), and exclusive (some have to be bought; some require the cheats; some are available only for a limited time).

If the basic structure of the game remains the same throughout—the avatar must continue to cross the road or river without getting hit or without pausing too long (the tardy get taken by an eagle)—certain sets of avatars are correlated with particular kinds of landscape and terrain. There is a "spooky" series, which includes a Mummy, a Wolf, the Mad Wizard, the Dark Lord, the Gravedigger, Ghost, Zombie, and many others. The accompanying terrain is dark and ghostly. There is a Korean series, which includes (among others) Daddy, Psy, the Korean BBQ, and the K-Drama Actor. The landscape is a densely packed Korean urban space. There is a Brazil series, which includes (among others) the aforementioned Brazil Chicken and the Capoeira exponent, but also a Carnaval dancer, a Jaguar, a Blue Macaw, a Marmoset, and a Football Player. The accompanying landscape looks something like an idealized Rio de Janeiro.

In addition to these aesthetic shifts, some avatars automatically perform certain characteristic actions, which again make no difference to the game structure, but offer little fillips of perceptual differences: the Yeti throws snowballs at cars, the sci-fi adventurer Epoch blows up trees, and so on. The audio effects also vary with characters.

If *Pokémon GO* demands often strenuous physical adventuring as integral to its play and *Resident Evil 4* requires the submission of the entire body, otherwise immobilized in a small space, *Crossy Road* is a game that can literally be played anywhere, as long as one has a screen. Its extreme structural simplicity nonetheless offers the proliferation of avatars as a kind of aesthetic supplementation, whereby the basic repetitions of tap and swipe are articulated with affects created by tiny perceptible differences between the avatars, which themselves, as multiple, function semiotically to create cognitive links of recognition to all sorts of other phenomena nominally external to the game.

Having outlined these three extremely diverse instances of the affordances and operations of contemporary video game avatars, what, if anything, binds them together? Are there any conceptual formulas able to account for their unity as avatars and their diversity as operations? What sort of account can be given of their appeal and their import?

In "The Question Concerning Technology," Heidegger famously argues that technology is a form of gathering (Heidegger, 1977). We can extend his analysis here by asserting that contemporary postconvergent communicational technologies are a gathering (or, if you prefer, an assemblage) and the transformation of an existing symbolic economy into a new kind of material bond. This is one of the things that Heidegger means by his assertions that "the essence of technology is nothing technological" and that "the essence of technology is enframing (*Gestell*)." For Heidegger, such a gathering and establishment of the frame of life by technology is not only a kind of ordering that renders certain kinds of commands otiose by inscribing them directly into possibilities for behavior and cognition, but is also a way of revealing. In its form of revelation, technology creates what Heidegger calls a "standing reserve" for which "regulating" and "securing" become the most determining general effects.

If we believe that such remarks hold for understanding the role played by avatars in modifying human behavior, that the avatar, as the primary interface with global networked digital technology, is a key way in which human behavior is now regulated and secured beyond the diversity of inherited and already existing forms of social and spatial governmentality, we need also to add a note regarding the *interpellatory* qualities of this figure, that is, the way in which such games make an appeal to their users. "Interpellation" is a term derived from legal discourse, where it at once means a form of summons, an interruption, and a constraint. We believe that this complex indicates what is crucial about the avatar: that they simultaneously summon their users, interrupt the continuum of everyday life, and constrain certain behaviors.

In social theory, the term received a new impetus from the theories of the French philosopher Louis Althusser in his famous essay, "Ideology and Ideological State Apparatuses" (Althusser, 2001). In that essay, Althusser makes a distinction between what he calls "Repressive State Apparatuses" (the police, courts, prisons, etc.) and "Ideological State Apparatuses" (the family, churches, schools, etc.). Whereas the former operate primarily (not exclusively) by forms of physical violence, the latter function primarily (again, not exclusively) by forms of inculcated behaviors, whose paradigmatic operation is precisely that of interpellation (see also Coleman, 2012, pp. 79–98; Dyer-Witheford & De Peuter, 2009).

Althusser's emblematic instance of interpellation is being hailed on the street by a policeman:

> *I shall then suggest that ideology 'acts' or 'functions' in such a way that it 'recruits' subjects among the individuals (it recruits them all), or 'transforms' the individuals into subjects (it transforms them all) by that very precise operation which I have called* interpellation *or hailing, and which can be imagined along the lines of the most commonplace everyday police (or other) hailing: 'Hey, you there!'*
>
> *Assuming that the theoretical scene I have imagined takes place in the street, the hailed individual will turn round. By this mere one-hundred-and-eighty-degree physical conversion, he becomes a subject. Why? Because he has recognized that the hail was 'really' addressed to him, and that 'it was* really *him who was hailed' (and not someone else).*
>
> **Althusser (2001, p. 118).**

While this is not the place to enter into the arcana of the discussions surrounding Althusser's theses, it is first of all worth noting that he does not use the term "ideology" as if it simply meant a motivated or inculcated form of misunderstanding (e.g., forms of unexamined belief) that further evidence or training would enable a person to see through or would be able to break from. On the contrary, there is no simple outside to ideology; we are all of us subject to its determinations. In this, Althusser's concept is compatible with Heidegger's notion of modern technology as enframing; it sets the terms for us all in ways that it is impossible simply to break with and whereby the terms of conflict and apparent dissension are themselves positions established in advance by ideology. One can be at once correct in one's beliefs (e.g., about how the world works), yet remain entirely ideologically saturated insofar as one's behaviors continue to conform to, to answer to, the policeman's call. Preprogrammed multiple positions are therefore at the heart of ideology, which works not according to a reduction to orthodoxy, but precisely by the subject recognizing itself in its address by an authority figure, which opens for it a topology of acceptable behaviors. Ideology in this sense establishes variable sets of comportments without requiring any particular psychological state or disposition for its continuing effectivity.

That said, it is also worth noting that Althusser's title and orientation are now substantially outdated: "Ideological State Apparatuses." Digital gaming clearly cannot be reduced to an ideology, even in the expanded sense Althusser gives it; it is no longer the state that is primarily at stake here, but deracinated multinational capitalist corporations acting expressly at a global level; finally, the word *apparatus* can only be insufficient to name the unthinkably complex actual and virtual systems that are our current media environment. Moreover, Althusser's celebrated formula for ideology, that is: "a 'Representation' of the Imaginary Relationship of Individuals to their Real Conditions of Existence" also needs to be modified under pressure of digital gaming.

What we would now like to say instead is that, first, the position of the policeman in Althusser's fable is better occupied by the avatar. Why? Because to enter the virtual world of any game whatsoever, one needs to uptake and accommodate oneself through the medium of the avatar. In doing so, one is integrated into the digital game world as if summoned (one can see the chiasmus or crossover between "worlds" as part of such a summoning), and, in doing so, one interrupts one's "real life," while necessarily constraining oneself by learning the game's affordances. Second, this makes the avatar the key operator for *the integration of the actual relationship of users to their virtual conditions of existence*. Avatars are interpellation machines that bring analog users into algorithmic worlds, thereby enabling not only a reorganization of the analog, but new transitions to be made between otherwise disjoint spaces.

Let's conclude by summarizing our key propositions. The avatar is currently the crucial aspect of the technical requirement to restructure each user's perception–cognition–action potentials each and every time a game is played. Each playtime leaves traces of the history of the player's own coming-to-be-able-to-play-in-playing—data itself harvested for vast big-data probability sets—which suggests that the affects the player experiences are the alibi for the extremity of what they are doing to themselves in playing. What is this paradox? The more one becomes master of a game, the more one must become an automaton that fuses with the algorithmic requirements of the game itself. In the era of video games, we are no longer in a dialectic of symbolic prohibition–transgression as motor of action, but submitted to pure algorithms for which nothing need be prohibited.

The avatar is the key device that effects this transition between zones, encouraging its user in turn to cross over virtual and actual spaces previously separated in reality. This is what we have called the FLIP complex of the avatar. Each avatar focalizes the user's attention through its deployment as the way into the game. Each avatar localizes its user by establishing virtually the actual sphere of acceptable movements, even if this localization requires extensive physical movement. Each avatar integrates its user into sets of behaviors that are correlated with the game's virtual operations. Finally, each avatar requires the reprogramming of its user, even if, as with *Crossy Road*, in a minimal fashion. Avatars, as FLIP elements functioning within a global assemblage of technology that today regulates and secures the actions of billions of human beings, are the central means by which individuals are interpellated as subjects into their virtual worlds.

REFERENCES

Althusser, L. (2001). *Lenin and philosophy and other essays* (B. Brewster, Trans.). NY: Monthly Review Press.

Apperley, T., & Clemens, J. (2016). The biopolitics of gaming: Avatar–player self-reflexivity in Assassin's Creed II. In M.W. Kapell (Ed.), *The play versus story divide in game studies: Critical essays* (pp. 110–124). Jefferson: McFarland & Co.

Apperley, T. (2013). The body of the gamer: Game art and gestural excess. *Digital Creativity*, 24(2), 145–156.

Böhme, G. (2012). *Invasive technification: Critical essays in the philosophy of technology* (C. Shingleton, Trans.). London: Bloomsbury.

Candy Crush (2012). King.

Coleman, B. (2011). *Hello avatar: Rise of the networked generation*. Cambridge: MIT Press.

Coleman, B. (2012). Everything is animated: Pervasive media and the networked subject. *Body & Society*, 18(1), 79–98.

Crossy Road (2014). Hipster Whale.

Dyer-Witheford, N., & De Peuter, G. (2009). *Games of empire: Global capitalism and video games*. Minnesota: University of Minnesota Press.

Flappy Bird (2013). dotGEARS.

Fordyce, Neale, R. T., & Apperley, T. (2016). Modelling systemic racism: Mobilizing the dynamics of race and games in everyday racism. *The Fibreculture Journal*, 27.

Frogger (1981). Konami.

Frow, J. (2012). Avatar, identification, pornography. *Cultural Studies Review, 18*(3), 360–380.

Fuller, & Jenkins, H. (1995). Nintendo® and new world travel writing: A dialogue. In S. G. Jones (Ed.), *Cybersociety: Computer-mediated communication and community* (pp. 57–72). Thousand Oaks: Sage Publications.

Heidegger, M. (1977). *The question concerning technology and other essays* (W. Lovitt, Trans. with intro.). New York: Harper and Row.

Miller, D. (2011). *Tales from facebook*. London: Polity.

Moore, K. (2015a). A situated approach to urban play: The role of local knowledge in playing Ingress. In *The refereed conference proceedings of the annual conference of the digital games research association of Australia*. Retrieved from https://www.academia.edu/13296463/A_Situated_Approach_to_Urban_Play_The_Role_of_Local_Knowledge_in_Playing_Ingress.

Moore, K. (2015b). Painting the town blue and green: Curating street art through urban mobile gaming. *M/C: A Journal of Media and Culture, 18*(4). Retrieved from http://journal.media-culture.org.au/index.php/mcjournal/article/view/1010.

Ndalianis, A. (2012). *The horror sensorium: Media & the senses*. Jefferson: McFarLand & Co.

Newman, J. (2002). The myth of the ergodic videogame: Some thoughts on player–character relationships in videogames. *Game Studies: The International Journal of Computer Game Research, 2*(1).

Niantic Labs (2016). Retrieved from https://support.pokemongo.nianticlabs.com/hc/en-us/articles/221957628-How-do-I-move-my-avatar-.

Shaw, A. (2015). *Gaming at the edge: Sexuality and gender at the margins of gamer culture*. Minneapolis: University of Minnesota Press.

Simanowski, R. (2016). *Digital humanities and digital media: Conversations on politics, culture, aesthetics and literacy*. London: Open Humanities Press.

Stiegler, B. (2009). Teleologics of the snail: The errant self wired to a WiMax network. *Theory Culture Society, 26*(2–3).

Stiegler, B. (2014). *The re-enchantment of the world* (T. Arthur, Trans.). London: Bloomsbury.

Virno, P. (2009). Natural–historical diagrams: The "new global" movement and the biological invariant. In L. Chiesa, & A. Toscano (Eds.), *The Italian difference: Between nihilism and biopolitics*. Melbourne: re.press.

CHAPTER 4

Avatar Lives: Narratives of Transformation and Identity

Denise Doyle
University of Wolverhampton, Wolverhampton, United Kingdom

You ask me what 'moving' or 'travelling' means to me: it is about transformation 'through' dreaming, through imagining. I am freer to dream when I am moving. And one has to journey to dream.
Wanderingfictions Story *in Doyle and Kim (2007, p. 214)*

Truth in her dress finds facts too tight. In fiction she moves with ease
Rabindranath Tagore (2011, p. 140)

INTRODUCTION

There is always a certain "discovery" of the self when moving through different cultures, spaces, or times. When you loosen your grip on your everyday humdrum realities, it is curious how quickly you move more freely, think more freely. There can be a sense of transformation through the experience of moving through space itself. Yet, as the Tagore quote previously mentioned suggests, an even greater freedom comes when we can imagine the truth through another kind of fiction, a fiction that expands our view of reality (as will be seen in Judith Schalansky's writing on remote islands). Since embracing the digital realm in the mid-1990s, many of my own digital arts projects of that time used travel as a starting point for the exploration of space, whether real, virtual, or imagined. With the pending 50th anniversary of the groundbreaking 1968 exhibition, *Cybernetic Serendipity: The Computer and the Arts* at the Institute of Contemporary Arts in London, artists continue to search out and explore the use of new technology for "creativity and inventiveness" (Reichardt, 1968). Susan Merrill Squier observes that it is the liminal lives that are "mingling existence and non-existence" (and the shifting, interconnected, and emergent quality of human life) that should demand our attention as powerful representatives of transformation (Squier, 2004, p. 5).

Boundaries of Self and Reality Online
ISBN 978-0-12-804157-4
http://dx.doi.org/10.1016/B978-0-12-804157-4.00004-9

Central to the virtual worlds experience is the mediation of the space through the body of the avatar (Doyle, 2011). Despite early promises for virtual reality (Rheingold, 1991), the body has never lost its significance or place in new technologies. Moreover, research conducted in the 1990s in the virtual reality work of artist Char Davies (1995), and even in the outer space exploration of dancer and choreographer Kitsou Dubois (1999), highlighted the question of what we mean by the virtual, the weightless, or even the immaterial body, from early research on virtual worlds and virtual reality (Damer, 1997; Heim, 1994; Heudin, 1999; Schroeder, 2002) to more recent research on the avatar that creates a bifurcated self (Morie, 2007), or even what can be considered as some form of phantom limb (Veerapen, 2011). Other research on the significance of the avatar has focused on virtual worlds as a mirror for our identity, whether it is the exploration of an idealized self (Schomaker, 2010) or another gender, race, or even another species (Cárdenas, 2010). This chapter concerns itself with digital embodiment and the construction of the self as avatar in the collaborative art practices that are emerging through new technological platforms and what curator Jasia Reichardt might term "other serendipitous manifestations" (1968). Using examples of a range of art projects, the chapter explores how technology can aid the exploration of new forms and senses of our own identity. The chapter will discuss two sets of art projects; the first series of earlier art projects focuses on exploring the new grounds and geographies of virtual space, and initial negotiations of the construction of the avatar and its connections to and between physical and virtual space, and a second series of more recent projects extending the notion of transformation through digitally constructed realities through the exploration of gender and identity transformations, constructions, and deconstructions.

ART AND VIRTUAL SPACE

There has been a relationship between art and virtual space at least since the Renaissance with the invention of linear perspective. More recently, in the field of Art and Technology, the relationship between art and virtual space appears implicit in its scope and engagement (Ettlinger, 2009; Grau, 2003; Lindstrand, 2007). However, Or Ettlinger describes the "fog of multiple meanings around the term the virtual" (Ettlinger, 2009, p. 6), and he suggests that, in fact, contemporary and digital art has lost its interest in the art of illusion and is only now marginally concerned with the pictorial. There is a history to the relationship between art and the virtual, which spans a number of decades from the early 1990s, from early experiments in virtual environments (Davies, 1995, 1998; Sermon, 1992), to the networked environments of the early 21st century (Zapp, 2002, 2005) and to the networked virtual spaces found in online virtual worlds such as *Second Life* (SL). There is an argument that as soon as linear perspective was invented, painting became another kind of virtual space, and in fact, Lindstrand suggests that "before the invention of linear perspective, spatial experience was detached from imagery. Once the tools to depict three-dimensional space on a two dimensional surface were developed, architecture and the understanding of space leaped into a new era" (Lindstrand, 2007, p. 354). For Lindstrand, the possibility for the viewer to imagine herself walking around inside a painting opened up a whole new chapter in art as well as causing a fundamental shift in the experience of space. Ettlinger would most certainly agree with this perception of space. In developing "The Virtual Space Theory," he states that at its heart lies "the interpretation of virtual space as the overall space which we see through pictorial images and of 'virtual' as describing any visible object which is located inside of that space" (Ettlinger, 2009, p. 6).

Considering the notion that the concept of space can be seen as Cartesian, "definable and contained" is at odds with the concept of space as lived, as experienced, such as the "Thirdspace" that Edward W. Soja (1996) describes, and is discussed further as follows. In *The Production of Space* (1992), Henri Lefebvre attempts to define the experience of space from both a metaphysical and an ideological perspective. Initially, he outlines two terms in relation to space, that of the *illusion of transparency* and the *illusion of opacity* (or the realistic illusion). Of the illusion of transparency, he writes that the emphasis of the written word is to the detriment of what he terms social practice. In what he describes as the grasping of the object by the act of writing, he suggests that this is supposed to bring the:

> ... non-communicated into the realm of the communicated ... such are the assumptions of an ideology which, in positing the transparency of space, identifies knowledge, information and communication ... The illusion of transparency turns out ... to be a transcendental illusion: a trap, operating on the basis of its own quasi-magical power.
>
> **Lefebvre (1992, pp. 28–29)**

In turn, the illusion of opacity, of substantiality, is philosophically closer to naturalistic materialism. However, and most interestingly, Lefebvre continues to say the two illusions are not necessarily in opposition to each other and do not "seek to destroy each other." Rather, he argues that "each illusion embodies and nourishes the other. The shifting back and forth between the two, and the flickering or oscillatory effect that it produces, are thus just as important as either of the illusions considered in isolation" (Lefebvre, 1992, p. 29). This flickering, from opaque to transparent to opaque again, these oscillations, suggest a complex system of relationships between a space and the objects found in that space. Yet, Lefebvre (1992, p. 29) writes that it is the texture of space that allows us to create space through social practice as sequences of acts that become a signifying practice in itself. Ettlinger's and Lefebvre's understandings of space appear at odds with each other.

An article by Axel Stockburger, *Playing the Third Place* (2007), extends Lefebvre's ideas to the work of Soja and his definition of what he terms the Thirdspace. As Stockburger notes, beyond the dualism of subject and object, Lefebvre suggests that spaces can be understood within the triad of the perceived, the conceived, and the lived. According to Stockburger, Soja "identifies perceived space (Firstspace) with the real, and conceived space (Secondspace) with the imaginary, leading to lived space (Thirdspace), as a field of both, imagined and real" (Stockburger, 2007, p. 232). Stockburger continues with his interpretation in the context of game space and describes the hybrid mix between real and imagined spaces created through digital game universes as resonating strongly with the concept of Thirdspace. He notes that "this insight is crucial because it defies the idea of computer games as merely 'virtual' or purely imaginary spaces. It is precisely the interaction between real and imagined spatiality that makes this medium so compelling and unique" (Stockburger, 2007, p. 232). A concept of space that suggests a mixed experience of both real and imagined spatiality proves to be useful when considering online and networked spaces, whether they are games-based or not.

The early use of virtual environments for artistic practice were explored in a series of projects undertaken at the Banff Centre, Canada in the early 1990s and subsequently documented in *Immersed in Technology: Art and Virtual Environments* (Moser & MacLeod, 1996). In the preface to the book, Douglas Macleod, the Project Director, likens this "moment of virtual reality" to a similar moment in time when Vertov's *Man with the Movie Camera* was released in 1929, cataloging the potential of the film medium (Moser & MacLeod, 1996, p. ix). Of particular note were works such as Brenda Laurel and Rachel Strickland's *Placeholder* (1993), the *Archaeology of the Mother Tongue* (1993) by Toni Dove and Michael Mackenzie, and the virtual reality performance, *Dancing with the Virtual Dervish: Virtual Bodies* (1994), by Diane Gromala and Yacov Sharir. These projects were particularly innovative in their exploration of virtual reality environments in an art context.

Artists such as Char Davies moved from painting to exploring virtual space in virtual environments in the early 1990s, resulting in the works *Osmose* (1995) and *Ephémère* (1998). In *Osmose*, the participant, or "immersant," must concentrate on their breath as a device to navigate vertically through the spaces represented. In *Landscape, Earth, Body, Being, Space, and Time in the Immersive Virtual Environments Osmose and Ephémère* (2003), Davies says that "within this spatiality, there is no split between the observer and the observed" (2003, p. 1). She argues that this is not tied to a Cartesian paradigm, but rather allows "another way of sensing to come forward, one in which the body feels the space very much like that of a body immersed in the sea" (p. 1). In this private virtual space, by "leaving the space of one's usual sensibilities, one enters into communication with a space that is psychically innovating … For we do not change place, we change our nature" [Bachelard (original, 1966) in Davies, 1997, p. 3].

THE AVATAR CONSTRUCT: AVATAR AND IDENTITY

An avatar is not object. Nor though is it subject. The avatar occupies an uneasy position between the two and destabilizes our sense of self within user-created environments

Heller (2015, pp. 156–157)

The virtual embodiment of people as avatars is a term used in many online worlds, according to anthropologist Tom Boellstorff (2008, p. 128). Avatar is the Sanskrit word that originally referred to the incarnation of a Hindu god and particularly the god Vishnu (Boellstorff, 2008, p. 128). However:

While avatar [...] historically referred to incarnation – a movement from virtual to actual – with respect to online worlds it connotes the opposite movement from actual to virtual, a decarnation or invirtualization.

Boellstorff (2008, p. 128)

He further suggests that as "avatars make virtual worlds real, not actual: they are a position from where the 'self' encounters the virtual" (Boellstorff, 2008, p. 129). Using the terms virtual, the real, and the actual, Boellstorff links his ideas to Henri Bergson's examination of the real and the virtual in the early part of the 20th century. Bergson makes this distinction between the real and the actual, which reframes his concept of the virtual. Whatever the change in use of the term avatar toward the virtual, how do we begin to examine this represented self in virtual space?

Figure 4.1 *Wanderingfictions Story*: Looking for India in *Second Life*, 2007.

My own virtual counterpart, or avatar, *Wanderingfictions Story*, has developed significantly since her "birth" in 2006. My interest in the notion of *Wanderingfictions Story* as a form of virtual traveler, moving between the physical and the virtual, traveling between the virtual and the imagined (and quoted at the start of this chapter) became the basis of a range of projects, including *Metadreamer* (2009), which will be discussed later in the chapter. In *"The body of the avatar: constructing human presence in virtual worlds,"* I reflected upon my avatar *Wanderingfictions Story*: "... if translated back into physical space, [she] would be over seven foot tall, brown skinned, with a wardrobe full of saris" (Doyle, 2011, p. 106) (see Fig. 4.1).

This representation of the self was a result of a performative writing experiment undertaken in 2007 with artist Taey Kim. Inspired by a particular description of "cyberspace," my virtual counterpart decided to search for "place" in SL, and, in particular, India, in response to a piece of text by writer Jay Griffiths: "There's no India in cyberspace, no jasmine, no gupshop, no sari, no desert [...] there's no nature in the synthetic element" (Griffiths, 2004, p. 269). *Wanderingfictions* strategy was to change her dress: "Yesterday I searched again for India and in a way found it. There was no Taj Mahal, no sign to tell me. I changed my clothes so I could imagine India a little more. It seemed to work" (*Wanderingfictions Story* in Doyle & Kim, 2007, p. 218). She goes on to explain her experience of flying in SL, already having added "wings" to her dress attire. Gaston Bachelard, writing in *Air and Dreams* [1988 (original, 1943), p. 27], suggests that when we dream of flight, wings are already a rationalization. This is an interesting consideration or reflection upon a number of features of the avatar and their potential adornment and expression; this will be taken up further later in the chapter. Yet there is no doubt the experience of developing *Wanderingfictions Story* in this way was a rewarding experience, both creatively and personally. How do we make sense of these opportunities for new forms of "transformation" being offered by new technologies?

ART, VIRTUAL GEOGRAPHY, AND THE AVATAR

The work that defines the early exploration of telepresence in telematic spaces by artists engaged with technology is that of UK-based artist, Paul Sermon, and his work *Telematic Dreaming* (1992), which Dixon describes as a "wonderful, exquisitely simple and ground-breaking installation [that] creates a type of magic, a sort of lucid dream" (2007, p. 220). Over the last two decades, Sermon has built upon this very simple concept of two geographically remote spaces being connected in time. In *Telematic Dreaming*, images of two beds, one in Finland and the other in England, are projected onto each other, enabling a real-time interaction with the performer in one space and the visitor in the other (Sermon, 1992). This new form of telematic experience enabled the participant to "travel," or rather to be "present," in another space through the use of technology. Susan Kozel writes an interesting account of her experience of being the performer in this piece in *Spacemaking: Experiences of a Virtual Body* (1994), noting that "telepresence has been called an out-of-body experience, yet what intrigues me is the return to the body which is implied by any voyage beyond it". She continues to discuss the claim of artists such as Myron Krueger that virtual technology changes what it means to be human and alters human perception, but suggests that it does not "simply refer to the voyage out, but the inevitable return and the lasting effect that the outward motion leaves on the reunited body" (Kozel, 1994).

A more recent project by performance artist and activist Joseph DeLappe was realized in the virtual world of SL. Inspired by a comment, or rather a criticism, by a player in *America's Army* that DeLappe was suffering from a "Gandhi Complex," he began researching the history of protest and Mahatma Gandhi's forms of protest; the result was the reenactment of Gandhi's 1930 "Salt March to Dandi" from the March 12 to April 6, 2008, in a durational performance in SL. Using a customized treadmill that controlled the Gandhi avatar, *MGandhi Chakrabarti*, DeLappe walked for 26 days to cover the 240-mile march, but this time in virtual space. A whole series of works were created as a result of the performance and the subsequent residency at the Eyebeam Gallery, New York (DeLappe, 2008a, 2008b). Acknowledging that the circumstances of the works came from the residency and the opportunity to experiment with the rapid prototyping facilities there, he, however, recognized that it was the time spent reenacting in SL that gave him the opportunity for other ideas to emerge. When interviewing DeLappe, he commented that "What's fascinating about these performance projects, this walking, gives you, number one time, this physical movement, and contemplating this reality as it is presenting in front of you" (DeLappe in Doyle, 2010, p. 244).

As to how the land would be traversed in SL and how this connected to Gandhi's actual march to Dandi in 1930, DeLappe comments that he was initially considering this as a geographical connection or interpretation. In the end, due to the nature of SL space being spatially discontinuous (with a number of mainlands and then a series of disconnected islands), DeLappe acknowledged in the interview that "it was impossible to make the route do that" (DeLappe in Doyle, 2010, p. 252). After beginning on the largest mainland (and traversing the land in a circular route), DeLappe teleported to ever decreasing masses of land. Sometimes he teleported to smaller plots of land, or islands, with random security systems, creating what he terms "a kind of involuntary navigation" that he did not expect. The navigation came through the recognition of presence on the grid. He explains that in the end, he decided to follow this form of navigation and responded by thinking:

> … let's see where I am and let's keep walking. That was definitely something I thought about, but I'm really glad I didn't do that perfect tracing of the map. Because, what I landed up doing, the primary navigation was, I would go from one group of green dots to the other, so I could interact with the residents and invite people to walk. That became a primary way of navigating after a while.
>
> **DeLappe in Doyle(2010, p. 252)**

Working within the realm of Art and Technology (and as an artist who engages with narrative as method), my own exploration of virtual space over the last decade has often been based on the retelling of narratives in a new context. An early practice-based project was to reinterpret Italo Calvino's *Invisible Cities* (1997) through an interactive artifact. The story was of Marco Polo's adventures to imagined cities, with Calvino providing the descriptions of the fantastic, symbolic, and often conceptually-based places. How do we travel without a map? Of note were my closing remarks, where

I suggested that the creation of a figure in the virtual space, that of Eleni, was worthy of further study, "… to produce Wandering Fictions for the web remained essential for the concept. The impact on the process, above technical constraints, of constructing a character to exist within this space was continually evident. The borders and boundaries of net space, if it has them, are not yet visible. A very different potential space could still emerge" (Doyle, 2000, p. 24). Following my introduction to SL in 2007, it was a relatively short time before I created *Wanderingfictions Story*. The origin of the maiden name was based on media archaeologist Siegfried Zielinksi's early writings on the Internet, in which he notes that:

> *In the motion of crossing a border, heterology encircles the impossible place, that is unlocatable, that is actually empty, that in practice is created in the motion of crossing the border […] this is what taking action at the border, that which I call subjective, targets in relation to the Net: strong, dynamic, nervous, definitely process-orientated aesthetic constructions, that are introduced into the Net as Wandering Fictions.*
>
> **Zielinski (1997, p. 285)**

Having already developed a number of artist projects utilizing and investigating SL as a space for artistic experimentation, in 2009 my interest in the notion of *Wanderingfictions Story* as a manifestation of, and from, virtual space became the basis of a new project, *Meta-Dreamer* (2009). After reflecting on DeLappe's *MGandhi* series, I began working with digital materialization expert Turlif Vilbrandt to create a series of digitally materialized objects of *Wanderingfictions Story*. By experimenting with digital processes that extracted data from SL and investigating different types of materials, attempts were made to represent jade and clouded glass, among other textures. The end result enabled the qualities of the figure to be cloud-like and ethereal as though *Wanderingfictions Story*, the meta-dreamer, is "almost there." The digital object was presented in the Golden Thread Gallery space (as part of the ISEA 2009 exhibition) alongside DeLappe's figure of *MGandhi 1* (2008a, 2008b). The visitor could also experience the virtual installation on Kriti Island that included the presentation of *Wanderingfictions Story*, the metadreamer, through captured images and her metadream writing (see Fig. 4.2).

In *Exploring Liminal Practices in Art, Technology and Science* (Doyle, 2015), I reviewed the digital materialization project *Meta-Dreamer* (2009) that explored the identity and development of the avatar, *Wanderingfictions Story*, in the context of the liminal lives discussed by Squier earlier in the chapter. In commenting on the work of anthropologist Victor Turner, she advocates

Figure 4.2 *Wanderingfictions Story* as Digital Object, Golden Thread Gallery, Belfast, 2009.

the "need to move beyond Turner's exclusively cultural framing to under-stand liminality not merely as a cultural state but as a *biocultural process*" (original emphasis) (Squier, 2004, p. 8). The translucent yet frozen properties of the digital objects materialized in *Meta-Dreamer* suggest a state of in-between, and perhaps even what Elizabeth Grosz describes as the "loci of emergence" itself (Grosz, 2001, p. 112). In the last 5 years, materialization costs have reduced and further material processes have developed, as evidenced by the work of Neri Oxman at MIT offering new research potential for the principle of avatar materialization.

OTHER GEOGRAPHIES

Ah, so you are a map maker! I wonder what remarks you make of the landscapes that you travel through? Do you have a system of classification at all? Of pattern-ing? Is it to 'capture' what it is to be here or to be there? I'm uncertain of my own geography. I don't even know where I live. Conceptually, that is. If we looked on the map I would not be able to point to it and say 'there, that is where I live, that is my home'. Perhaps this is something that happens with a virtual geography.

Doyle and Kim (2007, pp. 214–215)

Moving through space (and time) is our basic level of experiential knowledge as we exist in the physical world. Geographer Doreen Massey, in an essay responding to the work of artist Olafur Eliasson, attempts to illustrate a set of relationships between time and space by using a narrative account of a journey between Manchester and Liverpool in the UK. In the process of traveling, she suggests, "If movement is reality itself then what we think of as space is a cut through all those trajectories; a simultaneity of unfinished stories" (Massey, 2003, p. 111). Further, "Space has its times. To open up space to this kind of imagination means thinking about time and space together. You can't hold places and things still. What you *can* do is meet up with them … 'Here,' in that sense is not a place on a map. It is that intersection of trajectories" (original emphasis) (Massey, 2003, p. 111).

Two interesting points emerge from this argument; firstly, if each space has a particular time, as Massey implies, then it could be that virtual world spaces also have a particular time (or times) attached to them. Not only, then, could there be different sets of time–spaces that may be located in the SL, the space could enable a particular reflection upon different time–spaces as phenomenal experience. Secondly, if "place" can be considered to be an intersection of trajectories of unfinished stories, does this challenge our understanding and articulation of what place is? Is "place," in fact, physical at all?

An artist residency in India revealed that distinct folk art practices have developed in very specific regions and can even be linked to individual villages in the state of West Bengal. These folk art practices are intrinsically connected to (and are born out of) place. Certain parallels already exist between the virtual space of Kriti Island and the real places in West Bengal. *Wanderingfictions Story* (i.e., my avatar) "wanders" in her virtual place, just as the Bauls and Fakirs (i.e., minstrels) "wander" through their place in the eastern region of the state (having already inspired many of the writings of the well-known Indian writer and poet, Rabindranath Tagore). Professor of Philosophy Edward Casey considers that:

> There is no knowing or sensing a place except by being in that place and to be in a place is not, then, subsequent to perception … but is an ingredient of perception itself. Such knowledge, genuinely local knowledge, is itself experiential.
>
> **Casey (1997, p. 18)**

Yet Massey suggests that places should not be considered "as points or areas on map, but as integrations of space and time, as *spatio-temporal events*" (original emphasis) (Massey, 2005, p. 130). Perhaps an understanding of place should be multilayered and draw from a range of views in attempting to consider moreover the "specificity of place" itself (Massey, 2005, p. 130).

In her *Atlas of Remote Islands: Fifty Islands I Have Not Visited and Never Will*, writer Judith Schalansky (2010, p. 10) suggests that "the lines on a map prove themselves to be artists of transformation: they crisscross in cool mathematical patterns … they ensure the earth retains its physicality." Having never traveled to these real islands (and never intending to), Schalansky pieces together information and descriptions of these imagined, yet real places. Comparing the earth represented as a globe and through the atlas, she writes:

> … this Earth has no borders, no up or down, no beginning and no end [whereas] in an atlas, the Earth is as flat as it was before explorers pinned down the white spaces of enticingly undiscovered regions with contours and names, freeing the edges of the world from the sea monsters and other creatures that had long held sway there.
> **Schalansky (2010, p. 11)**

Rapa Iti, *Pingelap*, and *Clipperton Atoll* are but 3 of the 50 islands that are described by Schalansky (it is hard not to imagine Kriti Island to be the 51st of Schalansky's Islands, full of stories yet to be told). *Rapa Iti* is 40 square kilometers with 482 inhabitants and lies in the Pacific Ocean as part of French Polynesia. Marc Liblin, who lived near the foothills of the Vosges in France, dreamed that he speaks an unknown language. Eventually, he meets an old woman who speaks the old Rapa of her homeland. Liblin, "who has never been outside Europe, marries the only woman who understands him, and in 1983 he leaves with her for the island where his language is spoken" (Schalansky, 2010, p. 72). Seventy-five of the 250 inhabitants of *Pingelap* in the Caroline Islands see no color, "not the fiery crimson of the sunset, not the azure of the ocean … Silly talk about the gloriousness of color makes them indignant" (Schalansky, 2010, p. 98). *Clipperton Atoll*, with barely 2 km of land, is uninhabited. Schalansky suggests that the very construction of an island lends itself to narrative, or to stories in literature (everything becomes a stage):

> The absurdity of reality is lost on the large land masses, but here on the islands, it is writ large. An island offers a stage: everything that happens on it is practically forced to turn into a story, into a chamber piece in the middle of nowhere, into the stuff of literature.
> **Schalansky (2010, pp. 19–20)**

If *Kriti Island* were to be described in similar ways (if her stories could be told), the space (or place) would not be unlike the islands described by Schalansky (2010). When *Kriti Island* was specifically placed almost adjacent to the virtual island of *Symobia* in 2007, there was barely another island nearby. By 2013, it was as though Kriti has become part of an archipelago of islands. Beyond its locality, it was hard to determine the situation of *Kriti* with any geographical certainty. But when I try and "imagine" the differences and similarities between the real islands in Schalansky's atlas and *Kriti*, their differences seem to fade and their similarities strengthen, the island offering up a stage writ large.

GENDER, BIOTECHNOLOGIES, DRIFTING BODIES

The exploration of gender has found rich and fluid grounds in virtual worlds negotiated through avatar form. Arthur Kroker, writing in *Body Drift: Butler, Hayles, Haraway* (2012), comments on Donna Haraway's concept of the hybrid body, and that, in fact, it only knows the borderlines, the intersections, the unsituated: "Neither pure information nor pure flesh, the hybrid body knots the strange experience of being digital, being plant, being animal, being mineral into a beautiful labyrinth of knowledge" (Kroker, 2012, p. 14).

Further, he highlights how, when we explore: "different forms of life that appears when the borderline comes inside our bodies [...] we become the intersections, ruptures, and intermediations of our most creative imagination" (Kroker, 2012, p. 14). There are three art projects, all developed in SL, that, in many ways, reflect the sentiments of Kroker's observations of Haraway's hybrid body: *Becoming Dragon* (2009) by Micha Cárdenas, *The Adventures of Nar Duell* (2007–ongoing) by Lynne Heller, and *Meta_Body* (2011–ongoing) by Catarina de Sousa.

The work developed by artist Micha Cárdenas, *Becoming Dragon* (2009), questioned "the one-year requirement of 'Real Life Experience' that transgender people must fulfill in order to receive Gender Confirmation Surgery" through a mixed-reality performance (Cárdenas, 2010). For the performance, Cardenas 'lived' for 365 h immersed in SL via a head-mounted display, and during the year of research and development of the project, Cardenas began her own real-life hormone replacement therapy. She notes that both virtual worlds and biotechnology are each technologies of transformation and "offer the promise of becoming something else, of having a new body and a new life" (Cárdenas, 2010). This mixing of realities and ultimately mixing of genders in her performance piece focuses on the process of becoming, and she concludes that "the epistemological topology of becoming is shaped by the radical unknowability of the future" (Cárdenas, 2010).

An art project that perhaps creates as many questions as it may answer is the work of artist Catarina de Sousa, in partnership with her mother, and it focuses on the construction of embodied identity through the avatar where they have developed the concept of shared creativity through collective creation, distributed creation, and collaborative creation (de Sousa, 2012). This emerging method opens up new avenues to understand and explore the construction of gender and identity in virtual worlds. The project focused on two concerns:"the avatar as body/language open to experimentation and potency, and avatar building as a shared creative process and aesthetical experience" (de Sousa, 2015, pp. 187–188). Phase I of this participatory project involved the artists distributing 18 original avatars and a subsequent call for derivative artworks based on one of more the avatars. Full permissions were given to alter and develop the avatar representations. de Sousa writes that, "by distributing free and open material, further enabling users to experiment and express themselves through their avatar, actively inciting their transformation and the process of becoming in the liminoid space of the metaverse" (2015, p. 209).

In the exploration of identity and gender through the avatar in *The Adventures of Nar Duell* (2007–ongoing), Canadian artist Lynne Heller suggests the relationship between herself and her avatar is akin to that of a mother/daughter relationship, and explores issues of appropriation and the avatar as found object (Heller, 2015). She traces "a process of creating in SL from found object collage, through collecting/consuming practices and finally to the notion of the bought self, avatar representation in virtual worlds through consumerist artistic practice" (Heller, 2015, p. 140). Heller remarks that "when naming an avatar in Second Life you are confronted by the realization that you are creating an alter ego [...] the name you choose is on the only aspect of your avatar that can never change" (Heller, 2015, p. 150). As with *Wanderingfictions Story*, Heller's avatar name perhaps has influenced her approach to her artistic methods within the *SL* space. Further to this, Heller, while acknowledging the significance of embodiment, stresses how this is actually "advanced through the nurturing and aestheticisation of the avatar [and] is fundamental to the relationship between person and virtual representation" (Heller, 2015, p. 153). To reflect upon my own observations of developing *Wanderingfictions Story* as a persona, it was when I experimented with the body and representation of my own avatar that a more significant exploration of identity was undertaken. As Heller notes that:"SL is a petri dish under the microscope due to all the 'real' that people bring in to this virtual world" (Heller, 2015, p. 155).

Each of these art projects intentionally challenges our understanding of our identities as fixed and stable, questioning to an extent the process of nature that is echoed in the sentiment offered by Brian Eno:

We come from a cultural heritage that says things have a 'nature', and that this nature is fixed and describable. We find more and more that this idea is unsupportable

Eno in Ayiter and Ugajin (2015)

All of the projects imply either a birthing or a biotechnical process, and all highlight the potential of online worlds and, in particular, SL, as a platform that can transform the "real" that is brought into it.

CONCLUSION

Our multiple bodies [...] our proliferating identities will always follow paths into the future figured by the contingent, the complex and the hybrid

Kroker (2012, p. 144)

The potential of new technologies for exploring issues of transformation and identity by the artists discussed in this chapter point to new relationships in virtual space, experienced as real and sometimes offering entirely new hybrid experiences. As the real and the virtual, and the real and the imagined are no longer strangers (or opposites), it is also true that the physical and the virtual have become more firmly entangled. Whether traveled to physically, or in the imagination, the experience of a place can be as a mathematical pattern on a map, as a virtual island on a virtual grid, or even as a real place imagined. In the accounts of those that have experienced their virtual bodies, the heterogeneity of the experiences point toward a complex interweaving of the virtual and the physical, and that of the body with space and place. The question of what is real and what is fiction has always been a tenuous one, and this premise is demonstrated in the stories and descriptions of the islands on Schalansky's (2010) map. The narratives are written based on fact, and yet these embellished stories allow us to see the world slightly differently, revealing stories that allow us to make another sense of the world. Finally, transformation through exploring hybrid identities, were seen in a number of the works discussed. The UK Government's *Future Identities* report concludes that the Internet, rather than changing our identities, has been "instrumental in raising awareness that identities are more multiple, culturally contingent and contextual than has previously been understood" (Foresight, 2013, pp. 1–70).

Perhaps SL can be comfortably placed alongside this notion, and as one SL veteran noted, having "a wardrobe full of avatars" (Morie in Doyle, 2011) suited her many-faceted self.

REFERENCES

Ayiter, E., & Ugajin, E. (2015). Moving islands [rafts]: A collective art conglomeration in second life. In D. Doyle (Ed.), *New Opportunities for artistic practice in virtual worlds* (pp. 162–186). Hershey, PA: IGI Global. http://dx.doi.org/10.4018/978-1-4666-8384-6.ch008.

Bachelard, G. (1988). *Air and dreams: An essay on the imagination of movement* (E. R. Farrell & C. F. Farrell, Trans.). Dallas, TX: Dallas Institute Publications (Original work published 1943).

Boellstorff, T. (2008). *Coming of age in second life: An anthropologist explores the virtually human.* Princeton, NJ: Princeton University Press.

Calvino, I. (1997). *Invisible cities.* London: Vintage.

Cárdenas, M. (2009). *Becoming dragon [performance].* Retrieved from http://secondloop.wordpress.com/.

Cárdenas, M. (2010). Becoming dragon: A transversal technology study. In A. Kroker, & M. Kroker (Eds.), *Code drift: Essays in critical digital studies* (pp. 127–152). Victoria, Canada: CTheory Books. Retrieved from http://ctheory.net/articles.aspx?id=639.

Casey, E. S. (1997). How to get from space to place in a fairly short stretch of time: Phenomenological prolegomena. In S. Feld, & K. H. Basso (Eds.), *Senses of place* (pp. 13–52). Santa Fe, NM: School of American Research Press.

Damer, B. (1997). *Avatars! Exploring and building virtual worlds on the internet.* Berkeley, CA: Peachpit Press.

Davies, C. (1995). *Osmose [virtual reality environment].* Retrieved from http://www.immersence.com/osmose/index.php.

Davies, C. (1998). *Ephémère [virtual reality environment].* Retrieved from http://www.immersence.com/.

Davies, C. (1997). Changing space: Virtual reality as an arena of embodied being. In R. Packer, & K. Jordan (Eds.), *Multimedia: From Wagner to virtual reality.* New York, NY: Norton.

Davies, C. (2003). Landscape, Earth, body, being, space, and time in the immersive virtual environments Osmose and Ephémère. In J. Malloy (Ed.), *Women, art, and technology* (pp. 322–337). Cambridge, MA: MIT Press.

DeLappe, J. (2008a). *Reenactment: The salt satyagraha online.* Retrieved from http://saltmarchsecondlife.wordpress.com/.

DeLappe, J. (2008b). *Tourists and travelers [installation].* Brooklyn, NY: Eyebeam Gallery. Retrieved from http://eyebeam.org/events/tourists-and-travelers.

Dixon, S. (2007). *Digital performance: A history of new media in theater, dance, performance art, and installation.* Cambridge, MA: MIT Press.

Dove, T., & Mackenzie, M. (1993). *Archaeology of the mother tongue [installation].* Banff, Canada: Banff Centre for the arts. Retrieved from http://www.banffcentre.ca/bnmi/coproduction/archives/a.asp.

Doyle, D. (2000). *Wandering fictions 2.0: Eleni's journey* (Unpublished Master's thesis). Coventry, UK: Coventry University.

Doyle, D. (2010). *Art and the emergent imagination in avatar-mediated online space* (Doctoral dissertation). SMARTlab Digital Media Institute, University of East London (Accession Number).

Doyle, D. (2011). The body of the avatar: Constructing human presence in virtual worlds. In A. Ensslin, & E. Muse (Eds.), *Creating second lives: Community, identity and spatiality as constructions of the virtual* (pp. 99–112). New York, NY: Routledge.

Doyle, D. (2015). Exploring liminal practices in art, technology, and science. In D. Harrison (Ed.), *Handbook of research on digital media and creative technologies* (pp. 1–17). Hershey, PA: IGI Global. http://dx.doi.org/10.4018/978-1-4666-8205-4.ch001.

Doyle, D., & Kim, T. (2007). Embodied narrative: The virtual nomad and the meta dreamer. *International Journal of Performance Arts and Digital Media, 3*(2–3), 209–222. http://dx.doi.org/10.1386/padm.3.2-3.209_1.

Dubois, K. (1999). *Gravity zero [installation].* Retrieved from http://www.artscatalyst.org/gravity-zero.

Ettlinger, O. (2009). *The architecture of virtual space.* Ljubljana, Slovenia: University of Ljubljana Faculty of Architecture.

Foresight (2013). *Future identities: Changing identities in the UK: The next 10 years [Final project report].* Retrieved from https://www.gov.uk/government/publications/future-identities-changing-identities-in-the-uk.

Grau, O. (2003). *Virtual art: From illusion to immersion.* Cambridge, MA: MIT Press.

Griffiths, J. (2004). *A sideways look at time.* Tarcher Books.

Gromala, D., & Sharir, Y. (1994). *Dancing with the virtual dervish: Virtual bodies [installation].* Banff, Canada: Banff Centre for the arts. Retrieved from http://www.banffcentre.ca/bnmi/coproduction/archives/d.asp#dancing.

Grosz, E. (2001). *Architecture from the outside: Essays on virtual and real space.* Cambridge, MA: MIT Press.

Heim, M. (1994). *The metaphysics of virtual reality.* New York, NY: Oxford University Press.

Heller, L. (2007–ongoing). *Adventures of nar duell in second life [comic book series].* Retrieved from http://www.lynneheller.com/#/01/.

Heller, L. (2015). Found objects, bought selves. In D. Doyle (Ed.), *New opportunities for artistic practice in virtual worlds* (pp. 140–161). Hershey, PA: IGI Global. http://dx.doi.org/10.4018/978-1-4666-8384-6.ch007.

Heudin, J. C. (Ed.). (1999). *Virtual worlds: Synthetic universes, digital life, and complexity.* Reading, MA: Perseus Books.

Kozel, S. (1994). *Spacemaking: Experiences of a virtual body.* Retrieved from http://art.net/~dtz/kozel.html.

Kroker, A. (2012). *Body drift: Butler, Hayles, Haraway.* Minneapolis, MA: University of Minnesota Press.

Laurel, B., & Strickland, R. (1993). *Placeholder [installation].* Banff, Canada: Banff Centre for the Arts. Retrieved from http://www.banffcentre.ca/bnmi/coproduction/archives/p.asp#placeholder.

Lefebvre, H. (1992). *The production of space* (D. Nicholson-Smith, Trans.). Oxford, UK: Blackwell (Original work published 1974).

Lindstrand, T. (2007). Viva piñata: Architecture of the everyday. In F. von Borries, S. P. Walz, & M. Böttger (Eds.), *Space time play: Computer games, architecture and urbanism: The next level* (pp. 354–357). Basel, Switzerland: Birkhauser.

Massey, D. (2003). Some times of space. In S. May (Ed.), *Olafur Eliasson: The weather report.* London, UK: Tate Publishing.

Massey, D. (2005). *For space.* London, UK: Sage.

Morie, J. F. (2007). Performing in (virtual) spaces: Embodiment and being in virtual environments. *International Journal of Performance Arts and Digital Media, 3*(2–3), 123–138. http://dx.doi.org/10.1386/padm.3.2&3.123/1.

Moser, M. A., & MacLeod, D. (1996). *Immersed in technology: Art and virtual environments.* Cambridge, MA: MIT Press.

Reichardt, J. (1968). *Cybernetic serendipity: The computer and the arts [exhibition catalogue]*. Retrieved from http://cyberneticserendipity.com/cybernetic_serendipity.pdf.

Rheingold, H. (1991). *Virtual reality*. New York, NY: Summit Books.

Schalansky, J. (2010). *Atlas of remote islands*. London, UK: Particular Books.

Schomaker, K. (2010). *My life as an avatar*. Retrieved from http://www.kristineschomaker.net/#!my-life-as-an-avatar/csfq.

Schroeder, R. (Ed.). (2002). *The social life of avatars: Presence and interaction in shared virtual environments*. London, UK: Springer.

Sermon, P. (1992). *Telematic dreaming [performance installation]*. Retrieved from http://creativetechnology.salford.ac.uk/paulsermon/dream/.

Soja, E. W. (1996). *Thirdspace: Journeys to Los Angeles and other real-and-imagined places*. Malden, MA: Blackwell.

de Sousa, C. C. (2011–ongoing). *Meta_body*. Retrieved from https://delicatessensl.wordpress.com/meta_body/.

de Sousa, C. C. (October 2012). Mom and me through the looking glass. *Metaverse Creativity*, 2(2), 139–162. http://dx.doi.org/10.1386/mvcr.2.2.137_1.

de Sousa, C. C. (2015). Meta body: Virtual corporeality as a shared creative process. In D. Doyle (Ed.), *New opportunities for artistic practice in virtual worlds*. Hershey, PA: IGI Global. http://dx.doi.org/10.4018/978-1-4666-8384-6.ch009.

Squier, S. M. (2004). *Liminal lives: imagining the human at the Frontiers of biomedicine*. Durham, London: Duke University Press.

Stockburger, A. (2007). Playing the third place: Spatial modalities in contemporary game environments. *International Journal of Performance Arts and Digital Media*, 3(2–3), 223–236. http://dx.doi.org/10.1386/padm.3.2-3.223_1.

Tagore, R. (2011). *Stray birds* (G. Rosenstock, Trans.). Knockeven, Ireland: Salmon Poetry (Original work published 1916).

Veerapen, M. (2011). Encountering oneself and the other: A case study of identity formation in second life. In A. Peachey, & M. Childs (Eds.), *Reinventing ourselves: Contemporary concepts of identity in virtual worlds* (pp. 81–100). London, UK: Springer.

Zapp, A. (2002). *The imaginary hotel [installation]*. Retrieved from http://www.virtualart.at/database/general/work/the-imaginary-hotel.html.

Zapp, A. (2005). *Human avatars [installation]*. Retrieved from http://www.storyrooms.net.

Zielinski, S. (1997). Thinking the border and the boundary. In T. Druckery (Ed.), *Electronic culture: Technology and visual representation*. New York, NY: Aperture Foundation.

CHAPTER 5

Internet Use and Self-Development in Chinese Culture*

Zong-kui Zhou[1,2], Geng-feng Niu[1,2], Qing-qi Liu[1,2], Wu Chen[1,2]
[1]Key Laboratory of Adolescent Cyberpsychology and Behavior (CCNU), Ministry of Education, Wuhan, China;
[2]School of Psychology, Central China Normal University, Wuhan, China

With the exponential growth of information technology in the last two decades, especially the widespread availability of smartphones, the Internet has become an integral part of our daily lives. It plays an important role in how people acquire information, connect with friends and family, and consume entertainment worldwide. In China, the number of Chinese netizens has reached 688 million, which accounts for 50.3% of the Chinese total population, and 54% of these are below the age of 29 (Chinese Internet Network Information Center, CNNIC, 2016).

There are several features of Chinese Internet users. First, social network sites (SNSs) have been increasingly popular among Chinese Internet users. According to a related statistical report, social network sites have reached a usage rate of 61.7% in Chinese Internet users, and 57.9% SNS users use social network sites every day (CNNIC, 2014). A great many young adults and adolescents use social network sites for self-presentation (Liu et al., 2016; Niu et al., 2015a,b). Second, cyberbullying is increasingly common among Chinese Internet users, especially among Chinese adolescents (Hu, Fan, Zhang, Xie, & Hao, 2014; Zhou et al., 2013). Third, in contrast to cyberbullying, lots of Chinese Internet users, especially young adults and adolescents, are willing to engage in online altruistic behavior (Zhao, Zhang, Liu, Wang, & Zhou, 2012; Zheng & Zhao, 2015). Fourth, Internet use has been found to be closely associated with self-development of Chinese individuals. For instance, social network site use may have significant effects on self-esteem and self-identity (Liu, Sun, Zhou, & Niu, 2015; Niu et al., 2015a,b).

These features attract much research attention. Many studies have been conducted to explore influencing factors of Internet use behaviors, as well

---

* This chapter is partially supported by the Chinese National Social Science Foundation Project 11&ZD151.

Boundaries of Self and Reality Online
ISBN 978-0-12-804157-4
http://dx.doi.org/10.1016/B978-0-12-804157-4.00005-0

as the effects of Internet use on self-development of Chinese people. Based on the existing studies conducted among Chinese adolescents and college students, this chapter will explore Internet use and self-development in Chinese culture. We cite studies of non-Chinese people when it is necessary, such as when introducing some concepts or explaining some results, but most of the studies we use will focus on samples from Chinese individuals. In the first part, we will discuss three typical Internet use behaviors (i.e., social network site use, cyberbullying behavior, and online altruistic behavior) and the underlying influence factors. In the second part, we will explore the effect of Internet use on self-development, including self-esteem, self-identity, body image, social self-efficacy, and self-concept clarity. We look forward to contributing to a better understanding of Internet use and its association with self-development in Chinese culture.

INTERNET USE BEHAVIORS OF CHINESE ADOLESCENTS AND COLLEGE STUDENTS

Social Network Site Use and Its Influencing Factors

A social network site is defined as an online service platform that facilitates the building of social networks and social relations among people who share interests, activities, backgrounds, or real-life connections (Wikipedia, 2012). It provides personal profile pages where status, albums, notes, music, and videos can be shared, updated, and viewed by others; and it also offers instant online interactions supported by tools including pop-up windows and message boards. Excluding dating sites, there are approximately 200 active SNSs worldwide (Wikipedia, 2012), one of which is Facebook—the dominant social network service in the world. Since Facebook has been blocked in mainland China, most adolescents and college students in mainland China do not use it. Instead, some indigenous SNSs such as Renren, QQ zone, and WeChat are very popular in mainland China. These native or unique SNSs are major means for Chinese people to develop their own social relations online.

Indeed, social network sites are popular among teenagers and college students. As mentioned above, social network sites have reached a usage rate of 61.7% in Chinese Internet users, and 57.9% of SNS users use social network sites every day (CNNIC, 2014). SNSs have become a new way or medium for people, especially youngsters, to communicate with friends, acquaintances, and even strangers (Cooley, 2010). Thus, it is gradually exerting greater influence on individuals' development (e.g., interpersonal relationships) in various domains of life.

On the one hand, SNSs aim to encourage people to build and maintain their network of interpersonal relationships, which, to a large extent, has a profound impact on individuals' psychosocial adaptation (Valenzuela, Park, & Kee, 2009), such as to overcome shyness, reduce loneliness, improve self-worth or self-esteem, and promote subjective well-being (Ellison, Steinfield, & Lampe, 2007; Indian & Grieve, 2014; Valkenburg & Peter, 2007). Studies on Chinese adolescents and college students also indicate that individuals' self-presentation of the self on SNSs is positively associated with their self-identity, self-esteem, positive emotions, and perceived social support (Liu, Chen, & Zhou, 2015; Liu, Sun, et al., 2015; Niu et al., 2015a,b).

On the other hand, some research has indicated that SNS use is associated with negative psychosocial variables such as self-esteem or depression (e.g., Niu, Sun, Zhou, Kong, & Tian, 2016). Given the positive self-presentation bias in SNSs, SNSs are notorious for giving the impression that other people are happier and having better lives than we are (Chou & Edge, 2012). SNSs offer abundant opportunities for upward social comparison with detailed information about others and continually exposing oneself to SNSs could elicit envy and cause people to make worse self-evaluations. The inconsistency in the literature may be due to the fact that specific patterns of SNS use are not taken into account. Some Chinese scholars have started to focus on the potential benefits and drawbacks of different patterns of SNS use, such as passive SNS use (Chen, Fan, Liu, Zhou, & Xie, 2016). Passive SNS use involves consuming information without any comments or any attempts to provide social connection with others, and may lead to a negative self-evaluation and lower self-esteem, which in turn may undermine users' subjective well-being (Chen et al., 2016).

Reasons why Chinese adolescents or college students more frequently use social network sites such as Renren, QQ zone, and WeChat are explored in some studies. To explore Chinese adolescents' SNS behaviors, a group of 531 volunteer participants during their junior or senior middle school years in Beijing were investigated. Three important behaviors were identified: the management of privacy information, the extent of SNS usages, and the development of offline relations via Renren (Ji, Wang, Zhang, & Zhu, 2014). Researchers also found that most Chinese younger and older adolescents were likely disclosing real names and photos on SNSs. Their latent utilization, socializing, and privacy disclosure SNS behaviors were influenced by age, gender, personality, or attachment styles. Specifically, Wang, Jackson, Wang, and Gaskin (2015) explored the predictors of SNS use (i.e., QQ zone) concerning the influences of specific personality traits and motivations on SNS use by recruiting college students in Southwestern China. Participants answered the Sociability Scale, the Shyness Scale, the attitudes toward Internet use Scale, the Motivation Scale and the Internet self-efficacy. Results of the study showed that sociability, shyness, attitudes toward Internet use, motivation for using SNSs, and Internet self-efficacy predicted SNS use and the predictors were distinct depending on two major functions of SNS use: social and recreational function. Sociability, positive attitudes toward SNS use, social interaction motivation for SNS use and self-efficacy were significant predictors of SNS's social function. In contrast, shyness, positive attitudes toward SNS use, relaxing entertainment motivation and self-efficacy were significant predictors of its recreational function. Another study was conducted to examine the predictors of Chinese netizens' adoption intention of preadopters and postadopters on social network sites (Chang & Zhu, 2011). It uses the partial least squares (PLS) technique to analyze data from online surveys of netizens in China. The results indicated that positive attitudes toward SNS use, subjective norm, and perceived behavior control had significant effects on the adoption intention of pre-adopters and postadopters. Information, meeting new people, and conformity motivations had the same significant effects on preadopters and postadopters on social network sites. Although, entertainment motivation had a significant effect on preadopters, connecting with old friends had none. In contrast, connecting with old friends exerted significant effect on postadopters, but entertainment motivation did not.

Additionally, self-construal was found to be a factor that influenced social network site use. Self-construal refers to an individual's awareness of the relationship between the self and the surrounding environment (Markus & Kitayama, 1991). It can be divided into independent self-construal and interdependent self-construal. People with interdependent self-construal tend to accept group cultural values, and attach importance to others' opinions or the relationship between the self and others, while people with independent self-construal are inclined to accept individualistic cultural values, place emphasis on their inner thoughts and feelings, and portray themselves in terms of their inherent characteristics and goals (Markus & Kitayama, 1991; Wang & Wang, 2016). A study conducted in Taiwanese college students (Chang, 2015) demonstrated that interdependent self-construal was positively associated with social interaction orientation (such as responsiveness and self-disclosure), which further positively predicted different Facebook activities (e.g., responding to others and revealing oneself on Facebook).

In brief, social network sites are popular among Chinese adolescents and college students and have important impacts on their lives. Some essential factors such as demographic factors, personality traits, attitudes or motivations for SNS use, and self-construal are associated with individuals' SNS behaviors. Future research may elaborate specific SNS behaviors and explore the interactive effects of intrapersonal factors and situational factors both in physical and virtual environments on these behaviors in Chinese culture.

Cyberbullying Behavior and Its Influencing Factors

In recent years, with the prevalent use of information communication technologies (ICTs) in the lives of adolescents and college students, Internet and mobile phones are gradually shaping new forms for them to communicate and socialize with acquaintances or strangers. Compared with the advantageous aspects of the Internet, however, it also appears to be a dark side for adolescents to engage in antisocial behaviors, a typical form of which is defined as "cyberbullying" or "electronic bullying." Specifically, it refers to an aggressive, intentional act carried out by a group or an individual, using electronic forms of contact, repeatedly and over time against a victim who cannot easily defend him- or herself (Smith et al., 2008). People can harass, denigrate, abuse, or exclude others via different media, such as email, chat rooms, websites, text messaging, etc. Although three core features in traditional bullying (i.e., intention to aggress, power imbalance, and repetitiveness) may be still applicable to cyberbullying, some unique characteristics in the cyber context may make the manifestation of these features different. For example, the repetitiveness of bullying incident in the cyber environment can be presented by bystanders' or others' behaviors, such as commenting, liking, and retweeting, which may easily lead to a snowball effect. In the traditional form of bullying, the repetitiveness is mainly presented by the original perpetrators' repeated bullying behavior to the victim.

Cyberbullying is a relatively prevalent phenomenon in adolescents and college students as their universal usage of the Internet, especially using mobile devices to access to the Internet. A recent metaanalysis reviewed 80 studies written in English that reported corresponding prevalence rates for cyber and traditional bullying in adolescents (Modecki, Minchin, Harbaugh, Guerra, & Runions, 2014). The results indicated that the mean prevalence rate was 15% for cyberbullying involvement. Utilizing a sample of 1438 high school students from central China, Zhou et al. (2013) found that cyberbullying among high school students in the heartland of central China is relatively common. A total of 34.8% of participants reported having bullied someone and 56.9% reported having been bullied online. Furthermore, students in Hong Kong were also investigated, with 47.3% of students saying they had experienced cyber-victimization at least once and 31.2% of students saying they had cyberbullied others at least once (Leung & McBride-Chang, 2013). It appears that cyberbullying is a normal phenomenon in students' daily life (Hu et al., 2014; Hu, Fan, Zhang, & Zhou, 2013).

Both perpetrators and victims of cyberbullying tend to suffer from a lot of severe internalizing and externalizing problems (Cénat et al., 2014; Chang, Lee, Chen, et al., 2013; Chang, Lee, Chiu, et al., 2013; Hay & Meldrum, 2010; Mitchell, Ybarra, & Finkelhor, 2007). Some features in the cyber environment (e.g., anonymity, lack of a safe haven, potentially large breadth of audience) may make the impacts of cyberbullying especially strong for some young people and in some circumstances (Slonje, Smith, & Frisén, 2013). Research on Chinese students indicated that cyber-victims were more likely to experience depressive symptoms (Hu et al., 2013, 2014), lower self-esteem (Chang, Lee, Chen, et al., 2013; Chang, Lee, Chiu, et al., 2013), and lower levels of social competence, friendship satisfaction, and life satisfaction (Leung & McBride-Chang, 2013), which suggests that parents, educators, and scholars should pay more attention to this problem.

There are some essential factors investigated in the previous studies to influence Chinese students' cyberbullying behavior. Zhou et al. (2013) investigated the risk factors of cyberbullying by utilizing a sample of 1438 high school students from central China. Participants rated themselves on the Internet Usage Scale, the Cyberbullying Inventory, the Traditional Bullying Scale, the Motivation for Cyberbullying, Parents' and Teachers' Supervision, as well as demographics. The results indicated that gender, academic achievement, traditional victimization experiences, and online time, place, or behaviors were prominent factors. Specifically, boys are more likely to be both cyberbullying perpetrators and victims. Students with lower academic achievement are more inclined to be perpetrators of cyberbullying. Students who spend more time on the Internet, have access to the Internet in their bedrooms, have experienced traditional bullying as victims, and are frequently involved in instant-messaging and other forms of online entertainment are more likely to experience cyberbullying. Some of these results were also confirmed in a study by investigating junior high school students in Taiwan. For example, male students and instant messenger users experience more cyberbullying than female students and users of other technologies (Huang & Chou, 2010). However, Huang and Chou's (2010) study did not demonstrate that students' academic achievement was associated with cyberbullying. This may be because students' academic achievement is more valued in mainland China than in Taiwan. From this perspective, in mainland China, students' failure in academic performance is more likely linked with their development in other fields of lives, such as troubled peer relationships. Furthermore, a study was conducted to examine the effect of parenting styles on Chinese adolescents' cyberbullying perpetration. A total of 773 middle school students anonymously completed the S-EMBU, Narcissistic Personality Questionnaire, and Cyberbullying Inventory. The analyses revealed that parental rejection and overprotection positively correlated with cyberbullying, whereas parental emotional warmth negatively correlated with cyberbullying (He, Fan, Niu, Lian, & Chen, 2016).

To sum up, cyberbullying is a common phenomenon among Chinese adolescents and causes serious developmental consequences to them, including internalizing and externalizing problems. Some important factors have been found to be related to cyberbullying, such as age, time spent on the Internet, previous victimization experiences, and parenting styles. More research in the future should focus on the roles of personality traits, related factors both in family and school context, and other unique factors in cyber environment (e.g., anonymity, publicity) in cyberbullying among Chinese adolescents or college students.

Online Altruistic Behavior and Its Influencing Factors

Altruistic behavior is a form of prosocial behavior, which is voluntary and has the ultimate goal of increasing another's welfare (Batson & Shaw, 1991). With the popularity and rapid development of the Internet, altruistic behavior has been extended to the Internet environment, therefore researchers began to focus their attention on altruistic behavior in cyberspace (Amichai-Hamburger, 2008; Wright & Li, 2011). Online altruistic behavior is a kind of voluntary behavior which is manifested in the Internet, and in favor of other people and society but without expecting anything in return (Zheng, 2010). Organizing altruistic and voluntary activities to help people in need in cyberspace is a typical example of prosocial Internet behavior (Ma, Li, & Pow, 2011).

Amichai-Hamburger (2008) stated that the characteristics of the Internet are more conducive to the occurrence of altruistic behavior than those of offline. For example, anonymity made it easier for people to ask for help on the Internet, and immediacy made the altruistic behavior more effective (Zheng & Gu, 2013). This may be due to the disinhibition effect that makes people feel less inhibited by others' opinions or potential behaviors and social conventions, and the Internet might remove some possible barriers to help-seeking/giving. Unfortunately for so many published articles concerning Internet use among adolescents and college students, the author emphasized too much on its negative effects, such as problematic Internet use (Chen, Li, Bao, Yan, & Zhou, 2015), rather than its potential positive consequence such as online altruistic behavior. Take computer games as an example, the literature has stressed the association between game playing and aggression (Anderson & Dill, 2000), but there is some research that also revealed that those who spent more time playing computer games display more prosocial behavior (Mengel, 2014). Every coin has two sides, we should not neglect positive Internet use behavior.

In the mainland China, online altruistic behavior has got some scholars' attention. Zheng, Zhu, and Gu (2011) developed the Internet Altruistic Behavior Scale for Chinese college students. The scale consisted of 30 items, which had four factors such as online support, online guidance, online sharing, and online reminding. This scale showed satisfying reliabilities and validities, and has been used in most of the online altruistic behavior studies in mainland China (e.g., Liu, Chen, et al., 2015; Zhao et al., 2012; Zheng, 2013; Zheng & Gu, 2012).

Previous work that examined the influencing factors of online altruistic behavior has focused on personality, Internet communication motivation, online interpersonal trust, online social support, and self-esteem among other related concepts. Zheng and Gu (2013) found that extraversion, conscientiousness, openness, and self-esteem were positively associated with Internet altruistic behavior, whereas neuroticism was negatively associated with Internet altruistic behavior. Moreover, the association between the big five characteristics, such as openness, conscientiousness, neuroticism, and Internet altruistic behavior was mediated by self-esteem. In addition, Zheng (2012) found that higher levels of optimism were positively related to online social support and Internet altruistic behavior. Besides, online social support plays a partially intermediary role in the effect of optimism on Internet altruistic behavior. Zhao and Zhang (2013) examined the effects of Internet communication motivation and online interpersonal trust on college students' Internet altruistic behavior. The results revealed that Internet communication motivation and online interpersonal trust were positively related to Internet altruistic behavior, the effect of Internet communication motivation on Internet altruistic behavior was partially mediated by online interpersonal trust. Zhao et al. (2012) explored the mediating effects of online social support in the relationship between trait empathy and Internet altruistic behavior. The results indicated that college students' online social support played a full mediation effect on trait empathy and Internet altruistic behavior. Liu, Chen, et al. (2015) examined the impact of Internet use and Internet altruistic behavior, and found that Internet use, including online social interaction, Internet information behavior, and online game behavior, was positively correlated with Internet altruistic behavior—and the positive association between Internet use and online altruistic behavior was mediated by Internet use self-efficacy.

In summary, given some characteristics of the Internet (e.g., anonymity, immediacy), people can easily offer assistance to others online. In the Chinese culture context, an Internet Altruistic Behavior Scale was developed and frequently used in the studies in mainland China. In terms of the influencing factors of online altruistic behavior, the existing literature in China has revealed some important factors, including personality, Internet communication motivation, online interpersonal trust, online social support, and self-esteem.

However, online altruistic behavior research is still in its early stages. Current research on online altruistic behavior is currently only a simple analysis based on its conception, features, and influencing factors, and lacks of in-depth and systematic research (Zheng & Gu, 2012). More specifically, the present studies on online altruistic behavior should be interpreted in light of certain limitations. First, many of the previous studies were cross-sectional, and it is important to realize that cross-sectional design cannot support causal inferences. Future studies should adopt longitudinal or experimental designs to obtain more robust measures of the online altruistic behavior and its influencing factors. Second, most studies only focused on the helper in online altruistic behavior, and a very important future direction is to consider the recipients and help giver in cyberspace simultaneously. In other words, we did not take other disclosure targets (e.g., parents) into consideration. Future research is needed to examine whether the current findings generalize to other disclosure targets. Last, individual differences are also important to consider in regard to online altruistic behavior. Some potential moderator factors, such as gender and different types of online altruistic behavior, are especially informative for our understanding of positive Internet use behavior.

INFLUENCES OF INTERNET USE ON SELF-DEVELOPMENT OF CHINESE ADOLESCENTS AND COLLEGE STUDENTS

The development of the self is the core of individuals' development, and it has a significant impact on the development of individuals' other aspects, as well as individuals' social and psychosocial adaptations. The Internet provides a perfect platform for self-presentation and self-expression, in which users can take time to strategically present and construct an online personality through screenname, avatar, picture, and information-posting (Gu & Jin, 2012). Because online communication is often characterized by reduced auditory and visual cues, as well as the separation from those in real life to some extent, the Internet may encourage individuals to emphasize, change, or conceal certain features of their selves. Further, it provides an excellent space for identity experiments (Valkenburg & Peter, 2008; Zhang, Zhang, Xin, & Zhang, 2016). In addition, the feedback received from online friends will also promote self-reflection and self-assessment. Thus, Internet use may have a close relationship with self-development.

The self in psychological science is an umbrella term. Early researchers considered the self-concept clarity as a monolithic entity, whereas contemporary views of conceptions of the self have drawn a distinction between two components: content and structure (Campbell, 1990; Campbell, Assanand, & Paula, 2003; Campbell et al., 1996). The former refers to an individual's conceptions of who or what he or she is (i.e., the knowledge subcomponent, often termed domain-specific self-concepts, such as physical self and social self-efficacy) and feelings toward oneself (i.e., the evaluative subcomponent, often termed self-esteem), whereas the structural component refers to the organization and hierarchical ordering of the domain-specific self-beliefs and/or self-views (e.g., self-concept clarity). Existing studies on the influences of Internet use on self-development of Chinese individuals involve self-esteem, self-identity, body image (a form of physical self), self-efficacy as well as self-concept clarity. According to the contemporary views of conceptions of the self (Campbell, 1990; Campbell et al., 2003, 1996), self-esteem, self-identity, body image, and social self-efficacy belong to self-content, and self-concept clarity belongs to self-structure. Therefore, we will summarize existing research on the influences of Internet use on self-development of Chinese individuals into two parts: self-content (i.e., self-esteem, self-identity, physical self/body image and social self-efficacy) and self-structure (i.e., self-concept clarity).

Influences of Internet Use on Self-Esteem as a Form Self-Content

Self-esteem refers to one's general value judgment of worthiness (Rosenberg, 1965). Sociometer theory of self-esteem stated that changes in self-esteem help people to gauge whether or not social relationships are functioning properly (Leary, Tambor, Terdal, & Downs, 1995). Self-esteem fluctuates in response to social exclusion and social acceptance (Lamer, Reeves, & Weisbuch, 2015). Given the relevance of social network sites to a variety of social functions, the effect of social network site use on self-esteem has received increased attention in recent years. One Internet use behavior considered to have an effect on self-esteem was self-presentation on a social network site. Self-presentation and belongingness are two primary needs that motivate the use of social network sites (Nadkarni & Hofmann, 2012). Self-presentation on a social network site could be mainly classified into two types: honest self-presentation and positive self-presentation (Kim & Lee, 2011; Niu et al., 2015a,b). Honest self-presentation refers to present true information about oneself regardless of whether the information is positive or not, whereas positive self-presentation refers to presenting positive information about oneself. As social network sites are mainly used to maintain existing interpersonal relationships (CNNIC, 2014; Ellison et al., 2007) and most social network site friends were offline friends who knew or could know the presenter easily in real life, individuals would have to present true information about themselves in case others thought they were dishonest (Liu et al., 2016). Even positive information presented on social network sites can be thought of as true information, but maybe some negative information is not included (Yang, 2014; Yao, Ma, Yan, & Chen, 2014). A previous study showed that positive self-presentation had a direct effect on life satisfaction, while honest self-presentation had a direct effect on life satisfaction through the mediating role of social support (Kim & Lee, 2011). As for self-esteem, Gonzales and Hancock's (2011) behavioral experiment found that participants who updated their profiles and viewed their own profiles during the experiment reported greater self-esteem.

Against this background, some Chinese scholars examined whether self-presentation on social network sites would influence the self-esteem of Chinese individuals and the mediating process underlying the relation (Niu et al., 2015a,b). They conducted a survey in which scales for self-presentation on social network sites (including honest self-presentation and positive self-presentation), social support as well as self-esteem were inquired about. This was administered to 503 college students. The results indicated: (1) both honest self-presentation and positive self-presentation were positively correlated with social support and self-esteem; (2) positive self-presentation could directly and positively predict self-esteem, while honest self-presentation positively predicted self-esteem through the mediating effect of social support. These results suggest different types of self-presentation influence self-esteem with different mechanisms.

In another study, the SNS Honest Self-presentation Questionnaire, SNS Positive Feedback Questionnaire, and General Self-concept Questionnaire were administered to 554 middle and high school students. The results found that honest self-presentation, online positive feedback and self-esteem were significantly correlated with each other. Besides, honest self-presentation could positively predict self-esteem through the mediating role of online positive feedback (Liu et al., 2016). Online positive feedback could be considered as a special kind of social support different from traditional offline social support. Honest self-presentation not only could increase offline social support, but also increases online social support; and both online social support and offline social support contribute to the development of self-esteem.

In addition, different patterns of SNS use may have different effects on self-esteem. A recent study revealed that passive SNS use was especially harmful for users' self-esteem (Chen et al., 2016). Passive social network site use (e.g., just viewing others' post), as opposed to active social network site use, may not benefit so much from social network site use, such as receiving positive feedback from others. On the contrary, passive SNS users may more easily experience negative social comparison, which is detrimental to perceptions about the self and self-esteem. It is worth mentioning that, compared with children, adolescents are more sensitive to the social relationship in cyberspace because of the rapid development of social and self-consciousness in adolescence. The educators and parents should pay more attention to the effects of social network site use on adolescent self-esteem.

Therefore, the studies above suggest that both positive self-presentation and honesty self-presentation on social network sites have positive effects on self-esteem. Different types of self-presentation positively influenced self-esteem through different mechanisms. Moreover, people passively engaged in social network sites may experience a detrimental impact on their self-evaluation and self-esteem. Given the complexity of social network site use, it is especially important to consider different patterns of social network site use.

Influences of Internet Use on Self-Identity as a Form Self-Content

Self-identity was considered to be a stable and coherent perception of one-self. Both adolescents and young adults are in a special developmental stage to develop self-identity (Arnett, 2000). As Ecological System Theory increasingly gets more attention from developmental psychologists, researchers increasingly study self-identity in different developmental environments. In addition to a traditional offline environment, the Internet environment has become an important developmental environment of adolescents and young adults. A lot of individuals are increasingly using the Internet to experiment with their identity through pretending to be someone else when being online (Chai & Gong, 2011; Valkenburg & Peter, 2008). However, previous studies generated mixed conclusions on the association between online identity experimentation (pretending to be someone else in the Internet environment) and self-identity development. Some scholars found that online identity experimentation on social network sites significantly contributes to self-identity development (Zhao, Grasmuck, & Martin, 2008). Some found online identity experimentation was negatively correlated with self-identity, or online identity was not significantly correlated with self-identity (Matsuba, 2006; Valkenburg & Peter, 2008). Online identity experiments may promote the development of self-identity through bridging the gap between the ideal self and the true self, on the other hand, individuals may also receive some negative feedback on their identity experimentation (Chai & Gong, 2011).

Will online identity experimentation positively or negatively influence self-identity development of Chinese adolescents? Some Chinese scholars conducted a study to explore the effects of online identity experimentation on Chinese college students' self-identity as well as the underlying moderating and mediating mechanisms (Zhang et al., 2016). In their study, the Online Identity Experiments Scale, Self-identity Scale, Internet Behaviors Questionnaire, and Compulsive Internet Use Scale were administered to 275 college students. The results showed that: (1) the relationship between online identity experiments and self-identity was moderated by online social tendency. For individuals who had more friends in real life rather than online, online identity experiments significantly negatively predicted self-identity. However, for individuals who had more friends online rather than in real life, although high online identity experimentation still significantly negatively predicted the self-identity, moderate online identity experimentation was positively associated with self-identity; (2) compulsive Internet use played a completely mediating role between online identity experiment and self-identity. This study suggests that, as a whole, online identity experiments may be harmful to the development of college students' self-identity, but a moderate amount of online identity experiment activities could play a positive role in the development of self-identity.

Besides, online identity experimentation is not limited to pretending to be someone else in the anonymous Internet environment, since the Internet environment has had rapid development in recent years. Traditional CMC (computer-mediated communication) environments are characterized by anonymity and reduced cues (Kraut et al., 1998). However, SNSs belong to the latest generation of CMC environments (Antheunis, Valkenburg, & Peter, 2010). They are mainly used to maintain existing interpersonal relationships, and they encourage individuals to disclosure true information (CCNIC, 2014; Ellison et al., 2007). Lots of individuals explore possible identity through self-presentation on social network sites (Chai & Gong, 2011; Zhao et al., 2008), and not pretending to be someone else. Some researchers thus examine whether self-presentation on social network sites would affect the self-identity of Chinese individuals (Liu, Sun, et al., 2015).

In their study, a survey was conducted in which the SNS Self-presentation Questionnaire, SNS Positive Feedback Questionnaire, and Short Measure of Erikson Ego Identity Questionnaire were administered to 484 middle and high school students. The results showed that: (1) both positive self-presentation and honest self-presentation were positively related to online positive feedback as well as ego identity development; and (2) positive self-presentation had no direct effect on ego identity, it could only increase ego identity through the mediating role of online positive feedback while honest self-presentation not only directly and positively predicted ego identity development, but also positively predicted ego identity development through the mediating role of online positive feedback. This study suggests that self-presentation on social network sites has a positive effect on self-identity development, and different self-presentation strategies influence self-identity through different mechanisms.

The above two studies on the relationship between Internet use and self-identity discussed two different identity exploration behaviors of Chinese individuals in two different Internet environments. Pretending to be someone else online is more likely to lead to negative effects on self-identity development, whereas self-presentation on social network site tends to bring about positive effects on self-identity development.

Influences of Internet Use on Other Aspects of Self-Content

In addition to the aforementioned perspectives on self, the physical self is also an important part of self-consciousness and the development of self, which plays a central role in people's physical health, mental health, and psychological well-being (Hsu & Frank, 2015).

Chang, Lee, Chen, et al. (2013) investigated the relationship between Internet use and body image. A total of 2992 students in the 10th grade were recruited from 26 high schools in Taipei, Taiwan. They completed the Thin-ideal Media Exposure Scale, the revised Sociocultural Attitude Toward Appearance Questionnaire, the Multidimensional Body-Self Relations Questionnaire—Appearance Scale, questions about disorder eating behavior and body mass index. The results showed a negative association between the thin-ideal media exposure online and body image—thin-ideal media exposure online would significantly increase the likelihood of body dissatisfaction, which would further contribute to both restrained eating and unhealthy weight control behaviors.

Besides, researchers also have investigated the relationship between online communication and social self-efficacy. Social self-efficacy is a subjective evaluation and faith in an individual's sociability, which guides his or her behavior during interpersonal activities (Fan & Mak, 1998). As online communication is often characterized by reduced auditory and visual cues, the Internet may provide a safe interpersonal space and individuals may have more control in online communication. Thus, online communication may promote social skills and social self-efficacy. Li, Shi, and Dang (2014) examined the relationship between online communication and social self-efficacy. In this study, 574 college students with an average age of 20 were asked to complete the Psychological Need for Online Communication Scale, Shyness Scale, Social Self-efficacy Scale, and Subjective Well-being Scale. The results showed that the psychological needs satisfied by online communication can promote a person's social self-efficacy and subjective wellbeing. Meanwhile, the psychological needs satisfied by online communication can also influence individuals' status of shyness, which will decrease their social self-efficacy and lead to a lower subjective wellbeing. Moreover, Chinese female college students obtain less social self-efficacy from the satisfaction of psychological needs through online communication than their male counterparts did.

In addition to self-esteem and self-identity, Internet use behaviors seem to have complex effects on some aspects of self-content in Chinese individuals, such as social self-efficacy. Besides, self-content includes many other aspects such as academic self-concept and relationship self-concept. More studies are in need to make further explorations.

Influences of Internet Use on Self-Concept Clarity as a Form of Self-Structure

Self-concept clarity is defined as the extent to which one's self-concept is "clearly and confidently defined, internally consistent, and temporally stable" (Campbell et al., 1996, p. 141). As an important aspect of the self, recent studies have shown that, beyond domain–specific self-concepts and global self-esteem, self-concept clarity has made a unique contribution in predicting psychological wellbeing and adjustment (Steffgen, Silva, & Recchia, 2007).

A major developmental task for adolescents is to achieve a firm and unitary sense of self or identity. As mentioned above, the Internet offers individuals opportunities for self-discovery and self-validation by easily encountering a wide variety of people, which may further foster the development of self-concept clarity (Valkenburg & Peter, 2008; Zhang et al., 2016). But Valkenburg and Peter (2011) put forward the self-concept fragmentation hypothesis, stating that the ease with which possible identities can be crafted online may fragment adolescents' personalities. Thus, the many possibilities for self may confront them with people and ideas that may further disintegrate their already fragile personalities, and undermine the ability to coordinate the multiple facets into a coherent whole.

In online communication, social network sites stand out as the most popular and important platform of interpersonal interaction. Thus, researchers (Niu et al., 2016) examined the relationship between Qzone (which is the most visited social network site in China) use and self-concept clarity and the mediating role of social comparison, among Chinese adolescents. Adolescents with active Qzone accounts were recruited from two middle schools in central China to participate in this research, for a total of 679 participants. They completed the Scale for Social Network Site Use Intensity, Iowa–Netherlands Comparison Orientation Measure, and Self-concept Clarity Scale. The results showed that: (1) social network site use was positively correlated with social comparison orientation, but both social network site use and social comparison orientation were negatively correlated with self-concept clarity; (2) social comparison orientation partially mediated the relation between social network site use and self-concept clarity.

Internet Use and Self-Development in Chinese Culture   91

Although self-presentation on social network sites has positive effects on self-esteem, social network site use intensity could negatively influence self-concept clarity. Social network site use has mixed impacts on self-development of Chinese individuals. It exerts different or even opposite effects on different aspects of self.

CONCLUSION

This chapter discussed Internet use and self-development in Chinese culture. We summarized existing studies conducted among Chinese adolescents and college students. Social network site use, cyberbullying, and online altruistic behavior are three typical Internet use behaviors that have attracted much research attention. Sociability, positive attitudes toward SNS use, social interaction motivation for SNS use, self-efficacy and interdependent self-construal were significant predictors of SNS's social function, whereas shyness, positive attitudes toward SNS use, relaxing entertainment motivation, and self-efficacy were significant predictors of its recreational function. Gender, academic achievement, traditional victimization experiences and online time, place, or behaviors are prominent factors of cyberbullying. Individual characteristics such as extraversion, conscientiousness, openness, self-esteem, optimism, and trait empathy are positively associated with Internet altruistic behavior. Internet communication motivation, Internet use self-efficacy, online interpersonal trust, and online social support also have significant and positive effects on Internet altruistic behavior.

It appears that Internet use is closely related to self-development of Chinese individuals. We sum up research on self-content such as self-esteem, self-identity, body image, and social self-efficacy, as well as self-structure such as self-concept clarity. Both positive and honest self-presentations have positive effects on self-esteem and self-identity. Online social support plays a mediating role in the relationship between honest self-presentation on SNSs and self-esteem, as well as self-identity. But online identity experimentation, often termed pretending to be someone else in an anonymous Internet environment, significantly negatively predicts the self-identity. Thin-ideal media exposure online would significantly increase the likelihood of body dissatisfaction, whereas psychological need for online communication could promote a person's social self-efficacy. Moreover, social network site use intensity not only negatively predicts self-concept clarity, but also had an indirect effect on it through the mediating role of social comparison.

Finally, it is necessary to note that most of the studies we collect are based on cross-sectional questionnaire design, which cannot support causal inferences. Future studies should adopt longitudinal or experimental designs to obtain more robust conclusions. Furthermore, these results might be different across different cultures, which require more cross-cultural studies in the future.

REFERENCES

Amichai-Hamburger, Y. (2008). Potential and promise of online volunteering. *Computers in Human Behavior, 24*(2), 544–562.

Anderson, C. A., & Dill, K. E. (2000). Video games and aggressive thoughts, feelings, and behavior in the laboratory and in life. *Journal of Personality and Social Psychology, 78*(4), 772–790.

Antheunis, M. L., Valkenburg, P. M., & Peter, J. (2010). Getting acquainted through social network sites: Testing a model of online uncertainty reduction and social attraction. *Computers in Human Behavior, 26*(1), 100–109.

Arnett, J. J. (2000). Emerging adulthood. A theory of development from the late teens through the twenties. *American Psychologist, 55*(5), 469–480.

Batson, C. D., & Shaw, L. L. (1991). Evidence for altruism: Toward a pluralism of prosocial motives. *Psychological Inquiry, 2*(2), 107–122.

Campbell, J. D. (1990). Self-esteem and clarity of the self-concept. *Journal of Personality and Social Psychology, 59*(3), 538.

Campbell, J. D., Assanand, S., & Paula, A. D. (2003). The structure of the self-concept and its relation to psychological adjustment. *Journal of Personality, 71*(1), 115–140.

Campbell, J. D., Trapnell, P. D., Heine, S. J., Katz, I. M., Lavallee, L. F., & Lehman, D. R. (1996). Self-concept clarity-measurement, personality correlates, and cultural boundaries. *Journal of Personality and Social Psychology, 70*(1), 141–156.

Cénat, J. M., Hébert, M., Blais, M., Lavoie, F., Guerrier, M., & Derivois, D. (2014). Cyberbullying, psychological distress and self-esteem among youth in Quebec schools. *Journal of Affective Disorders, 169*, 7–9.

Chai, X. Y., & Gong, S. Y. (2011). Adolescents' identity experiments: The perspective of inter-net environment. *Advances in Psychological Science, 19*(3), 364–371.

Chang, C. (2015). Self-construal and facebook activities: Exploring differences in social interaction orientation. *Computers in Human Behavior, 53*(6), 91–101.

Chang, F. C., Lee, C. M., Chen, P. H., Chiu, C. H., Pan, Y. C., & Huang, T. F. (2013). Association of thin-ideal media exposure, body dissatisfaction and disordered eating behaviors among adolescents in Taiwan. *Eating Behaviors, 14*(3), 382–385.

Chang, F. C., Lee, C. M., Chiu, C. H., Hsi, W. Y., Huang, T. F., & Pan, Y. C. (2013). Relationships among cyberbullying, school bullying, and mental health in Taiwanese adolescents. *The Journal of School Health, 83*(6), 454–462.

Chang, Y. P., & Zhu, D. H. (2011). Understanding social networking sites adoption in China: A comparison of pre-adoption and post-adoption. *Computers in Human Behavior, 27*(5), 1840–1848.

Chen, W., Fan, C. Y., Liu, Q. X., Zhou, Z. K., & Xie, X. C. (2016). Passive social network site use and subjective well-being: A moderated mediation model. *Computers in Human Behavior, 64*, 507–514.

Chen, W., Li, D. P., Bao, Z. Z., Yan, Y. W., & Zhou, Z. K. (2015). The impact of parent-child attachment on adolescent problematic Internet use: A moderated mediation model. *Acta Psychologica Sinica, 47*(5), 611–623.

China Internet Network Information Center (CNNIC). (2014). *The research report on user behavior of Chinese social networking applications in 2014*. Retrieved from http://www.cnnic.net.cn/hlwfzyj/hlwxzbg/201408/P020140 822379356 6 12744.pdf.

China Internet Network Information Center (CNNIC). (2016). *The 37th statistical report of the development of Chinese Internet Network*. Retrieved from http://www.cnnic.net.cn/hlwfzyj/hlwxzbg/201601/P020160122469130059846.pdf.

Chou, H. T. G., & Edge, N. (2012). They are happier and having better lives than I am: The impact of using Facebook on perceptions of others' lives. *Cyberpsychology, Behavior and Social Networking, 2*, 117–121.

Cooley, S. (2010). Social networks and Facebook. *Mortgage Banking, 70*(6), 84–85.

Ellison, N. B., Steinfield, C., & Lampe, C. (2007). The benefits of Facebook "friends": Social capital and college students' use of online social network sites. *Journal of Computer-Mediated Communication, 12*(4), 1143–1168.

Fan, C., & Mak, A. S. (1998). Measuring social self-efficacy in a culturally diverse student population. *Social Behaviors and Personality: An International Journal, 26*(2), 131–144.

Gonzales, A. L., & Hancock, J. T. (2011). Mirror, mirror on my Facebook wall: Effects of exposure to Facebook on self-esteem. *Cyberpsychology, Behavior, and Social Networking, 14*(1), 79–83.

Gu, X., & Jin, S. H. (2012). Online self-presentation and its characteristics among Chinese adolescents: Preliminary study based on virtual ethnography. In *The 15th National Academic Congress of Psychology (Beijing, China)*.

Hay, C., & Meldrum, R. (2010). Bullying victimization and adolescent self-harm: Testing hypotheses from general strain theory. *Journal of Youth and Adolescence, 39*, 446–459.

He, D., Fan, C.Y., Niu, G. F., Lian, S. L., & Chen, W. (2016). The effect of parenting styles on adolescents' cyberbullying: The mediating role of covert narcissism. *Chinese Mental Health Journal, 24*(1), 41–44.

Hsu, Y. W., & Frank, J. H. L. (2015). The development and validation of the physical self-concept scale for older adults. *Educational Gerontology, 39*(7), 115–132.

Hu, Y., Fan, C.Y., Zhang, F. J., Xie, X. C., & Hao, E. H. (2014). The effect of perceived stress and online social support on the relationship between cyber-victimization and depression among adolescents. *Psychological Development and Education, 2*, 177–184.

Hu, Y., Fan, C.Y., Zhang, F. J., & Zhou, R. (2013). Behavioral characteristics of different roles in cyberbullying and relation to depression in junior students. *Chinese Mental Health Journal, 27*(12), 913–917.

Huang, Y. Y., & Chou, C. (2010). An analysis of multiple factors of cyberbullying among junior high school students in Taiwan. *Computers in Human Behavior, 26*(6), 1581–1590.

Indian, M., & Grieve, R. (2014). When Facebook is easier than face-to-face: Social support derived from Facebook in socially anxious individuals. *Personality and Individual Differences, 59*(2), 102–106.

Ji, Y., Wang, G. J., Zhang, Q., & Zhu, Z. H. (2014). Online social networking behaviors among Chinese younger and older adolescent: The influences of age, gender, personality, and attachment styles. *Computers in Human Behavior, 41*, 393–402.

Kim, J., & Lee, J. R. (2011). The Facebook paths to happiness: Effects of the number of Facebook friends and self-presentation on subjective well-being. *Cyberpsychology, Behavior, and Social Networking, 14*(6), 359–364.

Kraut, R., Patterson, M., Lundmark, V., Kiesler, S., Mukophadhyay, T., & Scherlis, W. (1998). Internet paradox: A social technology that reduces social involvement and psychological well-being? *The American psychologist, 53*(9), 1017–1031.

Lamer, S. A., Reeves, S. L., & Weisbuch, M. (2015). The nonverbal environment of self-esteem: Interactive effects of facial-expression and eye-gaze on perceivers' self-evaluations. *Journal of Experimental Social Psychology, 56*, 130–138.

Leary, M. R., Tambor, E. S., Terdal, S. K., & Downs, D. L. (1995). Self-esteem as an interpersonal monitor: The sociometer hypothesis. *Journal of Personality and Social Psychology, 68,* 518–530.

Leung, A. N.-M., & McBride-Chang, C. (2013). Game on? Online friendship, cyberbullying, and psychosocial adjustment in Hong Kong Chinese children. *Journal of Social and Clinical Psychology, 32*(2), 159–185.

Li, C., Shi, X., & Dang, J. (2014). Online communication and subjective well-being in Chinese college students: The mediating role of shyness and social self-efficacy. *Computers in Human Behavior, 34*(5), 89–95.

Liu, Q. Q., Sun, X. J., Zhou, Z. K., & Niu, G. F. (2015). Self-presentation on social network sites and ego identity: Mediation of online positive feedback. *Chinese Journal of Clinical Psychology, 23*(6), 1094–1097.

Liu, Q. Q., Sun, X. J., Zhou, Z. K., Niu, G. F., Kong, F. C., & Lian, S. L. (2016). The effect of honest self-presentation in online social network sites on life satisfaction: The chain mediating role of online positive feedback and general self-concept. *Journal of Psychological Science, 39*(2), 406–411.

Liu, Q. X., Chen, W., & Zhou, Z. K. (2015). Internet use and online altruistic behavior in college students: The role of Internet use self-efficacy and gender. *Psychological Development and Education, 6,* 685–693.

Ma, H. K., Li, S. C., & Pow, J. W. (2011). The relation of internet use to prosocial and antisocial behavior in Chinese adolescents. *Cyberpsychology, Behavior, and Social Networking, 14*(3), 123–130.

Markus, H. R., & Kitayama, S. (1991). Culture and the self: Implications for cognition, emotion, and motivation. *Psychological Review, 98*(2), 224–253.

Matsuba, M. K. (2006). Searching for self and relationships online. *CyberPsychology & Behavior, 9*(9), 275–284.

Mengel, F. (2014). Computer games and prosocial behaviour. *PLoS One, 9*(4), e94099.

Mitchell, K. J., Ybarra, M., & Finkelhor, D. (2007). The relative importance of online victimization in understanding depression, delinquency, and substance use. *Child Maltreatment, 12*(4), 314–324.

Modecki, K. L., Minchin, J., Harbaugh, A. G., Guerra, N. G., & Runions, K. C. (2014). Bullying prevalence across contexts: A meta-analysis measuring cyber and traditional bullying. *The Journal of Adolescent Health, 55*(5), 602–611.

Nadkarni, A., & Hofmann, S. G. (2012). Why do people use Facebook? *Personality and Individual Differences, 52*(3), 243–249.

Niu, G. F., Bao, N., Fan, C. Y., Zhou, Z. K., Kong, F. C., & Sun, X. J. (2015). The effect of self-presentation in online social network sites on self-esteem: The mediating role of social support. *Journal of Psychological Science, 38*(4), 939–945.

Niu, G. F., Bao, N., Zhou, Z. K., Fan, C. Y., Kong, F. C., & Sun, X. J. (2015). The impact of self-presentation in online social network sites on life satisfaction: The effect of positive affect and social support. *Psychological Development and Education, 31*(5), 563–570.

Niu, G. F., Sun, X. J., Zhou, Z. K., Kong, F. C., & Tian, Y. (2016). The impact of social network site (Qzone) on adolescents' depression: The serial mediation of upward social comparison and self-esteem. *Acta Psychologica Sinica, 48*(10), 1282–1291.

Niu, G. F., Sun, X. J., Zhou, Z. K., Tian, Y., Liu, Q. Q., & Lian, S. L. (2016). The effect of adolescents' social networking site use on self-concept clarity: The mediating role of social comparison. *Journal of Psychological Science, 39*(1), 97–102.

Rosenberg, M. (1965). *Society and the adolescent self-image.* Princeton: Princeton University Press.

Slonje, R., Smith, P. K., & Frisén, A. (2013). The nature of cyberbullying, and strategies for prevention. *Computers in Human Behavior, 29*(1), 26–32.

Smith, P. K., Mahdavi, J., Carvalho, M., Fisher, S., Russell, S., & Tippett, N. (2008). Cyberbullying: Its nature and impact in secondary school pupils. *Journal of Child Psychology and Psychiatry, 49*(4), 376–385.

Steffgen, G., Silva, M. D., & Recchia, S. (2007). Self-concept clarity scale (SCSS): Psychometric properties and aggression correlates of a German version. *Individual Differences Research, 5*, 230–245.

Valenzuela, S., Park, N., & Kee, K. F. (2009). Is there social capital in a social network site? Facebook use and college students' life satisfaction, trust, and participation. *Journal of Computer-Mediated Communication, 14*(4), 875–901.

Valkenburg, P. M., & Peter, J. (2007). Internet communication and its relation to well-being: Identifying some underlying mechanisms. *Media Psychology, 9*(1), 43–58.

Valkenburg, P. M., & Peter, J. (2008). Adolescents' identity experiments on the internet consequences for social competence and self-concept unity. *Communication Research, 35*(2), 208–231.

Valkenburg, P. M., & Peter, J. (2011). Online communication among adolescents: An integrated model of its attraction, opportunities, and risks. *The Journal of Adolescent Health, 48*(2), 121–127.

Wang, J. L., Jackson, L. A., Wang, H. Z., & Gaskin, J. (2015). Predicting social networking site (SNS) use: Personality, attitudes, motivation and Internet self-efficacy. *Personality and Individual Differences, 80*, 119–124.

Wang, Y., & Wang, L. (2016). Self-construal and creativity: The moderator effect of self-esteem. *Personality and Individual Differences, 99*, 184–189.

Wikipedia. (2012). *List of social networking websites.* http://en.wikipedia.org/wiki/List_of_social _networking_websites.

Wright, M. F., & Li, Y. (2011). The associations between young adults' face-to-face prosocial behavior and their online prosocial behaviors. *Computers in Human Behavior, 27*(5), 1959–1962.

Yang, C. C. (2014). *It makes me feel good: A longitudinal, mixed-methods study on college freshmen's Facebook self-presentation and self-development* (Unpublished Doctoral Dissertation). University of Wisconsin-Madison.

Yao, Q., Ma, H. W., Yan, H., & Chen, Q. (2014). Analysis of social network users' online behavior from the perspective of psychology. *Advances in Psychological Science, 22*(10), 1647–1659.

Zhang, M., Zhang, Y., Xin, Z. Q., & Zhang, Q. H. (2016). The relationship between college students' online identity experiment and self-identity: The role of online social tendency and compulsive Internet use. *Psychological Development and Education, 32*(1), 98–105.

Zhao, H. H., & Zhang, H. Y. (2013). College students' Internet communication motivation and Internet altruistic behavior: The mediating effects of online interpersonal trust. *Psychological Research, 6*(6), 92–96.

Zhao, H. H., Zhang, H. Y., Liu, Q. X., Wang, F. X., & Zhou, Z. K. (2012). College students' trait empathy and Internet altruistic behavior: The mediating effects of online social support. *Psychological Development and Education, 5*, 478–486.

Zhao, S., Grasmuck, S., & Martin, J. (2008). Identity construction on Facebook: Digital empowerment in anchored relationships. *Computers in Human Behavior, 24*(5), 1816–1836.

Zheng, X. L. (2010). *Internet altruistic behavior of undergraduates: Scale developments and multilevel analysis* (Doctoral Dissertation). Shanghai: Shanghai Normal University.

Zheng, X. L. (2012). A structural equation model for the relationship between optimism, anxiety, online social support and internet altruistic behavior. *Chinese Journal of Special Education, 11*, 84–89.

Zheng, X. L. (2013). The relationship between reality altruistic behavior and Internet altruistic behavior: The role of online social support. *Psychological Development and Education, 1*, 31–37.

Zheng, X. L., & Gu, H. G. (2012). Personality traits and Internet altruistic behavior: The mediating effect of self – esteem. *Chinese Journal of Special Education, 2*, 69–74.

Zheng, X. L., & Gu, H. G. (2013). Relationship between Internet altruistic behavior of undergraduates and Internet-behavior preference: Effects of class environments. *Studies of Psychology & Behavior, 11*(5), 690–696.

Zheng, X. L., & Zhao, W. (2015). Relationship between Internet altruistic behavior and hope of middle school students: The mediating role of self-efficacy and self-esteem. *Psychological Development and Education, 31*(4), 428–436.

Zheng, X. L., Zhu, C. L., & Gu, H. G. (2011). Development of Internet altruistic behavior scale for college students. *Chinese Journal of Clinical Psychology, 19*(5), 606–608.

Zhou, Z., Tang, H., Tian, Y., Wei, H., Zhang, F., & Morrison, C. M. (2013). Cyberbullying and its risk factors among Chinese high school students. *School Psychology International, 34*(6), 630–647.

CHAPTER 6

Beyond the Boundaries of the Game: The Interplay Between In-Game Phenomena, Structural Characteristics of Video Games, and Game Transfer Phenomena

Angelica B. Ortiz de Gortari[1,2,3], Mark D. Griffiths[4]
[1]University of Liège, Liège, Belgium; [2]University of Bergen, Bergen, Norway; [3]University of Hertfordshire, Hatfield, United Kingdom; [4]Nottingham Trent University, Nottingham, United Kingdom

The rewarding nature of video game playing can be observed through transfers in space, inducing, not only temporary visual, auditory, or kinesthetic sensations while playing, but resulting in sensorial imprints that suddenly occur after playing. Furthermore, virtual worlds are becoming more immersive, and games are lived and experienced rather than just being played on the screen. Arguably, there is a tendency among some individuals not to dichotomize between actual and nonactual worlds. We are beginning to witness an integration between the simulation of real-world environments, augmented reality games, and use of virtual reality headsets. Consequently, this challenges our concept of reality for two important reasons: (1) virtuality allows us to live parallel lives in nonactual worlds by adopting virtual identities and materializing fantasies (Ryan, 1999), and (2) the consequences of virtual immersion are capable of facilitating and/or stimulating postplay phenomena, which manifest as hallucinatory-like experiences, such as seeing or hearing elements from the game after playing. This poses challenges to individuals that, even though they are aware that the virtual elements (e.g., sounds, images) are not real, for a split second, they find themselves responding intuitively to those elements as if they are in the virtual world. In addition, the consequences of virtual immersion go beyond the virtual space and can influence the way we perceive and interact with the real world (Dill, 2009).

In studies with over 3500 participants, gamers have reported involuntary phenomena directly related to video game content that manifest as altered sensorial perceptions, spontaneous thoughts, actions, and behaviors, referred

Boundaries of Self and Reality Online
ISBN 978-0-12-804157-4
http://dx.doi.org/10.1016/B978-0-12-804157-4.00006-2

97

to as Game Transfer Phenomena (GTP). The structural characteristics of the game and the nature of the game activity appear to facilitate transfer effects (Ortiz de Gortari, Aronsson, & Griffiths, 2011; Ortiz de Gortari & Griffiths, 2014a,b,c; Ortiz de Gortari & Griffiths, 2015, 2016).

This chapter is a first attempt to map in–game phenomena and structural characteristics of video games, with transfers of game experiences manifesting in a number of modalities: altered perceptions, automatic mental processes, and behaviors with the purpose of stimulating future empirical work for hypothesis testing. This chapter also examines which phenomena, inherent to the video game world and elements in gameplay, appear to contribute to transfer of game experiences.

GAME TRANSFER PHENOMENA: A BRIEF OVERVIEW

A number of studies by the present authors have investigated the relationship between GTP and playing habits, individual characteristics and motivations for playing, as well as severity levels of GTP. In a sample of over 2000 gamers, playing habits, particularly (1) the length of the playing sessions (3 to 6 hours sessions), and (2) individual factors, such as having a preexisting medical condition and playing for immersion, exploration, customization, mechanics, and for escape from the real world, have been significantly associated with GTP (Ortiz de Gortari & Griffiths, 2015). Those with severe levels of GTP (i.e., experience GTP frequently and several types) were significantly more likely to (1) be students; (2) be aged 18–22 years; (3) have played video games every day in sessions of 6 hours or more; (4) have played to escape from the real world; (5) have a mental disorder, sleep disorder, or consider themselves as having dysfunctional gaming or gaming addiction; and (6) have experienced distress or dysfunction due to GTP (Ortiz de Gortari, Oldfield, & Griffiths, 2016).

A cross–cultural comparison showed that Spanish-speaking gamers (i.e., a sample with a large percentage of Latin American participants) were more likely to experience GTP that manifest as external or exogenous phenomena (e.g., involuntary movements of limbs as a response to external stimuli, verbal outburst, act out a behavior, change of behavior, seeing images with open eyes) than English-speaking gamers (Ortiz de Gortari, 2015b).

GTP have also been reported in over 400 unique video games, including old and modern games, in a large variety of video game genres (Ortiz de Gortari, 2015b). Among the most popular video game genres associated with severe levels of GTP are: massively multiplayer online role-playing games, strategy games, simulation games, and fighting games (Ortiz de Gortari et al., 2016). A higher level of engagement in the narrative has been suggested as being important for the occurrence of biased perceptions and experiences (e.g., thoughts about the game being triggered by physical objects, sounds, and/or music) (Poels, Ijsselsteijn, & de Kort, 2014).

No systematic analysis has ever been conducted in relation to the structural characteristics of video games associated with GTP, but some patterns have been observed among qualitative data (Ortiz de Gortari, 2015b). These are presented below according to each of the GTP modalities/submodalities:

- *Altered visual perceptions.* Afterimages of prolonged duration that arise recurrently, usually in the back of the eyelids, have been reported frequently when playing video games with monotonous patterns and repetitive gameplay. Perceptual neural adaptations to visual effects have been reported in relation to abrupt changes of colors and lights (e.g., eagle vision in *Assassin's Creed*) and visual effects (e.g., slow-motion effect in *Crysis*) (in eagle vision mode, all of the environment turns blackish, and relevant objects glow in different colors). Furthermore, motion aftereffects have been associated with music/dance video games and high-speed racing video games. Hallucinations involving the seeing of video game elements with open eyes or the misinterpretation of video game images appear to be more related to recurrent feedback images of specific video game elements such as maps, heads-up displays, power bars, and menus (Ortiz de Gortari & Griffiths, 2014a).
- *Altered auditory perceptions.* Recurrent replays of music (e.g., earworms) have repeatedly been reported by gamers who play games that use background music. Also, hallucinatory-like experiences, such as suddenly hearing a sound from the video game or misinterpreting real-life sounds have been reported in relation to repetitive sounds associated with fundamental activities within the game. Sounds reported by gamers include high-pitch and loud sounds (e.g., bullets, explosions, screams), but also more discrete sounds (e.g., lasers, the spreading of a net). Also, sounds embedded as rewards, alerts, or punishments have been reported. The content of hearing voices include instructions, commands, echoing voices, and whispers (Ortiz de Gortari & Griffiths, 2014b).
- *Body-related perceptions.* These experiences have been reported in video games that use effects of velocity, slow motion, constant, and/or fast movements. Stereotypical body movement, such as strafing (i.e., moving sideways) around corners, has been related to playing first-person shooter

games. Other examples include tactile hallucinations related to the haptic feedback of gamepads (Ortiz de Gortari & Griffiths, 2014a).

- *Automatic mental processes.* Repetitive activities in the game (e.g., climbing, jumping, running) and associations between visual and/or auditory cues and activities have manifested as thoughts, urges, and/or behaviors when the impulses are not held back. This also includes thoughts about using video game elements that have a function, such as elements of feedback (e.g., health bars, maps, bionic arms, hook) (Ortiz de Gortari & Griffiths, 2014c).
- *Automatic Behaviors.* Automatic behaviors include most video games that involve the simulation of real-life activities (e.g., driving, searching, jumping, climbing buildings) (Ortiz de Gortari & Griffiths, 2014c).

IN-GAME PHENOMENA RELEVANT TO GAME TRANSFER PHENOMENA

There is a lack of understanding of which in-game phenomena and structural characteristics of the video game lead to GTP experiences. Four core factors relevant for GTP to occur have been identified by the present authors: (1) sensory perceptual stimulation, (2) high cognitive load, (3) dissociative states, and (4) high emotional engagement (see Table 6.1 for overview of the in-game phenomena related to GTP). The factors proposed are based on analysis of gamers' self-reports concerning GTP (Ortiz de Gortari et al., 2011; Ortiz de Gortari & Griffiths, 2014a, 2014b, 2014c) and are supported by review of related literature. However, there they are preliminary in nature and thus warrant further empirical validation.

SENSORY PERCEPTUAL STIMULATION

Virtual immersion is characterized by sensorial stimulation due to the exposure to repetitive or recurrent synthetic stimuli (e.g., visual, aural, and haptic effects). Traditionally, perceptually related aftereffects have been associated with the use of highly immersive technologies, such as simulators and head-mounted displays (LaViola, 2000). However, research concerning GTP has found a large variety of perceptual distortions, misperceptions, and hallucinations with video game content when playing on a computer or TV screen. The main in-game phenomena suggested to be related to GTP concerning sensory perceptual stimulation are: (1) exposure to specific

Table 6.1 Overview of the in-game phenomena related to Game Transfer Phenomena (GTP)

In-game phenomena	Game Transfer Phenomena (GTP)	Examples
Sensory perceptual stimulation		
Special visual effects	Perceptual adaptations (e.g., perceive objects, environment, time distorted)	Seeing objects pixelated or floating, environments in monochrome color, intensified color, objects having a colored outline or a halo. Feeling time slowing down.
Monotonous gameplay	Hallucinatory-like phenomena (e.g., seeing images, hearing sounds, or feeling tactile and kinesthetic sensations)	Seeing video game images in the back of the eyelids; tactile feedback of the gamepad; feeling the pushing of the gamepad button; hearing music, sounds, or voices after playing
	Multisensory and induced synesthesia	Movements of fingers when hearing music or seeing images from the video game while hearing the music from the game or/and feeling moving of limbs.
Sensory discrepancies	Postural instability and lack of motor flexibility	Uncoordinated motor movements or feeling the body stiffen, such as arms moving upwards, automatically strafing (i.e., moving sideways) around corners after playing first-person shooter games.
	Vestibular adaptations	Illusion of body movement as feeling the movement from the video game when trying to fall asleep.
		Out-of-body–like experiences such as feeling as being in a "zombie state," the "mind getting disconnected from the body," and "like being in a hangover."

Continued

Table 6.1 Overview of the in-game phenomena related to game transfer phenomena (GTP)—cont'd

In-game phenomena	Game Transfer Phenomena (GTP)	Examples
High cognitive load		
Pairing between stimuli	Misperceptions	Thinking that birds in real life are fighter planes from a video game.
	False expectations	Interpreting events and responding to real-life objects using the logic of the video game.
	Misattribution errors	Seeing images from menus in conversations, maps in the corner of their eyes when looking for an address, or seeing tags above peoples' heads.
Engaging in repetitive problem solving	Lack of cognitive flexibility or perseverative mental states	Continued looking for patterns, trying to arrange objects in sets, or continued scanning for items from the video game in real-life contexts.
Dissociative states: Immersion and subjective sense of presence in the virtual world		
Feeling as if the game was real	Automatic associations between both worlds and source monitoring errors	Confusing memories from the video game with those from real life or confusing video game characters with real individuals, such as thinking that something needs to be done in real life when this actually needs to be done in the video game.
Simulation of body movements	Automatic motor activation when in real life encountering game-related cues associated with in-game actions	Involuntary movements of fingers or arms when wanting to use video game, feeling the urge to perform actions or body movements as in the video game in real life.

Table 6.1 Overview of the in-game phenomena related to game transfer phenomena (GTP)—cont'd

In-game phenomena	Game Transfer Phenomena (GTP)	Examples
Ownership and functionality of video game elements	Attachment to video game elements and wanting to use video game elements in real life	Feeling strange when not having video game elements in real life such as a bionic arm, thoughts popping up when wanting to resolve situations in real life using video game elements, to extreme cases where experiencing temporal inability to accomplish real-life tasks for not having the video game elements.
	Cognitive failures as slips of actions	Confusing video game controls and those from real-life machinery or vehicles, like looking for the R1 button for braking while cycling.
Embodiment of virtual entities that lead to	Depersonalization-like experiences	Feeling as being the game character, such as going to bed thinking being Batman or feeling as the character in the game when traveling in the subway.
	Body-related altered perceptions	Feeling shorter after playing a video game with a small character in a gigantic world.
High emotional engagement		
Rewarding and punitive features	Attention bias and overreaction toward game-related cues	Trivial stimuli become salient and capturing gamers' attention. Resulting sometimes in overreactions, such as ducking when seeing a security camera.
	Change of moods	Feeling relaxed or hypervigilant when encountering stimuli related to the video game.
Accomplishments in the video game	Feeling empowered and having irrational thoughts related to the video game	Gamers momentarily thinking they can climb buildings and actually trying to do it, or trying to break some object with only a finger.

visual effects that lead to perceptual adaptations, such as perceiving objects, environment, time, and/or body as distorted; (2) monotonous gameplay that leads to hallucinatory–like phenomena when seeing images, hearing sounds, feeling tactile and kinesthetic sensations, and/or multisensorial sensations that induce synesthesia as daytime or nighttime phenomena; and (3) sensorial discrepancies as precursors for out-of-body–like experiences, illusions of body movement, and uncoordinated body movements.

Specific Sensory Effects

The brain tends to easily adapt to the perception it receives (Harris, 1965), including such things as patterns and visual effects; therefore, perceptual adaptations can take place when virtual environments alter the person's vision, especially when there is prolonged exposure (LaViola, 2000). Playing video games can lead to visual aftereffects, and gamers have reported perceptual distortion of objects or environments (Ortiz de Gortari & Griffiths, 2014a). Such reports include: (1) seeing objects pixelated or floating, (2) seeing environments in monochrome color or intensified color, and (3) seeing objects cell-shaded with a colored outline or with halos.

Playing music or dance games such as *Guitar Hero* or *Rock Band* have been have found to provoke motion aftereffects, such as waterfall motion effects (Dyson, 2010). Given that the images of the game descend at a certain velocity, when gamers take away their eyes from the screen, they continue to see movement. Gamers have reported that their vision becomes "wavy" and that objects appear to "levitate" or "slowly moves upward" (Ortiz de Gortari et al., 2011; Ortiz de Gortari & Griffiths, 2014a). Furthermore, after playing games with high velocities or with slow–motion visual effects, gamers perceive time going slowly or moving slowly (Ortiz de Gortari & Griffiths, 2014a). For instance, one gamer explained:

> *"After playing 'Crysis' with infinite ammo for an extensive period of time, only blowing things up (which slow down the frame rate), I saw the world in a slower frame rate. It was kind of awesome. It was not incredibly slower or frustrating. It just felt a little stiffer. It lasted for maybe two days. I could induce intentionally when it started to wear off. It was awesome."*
>
> **Ortiz de Gortari and Griffiths (2014a, p. 102).**

Monotonous Gameplay

The playing of monotonous video games has been associated with seeing images, hearing sounds, and having kinesthetic sensations with video game content, and has been reported in a variety of circumstances. Various experimental studies have used stereotypical puzzle–tile games such as *Tetris* or *Alpine Racer* (i.e., a downhill skiing simulator) as a visuomotor learning task to investigate how daytime experiences are replayed during sleep onset (Stickgold, Malia, Maguire, Roddenberry, & O'Connor, 2000).

A number of studies have reported gamers seeing video game images at sleep onset (Kusse, Shaffii-Le Bourdiec, Schrouff, Matarazzo, & Maquet, 2012; Ortiz de Gortari & Griffiths, 2014a; Stickgold et al., 2000; Wamsley, Perry, Djonlagic, Reaven, & Stickgold, 2010). The visualizations are characterized by only seeing elements of the gameplay, rather than external elements, such as screens, keyboards, or gamepads (Kusse et al., 2012; Ortiz de Gortari & Griffiths, 2014a; Stickgold et al., 2000; Wamsley et al., 2010). Furthermore, the lack of emotional content in gamers' experiences at sleep onset suggests the absence of the participation of cerebral structures, such as the amygdala and the reward system (Kusse et al., 2012). A large number of these visualizations have been considered to be the result of hypnagogic states (i.e., the transactional period between being awake and falling asleep) (Mavromatis, 2010). This is one of the most common types of hallucination among the nonclinical population (Collerton, Perry, & McKeith, 2005), and is suggested to be mediated by implicit memory since even amnesic patients that do not recall having played the game have reported seeing such images (Stickgold et al., 2000). However, healthy gamers have also been known to incorporate features of previous versions of the same video game they have played in the construction of the images. This suggests that these experiences are not simply products of automatic replay of recent activity or exposure to sensory stimuli, but are also the result of activation of remote memories (Stickgold et al., 2000).

In a survey concerning GTP ($N = 2363$), 77% of the gamers reported having visualized or seen video game images in the back of their eyelids (Ortiz de Gortari & Griffiths, 2016). Seeing such images have been reported both at daytime and nighttime. When the images were seen for prolonged periods of time, it provoked sleep deprivation (Ortiz de Gortari et al., 2011; Ortiz de Gortari & Griffiths, 2014a). For example:

"I don't usually play it in the evening now…When I go to bed, I can see 'Tetris' shapes on the back of my eyelids and I try to make the shapes all fit together…It's sort of fun for a while but then I think "I need to sleep!"

Ortiz de Gortari and Griffiths (2014a, p. 100).

"Lumines, oh God. I play 3 days and I have seen those damn squares everywhere, even when my eyes open."

Ortiz de Gortari and Griffiths (2014a, p. 100).

Hypnotic proneness and visuospatial skills have been associated with afterimage persistence (Atkinson & Crawford, 1992); therefore, the "hypnotic properties" of the game that lead to trance states may be enacted (e.g., automatic playing, attention absorption, and flow states). Gamers have also reported multisensory experiences when trying to sleep, and they have felt movements of fingers or hearing music from the game while seeing the images (Ortiz de Gortari & Griffiths, 2014a). For instance:

> *"It's annoying, but very interesting. First this happened when started to play 'DDR' [Dance Dance Revolution], as I was falling asleep I would literally feel my feet moving with an image I made up of the game in my head. . . . Recently for 'Robot Unicorn Attack,' as I fall asleep, I picture the game blowing by in my head, with my fingers twitching (at least they feel like they are moving) to control the unicorn."*
> **Ortiz de Gortari and Griffiths (2014a, p. 101).**

Moreover, some gamers have reported synesthesia–like experiences. For instance:

> *"Playing so much 'Rock Band,' some songs make me see green, red, yellow, blue and orange notes in my vision."*
> **Ortiz de Gortari and Griffiths (2014a, p. 101).**

Additionally, gamers have reported sensations of tactile feedback of the gamepad, or they have felt themselves pushing the buttons of the gamepad (Ortiz de Gortari & Griffiths, 2014a). Tactile sensations related to the game were found in 41% of the participants in a survey on GTP (Ortiz de Gortari & Griffiths, 2016). Other gamers have continued to hear music, sound, and/or voices after video game playing as auditory imagery, inner speech, and hallucinations (Griffiths & Ortiz de Gortari, 2015; Ortiz de Gortari & Griffiths, 2014b). For instance:

> *"'Command & Conquer: Red Alert' was an exception. I used to wake up with 'Hell March' in my head for weeks after finishing the game."*
> **Ortiz de Gortari (2015b, p. 140).**

Sensorial Discrepancies

It is well-known that motion sickness symptoms (i.e., nausea, eyestrain, and visual discomfort) are the results of neural adaptations due to sensorial discrepancies and disrupted integration between different systems (e.g., vestibular, proprioceptive, tactile, and visual). Disruption in multisensory integration due to the virtual immersion has been suggested to be responsible for: (1) postural instability or motor flexibility (Murata, 2004),

(2) vestibular adaptations, and (3) out-of-body–like experiences (Seifert & Patalano, 1991).

Postural instability and lack of motor flexibility includes uncoordinated body movements, such as arms moving upwards automatically and feeling the body stiffen, which may be related to neural adaptions when experienced soon after playing (Ortiz de Gortari & Griffiths, 2014c). For instance:

> *"Many times! 'Quake 2,' made me literally strafe my way around corners in real life!"*
>
> *"I played 'Megaman' one to six. After this, my arms would come up automatically like they were going to push the reload save button. It was actually kind of embarrassing."*
>
> **Ortiz de Gortari and Griffiths (2014c, p. 442).**

Vestibular adaptations manifest as *illusions of body movement*, and are related to *out-of-body–like experiences*. During illusions of body movement, the constant movements or haptic perceptions (e.g., flying, bouncing, or tumbling in the game) persevere, and gamers report that they keep feeling the movement from the game when trying to fall asleep (Ortiz de Gortari & Griffiths, 2014a). This is similar to the feeling sailors have when they keep feeling the movement from the sea due to vestibular adaptation (i.e., Mal de Debarquement Syndrome or disembarkment syndrome; Cha, 2009). Bodily sensations of movement were reported by over half of all gamers by Ortiz de Gortari and Griffiths (2016). For instance:

> *"I would be playing tons of 'Armored Core,' and trying to fall asleep that night. I could 'feel' the constant movement of an arena fight because I had done the whole damn arena list before bed. I can liken this to feeling the waves at the beach after you get home."*
>
> **Ortiz de Gortari (2015b, p. 117).**

Researchers have suggested that disrupted sensorial processing (e.g., visual, vestibular, proprioceptive), which are easily stimulated by the virtual immersion, and inputs received from various systems, are important precursors of out-of-body experiences and autoscopy (Blanke & Mohr, 2005). Research on GTP experiences reported by gamers include reports of feeling like they are in a "zombie state," like the "mind is disconnect[ing] from the body," and "like being in a hangover" (Ortiz de Gortari, 2010). In a survey with 2362 gamers, almost half reported having perceived time and/ or feeling the body differently after playing a video game, and almost one-third felt as though the mind had disconnected from the body after playing (Ortiz de Gortari & Griffiths, 2016).

HIGH COGNITIVE LOAD

Playing a video game is a highly demanding activity that requires interactivity and involves the processing of visual and auditory stimuli, executive functions, and perceptual and motor skills (Powers, Brooks, Aldrich, Palladino, & Alfieri, 2013). The main in-game phenomena related to GTP in the cognitive load are: (1) pairing between stimuli that lead to attentional bias and hallucinatory-like experiences explained as misattribution errors, and (2) engaging in repetitive problem-solving that lead to perseverative mental states.

Pairing Between Stimuli

The incidentally learned associations via the repetitive pairing between cues and activities in the game (i.e., implicit learning) leads to gamers acquiring schemas or templates that later influence their interpretations of experiences or responses in the real world. Manifestations include (1) misperceptions, (2) false expectations, and (3) misattribution errors.

Misperceptions

Gamers have confused physical objects or sounds with those from the game, such as thinking that birds in real life are fighter planes from a video game (Ortiz de Gortari et al., 2011; Ortiz de Gortari & Griffiths, 2014a,b). In a survey, 46% had misperceived a real-life object with something from within a video game, and 65% had misinterpreted a sound in real life with something from a video game (Ortiz de Gortari & Griffiths, 2016). For instance:

> "For minutes I would confuse airplanes in the sky for [unmanned aerial vehicles] in 'Modern Warfare 2.'"
>
> **Ortiz de Gortari and Griffiths (2014a, p. 102).**

False Expectations

Gamers have expected that something will happen as in the game (Ortiz de Gortari & Griffiths, 2014c). As one gamer explained:

> "After a marathon of 'Grand Theft Auto,' I was driving and saw a car flipped upside down and thought 'Go! It is going to explode in 5 seconds!'"
>
> **Ortiz de Gortari (2015b, p. 174).**

Other gamers have performed actions expecting to find something from the video game. There is the extreme case of a gamer who found a barrel in a shopping store, and he broke it looking for bananas, as he would typically do when collecting points in the game *Donkey Kong* (Ortiz de Gortari & Griffiths, 2014c).

Misattribution Errors

Gamers have perceived internal thoughts as sensorial experiences. For example, gamers have seen menus in conversations, maps in the corner of their eyes when looking for an address, and tags above peoples' heads. Moreover, sometimes sounds or music related to the game have been heard as if coming from external sources (Ortiz de Gortari & Griffiths, 2014b). Some gamers have even checked if they left the console on because the music they heard was very vivid. For instance:

> *"I will wake up sometimes and check if my computer is off because I swear I heard videogame music coming out of my speakers. I need help."*
> **Ortiz de Gortari (2015b, p. 140).**

> *"After a 'Team Fortress 2' binge one day, I started hearing spies decloaking around the house. Would move my head around before I noticed what I was doing."*
> **Ortiz de Gortari and Griffiths (2014b, p. 64).**

Other gamers have reported hallucinatory-like experiences when hearing sounds from the game in real-life conditions that reminded them of the video game. One gamer heard the sound from the game that indicated that a monster was close by and started to look around and became scared.

Repetitive Problem-Solving

Engaging in repetitive cognitive operations (e.g., strategies) to solve problems in a video game facilitates the acquisition of action schemas. Specific tasks can be activated by specific environmental stimuli since strong associations have been established between stimuli and actions executed by video game playing (Ridderinkhof, Span, & Van Der Molen, 2002). When gamers are unable to override the action schemas learned in the game, they continue applying the strategies in real-life contexts that share salient features with the video game, showing perseveration or cognitive inflexibility (Ridderinkhof et al., 2002). However, ecological approaches that are strongly against cognitivist perspectives may argue that gamers are discovering specific affordances in real-life contexts where they apply learning based on their expertise as gamers (Linderoth, 2012). For instance:

> *"Once I stayed up all night to play 'Lemmings.' The next day, when I was trying to read, I kept trying to figure out how to get the lemmings across the sentences."*
> **Ortiz de Gortari and Griffiths (2014c, p. 442).**

> *"There is a large football court with some five meter high buildings around it when I then walk out in the football field I try to find all the weaknesses and strong points as well as hiding places then I sometimes wants to shout orders to my friends and start running into cover."*
> **Ortiz de Gortari et al. (2011, p. 22).**

More specifically, performing a highly demanding activity for a prolonged period of time, such as playing a video game, may lead to mental fatigue where the executive control can become compromised (Van den Linden, Frese, & Meijman, 2003). When the executive control is compromised, the individual responses are often guided by external stimuli, even when these responses are inappropriate (Van den Linden et al., 2003). Consequently, this type of cognitive failure may easily manifest as GTP (Ortiz de Gortari & Griffiths, 2014c). In research concerning GTP, gamers have reported perseverative mental states shortly after playing. They perceived physical objects as if they were, for example, *Tetris* pieces and they kept looking for patterns, trying to arrange objects in sets, or kept scanning for items from the video game in real-life contexts (Ortiz de Gortari & Griffiths, 2014c). For instance:

> "I played 'Vice City' and got all the hidden packages at once. When I quit playing I was looking in the corners of the rooms for hidden packages. It was really odd."
>
> **Ortiz de Gortari and Griffiths (2014c, p. 441).**

DISSOCIATIVE STATES

Daydreaming, fantasy, and absorption in recreational activities are considered a type of dissociation that are, in essence, a form of nonpathological dissociation, also referred to as "normative dissociation" (Butler, 2006). Both normative and pathological dissociations are characterized by "telescoping of the attentional field to concentrate on a narrow range of experience and the exclusion of other material (internal or external) from awareness, to some degree, from accessibility, which may result in a temporary lack of reflective consciousness" (Butler, 2006, p. 46). Engaging with entertainment media and intrinsically rewarding activities involves a variety of normative dissociative phenomena, including: (1) time distortion by losing track of time (Wood, Griffiths, & Parke, 2007); (2) states of flow that imply hyperfocus as intense focus and concentration in an activity, loss of reflective self-consciousness, sense of personal control or agency over the activity, and distortion of time (Csikszentmihalyi, 1991); and (3) absorption by being transported in the fictional story, leaving behind the sense of disbelief or judgment and suspending critical evaluations (Dill, 2009). However, two phenomena are characterized exclusively from the involvement in virtual environments: (1) immersion in a multisensory events, and (2) the sense of presence by feeling dislocated or detached from the physical location and feeling "in" the virtual space (Jennett et al., 2008).

Immersion

Higher degrees of immersion or presence in the virtual world imply greater detachment from the objective reality, particularly among individuals with dissociative tendencies or symptoms (Aardema, O'Connor, Côté, & Taillon, 2010). Total immersion in the game has led to derealization-like experiences when gamers still believe they are in the video game. This can be exemplified by the following experiences:

> *"I played more or less 18 hours 'Alien vs. Predator 2' in darkness. My father came in, I turned around and shout swearwords while clicking the trigger of the non-existent gun in my hands…He disconnected the plugs from the PC."*
>
> **Ortiz de Gortari (2015b, p. 190).**

> *"I was playing 'Star Wars: Knights of the Old Republic' about four hours straight. When I stood up I had a massive head rush. I thought I was a Jedi in a cave for about five seconds. I was worried that the giant birds in the game's caves were going to attack me. I was confused, and afraid."*
>
> **Ortiz de Gortari (2015b, p. 183).**

Presence

The subjective sense of presence requires interaction with the virtual surroundings rather than just looking at images on the screen (Slater & Wilbur, 1997). Presence is a core component of virtual embodiment including sense of agency and sense of body ownership (Kilteni, Groten, & Slater, 2012). The elements related to the subjective sense of presence in the virtual world that appear to be most relevant for GTP are: (1) sensory realism that facilitates associations and lead to source monitoring errors, (2) simulations of body movement that lead to automatic motor activation when in real life encountering game-related cues associated with in-game actions, (3) ownership and functionality of video game elements that lead to gamers wanting to use video game elements in real life, and (4) embodiment of virtual entities that lead to body-related altered perceptions and depersonalization-like experiences.

Sensory Realism

Memories of events in the virtual world share salient features (e.g., perceptual, spatial, temporal, semantic, and affective information) with those from the real world (Hoffman, Garcia-Palacios, Thomas, & Schmidt, 2001; Johnson, 2007). More specifically, similarities are enhanced by sensory realism (i.e., realistic representations of objects) (Jeong, Biocca, & Bohil, 2012) and perceived realism when the individual responds to stimuli as if they are real (e.g., suspending disbelief) (Hall, 2006). Sensory realism facilitates automatic associations between video game elements, real-life stimuli, and source monitoring errors when confusing memories from the real and the virtual world. For instance, gamers have reported confusing memories from the game with those from real life or confusing game characters with real individuals:

> *"Sometimes get my 'Sims' mixed up with people. 'Remember when you'....oh no, wait, that was my 'Sim.'"*
>
> **Ortiz de Gortari and Griffiths (2014c, p. 440).**

Another gamer found himself in a hardware store, trying to remember why he was there (but actually needed a light bulb in the video game). One study on GTP among gamers found that 43% had mixed up events from the video game with actual events in real life (Ortiz de Gortari & Griffiths, 2016).

Simulations of Body Movement

It is known that observing someone else's actions tends to evoke activation of the observed action's motor pathways (Borroni, Gorini, Riva, Bouchard, & Cerri, 2011). Studies have demonstrated that viewing an avatar picking up an object in a natural way resulted in activation of the mirror neuron system of the observer (Borroni et al., 2011). Many games involve simulation of body movements (e.g., jumping, running, walking), which, in a way, awakens the movement they represent, although this may be more relevant in realistic games.

The automatic activation of motor pathways during video game playing may heighten gamers' experiences related to movements of limbs when they want to use that particular video game element in real life contexts. For instance, one gamer involuntary moved his arm when he wanted to use a grappling hook to swing under a bridge. Almost half of over 2000 participants in a GTP survey reported reflexive body reactions associated with their video game playing (Ortiz de Gortari & Griffiths, 2016). Gamers have also expressed urges to perform behaviors or body movements as in the video game. For instance:

> *"There is a game called 'Assassin's Creed,' in which you move a lot in big crowds of people the method of doing so efficiently is that he kind of gently pushes everyone out of the way. I remember feeling an urge for doing so in a crowded street."*
>
> **Ortiz de Gortari et al. (2011, p. 23).**

Ortiz de Gortari (2015b) argued elsewhere that since video game elements (e.g., visual or auditory cues) are paired with activities, game-related cues in real-life contexts can trigger a well-learned sequence of responses where gamers need to hold back their impulses, and sometimes the encounters with game-related cues activate the visual or auditory cortex, leading to gamers seeing or hearing something from the game. In fact, a functional magnetic resonance imaging study showed that encounters with game-related cues showed a larger difference than fantasy television drama-related cues in activations of the brain areas related with control inhibition, particularly motor inhibition (Ahn, Chung, & Kim, 2015).

Other studies have showed that the mirror neuron system that becomes activated when hearing sounds is associated with specific movements (Kohler et al., 2002). Gamers also appear to have established associations between body movements used to control rhythm music games and music, leading to experiences where they reported automatic movements of fingers or legs when they heard a song related to the game. These experiences appear to be closely related to when pianists experience involuntary movements of their fingers for playing the song they are listening to (Haueisen & Knösche, 2001).

Ownership and Functionality of Video Game Elements

The bodily ownership or illusion of "owning" a rubber or virtual hand (and even someone else's body parts) have been induced experimentally by synchronous multisensory stimulation (Kilteni, Normand, Sanchez-Vives, & Slater, 2012; Petkova & Ehrsson, 2008).

Gamers have reported attachment to video game elements that typically provide a function in the game and that are used repetitively (e.g., health bars, maps, special items), and wanting to use video game elements in real life. One gamer reported that after having played as a virtual character with a bionic arm, he felt strange to not have the bionic arm in real life (Ortiz de Gortari et al., 2011). In addition, it has been reported that thoughts have popped up in gamers' minds when they wanted to resolve situations in real life using video game elements. For instance, there is the case of the gamer wanting to use the grappling hook, as mentioned previously. In extreme cases, some gamers have experienced temporal inability to accomplish real-life tasks due to not having the desired video game elements. One gamer explained how he got lost going to a friend's house after playing a video game because he could not find the way without the compass from the game (Ortiz de Gortari & Griffiths, 2016). In a GTP survey, 72% of gamers reported having wanted or felt the urge to do something in real life after seeing something that reminded them of the game. For instance:

> *"I got that urge though to climb and explore after I played 'Shadow of the Colossus'. Something that you really want to do, almost as if you must do."*
>
> **Ortiz de Gortari et al. (2011, p. 23).**

Cognitive failures, such as slips of actions (Norman, 1981), due to the repetitive use of video game elements to resolve problems in the video game, have also been reported. For instance:

> *"After playing too much 'Grant Thief Auto: San Andreas'. I was riding my bicycle and I need to brake. I thought: 'where is the R1 button for the handbrake'. I got scared when I just understand what had just happened."*
>
> **Ortiz de Gortari and Griffiths (2014c, p. 443).**

Embodiment of Virtual Entities

The embodied virtual entity is the representation of the gamer. This representation socializes, achieves, or fails, and as a consequence, emotions become attached to it (Li, Liau, & Khoo, 2013). There are different processes that take place during virtual embodiment. These include: (1) monadic identification with the game character or avatar creating the feeling for the gamer that he/she is the virtual entity, usually referred to as "I." This is different from the dyadic identification with traditional media that is more external or dualistic, where the viewer is observing an autonomous entity (Hefner, Klimmt, & Vorderer, 2007); (2) character attachment as "feelings of friendship and identification with a videogame character when an individual is willing to suspend disbelief, feels responsible for the game character and feels in control of the game character's actions" (Lewis, Weber, & Bowman, 2008, p. 516); (3) vicarious learning by imitating an attractive and rewarding model (Bandura, 1986); and (4) the Proteus effect, based on the self-perception theory (i.e., the observation of one's own appearance in the virtual world can lead to behavioral changes) (Yee & Bailenson, 2009, p. 196). The GTP research concerning the embodiment of virtual entities appears to have contributed to: (1) deperzonalisation-like experiences, and (2) altered perceptions of body.

Depersonalization-Like Experiences.

In extreme cases, case studies have been reported where gamers have lost contact with reality and personified video game characters. Forsyth, Harland, and Edwards (2001) reported the case of a man who was transferred from prison to a psychiatric unit because he thought he was the video game character. He was stealing vehicles and assaulting the owners with weapons. In GTP research (Ortiz de Gortari & Griffiths, 2014c), gamers have reported feeling as being the video game character. For instance, one gamer said he went to bed thinking he was Batman. Another said he felt like the character in the video game:

> "Our subway system here often announces stops and service announcements, and I swear it feels as if I'm Gordon Freeman going into work every morning."
>
> **Ortiz de Gortari (2015b, p. 183).**

Altered Perceptions of Body.

Even when the user topology, geometry (i.e., body shape, size, and symmetry), and social role do not match the virtual entity, the virtual embodiment can influence the gamer's perception of the self, thoughts, and behaviors (Biocca, 1999). Experimental studies have demonstrated how embodying a character with a big belly or enlarged arm leads to the self-perception of having a bigger belly (Normand, Giannopoulos, Spanlang, & Slater, 2011) or a larger arm (Kilteni et al., 2012). Moreover, playing with a young character leads to overestimating the size of objects and identification with child-related images when using the Implicit Association Test (Banakou, Groten, & Slater, 2013). In GTP studies, gamers have reported body-related altered perceptions (Ortiz de Gortari & Griffiths, 2014a). For example, one gamer reported having felt shorter after playing a game with a small character in a gigantic world. A GTP survey of over 2000 gamers showed that 49% had perceived time and/or felt their body differently after having played a video game.

HIGH EMOTIONAL ENGAGEMENT

Events in the video games tend to elicit the most primitive instincts, such as survival and aggression, although they also include more subtle mechanisms of empathy, nurturing, and creativity (Freeman, 2003). Emotional responses reported by gamers when playing include joy, relaxation, anger, fear, and depression (Ravaja et al., 2004). Research on violent video games has shown how affect can be temporarily modified, leading to decreases in empathy (Anderson, Gentile, & Buckley, 2007) or increases in hostility and anger (Arriaga, Esteves, Carneiro, & Monteiro, 2008; Barlett, Branch, Rodeheffer, & Harris, 2009). Some video games are able to provoke physiological arousal and certain degrees of sadness according to how proficiently the person plays video games (Ivarsson, Anderson, Åkerstedt, & Lindblad, 2013). Transfer of game experiences related to emotions are observed along the different manifestations of GTP, but the most important ones relating to high emotional engagement appear to be: (1) rewarding and punitive video game features that lead to attention bias, overreaction and change of moods, sometimes elicited by game-related cues; and (2) accomplishments in-game that lead to feeling empowered.

Rewarding and Punitive Features

Activities in video games are usually rewarded with points, sound effects, and level progression, or punished with the reduction of points, lives, and progression. Video games are designed as sequences of events that provide a schedule of series of reinforcements and punishments to achieve the goals in the game, creating the perfect conditions for conditioning behavior (Dill & Dill, 1999). Firstly, this has led to attentional bias and overreactions, given that physical objects simulated in the game acquire new or different properties, rewarding or aversive properties that are generalized to the original objects, via classical conditioning (Ortiz de Gortari & Griffiths, 2014c). In a GTP survey, almost half of the gamers had unintentionally acted differently in real-life situations because of something they had experienced in a video game (Ortiz de Gortari & Griffiths, 2016). For instance, gamers have ducked down when they saw a security camera. More specifically:

> "I ducked at helicopter after playing lots of 'Call of Duty 4.'"
> **Ortiz de Gortari and Griffiths (2014c, p. 444).**

Secondly, it has led to change of moods, triggered by game-related cues. For instance:

> "It was foggy and the church's bells stopped. It felt so docile, possibly my most relaxing moment that month…in 'Silent Hill 1' in the school after the boss fight, you play in hell and then wake up to this foggy, calm astonishing world."
> **Ortiz de Gortari and Griffiths (2014c, p. 445).**

Hypervigilant mood states have also been observed when gamers expect something to occur as would happen as in the game and acted based on it. For instance:

> "I was walking in the woods near my home and I just wanted to walk on the path because then its less likely to get attacked my mobs."
> **Ortiz de Gortari et al. (2011, p. 27).**

Accomplishments in the Video Game

Gamers have reported feeling empowered and stronger after playing to the degree that it has led to irrational thoughts. For example, some gamers thought for a moment that they could climb buildings and actually tried to do it, or tried to break an object using only their finger (Ortiz de Gortari, 2010). More specifically, as one gamer explained:

"If I go out after like playing 'Assassin's Creed' for six hours. I can look at the walls and building and thinking oh maybe I can climb there because when I am in the video game I can run in the roof and climb and it follows me to the real life."

Ortiz de Gortari et al. (2011, p. 20).

CONCLUSION

Virtual experiences have proven to be pervasive in many gamers' lives. The interplay of physiological, perceptual, and cognitive processes is evident among the different manifestation of GTP experiences. Studies have investigated individual factors and motivations for playing associated with GTP (Ortiz de Gortari & Griffiths, 2015, 2016; Ortiz de Gortari et al., 2016), but the present chapter is the first that has explicitly mapped in-game factors and in-game phenomena to transfer of game experiences.

The factors and subcomponents proposed in this chapter are preliminary in nature, but their identification opens new paths for interdisciplinary research. Greater understanding of the proposed factors may contribute to the identification of the precipitators of involuntary phenomena with video game content. This is particularly important with the progressive introduction of highly immersive technologies (e.g., virtual reality headsets such as *Oculus Rift*) that are expected to strengthen the effects of GTP (Ortiz de Gortari, 2015a). If specific GTP can be identified that are uncomfortable and lead to potentially negative outcomes, gamers might reduce or avoid the risks while, at the same time, identifying factors that can be used to develop video games that are more engaging and that can be used for therapeutic or learning purposes.

REFERENCES

Aardema, F., O'Connor, K., Côté, S., & Taillon, A. (2010). Virtual reality induces dissociation and lowers sense of presence in objective reality. *Cyberpsychology, Behavior and Social Networking, 13*(4), 429–435. http://dx.doi.org/10.1089/cyber.2009.1064.

Ahn, H. M., Chung, H. J., & Kim, S. H. (2015). Altered brain reactivity to game cues after gaming experience. *Cyberpsychology, Behavior and Social Networking, 18*(8), 474–479. http://dx.doi.org/10.1089/cyber.2015.0185.

Anderson, C. A., Gentile, D. A., & Buckley, K. E. (2007). *Violent video game effects on children and adolescents: Theory, research, and public policy.* Oxford, UK: Oxford University Press.

Arriaga, P., Esteves, F., Carneiro, P., & Monteiro, M. B. (2008). Are the effects of unreal violent video games pronounced when playing with a virtual reality system? *Aggressive Behavior, 34*(5), 521–538. http://dx.doi.org/10.1002/ab.20272.

Atkinson, R. P., & Crawford, H. J. (1992). Individual differences in afterimage persistence: Relationships to hypnotic susceptibility and visuospatial skills. *American Journal of Psychology*, *105*(4), 527–539. http://dx.doi.org/10.2307/1422908.

Banakou, D., Groten, R., & Slater, M. (2013). Illusory ownership of a virtual child body causes overestimation of object sizes and implicit attitude changes. *Proceedings of the National Academy of Sciences*, *110*(31), 12846–12851. http://dx.doi.org/10.1073/pnas.1306779110.

Bandura, A. (1986). *Social foundations of thought and action: A social cognitive theory*. Englewood Cliffs, NJ: Prentice-Hall.

Barlett, C., Branch, O., Rodeheffer, C., & Harris, R. (2009). How long do the short-term violent video game effects last? *Aggressive Behavior*, *35*(3), 225–236. http://dx.doi.org/10.1002/ab.20301.

Biocca, F. (1999). The cyborg's dilemma: Progressive embodiment in virtual environments. *Human Factors in Information Technology*, *13*, 113–144. http://dx.doi.org/10.1111/j.1083-6101.1997.tb00070.

Blanke, O., & Mohr, C. (2005). Out-of-body experience, heautoscopy, and autoscopic hallucination of neurological origin: Implications for neurocognitive mechanisms of corporeal awareness and self-consciousness. *Brain Research Reviews*, *50*(1), 184–199. http://dx.doi.org/10.1016/j.brainresrev.2005.05.008.

Borroni, P., Gorini, A., Riva, G., Bouchard, S., & Cerri, G. (2011). Mirroring avatars: Dissociation of action and intention in human motor resonance. *The European Journal of Neuroscience*, *34*(4), 662–669. http://dx.doi.org/10.1111/j.1460-9568.2011.07779.

Butler, L. D. (2006). Normative dissociation. *The Psychiatric Clinics of North America*, *29*(1), 45–62. http://dx.doi.org/10.1016/j.psc.2005.10.004.

Cha, Y.-H. (2009). Mal de debarquement. *Seminars in Neurology*, *29*(5), 520–527. http://dx.doi.org/10.1055/s-0029-1241038.

Collerton, D., Perry, E., & McKeith, I. (2005). Why people see things that are not there: A novel perception and attention deficit model for recurrent complex visual hallucinations. *The Behavioral and Brain Sciences*, *28*(6), 737–757. http://dx.doi.org/10.1017/S0140525X05000130.

Csikszentmihalyi, M. (1991). *Flow: The psychology of optimal experience*. New York: Harper Perennial.

Dill, K. E. (2009). *How fantasy becomes reality: Seeing through media influence*. Oxford, UK: Oxford University Press.

Dill, K. E., & Dill, J. C. (1999). Video game violence: A review of the empirical literature. *Aggression and Violent Behavior*, *3*(4), 407–428. http://dx.doi.org/10.1016/S1359-1789(97)00001-3.

Dyson, B. J. (2010). She's a waterfall: Motion aftereffect and perceptual design in video games involving virtual musicianship. *Perception*, *39*(1), 131–132. http://dx.doi.org/10.1068/p6607.

Forsyth, R., Harland, R., & Edwards, T. (2001). Computer game delusions. *Journal of the Royal Society of Medicine*, *94*, 184–185.

Freeman, D. (2003). *Creating emotions in games: The craft and art of emotioneering*. Indianapolis: New Riders.

Griffiths, M. D., & Ortiz de Gortari, A. B. (2015). Musical hallucinations: Review of treatment effects. *Frontiers in Psychology*, *6*, 1885. http://dx.doi.org/10.3389/fpsyg.2015.01885.

Hall, A. (2006). Viewers' perceptions of reality programs. *Communication Quarterly*, *54*(2), 191–211. http://dx.doi.org/10.1080/01463370600650902.

Harris, C. S. (1965). Perceptual adaptation to inverted, reversed, and displaced vision. *Psychological Review*, *72*(6), 419–444. http://dx.doi.org/10.1037/h0022616.

Haueisen, J., & Knösche, T. R. (2001). Involuntary motor activity in pianists evoked by music perception. *Journal of Cognitive Neuroscience, 13*(6), 786–792. http://dx.doi.org/10.1162/08989290152541449.

Hefner, D., Klimmt, C., & Vorderer, P. (2007). Identification with the player character as determinant of video game enjoyment. In L. Ma, M. Rauterberg, & R. Nakatsu (Eds.), *Entertainment computing – ICEC 2007* (Vol. 4740) (pp. 39–48). Berlin: Springer.

Hoffman, H. G., Garcia-Palacios, A., Thomas, A. K., & Schmidt, A. (2001). Virtual reality monitoring: Phenomenal characteristics of real, virtual, and false memories. *CyberPsychology & Behavior, 4*(5), 565–572. http://dx.doi.org/10.1089/109493101753235151.

Ivarsson, M., Anderson, M., Åkerstedt, T., & Lindblad, F. (2013). The effect of violent and nonviolent video games on heart rate variability, sleep, and emotions in adolescents with different violent gaming habits. *Psychosomatic Medicine, 75*(4), 390–396. http://dx.doi.org/10.1097/PSY.0b013e3182906a4c.

Jennett, C., Cox, A. L., Cairns, P., Dhoparee, S., Epps, A., Tijs, T., et al. (2008). Measuring and defining the experience of immersion in games. *International Journal of Human-Computer Studies, 66*(9), 641–661. http://dx.doi.org/10.1016/j.ijhcs.2008.04.004.

Jeong, E. J., Biocca, F. A., & Bohil, C. J. (2012). Sensory realism and mediated aggression in video games. *Computers in Human Behavior, 28*(5), 1840–1848. http://dx.doi.org/10.1016/j.chb.2012.05.002.

Johnson, M. K. (2007). Reality monitoring and the media. *Applied Cognitive Psychology, 21*(8), 981–993. http://dx.doi.org/10.1002/acp.1393.

Kilteni, K., Groten, R., & Slater, M. (2012). The sense of embodiment in virtual reality. *Presence: Teleoperators and Virtual Environments, 21*(4), 373–387. http://dx.doi.org/10.1162/PRES_a_00124.

Kilteni, K., Normand, J.-M., Sanchez-Vives, M. V., & Slater, M. (2012). Extending body space in immersive virtual reality: A very long arm illusion. *PLoS One, 7*(7), e40867. http://dx.doi.org/10.1371/journal.pone.0040867.

Kohler, E., Keysers, C., Umilta, M. A., Fogassi, L., Gallese, V., & Rizzolatti, G. (2002). Hearing sounds, understanding actions: Action representation in mirror neurons. *Science, 297*(5582), 846–848. http://dx.doi.org/10.1126/science.1070311.

Kusse, C., Shaffii-Le Bourdiec, A., Schrouff, J., Matarazzo, L., & Maquet, P. (2012). Experience-dependent induction of hypnagogic images during daytime naps: A combined behavioural and EEG study. *Journal of Sleep Research, 21*(1), 10–20. http://dx.doi.org/10.1111/j.1365-2869.2011.00939.

LaViola, J. A. (2000). Discussion of cybersickness in virtual environments. *SIGCHI Bulletin, 32*(1), 47–56. http://dx.doi.org/10.1145/333329.333344.

Lewis, M. L., Weber, R., & Bowman, N. D. (2008). "They may be pixels, but they're MY pixels:" Developing a metric of character attachment in role-playing video games. *CyberPsychology & Behavior, 11*(4), 515–518. http://dx.doi.org/10.1089/cpb.2007.0137.

Li, D. D., Liau, A. K., & Khoo, A. (2013). Player–avatar identification in video gaming: Concept and measurement. *Computers in Human Behavior, 29*(1), 257–263. http://dx.doi.org/10.1016/j.chb.2012.09.002.

Linderoth, J. (2012). Why gamers don't learn more: An ecological approach to games as learning environments. *Journal of Gaming & Virtual Worlds, 4*(1), 45–62. http://dx.doi.org/10.1386/jgvw.4.1.45_1.

Mavromatis, A. (2010). *Hypnagogia: The unique state of consciousness between wakefulness and sleep.* London, UK: Thyrsos Press.

Murata, A. (2004). Effects of duration of immersion in a virtual reality environment on postural stability. *International Journal of Human-Computer Interaction, 17*(4), 463–477. http://dx.doi.org/10.1207/s15327590ijhc1704_2.

Norman, D. A. (1981). Categorization of action slips. *Psychological Review, 88*(1), 1–15. http://dx.doi.org/10.1037//0033-295X.88.1.1.

Normand, J.-M., Giannopoulos, E., Spanlang, B., & Slater, M. (2011). Multisensory stimulation can induce an illusion of larger belly size in immersive virtual reality. *PLoS One, 6*(1), e16128. http://dx.doi.org/10.1371/journal.pone.0016128.

Ortiz de Gortari, A. B. (2010). *Targeting the real life impact of virtual interactions: The game transfer phenomenon 42 video games players' experiences* (Master's thesis). Retrieved from DiVA database. (59225).

Ortiz de Gortari, A. B. (2015a). What can game transfer phenomena tell us about the impact of highly immersive gaming technologies? In *Proceedings from ITAG '15: 2015 International conference on interactive technologies and games* (pp. 84–89). Nottingham, UK: IEEExplore. http://dx.doi.org/10.1109/iTAG.2015.15.

Ortiz de Gortari, A. B. (2015b). *Exploring game transfer phenomena: A multimodal research approach for investigating video games' effects* (Doctoral thesis). Retrieved from IRep database (27888).

Ortiz de Gortari, A. B., Aronsson, K., & Griffiths, M. D. (2011). Game transfer phenomena in video game playing: A qualitative interview study. *International Journal of Cyber Behavior, Psychology and Learning, 1*(3), 15–33. http://dx.doi.org/10.4018/ijcbpl.2011070102.

Ortiz de Gortari, A. B., & Griffiths, M. D. (2014a). Altered visual perception in game transfer phenomena: An empirical self-report study. *International Journal of Human-Computer Interaction, 30*(2), 95–105. http://dx.doi.org/10.1080/10447318.2013.839900.

Ortiz de Gortari, A. B., & Griffiths, M. D. (2014b). Auditory experiences in game transfer phenomena: An empirical self-report study. *International Journal of Cyber Behavior, Psychology and Learning, 4*(1), 59–75. http://dx.doi.org/10.4018/ijcbpl.2014010105.

Ortiz de Gortari, A. B., & Griffiths, M. D. (2014c). Automatic mental processes, automatic actions and behaviours in game transfer phenomena: An empirical self-report study using online forum data. *International Journal of Mental Health and Addiction, 12*(4), 432–452. http://dx.doi.org/10.1007/s11469-014-9476-3.

Ortiz de Gortari, A. B., & Griffiths, M. D. (2015). Game transfer phenomena and its associated factors: An exploratory empirical online survey study. *Computers in Human Behavior, 51*, 195–202. http://dx.doi.org/10.1016/j.chb.2015.04.060.

Ortiz de Gortari, A. B., & Griffiths, M. D. (2016). Prevalence and characteristics of game transfer phenomena: A descriptive survey study. *International Journal of Human-Computer Interaction, 32*(6), 470–480. http://dx.doi.org/10.1080/10447318.2016.1164430.

Ortiz de Gortari, A. B., Oldfield, B., & Griffiths, M. D. (2016). *An empirical examination of factors associated with game transfer phenomena severity. Computers in Human Behavior, 64*, 274–284. http://dx.doi.org/10.1016/j.chb.2016.06.060.

Petkova, V. I., & Ehrsson, H. H. (2008). If I were you: Perceptual illusion of body swapping. *PLoS One, 3*(12), e3832. http://dx.doi.org/10.1371/journal.pone.0003832.

Poels, K., Ijsselsteijn, W. A., & de Kort, Y. (2014). World of Warcraft, the aftermath: How game elements transfer into perceptions, associations and (day)dreams in the everyday life of massively multiplayer online role-playing game players. *New Media & Society, 16*, 1–17. http://dx.doi.org/10.1177/1461444814521596.

Powers, K. L., Brooks, P. J., Aldrich, N. J., Palladino, M. A., & Alfieri, L. (2013). Effects of video-game play on information processing: A meta-analytic investigation. *Psychonomic Bulletin & Review, 20*(6), 1055–1079. http://dx.doi.org/10.3758/s13423-013-0418-z.

Ravaja, N., Saari, T., Salminen, M., Laarni, J., Holopainen, J., & Järvinen, A. (2004). Emotional response patterns and sense of presence during video games: Potential criterion variables for game design. In *Proceedings from NordiCHI '04: Proceedings of the third Nordic conference on human-computer interaction* (pp. 339–347). New York, NY: ACM. http://dx.doi.org/10.1145/1028014.1028068.

Ridderinkhof, K. R., Span, M. M., & Van Der Molen, M. W. (2002). Perseverative behavior and adaptive control in older adults: Performance monitoring, rule induction, and set shifting. *Brain and Cognition, 49*(3), 382–401. http://dx.doi.org/10.1006/brcg.2001.1506.

Ryan, M. L. (1999). Immersion vs. interactivity: Virtual reality and literary theory. *SubStance*, *28*(2), 110–137.

Seifert, C. M., & Patalano, A. L. (1991). Memory for incomplete tasks: A re-examination of the Zeigarnik effect. In *Proceedings from CogSci '91: Proceedings: Thirteenth annual conference of cognitive science society* (pp. 114–119). Chicago, IL: Erlbaum.

Slater, M., & Wilbur, S. (1997). A framework for immersive virtual environments (FIVE): Speculations on the role of presence in virtual environments. *Presence: Teleoperators and Virtual Environments*, *6*(6), 603–616. http://dx.doi.org/10.1162/pres.1997.6.6.603.

Stickgold, R., Malia, A., Maguire, D., Roddenberry, D., & O'Connor, M. (2000). Replaying the game: Hypnagogic images in normals and amnesics. *Science*, *290*(5490), 350–353. http://dx.doi.org/10.1126/science.290.5490.350.

Van den Linden, D., Frese, M., & Meijman, T. F. (2003). Mental fatigue and the control of cognitive processes: Effects on perseveration and planning. *Acta Psychologica*, *113*(1), 45–65. http://dx.doi.org/10.1016/S0001-6918(02)00150-6.

Wamsley, E. J., Perry, K., Djonlagic, I., Reaven, L. B., & Stickgold, R. (2010). Cognitive replay of visuomotor learning at sleep onset: Temporal dynamics and relationship to task performance. *Sleep*, *1*(33), 59–68.

Wood, R. T., Griffiths, M. D., & Parke, A. (2007). Experiences of time loss among videogame players: An empirical study. *CyberPsychology & Behavior*, *10*(1), 38–44. http://dx.doi.org/10.1089/cpb.2006.9994.

Yee, N., & Bailenson, J. N. (2009). The difference between being and seeing: The relative contribution of self-perception and priming to behavioral changes via digital self-representation. *Media Psychology*, *12*(2), 195–209. http://dx.doi.org/10.1080/15213260902849943.

CHAPTER 7

The Self–Other Topology: The Politics of (User) Experience in the Like Economy

Tony D. Sampson
University of East London, London, United Kingdom

> *All those people who seek to control the behaviour of large numbers of other people work on the experiences of those other people. Once people can be induced to experience a situation in a similar way, they can be expected to behave in similar ways. Induce people all to want the same thing, hate the same things, feel the same threat, then their behaviour is already captive - you have acquired your consumers or your cannonfodder.*
>
> **R.D. Laing (1967, p. 80).**

In this chapter, I will argue that the politics of experience R. D. Laing described back in the 1960s has been dramatically intensified by social media networks, and continues, as Laing did, to test assumptions about the discreteness of the self/other relation. My contention is that this relatively recent escalation of mediated social connectivity becomes manifest in two specific ways, both of which challenge a self-concept widely understood as a phenomenal self-experience, that is to say, a self-model structured through representations of the external world experienced from a first-person perception. To begin with, the already fragile sense of the self/other relation Laing famously developed has become interwoven with the inventions of a networked experience economy based on collective mimicry and sharing. This is the *Like* economy in which shared experiences have acquired value and become ever more staged by social media marketing strategists. Indeed, through such devices as friending, liking, and sharing, social media businesses can now better mobilize and manipulate the contagiousness of shared experiences on a network so that they can be worked on in ways that produce new modes of what Laing describes above as captive behavior. This is a very different kind of self-model to that conventionally analyzed by media theorists interested in critiquing the alienating influence of marketing on, for example, self-identity and personal choice. It is necessary therefore to

Boundaries of Self and Reality Online
ISBN 978-0-12-804157-4
http://dx.doi.org/10.1016/B978-0-12-804157-4.00007-4

rethink how Laing's alienating politics of experience now arises from new kinds of commodity production focused increasingly on shared experiences rather than the phenomenal self-model typical of conventional critiques of consumerism mediated through old media forms. To fully grasp the extent to which social media affects the self/other relation in this way, the chapter will discuss an alternative concept of social relationality that intervenes in the seemingly intuitive sense of the phenomenal self.

Secondly, in this age of social media, it would seem that the phenomenal experience of self has become increasingly forced into commercialized spaces, like those facilitated by relational databases (Greenfield, 2006, p. 81). The aim is to harvest personal data in order to compare such things as personal preferences and purchase intent with others stored in database assemblages. This is not, however, necessarily an entirely new social experience. Indeed, we might say that the widespread use of these relational technologies simply draws attention to the extent to which the phenomenal model of self fails to fully capture how much of the self/other relation is already developed through shared experiences. In other words, phenomenality fails to grasp how the sense of self has always been "etched" with the behaviors and experiences of the other (Thrift, 2008, p. 237), and relatedly, shaped by the sensory environments in which self and other come together in relation. The theoretical approach in this chapter is, as such, intended to challenge the conventional, yet problematic, split between the psychological experience of self (the so-called inner world of experience) and the shared social self (the experience of the outer world) in ways that Laing only hints at. As he argues, the "relation of experience to behaviour is not that of inner to outer" (Laing, 1967, p. 18). Experience is not "inside" the head; experience is "out there in the room" (p. 18). The point is that social media does not create an inner self-identity, but rather intensifies the collapsing of inner and outer worlds mediated through experience. To be sure, we no longer encounter mediated experiences merely inside our heads or in rooms. Social media transports shared experiences beyond interpersonal spaces, beyond the group, even beyond the mass media encountered in the television room. As follows, shared experiences can potentially produce an added value that social media strategists, political campaigners, and marketers are becoming especially attuned to, enabling them to work on experiences, as Laing puts it, as mentioned previously. To be sure, rather glibly perhaps, we might venture to say that the self/other relation on social media becomes divisible in more ways than Laing (1990) famously imagined back in 1959, making the networked experience of self and other increasingly fluid and permeable to manipulation by those who look to control it. This newly mediated and frequently replicated experience is grasped in this chapter through the concept of a *self–other topology*.

The ensuing discussion begins by exploring two examples of how the self/other relation has been conventionally critiqued using phenomenal self-models. It then goes on to set out how Laing's alienating politics of experience challenges this convention before drawing on theories of affect and imitative social relationality that similarly intervene in phenomenal self-models. Indeed, the counterintuitive notion that the self–other topology is not an entirely new experience can be explained through theories that date back to the origins of sociology in the late 19th century. This approach is then updated by initially expanding on what Protevi (2010), following Wexler's (2008) contemporary neurobiological approach, calls *radical relationality*. As will be discussed in the following, this is a concept of social relationality that grasps the experience of self by way of the looping interactions established between self, other, and sensory environments of encounter. Finally, the self–other topology is more clearly mapped onto recent efforts made by social media marketers to work on consumer experiences by triggering and steering emotional contagions.

CONSUMERS, CANNON FODDER, AND SOCIAL MEDIA

Before going on to explore the theoretical concerns of this chapter, it is important to introduce a contemporary context to Laing's epigraph. To begin with, although his politics of experience were conceived of in an analog mass media world, we cannot help but notice how it has striking similarities to today's social media contagions of conformity. Indeed, I contend that we should perhaps be more concerned. This is because Laing's idea that the masses could be induced to experience certain situations in the same way, and that desires, feelings, and behaviors could be made captive, and therefore controllable, is more of a palpable reality now than it was back in the 1960s. Back then, communication theorists, trying to make a similar point to Laing, had trouble providing tangible causal correlations between the medium, the message, and the affected minds of the masses. Although evidently, the masses were vulnerable to influence via the mediated messages of advertisers and political campaign strategists alike, the postwar media effects models theorists adopted were, it seems, blunt instruments intended to determine concrete causal links between efforts to persuade and resultant changes in mass thinking and behavior.

Today, the situation needs to be more subtly grasped, not because the message of the marketer or political campaigner has radically changed, but since the media through which social influence spreads has become more sophisticated, ubiquitous, and fit for purpose. Simply put, the media experience has, on one hand, become increasingly intimate, and on the other hand, social influence tends to spread more because it has so many more vectors for contagion. It is not that past attempts to influence did not capitalize on the contagiousness of emotional messages. The infamous *Daisy Girl* ad from Lyndon Johnson's 1964 campaign had a potent emotive message that "went viral before there was a 'viral'" (Killough, 2014). Intimacy on social media is, however, differently realized because these seemingly viral connectivities have become more readily available to strategists intent on spreading content to specific target groups. Emotional messages are no longer simply modeled according to how they are broadcast, or *injected*, into the living rooms of the masses; they can now be observed spreading over vast distances through complex networks of intimacy experienced between friends, for example. It is these complex networks that have become far more vulnerable to manipulations resulting from the data assembled and mined from self–other encounters.

What Laing significantly adds to the analysis of social media is a novel way of grasping how influence spreads through mediated experiences shared between self and other on a network. Indeed, a renewed focus on shared experiences that are already in relation, rather than the direct causal media *effects* on an individual or group mind, provides a potentially richer insight into how marketers and campaigners can effectively work on people. The updated notion of the politics of user experience (UX) can be applied as much to the cannon fodder required for political power as it can to the consumption of commodities and brands. This is why Donald Trump, in his 2016 presidential campaign, for example, employs a director of social media rather than spending the huge amounts his rivals set aside for TV ads (Parkinson, 2015). It is important to stress that Trump's social media strategy does not necessarily need to affect or change individual minds. The idea that Trump is, in some way, capable of creating a particular kind of quasifascistic voter ignores the fact that social media is already full of people liking and sharing similar opinions brought about by often complex reasons and circumstances. Indeed, perhaps Trump's incendiary bigoted rants on Twitter, Facebook, Instagram, YouTube, Vine, and Periscope simply tap into, and make more traceable, an already emerging sense of shared alienation that readily feeds into political populism. But setting the multifaceted explanations for the spread of political populism aside, what is more important here is to grasp the capacity of the social media strategist to mine the data from these mediations of experience and provide a vector on which they can be cultivated. That is to say, strategists are able to exploit preexisting and emergent experiences so that they can be further induced, alienated, and uniformly stirred into action in ways that Laing describes.

I will return in the following sections to look again at how marketers are manipulating emotional experiences that are always already in relation on social media. The point is to draw attention to how recent efforts by Facebook to measure the extent to which the algorithmic filtering of emotional content can trigger massive-scale contagion among readily accessible social groups supports a shift in theoretical interest from the creation of a phenomenal self (Trump's creation of a quasifascistic voter, if you like) to a more nuanced approach looking at the significance of manipulable self–other relations in the politics of experience.

THE CREATED SELF

The link between the marketing of shared experiences and an alienated self-model is already well-established in Marxist media theory and semiotic analysis in particular. Take, for example, Williamson's (1978) important work on advertising in the 1970s. The relation established between self, other, and the marketing of commodities through advertisements is crucial to Williamson's account, in which she argues that the consumption of adverts leads to the *creation* of an alienated self concept. By evoking Lacan's mirror phase, Williamson (1978, pp. 63–64) explains how the *created self* emerges from the experience of the unobtainable other that appears in an advert (e.g., the perfectly airbrushed complexion of a Chanel model or the fabricated joyful encounters with Pepsi People). It is argued that such adverts act as an external mirror of the world in which the phenomenal self encounters, mimics, and internalizes an illusory representational world produced by the advertiser. Continuing to follow a Lacanian-influenced account of mimicry, the person is, at first, so captivated by the external environment that it becomes her camouflage. In other words, mimicry is the capture of the organism by the environment rather than some evolutionary necessity to mimic surroundings in order to survive in the world. But eventually this loss of self to the external world (acquired through captivation) is transferred from the externality of the environment—bodily affects, camouflage, etc.—to the inner world of Lacan's narcissistic ego and its false identification with the other. This is how, in short, bodily affects become phenomenalized in Lacan's mirror stage. This is also, accordingly, a representation of the world that is both false and alienating, yet nonetheless desirable, not least because it satisfies a *natural* inclination for a unified phenomenal sense of self.

Although the influence of Lacanian analysis has somewhat diminished over time, according to a more recent study of adolescent photo sharing on social media, the self and its interaction with others in the external world is similarly considered as "integral to the creation and continuation of a stable harmonious self-concept" (Drenten, 2012, p. 15). Without appealing to psychoanalytic alienation, adolescents are nevertheless assumed to upload and share photos of themselves adorned in various products as a way to crystalize the formation of a self-identity to present to others (p. 6). This account of identity creation relies heavily on a supposition that although self-identity opens up to social relations, the inner sense of self is distinct from the external world. The notion that adolescents mimic others they encounter, by way of adorning similar clothes, is, it seems, missing from this self-model. Like Lacan's mirror stage, the relation to the other in photo sharing functions mainly as a kind of collective *mirror* that helps the adolescent grapple with the phenomenal question of *Who am I*? Group associations are clearly important, but the self concept is defined predominantly by reflective internal choices made about these social encounters, alongside apparently willful consumption preferences for clothing, jargon, and music taste, for example. Despite offering a differently oriented interpretation of the external world, especially in terms of personal autonomy, this account similarly grasps mimicry of the other as something that Williamson (1978) says, "enter[s] you, and exist[s] inside rather than outside your self-image" (p. 48).

MIMICRY WITHOUT (REPRESENTATIONAL) MIRRORS

To begin to unravel these phenomenal accounts, it is important to briefly note here the significant influence of Caillois on Lacan's theory of how the mimicry of the sensory environment becomes internalized as an alienated sense of self. Caillois's (1984) work on insects, fish, octopuses, and mantises challenges the prevalent idea that mimicry is an instinctual form of protective immunity brought about by threats posed to the organism from the outside world. Rather than seeing these surface mimicries as protection against the external threat of the other, Caillois alternatively points to the many vulnerabilities that arise when the surface of an organism takes on the visual properties of its environment. For example, the remains of mimetic insects are, he observed, as abundant in the stomachs of predators as those that cannot change their visual appearance (Caillois, 1984, pp. 24–25).

This observation prompts Caillois to rethink the organism's mimicry of the environment not as a survival tactic, but as a capture of the subject in the spatial coordinates of its surroundings, this is, what we might call here the capture of the individual in a *topological environment*.

It is through this notion of topology, as well as a conflated theoretical move toward affective relationality, that we can radically depart from the phenomenal experience of self apparent in Lacan. As Parikka (2010, pp. 97–98) notes, Caillois's mimicry is all about "bodies in interaction" with the environment, that is to say, a relation exists between the haptic visual properties of space inhabited and the affected body. This notion of *affective relationality* counters, in many ways, Lacan's mirror stage insofar as it draws attention to the porous nature of the inside/outside relation to such an extent that the representational *I* (the phenomenal sense of self) is replaced by the space of the environment (Parikka, 2010, p. 104). The inner and outer world of phenomenological experience is therefore collapsed into an external world of affective relationality that disturbs the relation between personality and space. As Parikka (2010, p. 100) puts it:

> The reflective mind is forced to follow the noncognitive knowledge and motility of the [affected] body… [Caillois thus provides] a nonphenomenological mode of understanding the lived topology of the event.

Indeed, more directly, Caillois (1984, p. 28) similarly contends that:

> [T]he feeling of personality, considered as the organism's feeling of distinction from its surroundings, of the connection between consciousness and a particular point in space, cannot fail under these conditions to be seriously undermined.

It is the intersection between these radical notions of topological affective relationality and Laing's politics of experience that require further explication.

THE POLITICS OF AFFECTIVE EXPERIENCE

Although with one foot firmly rooted in phenomenal experience, Laing's appeal to *social phenomenology*, or a science of persons, helps him to move on to the relational aspects of social encounter. Initially, in *The Divided Self*, Laing (1990) famously argued that the self needed to be analyzed away from the debates concerning norms and anomalies in mental health. The problem of the schizoid is identified as a problem with relating to the world, that is to say, the alienated outsider is estranged as much from society as she or he is from his or her own sense of individual self. It is not solely the inner self, but the relations established with the external world that constitute the sickness. It is indeed a sick relation that results in an alienated sense of self. It is, nonetheless, in *The Politics of Experience* that the problem of the self/other relation moves away from issues directly related to mental health and really begins to resonate more deeply with the problematic encounters with social media experienced today.

To grasp the full force of Laing's analysis in this context, it is helpful to begin by further breaking it down into the following two component parts. Firstly, he draws attention to an axiomatic understanding of how "behaviour is a function of experience; and both experience and behaviour are always in relation to someone or something other than self" (Laing, 1967, p. 20). People in relation to each other subsequently find that their behaviors are mediated by their experience of the other. Secondly then, Laing argues that people are "not self-contained" (p. 25). We are not merely affected by our own reflections on the external world, but we have effects on, and are affected by, our sensory encounters. More significantly, he also begins to remove the boundary lines between self and other. In a nutshell, Laing sees "each of us" as "the other to the others" (pp. 25–26).

Although still working from within the parameters of phenomenology, the double claim that (1) we are in relation since behaviors are mediated by experience, and (2) people are not self-contained begins to challenge a number of the tenets of the phenomenal self-model. From the outset, the structures of consciousness are no longer simply explained from a first-person perspective. Experience is not intentionally directed by one person toward objects or others encountered in the world. There is arguably no need for an internalized representational mirror to convey experiences through the filters of meaning and content alone. On the contrary, as I argue in the following sections, affective relations can be established in encounters that sidestep a representational dimension of experience. Affect can be, like this, *nonrepresentational*. Simply put, the structuring of consciousness (if indeed structuring is the right term) is better grasped by the affected relationality of shared experiences. The representational sense of self preferred by the phenomenologist (and made explicit in the phenomenal self-model) is, as such, substituted by a *radical relation*.

This leap from a phenomenal sense of self to a radical theory of social relationality is, evidently, a counterintuitive grasping of how we appear to experience the world. Unless we are the schizoid subjects of Laing's research, most of us will, of course, recognize the external world from an apparently coherent first-person perspective. However, the phenomenal world, as it seems to be represented to us, is built on a number of philosophical assumptions brilliantly confronted in the work of Bergson (1911). As Bergson argues, on one hand, the world does not necessarily appear to us as realists might have it, as the real thing, but rather as an *image* of the real thing (this is how, for example, the eye and the brain make sense of the world pictorially). But on the other hand though, we also need to question an idealist assumption that our perception of matter somehow produces a representational dimension through which the phenomenal self experiences the external world. Why should we assume that matter has some magical property that produces representations that mediate the world to an inner phenomenal self? It is this latter assumption embedded in phenomenological approaches, it would seem, that Bergson-inspired Deleuzians most vehemently disagree with. In a nutshell, the Bergsonian brain is not involved in the production of representations that mediate between subjects and the objects they encounter, but is an image among other images. That is to say, the brain and the object encountered are pictorial without being representational. Indeed, Massumi's (in Deleuze & Guattari, 1987) definition of affect focuses on a relational capacity to affect (and be affected) to such an extent that he finds the experience of the world in prepersonal feelings rather than appearing as subjective representations. For Massumi, experience is not subjective at all, but corresponds to a passage from "one experiential state of the body to another and implying an augmentation or diminution in that body's capacity to act" (in Deleuze & Guattari, 1987, p. xvi). It is my contention here that Massumi's affective encounter between bodies is one way in which we might grasp the power of Laing's controlling mediated experience of relation without primary recourse to subjective phenomenality.

SELF, OTHER, AND IMITATION

Another way in which we might further theorize Laing's politics of experience, and by doing so, more readily connect it to the social media age, is to briefly revisit the foundational sociological work of Gabriel Tarde. It is not surprising to discover that Tarde has also had a big influence on Deleuze and Guattari's work (Dosse, 2010). In many ways, he prefigures a Deleuzian affect theory by drawing attention to an infra-level of communication experienced through *unconscious associations* with others (Sampson, 2012, pp. 17–60). But more than this, Tarde's (1903) foregrounding of microsocial imitation, as a process that brings self and other into relation, directly challenges the phenomenal model of self. Ostensibly, Tarde's thesis begins at the same point as Lacan, insofar as he grasps social relationality through mimicry, or imitation, more specifically. Indeed, in Tarde's social theory, social relations do not emerge as a macrosocial whole that somehow transcends the interactions of individuals, and as a result, determines those interactions, but instead comes together entirely through microlevel imitative interactions. Significantly, for Tarde, there is no determining higher level of a society. Society is microimitation and microimitation is society, through and through. In short, society is a process of social adaptation produced by the imitation of examples, examples that are copied and passed on.

However, unlike Lacan, this tendency toward the social imitation of examples does not result in the kind of mental internalization we find in the mirror phase. Tarde's social subjects do incarnate the mental and physical examples of others, but his society of imitation produces a porous self/other relation that acts as a social medium for further imitations. This is a social porosity Tarde considered to be established between the cells in different brains acting on each other. Like this, the concurrence of Tarde's imitation thesis with a contemporary understanding of "a brain circuitry that fires when we either perform a given action or see someone else perform the same action" has already been noted (Lakoff, 2008, p. 39). Not unlike Deleuze then, in his time, Tarde (1903, p. 88) demonstrates a deep commitment to the science of the brain by drawing on the British psychiatrist Maudsley's theory of an innate tendency to imitate in the nervous system as a basis for understanding how one brain might captivate the desires and beliefs of others. Nevertheless, Tarde's imitative brain should not be grasped here as a genetically determined (or neurocentric) image of thought. Unlike the recent hyperbole surrounding the so-called mirror neuron hypothesis, which can tend to reduce imitation to an exclusively genetic level, the Tardean brain is, in fact, a *social brain* that loosens the crude distinction often made between discrete biological and cultural interpretations of brain functioning. It is an assemblage brain in which biological cells are captivated with the imitative social traces of the other. Indeed, as Brennan (2004) similarly argues, what is passed on in *affective atmospheres* is perhaps social before it becomes biological. The brain is, like this, a point of exchange where the biological and sociological distinction begins to blur to such an extent that it cannot not be distinguished between. So although Tarde's theory of desire and belief refers to cerebral imitation functions, these are not significantly located *inside* the brain, in a particular network of neurons, for example. They are rather understood as a vital force wherein the brain reaches out to the social world. This is a brain in relation.

In a later work, Tarde (1968) continues to develop his imitation thesis to conceive of two kinds of individuality that directly challenge the phenomenal self-model. Significantly, he identifies a continuum of social relations established between the organic, psychological sense of *myself* and the *social individual*. The former is not grasped as a self-contained entity at a certain level of a layered social model, but rather considered in relation to the latter by way of imitative social processes. These are imitative relations established and maintained through transversal relations at all levels rather than limited to discrete social categories. In short, Tarde's theory resonates with Laing's point above. Rather than thinking in terms of personal identity, for example, we should instead look to a self that is being made by the affects of others.

Tarde's tendency to learn on the brain sciences to explain how imitative processes might occur in the cellular interactions between brains must not be misinterpreted as a neurocentric rendering of the self/other relation. The sense of self and other is not, as such, located *inside* the brain. That is, sense making does not precede on a journey from the inside of phenomenal experience to the external world. On the contrary, what Tarde points to is a *social brain* that is in a constant looping relation to the sensory environment. Like one of Caillois's mimicking insects, the social brain is captured in a topology, which establishes a relation between brains, bodies, and the sensory environment in which encounters occur.

RADICAL RELATIONALITY

In a self–other topology, the sense of self is not a fully formed subjectivity, that is, the self *we* perceive of filtered through meaningful representations that inform *us* of who *we* are. Importantly then, following Tarde, a self–other topology is not structured by language. To be exact, prior to language, the social brain reaches out to the external world by way of imitation. There are indeed interesting intersections, in this respect, between Tarde's social brain and Wexler's (2008) more recent work on the interactions between the brain and culture. To begin with, both similarly contend that language is not an essential property of the brain, but an effect of imitative sensory environments. As Wexler contends, if all living people were rendered permanently speechless and illiterate, their offspring and succeeding generations would be unable to speak, despite having normal brains. Language, assumed to be the most distinctive of all human characteristics, would be lost to the human species (Wexler, 2008, pp. 117–19). It is indeed a deep ontological commitment to imitation, not language, which becomes the universal principle of both Tarde's social brain and Wexler's brain and culture thesis. As Wexler (2008) puts it, imitation is "consistently operative throughout the moment–to–moment unfolding of everyday life" (p. 115). We might say that the imitations of the social brain are prior to language and its grip on our perception of the external world. To be sure, without imitation, language would surely never have thrived and we would have no words to describe who we are. Without language, this kind of sense making, which appears to be an internal dialog with our self, would perhaps be experienced as little more than a physiological sensation.

Following Protevi's (2010) reading of Wexler in conjunction with Deleuze, we further see how the inside/outside relation of phenomenality can be substituted by a *radical relationality*, that is to say, "being human is composed of relations; we do not 'have' relations, but we are relations all the way down" (p. 174). Indeed, radical relationality helps us to rethink the sense of self in a number of significant ways that further challenge the phenomenological journey from the inside to the outside. Firstly, Wexler (2008) notes how neuroplasticity becomes open to varying degrees of change, over time, occurring in a *neuro–environmental emergentism*, that is, the intricate connections and patterns established between neurons are "determined by sensory stimulation and other aspects of environmentally induced neural activity" (Wexler, 2008, p. 22). The transformation of the plastic brain is thus always open to the outside. Secondly, radical relationality reverses the polarity of the phenomenal self. Instead of beginning with the internal representation of an external world considered too complex to experience objectively, we find that it is the sense of subjectivity that may well be imaginary. In other words, the sense of self (as grasped as a substantive part of who we are) is the imagined outcome of the speed of sensory processing being too slow to perceive anything more than the self as an individuated substance embedded in the brain. So, rather than rendering the brain an individuated substance, bequeathed with fixed properties, like self-identity, Protevi (2010) contends that subjectivity is made in the tendency to partake in a "pattern of somatic and social interaction" (p. 173). It is not, therefore, the representations of the individuated self that determine how the external world is perceived, but rather "the interaction of intensive individuation processes that forms the contours of the virtual field" (p. 175).

Thirdly, radical relationality challenges the phenomenal self-model (grasped from the inside out) with a novel perspective in which what is internalized is a pattern of interaction. This is radical because, as Wexler writes:

The relationship between the individual and the environment is so extensive that it almost overstates the distinction between the two to speak of a relation at all.
Wexler (2008, p. 39).

Bodies and brains are in constant processual exchanges with the environment, which, although appearing to be masked by an individual's "exaggerated sense of independence," carried in a fleeting memory that considers our uniqueness to be a property of who we are, nevertheless, make us little more than an effect of the sensory environment (Wexler, 2008, pp. 39–40). Therefore, what Protevi significantly extracts from Wexler's plastic brain thesis is an emergent subjectivity in the making, not understood as the outcome of complex malleable brain functions, but from a "differentiated system in which brain, body, and world are linked in interactive loops" (Protevi, 2010, p. 173). Wexler's entire project is consequently underlined by his intention to:

Minimize the boundary between the brain and its sensory environment, and establish a view of human beings as inextricably linked to their worlds by nearly incessant multimodal processing of sensory information.
Wexler (2008, p. 9).

Again, in addition to Protevi's reading, Wexler (2008, pp. 113–121) continues to foreground the ubiquity and automaticity of imitative processes as key to understanding subjectivity in the making as an effect of the sensory environment. It is through the close bonds a child makes with a range of caregivers, he claims, that the imitation of example persists through social relations, building a kind of scaffold subjectivity in the making inhabits. Again, the extent to which the imitation of example occupies the interactive loops that compose subjectivity in the making suggests a distinctive Tardean aspect to the plastic brain's interaction with the sensory environment.

ALIENATION IN THE SHARED EXPERIENCES OF SOCIAL MEDIA

We are born into a world where alienation awaits us (Laing, 1967, p. 12).

Laing's (1967) various references to Marx, Kierkegaard, Nietzsche, Freud, Heidegger, Tillich, and Sartre as philosophers of alienation sets up the philosophical backdrop of his politics of experience, and by doing so, helps us to grasp how alienation might work in the experiences of the *Like* economy. Indeed, by briefly concentrating on a Marxist perspective, we find a useful way to bring Laing's thesis into the social media age by aligning it to a new, alienating economic space of commodity production developing around shared experiences. To fully grasp the paradigmatic shift proposed in this experience economy, we need to initially understand how it owes more to a mode of capitalism invented by Walt Disney than it does Henry Ford (Pine & Gilmore, 2011, pp. 17–24). That is to say, the focus of economic activity shifts significantly from the production of commodities mass assembled in a factory (a car or birthday cake) to the added value of experiences related to the commodity (in-car entertainment or a birthday party at McDonald's). These experiences can include those that were previously outside the marketplace, but are readily transformed into new commodities. On one hand, it is the experience that supplements the commodity. Marketers are indeed more attuned to the idea that it is the experience of the commodity itself that often captivates the consumer. At its most deep-seated though, on the other hand, the experience economy can commoditize pure experiences that do not have to refer back to a tangible commodity. For example, the value extracted from liking a post on Facebook does not necessarily relate in any palpable way to a product.

It is this transformation in commodity production that arguably leads to the kind of mediated experiences social media presents to consumers today. Indeed, in the old Fordist model of capitalism, it would be the software that made its way from the production line to the consumer. But in the experience economy, software is not the commodity; it is the free engine that facilitates the mediation of shared experiences. By freely using Facebook software, for example, the experience of friendship is captured as a commodity and prompted into action through the sharing and liking of others' content. It is this experience that is then sold on to marketers to extract value from. It is of little surprise, perhaps, that the businesses that have developed alongside social media software have become collectively known as the UX industry. It is these conglomerates of designers, big data researchers, network strategists, and marketers that produce the sensory environments in which experiences are shared and cultivated. But how can this focus on experience possibly be alienating in the way that Laing describes?

SOCIAL MEDIA CONTAGION

For good reason perhaps, Carr (2014) described it as a "bulletin from a dystopian future." He was referring to an experiment Facebook carried out in 2014 involving the manipulation of the emotional content of news feeds and measuring the effect these manipulations had on the emotions of

689,003 of its users in terms of how contagious they became (Kramer, Guillory, & Hancock, 2014). The researchers who carried out the experiment found that when they reduced the positive expressions displayed by other users, they produced less positive and more negative posts. Likewise, when negative expressions were reduced, the opposite pattern occurred. Although the recorded levels of contagion were rather paltry, the researchers concluded that the "emotions expressed by others on Facebook influence our own emotions, constituting experimental evidence for massive-scale contagion via social networks" (Kramer et al., 2014). Indeed, even if this contentious and ethically unsound attempt by Facebook to influence moods produced meager evidence of rampant contagion, the design and implementation of the experiment itself should alert us to a potential mode of mass manipulation of the kind Laing refers to, as mentioned previously. As Carr (2014) further remarks, the uncannily titled *Experimental Evidence of Massive-Scale Emotional Contagion through Social Networks* draws attention to the way in which the cultivation of big data assemblages by marketers treats human subjects like lab rats while also pointing to the widespread nature of manipulation by social media companies. "What was most worrisome about the study," Carr (2014) contends, "lay not in its design or its findings, but in its ordinariness." This kind of research is indeed part of a "visible tip of an enormous and otherwise well-concealed iceberg" in the social media industry (Carr, 2014). To be sure, the one thing that both the disparagers and apologists for Facebook seem to agree on is that user manipulation of this kind is rife on the Internet.

Social media provides a perfect test bed, or nursery, for cultivating and triggering emotional contagions, since users are predisposed to share emotional experiences in exchange for the benefits of a software tool that allows them to share the positive and negative experiences of encounters with others. It is indeed this mostly unconscious inclination to assume the feely experiences of others and pass them on as shared emotions that is of obvious interest to marketers and strategists who look to control affective relationalities online. Notwithstanding the small media storm that emerged after this particular attempt to manipulate emotions, many users of Facebook will be oblivious of their participation in attempts to manipulate shared experiences. Moreover, they will be unaware of their inclination to respond to emotional suggestion in such an apparently porous and imitative fashion. This is clearly an attractive proposition to marketers who wish to avoid transparently marketing to people in the way that advertisers have traditionally done so through discrete media forms.

The point is that this trend toward steering shared emotional experiences through social media presents a very different kind of commodification to that commonly attributed to the phenomenal self-model. This is no longer simply a process involving the commercial colonization of an alienated inward-looking self, as Williamson described it. On the contrary, this is the commodification of shared experiences in the external world. It is the capture of the self/other relation in a topology of sensory experiences designed and primed by a burgeoning experience industry. Moreover, these staged productions of emotional contagion demonstrate the extent to which the border that divides self from other is perhaps an illusion. It may be the case that we still experience our interactions on social media from the first-person perspective, but this is arguably a phenomenal misconception, which secretes us from the looping interactions of the social topologies we become ensnared in. We might say that the self is submerged in the radical relationality of social media, which prompts into action the propensity to mimic the sensory environments we inhabit.

Emotional contagion is an example of the self–other topology. It is the social in relation and externalized via experience beyond personal control. It leads to a very different kind of alienation to that previously grasped as internalized via a mirror representation of the world. These are our shared experienced that are worked on in the commercial domain. These are our shared experiences that are captured in a topology and used to induce us to share more experiences, mimic them, and behave in certain ways. Is it any surprise then to find out that once we become caught up in these contagious topologies that many of us begin to believe in the same things, desire the same things, hate the same things, love the same things, and feel the same threats and opportunities? We are, using Laing's terms, the new captives and consumers, the cannon fodder of social media.

REFERENCES

Bergson, H. (1911). *Matter and memory*. London, UK: Allen & Unwin.
Brennan, T. (2004). *The transmission of affect*. Ithaca, NY: Cornell University Press.
Caillois, R. (1984). Mimicry and legendary psychasthenia. (J. Shepley, Trans.). *October, 31,* 17–32 (Original work published 1936).
Carr, N. (2014). The manipulators: Facebook's social engineering project. *The Los Angeles Review of Books*. Retrieved from http://lareviewofbooks.org/essay/manipulators-facebooks-social-engineering-project#.
Deleuze, G., & Guattari, F. (1987). *A thousand Plateaus: capitalism and schizophrenia* (B. Massumi, Trans.). Minneapolis, MA: University of Minnesota Press (Original work published 1980).
Dosse, F. (2010). *Gilles Deleuze and Felix Guattari: Intersecting lives*. New York, NY: Columbia University Press.

Drenten, J. (2012). Snapshots of the self: Exploring the role of online mobile photo sharing in identity development among adolescent girls. Close. In *Online consumer behavior: Theory and research in social media, advertising, and e-tail*. New York, NY: Routledge.

Greenfield, A. (2006). *Everyware: The dawning age of ubiquitous computing*. San Francisco, CA: New Riders.

Killough, A. (September 8, 2014). *Lyndon Johnson's 'Daisy' ad, which changed the world of politics, turns 50*. CNN. Retrieved from http://edition.cnn.com/2014/09/07/politics/daisy-ad-turns-50/index.html.

Kramer, A. D. I., Guillory, J. E., & Hancock, J. T. (2014). Experimental evidence of massive-scale emotional contagion through social networks. *Proceedings of the National Academy of Sciences of the United States of America, 111*(24), 8788–8790. http://dx.doi.org/10.1073/pnas.1320040111.

Laing, R. D. (1967). *The politics of experience and the bird of paradise*. London, UK: Penguin.

Laing, R. D. (1990). *The divided self: An existential study in sanity and madness*. London, UK: Penguin.

Lakoff, G. (2008). *The political mind: A cognitive scientist's guide to your brain and its politics*. London, UK: Penguin.

Parikka, J. (2010). *Insect media: An archaeology of animals and technology*. Minneapolis, MA: University of Minnesota Press.

Parkinson, J. H. (2015). *Can Donald Trump's social media genius take him all the way to the White House?* The Guardian. Retrieved from https://www.theguardian.com/technology/2015/dec/23/donald-trump-social-media-strategy-internet-republican-nomination-president.

Pine, B. J., & Gilmore, J. H. (2011). *The experience economy* (Updated Edition). Boston, MA: Harvard Business School Press.

Protevi, J. (2010). Deleuze and Wexler: Thinking brain, body and affect in social context. In D. Hauptmann, & W. Neidich (Eds.), *Cognitive architecture: From bio-politics to noo-politics; architecture & mind in the age of communication and information* (pp. 168–183). Rotterdam, Netherlands: 010 Publishers.

Sampson, T. D. (2012). *Virality: Contagion theory in the age of networks*. Minneapolis, MA: University of Minnesota Press.

Tarde, G. (1903). *The laws of imitation*. New York, NY: Holt & Co.

Tarde, G. (1968). *Penal philosophy*. Montclair, NJ: Patterson Smith.

Thrift, N. (2008). *Non-representational theory: Space/politics/affect*. London, UK: Routledge.

Wexler, B. E. (2008). *Brain and culture: Neurobiology, ideology and social change*. Cambridge, MA: MIT Press.

Williamson, J. (1978). *Decoding advertisements: Ideology and meaning in advertising*. London, UK: Boyars.

CHAPTER 8

The Shadow of Technology: Psyche, Self, and Life Online

Michael A. Beier
Psychotherapist in Private Practice, Basalt, CO, United States

A high degree of technological influence in contemporary life is an indisputable reality. In fact, technological influences reach well beyond America and Europe and are now global forces, influencing the lives of even the most disenfranchised, remote, and impoverished peoples on the planet. Technology in general, and an intense Internet presence in particular, has become an integral part of daily living and carries an unquestionable and an often-unchallenged power. Humans have always utilized and applied technological means to life and to the environment around them, but never in human history has technology been so intimately involved with the very fabric of existence. In addition, the pace of technological development has been so rapid that humans have not had sufficient time to understand on a fundamental level (i.e., physiologically and psychologically) what it means to consistently have technology this close to the vest and involved in everything from the most trivial to the most intimate parts of life.

In this ever-expanding milieu of technological reality, and considering the magnitude of the deep psychological implications, it is fascinating that the phenomenon of technology often goes largely unscrutinized and is accepted as a part of human experience; in fact, a guarantor of a human future with both unconscious and transcendent qualities attached to it. Since the psychological implications of various technologies are numerous and our understanding of such implications is still developing, further scrutiny and critical discussion seem warranted. In this chapter the main focus is on digital technology and the Internet research that emphasizes the shadow side of technology and of life online, and clearly reminds the reader that technology, in addition to helping us, also brings us suffering. As such, an investigation of shadow helps us honestly evaluate at what cost humanity accesses the technological smorgasbord of life-prolonging,

Boundaries of Self and Reality Online
ISBN 978-0-12-804157-4
http://dx.doi.org/10.1016/B978-0-12-804157-4.00008-6
141

efficiency-building, and comfort-increasing inventions, platforms, and gad-getry. The cost here is measured in psychological suffering and maladaptation.

Depth psychology offers a unique view of this subject, especially if approached from the vantage point of the psyche and the shadow: The very premise of depth psychology is an acknowledgment of the reality of psyche, not just conceptually, but also experientially. Psyche, according to Jung, is the beginning and end of all human cognition and experience and empha-sizes depth, authenticity, slowness, and interiority.

Kaufman-Osborn (1997) reminded us to reflect on the number of "arti-sanal artifacts," "the sheer multiplicity, the overwhelming proliferation, of devices we employ each day, from the moment we tumble from our beds to the moment we wearily return" (p. 22). This is a healthy exercise in moni-toring the role of technology in everyday life, of bringing consciousness to our interaction with technological devices, and of putting technology in its place. This last phrase is from psychologist Sherry Turkle (2011) who has spent most of her career investigating the psychological implications of dig-ital technology. She wrote: "We don't need to reject or disparage technol-ogy. We need to put it in its place." (pp. 294–295). However, putting technology in its place is a difficult task, exactly because we, as a culture, have been so thoroughly seduced by, and enmeshed in, technology's power and promise. The technological reality of contemporary Western life, Turkle (2011) pointed out, is a classic double bind. We use technology to make life simpler, yet at times technology makes life more complicated. Strapped for time, we reach out to technology to help us cope, only to discover that the technological fix we created places other demands on us, demands that are new, often challenging, and sometimes taxing. Following this continued logic, the answer lies in another technological fix and the pattern continues with no end in sight. As Turkle (2011) stated, we ask less of people—of each other—and more of technology, hoping to find answers to the big questions in life, eliminating the complexities of relationships, and maintaining con-trol at all times—all while remaining connected to the world around us. Turkle (2011) aptly stated:

> We fill our days with ongoing connection, denying ourselves time to think and dream. Busy to the point of depletion, we make a new Faustian bargain. It goes something like this: If we are left alone when we make contact, we can handle being together (p. 203).

Putting technology in its place by helping to better understand some of its complex psychological implications is exactly the goal of this chapter;

it presents a Jungian or depth psychological view of some of the challenges to self presented by digital technologies and life online, and the subsequent changes in behaviors, perceptions, and priorities.

The draw and popular appeal of the scientific and technological paradigms, and the ideology of progress, are intimately intertwined with the collective as well as personal psychological environments of our age. Jung (1970) characterized the 20th century as a "time of dissolution and chaotic disorder" (p. 221) and this has only accelerated in the 21st century. James Hollis (1995), a Jungian analyst, demonstrated that the (post)modern person is in an unenviable position, psychologically speaking. In a society where the traditional role of institutions of meaning and value (e.g., church, community, etc.) is greatly diminished; a person finds him- or herself flapping like a flag in the wind, busying him- or herself from fad to fad, with nothing psychologically sound and substantial upon which to pin existential and survivalist hopes. Hollis wrote: "We are condemned to freedom, though the whiff of existential angst is enough to blow many off course, back to some safe ideological heaven" (p. 36). Hollis has gone to great lengths to aptly describe the vacuum of meaning-supplying institutions and the subsequent desperation and disorientation, which appears to afflict so many human beings in contemporary Western culture. In our culture, Hollis stated, with the loss of mythology, what are available are ideologies, namely: materialism, hedonism, and narcissism (Hollis could well have added technology specifically to this list). Hence, the experience of postmodernism is "the anguish of yearning from within our estrangement" (p. 25) and with little to meaningfully guide a person through the journey of life. Despite unprecedented material comforts and a smorgasbord of technological gadgetry, the life of the (post)modern is isolated, lonely, and often experienced as deeply meaningless.

The German philosopher and playwright Goethe wrote his Faust to underscore the plight of humanity and used Faust as the poster child for the postmodern human being and the difficult psychological landscape associated with life in our era. As pointed out by Hollis (1995), Goethe presents Faust in the play in a suicidal depressive state and ridden with anxieties. We also find Shakespeare's Prince Hamlet in a similar terrible condition in the famous play. Importantly, yet tragically, both of these characters sought the solution to their misery and existential anguish by embracing and immersing themselves in the archetype of the shadow.

James Hillman (1997) wrote about how humans respond to the contemporary crisis of meaning and faith and, somewhat humorously listed the options available to the postmodern human being. Hillman wrote that a psyche in crisis has the following options to choose from as new centers or ideologies capable of infusing modern life with some profundity, gravitas, or meaning. He wrote:

> Hellenism's many [gods] or Hebrewism's one [God] are not the only ways out of the psyche's pathological dilemma: There is flight into futurism and its technologies, turning East and inward, going primitive and natural, moving upward and out altogether in transcendence (p. 3).

Thus, many a person has tried, and many are in this very moment trying, to deal with the existential vacuum and emptiness inside by seeking refuge in the technological world, resorting to some sort of obsessive or addictive behavior related to technology. Some behaviors that are now commonplace include watching movies for days (i.e., binge watching), endless chatting on a social media, excessive online dating or gaming, addictions to pornography, or general problematic preoccupation with handheld technologies. Many a patient presents in the offices of his or her doctors and therapists with any number of symptomologies, and most frequently the presenting problem is either an experience of unexplainably elevated anxiety or debilitating depression—or a painful combination of the two.

TECHNOLOGY AND ITS DISCONTENTS: SHADOW AND TECHNOLOGICAL PATHOLOGIES SHADOW

A clearer understanding of the concept of shadow will be defined here in order to lay the proper foundation for further discussion on the topic. Shadow is Jung's term for what is more commonly referred to as the dark side or the dark passenger. It is the parts inside us that we are not proud of, do not wish to look at, and generally try to forget about. Jung always had slightly varied definitions for his concepts. This happened because of the very nature of his pioneering work and because he adjusted and refined concepts over time as his own understanding of them evolved. Sharp (1991) paraphrased Jung's definition of shadow as "composed for the most part of repressed desires and uncivilized impulses, morally inferior motives, childish fantasies and resentments" (p. 123). Sharp added that the unacknowledged personal characteristics of the shadow are frequently experienced in others through projection.

Jung wrote the following about shadow:

> The shadow is a moral problem that challenges the whole ego-personality, for no one can become conscious of the shadow without considerable moral effort. To become conscious of it involves recognizing the dark aspects of the personality as present and real.

> **Jung, as cited in Sharp (1991, p. 123)**

In addition, Jung was quick to point out the danger of the unacknowl-edged shadow in a person, phenomenon, or culture. His view of such dan-gers are explained in the following pertinent quote:

> *Recognition of the shadow is reason enough for humility, for genuine fear of the abysmal depths in man. This caution is most expedient, since the man without a shadow thinks himself harmless precisely because he is ignorant of his shadow. The man who recognizes his shadow knows very well that he is not harmless, for it brings the archaic psyche, the whole world of the archetypes, into direct contact with the conscious mind and saturates it with archaic influences.*
>
> **Jung (1966; para 452)**

Jung, however, also acknowledged sides of the shadow that were not wholly unacceptable and frightening to the ego. He came to understand that shadow included creative and natural instincts and desires, which had long been buried in the unconscious. The creative aspects of shadow are important as they pertain to technology and the technological paradigm. Jung wrote:

> *If it has been believed hitherto that the human shadow was the source of all evil, it can now be ascertained that…[the] shadow, does not consist only of morally rep-rehensible tendencies but also displays a number of good qualities, such as moral instincts, appropriate reactions, realistic insights, creative impulses etc.*
>
> **Jung, as cited in Sharp (1991, p. 125)**

Hillman (1998), too, wrote something important about the shadow that pertains exquisitely to the subject of technology. He wrote:

> *The cure of the shadow is on one hand a moral problem, that is, recognition of what we have repressed, how we perform our repressions, how we rationalize and deceive ourselves, what sort of goals we have and what we have hurt, even maimed, in the name of these goals (p. 242).*

In other words, Jung and Hillman remind us that the gifts of shadow are understanding and insight. If we investigate shadow, we have the possibility to understand why and how we repress certain aspects of technology and why we have chosen to perhaps overevaluate other aspects. One could say that the shadow can educate us about the heavy one-sidedness of the public and academic discourse of technology in our society by bringing conscious attention to this particular area. Shadow can teach us about why we insist on seeing predominantly one side of the archetype and focus on the quali-ties of the total archetypal message. This balancing act is the work and *raison d'etre* of depth psychology as a school of psychology in service to the *anima mundi* and, according to Jung, the task of each individual as well.

From the practice of psychodynamic psychotherapy, we know that the shadow is often the *prima materia* of the psychotherapeutic work. This is where the real "meat" is and, while looking at it is hard, it ultimately leads to a greater understanding and consciousness. So, the true gift of the shadow is that it allows for a deeper understanding of a given phenomenon and hence invites a deeper level of consciousness to flourish. Alternatively, if the lessons available through seeing a more complete picture and through investigating shadow are not learned, then there are serious and often tragic repercussions, especially as it pertains to the delicate balance between human psychology and technology. It is well illustrated by what Jung (1969) wrote:

> Western man has no need of more superiority over nature, whether outside or inside. He has both in almost devilish perfection. What he lacks is conscious recognition of his inferiority to the nature around and within him. He must learn that he may not do exactly as he wills. If he does not learn this, his own nature will destroy him. He does not know that his soul is rebelling against him in a suicidal way (p. 237).

The concept of shadow is perhaps one of the most important contributions of Jung's entire body of work. While this can seem like a bold statement, it is clear that Jung's concept of shadow is the first real attempt to give a place to the obvious and ever-pervasive, so-called dark, qualities of human beings in a way that is not taught or accepted within the traditional Judeo-Christian duality of good and evil. Previously, Freud had alluded to such qualities, though in a mono-dimensional manner, as repressed aggressive and sexual impulses surfacing in certain unwanted behaviors (Gay, 1995). Jung, on the other hand, with his concept of the shadow, allowed for humans to be inclusive of all parts: Without pathologizing, he invited humans to acknowledge, confront, and ultimately accept the inevitable darker sides of human nature. Jung realized that shadow encounters were difficult for the ego to handle, yet necessary for psychological growth, or individuation, which was Jung's preferred metaphor for the life-long process toward wholeness.

SHADOW OF TECHNOLOGY: AN ONLINE LIFE

As previously stated, the shadow of technology is something that is less frequently discussed in the predominantly optimistic narratives surrounding technology and the progress and benefits it is bringing to humanity. However, in the 20th century, some shrill and critical discussions centered on chemical, biological, and nuclear weapons developed for warfare and their potential for destruction of humanity and the planet. Today, many view the Frankensteinian potential of artificial intelligence (AI) and genetically modified organisms (GMOs) as shadow features of technology and scientific "progress," though they would probably not use the term shadow in this context. Also, the dark corners of the Internet, where weapons, drugs, and child pornography, along with other dark and destructive materials, can be found and purchased are shadow features of the ever-expanding online world. These, of course, are the major and obvious shadow features that can be spotted by most.

However, there are also other shadow areas of our daily use of digital technologies that are more insidious, which manifest in our personal lives and negatively impact our relationships—with ourselves and those around us. We need to ask the obvious question, how can too much of a supposedly good thing become a shadow problem? In the world of psychology, we can detect and judge unacknowledged shadow by the suffering and dysfunction it brings to our lives. Glen Slater (2007), a Jungian, wonderfully articulated that in his view "psychopathology has functioned as the canary in the mineshaft of technology" (p. 181).

Rosen (2012), a long time explorer of the complicated landscape emerging between the psyche and digital technology, explained that a generalized "overreliance on gadgets and websites has created an enmeshed relationship and that this relationship can cause significant problems in our psyche" (p. 4). He pointed to technology-induced suffering in the following diagnostic categories: panic and anxiety disorders, obsessive–compulsive disorders, mood disorders, addictive behaviors, and personality disorders primarily of the narcissistic kind. Rosen's work included both his own research and metaanalysis of the work of many other scholars throughout the Western world. Rosen (2012) wrote that one of the goals of his book was to discuss "the psychological impact of technology and scientific research demonstrating how specific media and technologies can and do to promote mental imbalance" (p. 6). These mental imbalances are what Rosen termed *iDisorders*. They could also be referred to as technological neuroses.

Jung (1970) is quoted as saying that neurosis is a wounded or offended god, or that neurotic symptomology is suffering that has not yet found its meaning. Depth psychology, in general, and Jungian psychology in particular, are psychologies of meaning, which is to say there is a specific focus on existential issues and on the overarching question of meaning. Hollis (2000) noted that Jung's "wounded god" is "a metaphor for the depth dynamics of the soul which is repressed, split off, projected" (p. 99). This is how pathology can best be viewed from a depth perspective. In depth psychology, the word *pathology* is used most frequently in the meaning of "suffering" as opposed to psychiatric labels of "sickness," "abnormal," or even "defective."

When life online demands constant attention and begets a monopoly of time both in the work and private spheres, priorities and behaviors become one-sidedly focused on the external. Email and text messages now demand almost immediate response and for most people a short timeframe for replies is expected. The boundaries between work and free time have become increasingly blurred with SmartPhones guaranteeing 24/7 online access to everything from movies to work email accounts. We struggle just to keep up as the demands, spoken and unspoken, for immediate responses to communication seem to increase in speed. On social media, posts are carefully edited, photos judiciously judged and cropped, and friends, associations, and events meticulously chosen. All this in order to assemble and ultimately maintain a self-created image or a staging of oneself as a person. It is the image one shows the world or the persona, or self, one attempts to proliferate in the online universe. Usually this online persona portrays self-confidence, social popularity, beauty, success, and an exciting life style, etc. It is an illusion of a "real" life, but a necessary fiction for the ego to feel good and safe, and for the maintenance of that certain persona. It is also a display case of our personal and collective narcissism.

The keyword of the shadow premise of our online self that is presented in this chapter is inauthenticity. The definition of inauthenticity used here simply means "not real, not accurate, and not sincere." Inauthenticity is a shadow feature by virtue of its lack of truth and the unconscious dynamics at play.

Hence, one of the problems with our online relationships is that in a deeper sense they are not *really* real. Not real in the sense that meaningful and enriching relationships cannot be turned on and off according to the whims of the day. Also, meaningful and lasting relationships take actual work and effort in order to be nourished and for them to flourish. For a relationship to supply meaning to psyche, a quick check-in and a picture of the latest adventure will not suffice. Social media is not by definition a problem or a platform, which causes psychological distress. Life on social media is not necessarily "one big lie," but for most people it is a construct: A construct or fiction where a targeted and carefully cultivated narrative is created and maintained toward a specific audience. It is a constructed self, or an online self, the goal of which is to portray a person not as he or she is, but how a person would like to be viewed by the world. In other words, the online self is often inauthentic or at the very least heavily one-sided.

Many users can handle it and regulate its use without any problem. For them, checking social media is part of their daily and largely unproblematic online routine. However, segments of people cannot seem to regulate social media usage and tend toward a problematic and artificial relationship with the platforms and their contents. Many of these eventually show up in the consulting rooms of therapists and psychologists because they realize and suffer the impacts of their dysfunction.

To further discuss the issues of inauthenticity, much online communication is impoverished and overly simplistic. Humans rely on communication in order to survive and thrive. The majority of such communication is nonverbal. In online communication, many cues are missed either because the communication is in writing and pictures or because, even when faced with one another on the screen, it is only a partial picture of the person compared to face-to-face communication. In addition, the personal responsibility of thoughtful communication is diminished by anonymous chats and other means leading to misunderstandings and, in worst-case scenarios, to outright cyber bullying and psychological injuries. Not to mention that communicating effectively and meaningfully in 140 characters or less is not an easy thing to do. If this is the communication environment the online self is navigating, this is not conducive to the enhancement of essential communication skills. As a general rule, viewed from a depth psychological standpoint, better and more thoughtful communication might be helpful to us as individuals and even as a species. Regardless of whether or not digital communication is the way of the future, impoverished and oversimplified communication, fraught with potential for misunderstanding or injury, is not a step forward but a shadow feature of modern communication styles.

Procrastination and avoiding facing the complex realities of life is another shadow feature in regard to life online and the role of social media. As the effective flight from boredom as well as action in life is at our fingertips all the time, technology, and life online in particular, often becomes the perfect distraction and excuse in order not to move forward. Some astonishing clinical examples of this are richly illustrated by Turkle (2011) in her book, where the reoccurring theme it that the return to real life by cyberobsessed subjects is a letdown compared to the constant stimulation of online life. In frightening (though extreme) clinical examples, actual life is largely ignored and life is moved online—with serious consequences for the people involved.

Life online also shines a cold light on the hot topics of the shadow sides of and the fractured and disbursed nature of modern family. Turkle (2011) mused about how, for young people, "computers and mobile devices offer communities, when families are absent" (p. 178). Many a therapist will recount stories where families report spending most evenings scattered in different rooms of the home, each person on a separate, and at times multiple, devices for the purpose of entertainment. There is very little interaction and communication happening between family members except for a bare minimum of practical and logistical coordination. The topic of the technological influence on family cohesiveness is a topic that alone deserves tremendous scrutiny and psychological research effort.

Most importantly, our unconscious fear of loneliness and abandonment will never be cured by digital technology or even the most vigorous and attractive online life. Turkle (2011) stated that humans now use the network to defend against loneliness and control the intensity of connections. "Technology makes it easy to communicate when we wish and to disengage at will" (p. 13). The common projection on social media is that this is a cure for feelings of loneliness—isolation. However, feeling lonely, and at times abandoned, is a part of the human condition. These feelings do not have to be destructive and devastating. Most likely, they are temporary and, if they are not, perhaps strengthening the ego; or searching for a solid existential footing by dealing with them in psychodynamic therapy is the best recommendation. Relationships and interactions are inherently complex and bring some (if not most) people anxiety. No amount of technology and self-staging online can fundamentally change that. However, it can create environments where more distant and simpler ways of communication are available and where hiding one's true self is easier. However, this is not likely to be a favor to anyone fearing the complexity of actual life, relationships, and social interaction. Real life can only be conquered by trial and error—in actual life. We also call this a part of the process of individuation.

Again, the question of authenticity, hence, looms large over the whole debate of life online and the psychological implications of social media and Internet use. How authentic are our online relationships? Do we as technology consumers begin to believe in the fantasy that we portray in our online selves and how does this influence the authenticity we have in relationship to ourselves?

Many online platforms are literal playgrounds for all kinds of shadow behaviors. This is especially true if platforms can be accessed anonymously. People do and say all the things online they would not be able to do or say in normal life. Perversions can be fed and explored and behaviors engaged in that would otherwise be considered unacceptable.

There is an ongoing academic as well as clinical discussion on the relationship between narcissism and online/social media usage. According to

Rosen (2012), the use of social media encourages narcissistic expression, and even reinforces narcissistic character traits. Turkle (2011) wrote about the Internet frontier and narcissism, that "like a sleek, gym-toned body, an appealing online self requires work to achieve" (p. 251). Rosen (2012) particularly mentioned the ability of the narcissist to collect "trophy friends" on social media sites. This type of friend is used as an image enhancer and makes for a good platform for the narcissist to bask in "public glory" (p. 24). Narcissists post frequently on social media, thinking that it is only natural that everyone is interested in every little thing they do down to the most habitual and tedious. Rosen (2012) mentioned that narcissistic individuals tend to post updates using sentences containing an overwhelming amount of personal pronouns. Posting will flow throughout the day and always contain lots of "I," "me," or "mine."

Rosen (2012) theorized those whole generations of children born after 1980 (and known as Millennials, Net generation, and iGeneration) are essentially more narcissistic than previous generations due to the confluence of technology and parenting styles emphasizing self-expression. Research quoted in Rosen's book found that postmillennial college students scored significantly higher on the narcissism scale compared to a cohort surveyed 20 years earlier. The researchers warned of a "narcissism epidemic" (p. 28) in America, where self-glorification and appearances of success led to a veritable flight from reality into a psychological "la-la land" of grandiose fantasies. Among factors deemed to have contributed to this epidemic of narcissism were "permissive parenting, celebrity culture, and the Internet" (as cited in Rosen, p. 28).

It seems clear that presenting a carefully styled self-portrait and keeping most communication casual and superficial is the perfect environment for narcissism. The narcissist is not interested in going too deep—risking the exposure of an insecure and imperfect self. The online self is just enough to comfortably show the world while remaining in control. The narcissist will also go through great pains in presenting a self-styled image of success and perfection. This will usually hold until it is challenged and exposed for the varnish-thin layer of truth that it is. Simplistic, juvenile, and highly controllable narratives are exactly what narcissists do, and texting and social media platforms are ideal for it. Turkle (2011) suggests that the culture as a whole, and with the influence of many of our technological gadgetry, tempts youngsters "into narcissistic ways of relating to the world" (p. 179). In other words, we are potentially conditioning new generations to interact with their surroundings in a defensive way, where they can feel in control and spend much energy on the highly manicured online self-narrative that is presented to the world. In the worst-case scenario, we could say that it appears that the shadow components of some of our technological platforms and interactions are a veritable breeding ground for narcissism.

THE WOUNDED GODS AND NEUROSES

Jung's concept of individuation is the opposite of inauthenticity. It is the difficult and ever-ending search for wholeness and, ultimately, meaning in life. So, working as a human being toward wholeness is by definition an authentic process. It requires investigating and ultimately facing one's projections, delusions, denials, and places of inflation. To be authentic requires facing the shadow head on.

The process can only be engaged in with vigor, sincerity, and an abundance of patience, and it requires paying attention to one's inner world over a prolonged period of time. By inner world is meant thoughts, images, intuitions, dreams, and fantasies. The key to this is self-awareness. Self-awareness can only be developed over time by paying attention and shying away from the endless noise and distractions in the outer world—of which digital technology is a major part. The shadow part of many of our gadget technologies, the Internet, and all our games and texts, is that we fear boredom and even the smallest break in the constant stream of information and mentation. Digital technology has the potential to fill our every waking moment—and not necessarily with anything important, developmental, or useful. However, if we do not take an occasional break from our technologies and our busy lives, we have a hard time checking in with how we are really doing, really feeling, and what we are really experiencing. In other words, we are prevented from having an authentic relationship with ourselves. If we have a predominantly inauthentic relationship with ourselves, we cannot know ourselves deeply and we cannot easily develop. When we do not develop, or remain a stranger to ourselves, the most significant psychological consequence will eventually be a sense of emptiness, clinical depression, and anxiety. Jung (1970) said: "the unconscious has a thousand ways of snuffing out a meaningless existence with surprising swiftness" (p. 474) and psyche will ill-tolerate this without physiological or psychopathological manifestations.

Clinically speaking, in depth psychology, anxiety, for example, is not necessarily considered pathological. The true pathology can develop from the ways in which a person attempts to control and manage elevated levels of anxiety. In depth psychology, anxiety could be considered more of a messenger (e.g., a feature of the Greek god Hermes), letting the person know that something is not quite right, being ignored, or something is seeking expression through a person but not finding the proper outlet. Oftentimes, anxiety is a sign of a major change needing to, or about to, happen in a person's life—or a person's inability to accept the occurrence of such a major change. Psychologically, one might say that the experience of anxiety also implies, as mentioned by Hillman, that the ego is stuck in a position and is being asked to change something important and fundamental. However, the ego is having a hard time adjusting to the message and changing accordingly.

Much of the human condition can provoke anxiety: work, money, sex, marriage, aging, and most certainly death. All of these ingredients, and many more not mentioned, have a way of increasing a person's experience of anxiety and perhaps even panic. Symbolically speaking, the presence of the Greek god Pan is in every hospital, in every office, in every home, in every bedroom, and on every airline flight. Hermes and Pan are both present when thresholds are being crossed, new territory explored, and new decisions made. In addition, the speed at which life happens in contemporary times seems to provoke anxiety in and of itself.

Archetypally, the ancients spent much time and energy on ritual and devotion to their gods in order to ensure that there was harmony between the human and the divine realms. Not paying proper attention to a particular deity was certain to cause friction and disharmony between the realms. Ultimately, to offend a god, using Jung's parlance, is a very serious deed often with terrible consequences. The Olympian gods were often vengeful, mean, and petty. However, symbolically, they retain their rightful place in mythology; and depth psychology stresses their importance, because in mythology and fairy tale (for example), a road map is presented of the human condition and the challenges of life. Even if the language or guise of mythology seems anachronistic to the modern person (e.g., because of our preference for interpreting and understanding things literally), the themes and motives are highly relevant to human life and instructive of psychological development to this day.

So, in anxiety, for example, many different deities can be offended depending in which realm the heart of the problem lies: In the realm of the marriage it might be Hera; in PTSD anxiety it is Mars; in denying of the role of religion, mythology, and spirituality in human life, the entire band of Olympian gods are offended, and so forth. If a person ignores Hermes by ignoring the message in the anxiety, Hermes's son Pan is there to impose his reign on the offending party. In the techno–industrial paradigms' continued and systematic ignoring of psyche lies the risk of offending Eros himself, because of his fondness of her. Long ignoring the beloved of Psyche will certainly have consequences; in depression what can be clinically observed is the withdrawal of Eros (i.e., life force). Honoring the deity is honoring the message in the symptom and even the symptom itself. This is not an easy thing to ask of a contemporary human being, but of vital importance for personal growth and wellness.

THE PLACE OF PSYCHE IN A TECHNOLOGICAL WORLD?

While knowing full well that psyche is a concept agreed upon among a certain group of students of psychology—a type of metaphor based on common interior experiences and stirrings that otherwise lack definition— the true depth psychological questions, which as yet remain unanswered, really are: What might psyche want or what is it trying to tell us in regard to the neuroticism and suffering around technology in our era?

Giegerich (2007) asked an important question: "Is technology not the very opposite of soul, namely absolutely soulless, cold, abstract, the result of ego machinations?" (p. 1). While Giegerich does not exactly give a simple answer to this question, a reasonable depth psychologist, who sees the suffering of contemporary clients in their practices, would have to add additional questions: Is technology making the soul sick or is the technological reality a symptom, a means by which psyche shows her suffering, her unhappiness? Is technology a pathological manifestation of the individual and collective psyche in our contemporary world?

In working extensively with dreams, technology as shadow shows up frequently in the dream imagery. This is important because, as Romanyshyn (1989) reminded us: "Dreams shadow waking life and what we, individually and collectively, cannot bear in conscious life we dream" (p. 13). He also reiterated that "to attend to the cultural dream of technology, then, is to attend to the shadows and silences of technology" (p. 13).

Is technology resulting in the atrophy of psyche? Is it the first or final nail in the coffin of psyche and symbolic of the demise of depth psychology, as predicted by Giegerich (2007). Or does technology force psyche to show up in different guises, to alter where and how it gets nourished? Science and technology belong to the world of the ego. The destruction in the world we see is the result of overidentification with the ego and disregard for the messages of psyche—a disconnect from the self.

Obviously, it is hard to say at this point that one can point to something uniformly being neglected in people who overuse digital technology. Is it social relations? Is it a connection with nature, is it being indoors instead of outdoors, playing, hiking, drinking coffee? This cannot be established with any certainty at this point, but from the point of view of depth psychology these are grave concerns.

Also, from the point of view of depth psychology, however, it seems fair to say that the suffering that shows up in psychotherapeutic treatment is most frequently of a profound existential nature. This is why Hollis (1995) work is so essential in an attempt to understand and address the common ills of modern life. Psyche seems perhaps like she is rebelling against being saturated with violent (and/or pornographic) content on television, in movies, on the Internet, and in video games. Perhaps psyche mostly rebels against being totally ignored in contemporary life. Interiority, ritual, silence, and connection to nature seem to be the main troth of psyche. In the modern technological world, she is being fed cotton candy at best. On the surface it is sweet and compelling, but deep down, the techno–industrial world fails to nourish.

The goal of depth psychotherapeutic work, then, is to pay appropriate attention to psyche, perhaps nourish it or permit its reoccurrence or reappearance in the archetypal stirrings of old. If the individual and the collective psyche are not listened to, the consequences are likely to be severe both on an individual and a collective level.

CONCLUSION AND IMPLICATIONS

Our search for tribe, community, and wholeness has gone outward and online. This has happened not just opportunistically as digital technology has developed, but also as other avenues have failed to provide what was wished for. A seemingly appropriate tool for fighting the anxieties and loneliness, which invariably emerge when an overall existential framework no longer exists and all individual attempts to put structures in its place, no matter how inventive and creative, ultimately fails. It is the disorienting and painful simultaneous bankruptcy of meliorism and Cartesian dogma. From a therapist's chair, the modern self seems, in a sense, to be in crisis-management mode. Hence, the shadow online version of self is often a juvenile, simplistic, and narcissist expression of parts of a personality. In the meantime, we have rejected all things old, slow, and mysterious (along with the overtly childish and/or feminine) by focusing on their negative attributes. Mythology and religion are deemed anachronistic, illogical, and pointless by our modern dualistic and positivistic mindset. There is a failure to recognize that mythology and religion are only diminished in value if taken too literal, but otherwise provide great insights into the human condition. However, such notions belong to an erratic, cruel, and primitive past that we have long overcome and replaced with the rational technological world of the future. Despite widespread denial, as we left the 20th century behind, we can only conclude, that, generally speaking, technology has not helped make the world a more peaceful and stable place, but made the potential for destruction on all levels, much the greater.

From the perspective of depth psychology, one could state that many of the shadowy digital experiences mentioned (e.g., being connected, net-worked, gaming, multitasking, self-staging) in relation to the self are roughly the equivalent of what cotton candy is to a body requiring nutrition. It appears at this point that it is essentially empty calories, which, in the best of cases, mostly speak to and exercise the more superficial layers of the per-sonality (or the self), and, in a worst-case scenario, traps and arrests people in the world of ego and persona. From a Jungian viewpoint this is a tragedy because it hinders the psycho-archeological work of engaging with the rich deeper layers of the psyche and becomes a serious obstacle to the process of individuation. Jung was clear beyond any doubt when he repeatedly stated that humans cannot tolerate living a superficial life lacking in meaning. We suffer the culture-wide indifference toward, and subsequent mummification of, psyche. The consequences of such a life are psychopathological manifes-tations of a wide-ranging nature; as psyche rebels all kinds of behavioral problems emerge and severe addictions ensue.

At the core, human beings are meaning-seeking and ultimately meaning-creating creatures trying to make sense of their own place in an increasingly complex world. If the search for meaning becomes difficult and dry, then meaning will be projected or infused into something, and hence created in order to restore a meaning-providing paradigm in a cosmology. This will reduce existential angst and order the world in a way that allows an individual to make sense both of the world and of their own existence. Hence, in a world that is always connected, we experience loneliness and dis-ease more strongly than ever before. The illusion of the technological fix that cures all is still going strong—even as it operates mostly on an unconscious level—even if we constantly experience how we employ ever more creative technological fixes to previous fixes to keep the illusion going. Technology, digital or otherwise, does not really have the power to change anything substantial. Perhaps it would be useful to merely view technology as an elaborate toolbox. The only real fix is a change in human consciousness and how we employ the tools that technology does provide for us. So as technology will never be able to save us from ourselves, it can provide us with valuable tools to help us along on a better path.

Realizing this is the challenge to us all in contemporary life, especially as the lines between life online and offline are increasingly getting blurred. We need to gather more information, be critical, and self-aware. Ultimately, it may be wise to remember what Jung (1967) reminded us: "Our freedom extends only as far as our consciousness reaches" (p. 117).

REFERENCES

Gay, P. (1995). *The Freud reader*. New York, NY: Norton.

Giegerich, W. (2007). *Technology and the soul* (2nd ed.). New Orleans, LA: Spring.

Hillman, J. (1997). *Archetypal psychology*. New York, NY: Spring.

Hillman, J. (1998). *Insearch: Psychology and religion*. New York, NY: Spring.

Hollis, J. (1995). *Tracking the gods*. Toronto, Canada: Inner City Books.

Hollis, J. (2000). *The archetypal imagination*. College Station, TX: Texas A&M University Press.

Jung, C. G. (1966). The practice of psychotherapy. In H. Reid, M. Fordham, G. Adler, & W. McGuire (Eds.), *The collected works of C. G. Jung* (Vol. 20) (R. F. C. Hull, Trans.). Princeton, NJ: Princeton University Press.

Jung, C. G. (1967). The symbolic life. In H. Reid, M. Fordham, G. Adler, & W. McGuire (Eds.), *The collected works of C. G. Jung* (Vol. 18, pp. 267–280) (R. F. C. Hull, Trans.). Princeton, NJ: Princeton University Press.

Jung, C. G. (1969). The structure and dynamics of the psyche. In H. Reid, M. Fordham, G. Adler, & W. McGuire (Eds.), *The collected works of C. G. Jung* (Vol. 8, 2nd ed.) (R. F. C. Hull, Trans.). Princeton, NJ: Princeton University Press.

Jung, C. G. (1970). Mysterium coniunctionis. In H. Reid, M. Fordham, G. Adler, & W. McGuire (Eds.), *The collected works of C. G. Jung* (Vol. 14, 2nd ed.) (R. F. C. Hull, Trans.). Princeton, NJ: Princeton University Press.

Kaufman-Osborn, T. (1997). *Creatures of prometheus*. Lanham, MD: Rowman & Littlefield.

Romanyshyn, R. (1989). *Technology as symptom and dream*. New York, NY: Routledge.

Rosen, L. (2012). *iDisorder: Understanding our obsessions with technology and overcoming its hold on us*. New York, NY: Palgrave Macmillan.

Sharp, D. (1991). *C. G. Jung lexicon*. Toronto, Canada: Inner City Books.

Slater, G. (2007). Cyborgian drift: Resistance is not futile. *Spring, 75*, 171–196.

Turkle, S. (2011). *Alone together: Why we expect more from technology and less from each other*. New York, NY: Basic Books.

SECTION B

Simulation or Reality?

CHAPTER 9

The Video Gaming Frontier

Jayne Gackenbach, Dylan Wijeyaratnam, Carson Flockhart
MacEwan University, Edmonton, AB, Canada

Video games have held a tentative place in society, perching on the fringes of culture and popular opinion, leading to many misgivings about what they have to offer the world beyond play. There have been many times that video games have been blamed for violence or misfortune in the news, and this has caused a primarily negative reaction to video games. In the past five years more and more researchers and scientists have looked into the existence of benefits from video games in our lives. This "frontier" of gaming, as we can call it, is an ever-expanding border made up of all the new advances in gaming that is quickly moving to encompass all aspects of our lives. Starting in a small corner of society, supposedly played by undesirables and miscreants, video games have now moved into the realms of artistic expression and useful tools. This expansion of scope has led to improved societal opinions surrounding video games.

Originally, video games were hard to access for many people, either due to the high initial cost of one of the many consoles or computer systems, or the complexity of the games and time commitment to play. These barriers limited the amount of people who could play, but have been overcome in the explosively expanding mobile industry. This expanding gaming frontier encompasses many areas of society, and with mobile devices now connecting many people on this planet, game developers and researchers have an unparalleled opportunity to use games. In fields like medicine, education, business, and politics, or "serious games," video games may aid human lives in ways we never would have dreamed. This chapter will explore the ways that video games are expanding our understanding of ourselves as individuals, including improving our dream life and improving society as a whole, as well as the ways that video games are being put to work to aid us in daily life.

THE INDIVIDUAL

The gaming experience is, in and of itself, usually a solitary one. Even when playing with friends or allies, a gamer is always aware of their own skills and

Boundaries of Self and Reality Online
ISBN 978-0-12-804157-4
http://dx.doi.org/10.1016/B978-0-12-804157-4.00009-8

those playing with or against them. Most games seek to challenge the individual, even when working in team situations, constantly seeking to test the mettle of those who would walk the path of the video game elite. However, how the individual can be influenced by playing video games is not subject to just one area of science. This part of the chapter will be looking at how the individual is affected by video game play in a variety of areas, from health and development to social well-being. Since video games typically involve quite a bit of sitting and not exercising, they have carried a more negative association as far as health outcomes. In many cases, the media attention and research interest have reflected this negative association; however, as time has passed, more effort has been made to explore the possible wide-ranging benefits of moderate to low amounts of video game play.

A major review of current video game play research by Jones, Scholes, Johnson, Katsikitis, and Carras (2014) made the case that video game play has much to offer in the realm of mental health, even going so far as to say it can help a person to flourish. The researchers state that "flourishing mental health has been defined as a combination of feeling good and functioning effectively resulting in high levels of mental well-being" (p. 1). To explore how video games affect players' mental well-being, the team used Seligman's model of well-being, which contains five elements that contribute to an adult's flourishing mental health. Seligman claims that this flourishing level of mental health should be clearly visible in people as happiness or satisfaction with their lives as well as feeling that their life has purpose and meaning (Seligman, 2011).

This review argued that moderate, and sometimes low, levels of video game play can have a positive influence on well-being. Specifically, video game play has been shown to improve mood, reduce emotional anxiety, improve emotional regulation, increase feelings of relaxation, and reduce stress. Most importantly, moderate play has been shown to be linked with better health outcomes than either excessive video game play or no play at all. There is a lack of negative effects for the majority of younger players, and instead, video game play is associated with greater self-regard toward one's intelligence, computer skills, and mechanical ability. The experience of feelings of competence, autonomy, and relatedness during video game play has been linked with higher self-esteem and certainly to greater success in life. These elements make up the necessary ingredients for an adult to have a positive sense of well-being, which is noted by Jones et al. (2014).

Given the positive effects of gaming, concern continues regarding any modeling influences on subsequent aggressive behavior, including desensitization to violence. This has been the primary issue supporting the antigaming voices. In 2013, Ferguson argued that there were several problems with the research connecting video game play to subsequent aggressive behavior. These ranged from a third variable effect to various media influences. More recently, both the American Psychological Association and the American Academy of Pediatrics have both warned against violence in media effects on children (Scutti, 2016). However, Ferguson, along with over 200 other social scientists, have argued that these societies need to put aside their outdated policies in favor of the more recent body of research. Specifically, DeCamp (2015) concluded:

> In terms of what does seem to matter in predicting violent behavior, other social factors account for the vast majority of the predictive power of the models. Though not significant in all models, seeing or hearing violence at home, having a sensation-seeking personality, experiencing less parental monitoring, and having lower levels of parental attachment are all relatively strong predictors of violent behavior and weapon carrying (p. 302).

When he added video game play to the prediction equations, it did not contribute anything significant. In other words, as earlier pointed out by Ferguson, gaming by itself does not predict aggressive behavior.

One possible negative effect of video games on the self is gaming addiction, or what the Diagnostic and Statistical Manual, 5th edition (DSM-V) is calling "Internet Gaming Disorder" (Sarkis, 2014). While the DSM doesn't officially list Internet Gaming Disorder, it is classified as a condition for further study, meaning that pending further research into the condition, it may or may not be included in the next edition of the DSM. This disorder is thought to be prevalent in males aged 12 to 20 (Sarkis, 2014). Internet Gaming Disorder falls into three classifications: mild, moderate or severe, depending on how much time is spent playing the games and how intensely they impact an individual's functioning. Based on further research, an individual would be classified as suffering from Internet Gaming Disorder if they meet five of the following, taken from Sarkis, 2014:

1. Preoccupation or obsession with Internet gaming.
2. Withdrawal symptoms when not playing Internet games.
3. A buildup of tolerance (more time needs to be spent playing the games).
4. The person has tried to stop or curb playing Internet games, but has failed to do so.
5. The person has had a loss of interest in other life activities or hobbies.
6. A person has had continued overuse of Internet games even with the knowledge of how much they impact a person's life.
7. The person lies to others about his or her Internet game usage.
8. The person uses Internet games to relieve anxiety or guilt.
9. The person has lost or put at risk an opportunity or relationship because of Internet games.

While there are many positive effects from gaming, repetitive and/or excessive use of games can cause disruption and impairment in an individual's functioning. The fact that the DSM is encouraging further research into this issue illustrates that there is still a dark side to gaming that needs to be explored. Addiction of any kind is detrimental, and Internet usage and gaming are no different. As with most things in life, in order to reap the benefits and positive effects of gaming, moderation, and a balance with nongaming activities is encouraged in order to remain mentally and physically healthy.

Given the increasing awareness of the positive effects of gaming from emotional and motivational perspectives as well as the classic improvements in various cognitive and spatial skills (Boot, Kramer, Simons, Fabiani, & Gratton, 2008), it may not be surprising that on a deeper psychological level, these positive consequences are observed. Here, we speak specifically of dreams. Over the last decade, our laboratory has been exploring the associations between video game play and subsequent nighttime dreams. Despite the general western societal dismissal of dreams as unimportant, the reality in today's dream research community is that dreams are crucial for memory consolidation, information processing, creative inspiration, and emotional regulation. Thus, dreams can impact us profoundly; as in the case of posttraumatic stress, dreams can enlighten and enliven our perspectives on our deep unconscious as in lucid dreams. We have found an association between gaming and lucid dreams as well as in the ability to control nighttime dreams. This association between dream control and gaming has led us to suggest a nightmare protection effect for gamers, that is, by playing video games during the day, especially combat-centric ones, we have found in several studies that these young men and women fight back at night in the most common nightmare dream scenario, chase dreams. Thus, while they may call the experience a "nightmare," they also find it fun and emotionally uplifting, if not empowering (see Bown & Gackenbach, 2015 for a summary).

This compelling case from a student illustrates these relationships:

When I was about 19 or 20 years old I, a former protestant, experienced a loss of faith in religion due to a number of factors including … a startling, terrifying fear that I might die and all my memories, visions, passions and experiences would be gone with me forever and my world would suddenly come to an end. The existential crisis I experienced worried me greatly, and thoughts of dying, nihilistic thoughts of not having a purpose at all, and feelings of helplessness pervaded my thoughts at all hours of the day no matter how hard I tried to suppress them.

Around this same time,…it was at home where I would find the closest thing to solace as I would play immersive video games like Mass Effect where technologically constructed alternative realities drew in the player, demanded undivided attention and cultivated absorption. Whenever I played these more complex games that fully engaged me for more than an hour I would forget about real world concerns like mortality and focus instead on the rules, conventions and objectives of the games. Whenever I finished playing I would start thinking about existential matters again, and subsequently worry again, so I played almost obsessively as often as possible.

Most interestingly, at night some very peculiar, unusual and frightening events would occur almost routinely: … but … I would sometimes, mercifully become aware that I was simply experiencing a nightmare, and instead of waking up (where I'd be less distressed, but still preoccupied with existentialism), I would think of Mass Effect scenarios such as walking through the "citadel" map, firing assault rifles and taking cover with allies - basically implanting myself in the fictional reality. Throughout these dreams, I primarily utilized the fictional biotic energy field attacks on Turian (alien) enemies, and imagined myself in Mass Effect plot lines I was working towards in the game, and my sense of comfort and calm was almost normal. I knew that I knew I was dreaming because I would remind myself not to get overzealous and "wake up", and to hold out for as long as possible. Essentially, I was escaping my nightmares by drawing upon more pleasant possibilities within the unconscious state …

VIDEO GAME–BASED INTERVENTIONS: HEALTH

To begin with, one of the longest held assumptions concerning video games has been that it comes hand-in-hand with low levels of physical activity. However, the biggest players of video games, the eSports athletes who can play up to 12h of video games a day to practice, exercise daily and rigorously. While it is often largely sedentary for most players, new technologies are seeking to blend physical activity with enjoyable game play.

The ever-increasing prevalence in younger generations of electronic device use is concerning for many reasons, one being the loss of physical activity. Some countries have shown that many children are getting less than the recommended dose of varied physical activity in any given day (Colley et al., 2011). Some studies look at the fundamental movement skill development in children, which include the ability to run, jump, catch, hop, and kick. These skills are not naturally acquired and must see the children engaging in them to learn them. As the numbers of children using devices continues to increase, new ways must be developed to bridge this growing gap. One promising technology is the use of active video games: systems such as the Microsoft *Kinect*, Playstation *Move*, or the Nintendo *Wii* or *WiiU*. All these systems involve video games requiring the player to move their arms, legs, and sometimes whole body (Barnett, Bangay, McKenzie, & Ridgers, 2013). These systems have been around for a few years, and while things like the *Wii Fit* tried to create a new niche for video games to fill, the trend did not last. While little research has been done concerning why fitness games fail to make a large impact in the gaming community, recent evidence, such as *Xbox* shutting down their fitness program on the new *Xbox One*, points to at least its economic failure. A newer form of active video games that seeks to appeal to the explosive use of mobile devices for gaming is augmented reality. At first, this was much simpler, being games or tools that could overlay images onto maps or pictures that could then be interacted with between friends and associates. Now, video game developers can utilize the real world by overlaying images in players' phones to get them to play a game using the real world as the environment. An example is Google's augmented reality world domination game, *Ingress* (Niantic, 2016a, 2016b). *Ingress* is a massively multiplayer online location-based game that forces players to choose a side between the two teams of the "Enlightened" and the "Resistance." It is an espionage-themed game, which tasks players with going out in the real world and using landmarks that appear in the game as portals. Once at these portals, players can get items or hack the location for their team (Ferrazzino, 2015).

Pokémon Go is a game that has recently come out and has already garnered much news. Pokémon has been around for many years, first in the form of Japanese manga, then a trading card game, and finally as television cartoons and video games. Its popularity exploded in North America and around the world in the early days of its release, and it has held a popular longstanding place among fans and gamers alike. This new game, *Pokémon Go*, uses the same augmented reality technology as the previously mentioned game; however, it uses the much loved brand of the *Pokémon* series and style to get players to travel the actual world looking to capture and battle *Pokémon* rather than engaging only within a virtual environment. The game has been so popular that in the few countries it is currently out in, there have been rampant server issues as too many players have tried to log on and use the game. In addition, the game is causing ripples in society, and gamers are occasionally being directed to go into places they are not allowed. These places range from police stations and hospitals to morgues and churches, all in the name of catching the rarer and rarer *Pokémon*. This game most definitely has players moving about in the world, engaging with one another in all sorts of places, and sometimes forcing people of differing views and places in society to come together. News stations, which rarely cover video games, are talking about *Pokémon Go*. They comment that the game shows how parents can bridge the gap to engage in a fun and effective play with their kids. While good in many ways, it is a very simplistic, goal-driven method that does not allow for improved exercise frequency or duration that some serious games offer, but it is an excellent way to get the kids out of the house.

Needless to say, this has led to an active area of research called active video games. It has become one of the focuses of research in the Games for Health community and journal since its inception in 2012 (Bohm, Hartmann, & Bohm, 2016). Indeed, de Boer, Adriani, van Houwelingen, and Geerts (2016) point out that their Game Maturity Model will "forecast … that within 5 years the use and development of applied games will have a role in our daily lives and the way we organize health care that will be similar to the role social media has today" (p. 87).

Video games are assisting in therapies and rehabilitations of various kinds. They may aid in improving education and training through new ways to reach youth and by increasing motivation in grueling training sessions. A group of researchers has called for major changes to the way society approaches e-therapies and related game-based interventions and therapies. Fleming et al. (2016) call for faster mobilization, development, and implementation, as well as greater access for the masses to therapeutic games.

An early example of using a video game therapeutically was developed for attention deficit hyperactivity disorder, or ADHD (Rivero, Nunez, Pires, & Francisco, 2015). As one of the most diagnosed childhood behavioral disorders, ADHD has seen many different approaches taken to combat it since it first began to be diagnosed in school-age children. As such, researchers were curious if video games could be used as a "neuropsychological rehabilitation and intervention tool" (Rivero et al., 2015; p. 1). Individuals with ADHD tend to have a wide array of everyday problems, including problems with regulating emotions, problems with appropriate behavior, and difficulty in social situations. In the past, ADHD has been combated by using combinations of interventions of varying degrees and effects. Some studies have shown that video game play promotes an "optimal cognitive performance" by providing constant feedback and improving focus and attention in the participant. As well, it aids in controlling inhibitions and increasing the mental arousal state of the person with ADHD, which increases greatly the motivation that people have when engaging in tasks.

Another much diagnosed disorder in young children is autism spectrum disorder (ASD), which is still not fully understood and often treated improperly or ineffectively. Treatment for ASD is usually costly, intensive, and time-consuming, which unfortunately leads toward the difficulty of managing and caring for children with ASD over the long term. As computer technology has improved, a home-based approach, via a video game intervention, has emerged. Bono et al. (2016) developed a gaming system that can operate on its own but allow for interventions by therapists and caregivers while also being employed in a solitary setting with the child. It has been developed by looking closely at two pivotal skills that have been linked strongly to ASD: imitation and joint attention. Eleven specific games have been developed for very young children suffering from ASD (U. of M. Department of Psychiatry, 2016). Its use allows the therapist to tailor the child's initial difficulty levels and then monitor what they are doing well on and what they are struggling with. This is easily and quickly adjusted in-game by the therapist. The researchers found that the greatest clinical benefits from this game-based intervention were the quick increase in ability that children showed in regards to imitation and joint attention skills. The game platform also allowed the therapist to create a scenario where the spontaneous, usually solo, activity of video games was easily pushed to become a shared activity leading to greater social interactions (Bono et al., 2016).

Video games work greatly at creating inclusive environments where players can feel comfortable discussing sensitive subjects. Bono explains that childhood abuse is a subject that few wish to recognize and even fewer victims seek treatment for. It may be that this is another area where gaming may be useful. In creating an environment where all parties may engage in safe talk, child sexual abuse may be talked about as the very significant societal problem it is. The main problem of abuse comes not just in the horrific moment, but also in the horrible negative effects that crop up in the years that follow. People who experience sexual abuse as children experience negative impacts for the rest of their lives, and these individuals have shown higher risks for a host of health problems. The younger generation gravitates toward video games as a safe place to discuss sensitive material in an anonymous fashion, demonstrating the usefulness of video games' popularity with this demographic. As well the subject material of abuse in any form is one that is generally met with uncertainty by teachers, and as such, this platform allows teachers to operate outside of their comfort zones while ensuring proper engagement with the subject material.

An example is *Orbit* (Stieler-Hunt, Jones, Rolfe, & Pozzebon, 2014). Problems in past interventions and programs had revolved mostly around issues of adult involvement, that is, not including adults at any point in the interventions seemed to convey to the participants that adults bore no responsibility for the children's protection. The *Orbit* program includes adults by providing supportive and educative information for families and community members. *Orbit* focuses on breaking down barriers to telling and sharing. The overall focus the authors describe while making the game was to make one of its primary goals that of building healthy self-concepts in the children while also making the game relatable and engaging for all players.

Orbit is an adventure game centered on a spaceship named Sammy who has become emotionally distant from its concerned crew. The crew consists of a number of aliens and robots, but the game truly begins when an earth child beams aboard the ship and has to try all they can to help the crew and ship out. Throughout the game, the child can teleport helpful adults from their life onto the ship to aid in helping Sammy, gradually helping Sammy to recognize how to begin the recovery process. The five chapters of the game are centered on major themes concerning this issue and are titled togetherness, listening, understanding, belief, and finally courage. The researchers showed that in order to work appropriately, the game *Orbit* would have to break free of certain limitations that interventions and treatments in the past had fallen short to.

Another shortfall that past interventions had fallen to was their hesitation to harm children by exploring the sensitive subject material. Too often, programs dance around, addressing what exactly abuse entails in order to avoid scaring children; *Orbit* instead will focus around breaking down barriers to telling and sharing. The overall focus the authors describe while making the game was to make one of its primary goals that of building healthy self-concepts in the children while also making the game relatable and engaging for all players (Stieler-Hunt et al., 2014).

Another game addresses one period of difficulty in families, the teen years. Familial bonds can be strained as budding youth chafe under the care of their parents. A surprising example of how this might be helped is a game called *Knowing You, Knowing Me* (Katsikitis, Jones, Muscat, & Crawford, 2014). It is an interactive game focusing upon problems that can arise between mothers and daughters. This game has been developed as a resource to increase the positive communications skills between daughters going through puberty and their mothers. *The Knowing You, Knowing Me* game contains tools and opportunities to develop healthy mother daughter communication, build respect and trust between parent and child, teach individuals how to negotiate set limits, and how to discuss values and analyze difficult situations.

It has been shown that video games have also been able to tackle other health issues, such as pain. Simplistic ancestors to the virtual reality and augmented reality have provided relief. A good example of this can be seen in the treatment of phantom limb pain. This is an experience described by those who undergo an amputation. They feel intense pain and sensation from the severed appendage. Mirrored therapy in the past has been employed to combat the pain. A person places a mirror between arms so that the person sees two complete arms when they look down. By moving the still whole arm, the brain of the person believes that they still possess both arms, and a remediation of symptoms seems to occur. More recently, virtual reality has been used as a more effective method. However, the problem that was systemic to the mirror therapy is the requirement that the person have at least one healthy appendage in order for the effect to take place. Ortiz-Catalan, Sander, Kristoffersen, Hakansson, and Branemark (2014) looked to see if they could improve this therapy using the improved visuals and higher degree of realism that virtual reality provides, coupled with other advancements. By using a game-like scenario, the researchers were able to improve participant engagement and motivation in using the new tool. People using the new intervention reported increased pain reduction after the sessions and an increasing amount of complete pain-free moments that, to many sufferers, had been a completely new sensation (Ortiz-Catalan et al., 2014).

These are but a few of the health applications of gaming. The field is exploding with the launching of a new journal, *Games for Health*, focusing on gaming in health fields from training to therapy. The website explains that this journal is "a bimonthly peer-reviewed journal dedicated to the development, use, and applications of game technology for improving physical and mental health and well-being. The Journal breaks new ground as the first to address this emerging, widely-recognized, and increasingly adopted area of healthcare" (Games for Health, 2016). Games for Health was founded in 2012 with articles offering a wide range of research results, including implications for public policy.

VIDEO GAME–BASED INTERVENTIONS: EDUCATION AND TRAINING

This next section looks at how education is being influenced by video games. Here, education is loosely defined as activities that are conveying new information to the players and helping them to retain and understand it. This also affects training or acquiring new skills. Video games are excellent arenas for training and learning, being rife with environments that are full of challenges and lessons of varying goals and rewards. They are overflowing with opportunities that provide chances to increase players' efficacy in virtual skills, which are transferable to real-world skills. It may seem that the only thing games can train people to do is to drive like Jason Statham, made famous by the *Transporter* series of movies, or shoot bad guys like James Bond. In fact, video games offer a wide and varied tool set to help players prepare for the real world.

Video games have been shown to offer insightful opportunities for players to engage in physical activity in this age of electronic saturation. This ability for video games to encourage children to engage and learn even when the subject matter may be sensitive or boring is a huge boon for trainers and educators alike. Lorenz, Gleich, Gallinat, and Kuhn (2015) looked at how video games utilized the reward system to increase motivation and training outcomes, namely, how video games hold very intricate reinforcement and reward schedules within their inner workings that can greatly increase the motivation felt by those trying to engage in the material. The longitudinal research study wanted to specifically see if indeed video games have an effect on the reward system in the brain and if this could be harnessed to increase the motivation to learn. Indeed, the authors were able to say that on some level, video games do indeed affect the reward system under certain conditions (Lorenz et al., 2015). The very ability to affect motivation is a hugely underestimated tool, especially when taken in context of all the training and new skills that some people must learn and go through. In regards to medical conditions, this is most evident, as people with new injuries must sometimes relearn new ways of doing once very simple tasks or suffer through grueling rehabilitation sessions of which motivation can be a crucial factor in success.

Increasing the motivation in those who must go through these difficult scenarios could be of huge benefit to the patient. An example of games being used to aid in the training of those with medical conditions can be seen in the case made by Connors, Chrastil, Sanchez, and Merabet (2014). They examined a game to assist in the training of navigation and spatial cognition skills in blind adolescents. They reported a high success rate among the youth, suggesting that the game had definitely improved their ability to develop spatial maps as well as to navigate within the spatial "quests." The researchers concluded that this type of game-based training can improve the lives of blind individuals everywhere as well as making it possibly fun (Connors et al., 2014).

To play video games is to engage in a dialogue with the self, as video games seek to tease out that which makes us "tick" as individuals. It is through play that we can better understand ourselves, and video games now are going beyond this to improve or heal that which we are. While gaming is linked to the individual, we are not just solitary creatures, and anything that can affect us can have wider ranging implications for groups or tribes. What affects us alone affects the whole. Thus, we turn to how video games are influencing human societies.

SOCIETY AND CULTURE

Although not the first video game ever created, *Pong* (1972) is often credited with igniting the video game industry into the multibillion dollar business it is today. When *Pong* came out, it drew people to arcades in droves for the chance to experience this simple yet addicting and wildly entertaining game. *Pong*, and video games as a whole, gave people the opportunity to interact with a digital world in a way that they had never before experienced. Then, when Atari brought the game into people's homes in 1977, culture shifted again as people no longer needed to leave the comfort of their homes to play video games. As consoles became more advanced and games themselves became more complex, people found new ways to interact with video games. Since then, the industry has continued to move forward in leaps and bounds, shaping our culture every step of the way. Today, it is a seemingly impossible task to find someone who has never encountered a video game at some point in his or her life. In fact, a 2015 survey in the US found that "155 million Americans play video games, and 42% of all Americans play video games for 3 or more hours per week" (ESA, 2015, p. 2). Another survey in Canada found that 19 million Canadians (54% of the population) identified themselves as gamers (ESAC, 2015). With the recent explosion of the smartphone and games like *Pokémon Go*, *Candy Crush*, *Clash of Clans*, and *Mobile Strike*, the number of gamers is on a steady incline. We will now consider the subculture created by video games, how games are being used as social platforms, how the gender gap in gaming is disappearing, and why eSports might be the next big thing. Overall, we will argue that video games are having large effects on our culture.

VIDEO GAME CULTURE

Before we talk about the impact of video games on our culture as a whole, it's important to look at how video games have created a sort of subculture of their own. Try to think of a typical "gamer." What images come to mind? The prevailing stereotype among older generations is that of an acne-covered teenager sitting in the basement, tightly gripping a controller a few feet away from the television. Maybe they have a headset on, and maybe there are piles of empty pizza boxes and soda cans lying around the room. While this image is still somewhat prevalent in popular media, in reality, the subculture of gamers is much more diverse. Game culture encapsulates a wide demographic of people who interact with video games, from casual gamers who play on their phones to those who self-identify as "hard-core gamers." Gaming has a large social aspect to it. Whether playing casually with friends or competitively on a global scale, the rise of the Internet and the influx of multiplayer games has greatly increased the social aspect of gaming. Typical of game culture is the local area network party, where individuals gather together, usually in a house, and play together. Alternatively, competitors and teammates can play the same game together online, which eliminates the need for geographical proximity. It's really quite incredible to think that today you can be talking to one of your teammates as you play together online, and they could be halfway around the world!

Gaming culture has also developed a language, usually comprised of abbreviations, to communicate game specific ideas. Many of these phrases have worked their way into popular language, such as the term "noob" (an abbreviation of the term newbie), meaning someone who is new to an experience and displays a lack of skill, or the term "pwn," meaning to totally defeat or dominate. These phrases, originally exclusive to video game culture, are now a part of everyday language, used by people who might otherwise have never experienced any aspect of game culture. Language is not the only thing that has spilled over from the video game culture to the real world; some games have become cultural phenomena in and of themselves. When we consider ourselves a fan of something, or identify membership with a particular group, we often wear clothing or buy items that represent that loyalty. This is expected with sports teams and bands, and now it is common among gamers. While there are extensive "die hard" fan communities of classic games, like *Mario* or *Pacman*, more modern games are making just as big a splash. A good example of this is the *Angry Birds* franchise. What started as a free smartphone game in 2009 has exploded into a massive, ever-expanding, loyal following. The series has reached over 3 billion downloads with 14 different variations of the original *Angry Birds* game (Robertson, 2015). Today you can buy *Angry Birds* stuffed animals, t-shirts, action figures, dishes, books, food, drink, and playsets. The game earned an animated TV series, released March 16, 2013, which spawned three subsequent series. Toy giant Lego released an *Angry Birds* toy series. Even the epic saga Star Wars has *Angry Birds*–themed toy sets and memorabilia based on the *Angry Birds*–Star Wars spinoffs of 2012 and 2013. This cultural fascination with *Angry Birds* has become so big that it received its own major motion picture in 2016, starring big name actors like Bill Hader, Jason Sudekis, and Peter Dinklage, which, at the time of this writing, has grossed over 344 million dollars worldwide in 2 months (IMDb, 2016; Box Office Mojo, 2016). This is not the first game to become a cultural phenomenon, and it certainly won't be the last.

Recently, we saw the explosion of *Pokémon Go*, which was discussed briefly in the beginning of this chapter. It is an augmented reality game that uses the smartphone's camera and location services to allow users to find, catch, train, and battle Pokémon in the real world. The game sounded exciting when it was in development, but nobody could have predicted just how big it would become. Within its first week of release, the game became the most downloaded app on the Apple App Store of all time, generating over 10 million downloads on Apple and Android devices; in less than a month, to date, it has over 75 million downloads. The game currently has 20 million daily active users in the US alone, which is more active users than Twitter, Snapchat, Instagram, Tinder, or Facebook! Through in-game purchases, the game generated almost $5 million in its first day. To date, the game has generated an estimated $75 million, with the amount rising every day. *Pokémon Go* is gaining popularity at such a rapid pace that it's extremely difficult to track the stats accurately. Aside from the obvious impact on users of the game, the effects of *Pokémon Go* are spreading to those outside the game. Businesses near Pokéstops (a place where players can replenish items) or near Pokémon themselves have seen significant increases in their foot traffic and subsequent revenue. When one of the authors was driving home from work the other day, an ad on the radio from a local car dealership promised a large amount of Pokécoins to buy a car! The augmented reality feature of this game encourages people to go outside and actively look for Pokémon; thus, it's doing a lot to change the perception of what a video game is, as previously mentioned. No longer is it sitting at home in front of the television. Now, you can be out for a jog as you hunt the local river valley trails for Pokémon! Also, the game doesn't require a certain amount of skill or a familiarity with the Pokémon franchise. Casual players can pull their phone out whenever they want and search their immediate surroundings for Pokémon. The fact that the app itself is free has allowed anybody to download it, and for some people, they are getting their very first taste of video games. As video games become more accessible and find new ways to engage and entertain us, the impacts of these games on our cultures will continue to amaze us.

One of the most striking cultural aspects of gaming is the existence of clans. Sometimes known as guilds or factions, these are organized groups of people who regularly play together and are typically focused on a certain game. Members of clans often develop close friendships, despite sometimes never seeing each other in person. Clans can be highly competitive, and many clans host online tryouts to determine whether or not an individual will be accepted (Smith, 2014). This results in a group of similar individuals, all highly competitive and passionate about a particular game. As we will see later, clans that are exceptionally good will often go on to compete in major eSports tournaments. Competitive teams like these will often require the clan members to move in together in order to maximize practice time and allow teammates to learn each other's play style in order to perfect effectiveness in game (Smith, 2014). Especially seen through clans, game culture replicates many of the social elements we commonly find in society. Gamers have found a way to make their own presence known among other subcultures, like film and music. In doing so, they have created an awareness of video games and encouraged other people that there is an accepting group awaiting them. Some gamers, but certainly not all, are socially marginalized individuals. Being a part of gaming culture gives these individuals a sense of identity and belonging, and more importantly, it allows them to live out their passions and enjoy gaming in a community of like-minded individuals who support and accept them.

SOCIAL MOVEMENTS

Another way in which video games have shaped our culture is through their ability to reach a wide and diverse group of people in order to affect social change. One way this is currently being accomplished is through the actual content of the games that are being produced. Founded in 2004, *Games for Change* is a nonprofit organization keen on using video games for social good. They produce what they call "social impact games" that can be used to further humanitarian efforts and educate players about important social topics. These games cover a wide variety of topics and continue to follow current social trends in order to keep their gamers on the cutting edge of what is happening in our world (Games for Change, 2016).

Video games are now being used to raise awareness about important issues affecting our lives. One of these is climate change. Climate change is a strongly scientifically supported phenomenon with one line of thinking about its cause being human interventions. Thus, educating the younger generations about the ramifications of our effects on the planet is very important. Currently, there is a competition for developers to create a game that will serve as a means to teach gamers about the impact their actions have on the planet. As if implementing social change wasn't incentive enough, the winning game developer is awarded $10,000. One finalist in this competition is a game called *Eco*, developed by John Krajenski (Boudreau, 2016). In *Eco*, the player finds his or her self in a utopian jungle planet where they must create a civilization and develop technology in order to save the planet from an incoming meteor. They must also consider their actions in light of their effects on the environment (Malo, 2016). When John pilot tested this game with middle schoolers in the US, they became excited and impassioned at the idea of controlling pollution and preserving the planet (Malo, 2016). Not only did they enjoy the testing period, many students continued playing the game once the testing was over! Games like this have found a way to bridge the gap between education and entertainment, creating a new genre of games aptly named "edutainment."

RACE

In the early days of video games, the majority of the characters like Link, Duke Nukem, and Mario were Caucasian. Even today, most big title games have the character take control of a Caucasian male protagonist. Some of the most recognizable characters, such as Marcus Fenix (*Gears of War*), Gordon Freeman (*Half-Life*), Sam Fisher (*Splinter Cell*), Vault Boy (*Fallout* series),

Ryu (*Street Fighter* series), Nathan Drake (*Uncharted*), Agent 47 (*Hitman*), Solid Snake (*Metal Gear Solid*), and almost any protagonist in the *Assassins Creed* or *Call of Duty* franchises are all Caucasian. A survey of 150 video games spanning 9 platforms in 2011 found that only 3% were Hispanic and less than 11% African American (DeLoria, 2011). The study also found that nonwhite characters were more likely to be sidekicks or villains, as opposed to protagonists. Other researchers looked at the top 20 most popular games of 2009 and found that 74% of the leading characters were white (Mou & Peng, 2009). A study from 2002 found that 56% of human characters were white; however, when solely the heroes of these games were analyzed, a whopping 87% of all heroes were white (Conditt, 2015). Another study found that when African Americans were portrayed in video games, they were limited to a small number of genres: sports and gang/crime games (Williams, Martins, Consalvo, & Ivory, 2009). The portrayal of race in gang/crime titles warrants further discussion. Classic examples of this can be seen throughout the *Grand Theft Auto* franchise, particularly in the most recent iteration, *GTA V*. Players have the opportunity to experience the lives of three different characters, switching between them as the story progresses. One of these characters is Franklin Clinton. Franklin never knew his father, and his mother is battling a cocaine addiction. His life is full of crime, dope dealing, and gang-banging, three things that popular media have associated with this particular race for a long time. While his character does somewhat evolve throughout the course of the game, this is a fairly typical (although factually inaccurate) representation of African Americans in video games. It is not the opinion of the authors that *all* video games negatively portray African Americans, as characters such as Augustus Cole (*Gears of War*) do well to speak against that stereotype. Rather, there seems to be a common trend in video games to propagate racial stereotypes. The problem lies in the fact that people playing these games start to adopt the racist ideology that is perhaps unwittingly presented by these games. Previously, we saw the significant effects of video games on the self, and this particular effect is one we need to stop.

One reason for this racial stereotyping could be due, in part, to the racial inequality of game developers. The International Game Developers Association surveyed 2202 developers worldwide in 2014 and found that 79% of those who responded were white. Amazingly, only 2.5% of those that responded were black (Conditt, 2015). This number is up just half a percent since the last survey in 2005 (Conditt, 2015). This dominance by Caucasians in the game developer community could be one of the main reasons there is a large amount of racial stereotyping in games. An accurate representation of black characters and games with black protagonists are not created because there is a significant lack of black game developers who can tell that story. Video games have begun to include more protagonists of color, but there is still a lot of work to be done in order to rid the industry of racial stereotypes and racial inequality among characters.

GENDER

When video games first emerged among consumer markets, they were very clearly targeted toward boys. Popular games like *Super Mario Bros.* and *Legend of Zelda* applied the all too common archetypes of "male protagonist hero figure" and "damsel in distress." The storyline is very familiar. The hero must fight his way through various minions and challenges in order to save the princess, who is helplessly trapped by the bad guy. These games were designed for, and marketed to, a male audience. Even games featuring a female protagonist, like the *Lara Croft: Tomb Raider* franchise, were still targeting a male audience through their comically overplayed sexualization of female characters (Ivory, 2009). Females who played video games were often looked down upon, as they were trying to make a name for themselves in a male-dominated arena. Thankfully, the industry has come a long way since then, and today video games are fairly equally played by men and women. In 2015, gamers in the US were 56% male and 44% female (ESA, 2015). In Canada, the gender gap is even smaller, with 52% male and 48% female (ESAC, 2015).

Even with glaring evidence that women make up close to half the population of gamers in North America, sexist attitudes are still prevalent in the majority of today's gaming communities. The basic argument of this sexism is that men are better gamers than women. However, recent research is suggesting something quite different. Shen, Rabindra, Cai, and Leavitt (2016) tracked several thousand players in two massive multiplayer online role-playing games (MMORPGs). They controlled for differences in playing time, character choice, and membership in a player's guild. Once the data was analyzed, they found no gender difference for performance in game; women were progressing from level to level just as fast as men.

Today, game developers are creating games where gamers can play as strong female protagonists, such as *Rise of The Tomb Raider*, *Mass Effect Andromeda*, and *Mirror's Edge: Catalyst*. Today, major title game series like *Halo* still portray a male protagonist in their storylines; however, with the dominant force of online play in titles like this, gamers now have the ability to customize the look of their character and associate a male or female gamer tag with their character to personally represent themselves online. Unfortunately, there is still a prevailing negative attitude toward female gamers in online communities, so much so that female gamers will often elect not to use their microphones and engage in in-game conversation in order to mask their gender. One female gamer summarized her experiences in the game *Ragnarok Online* as being harassed, asked to show her breasts, and being badgered about her relationship status until she felt physically unsafe (Samin, 2015).

Things got particularly awful for female game developers and fellow gamers in 2014, when a personal dispute became public. Controversy arose after a former boyfriend of game developer Zoe Quinn falsely accused her of beginning a relationship with a journalist for positive coverage. Supporters of Quinn's ex-boyfriend organized under the movement "Gamergate." What followed was a mass attack on women in the video game industry, threatening assault (both physical and sexual) and murder. While members of Gamergate claimed to be fighting against political correctness and unethical journalistic practices, any real message they did have was lost in the myriad of violently misogynistic ideology. The movement was primarily executed on Twitter, with individuals attaching the Gamergate hashtags to offensive, threatening tweets directed at women in the video game industry. Their intended message still remains unclear, but the message most people received from Gamergate was simple: gaming is for men and women don't belong here. Unfortunately, this statement fails to capture the visceral harassment that stemmed from Gamergate, and yet it perfectly encapsulated the majority of online gaming culture that opposes female presence in gaming. Gamergate proved that there is significant work to be done to remove the prevalent sexist attitudes among male gamers and further reinforced the notion that sexism is very much alive in the current culture of gaming.

As mentioned earlier, Games for Change have made a significant effort to increase the female presence in gaming, and have done so by creating games that empower female characters and deal with the sorts of real-life issues young women today are facing. *Wonder City* is a game targeted at 8- to 13-year-old girls. In the game, players control a high-school girl who has the ability to grant super powers to people (Games for Health, 2016). Throughout the story, players make a series of decisions that will unlock their "style of heroism." The game encourages self-exploration and self-expression in the player as she becomes a female superhero throughout the course of the game. Games such as this one are not only helping females find their voice in the gaming community, but also teaching them to be proud of who they are and encouraging prosocial behavior in schools as well as everyday life. We are seeing a shift in game developers and designers attempting to push for a more gender-equal platform for games. We have already seen a major shift in our culture where video games are now more widely played by females compared to previous years, and we have seen that females are equally successful as men in MMORPGs, though further research with different genres of games is needed. Positively empowering young women through video games has a direct impact on the type of people they will grow up to be. This is bound to have significant impacts on our culture as game developers continue to push for gender equality in gaming.

eSPORTS

One of the biggest impacts we have seen in our culture due to gaming has been the rise of competitive gaming. What started as friends battling each other to post the highest score has now turned into an international sport. Stadiums of people gather to watch both teams and individual players compete to win their share of prize pools reaching upwards of 18 million dollars. Video games are no longer a hobby; for some, they have become a full-time job as evidenced by Riot Games, who pay players in their *League of Legends* championship series a salary. The most popular genres associated with eSports are: "real-time strategy, fighting, first-person shooter, and multiplayer online battle arena (MOBA)" (eSports, 2016). The more popular tournaments are live-broadcast and garner a large viewership from dedicated fans. The pace at which eSports is growing in popularity and membership is staggering. In 2015, eSports revenue totaled $325 million worldwide (NewZoo, 2016). So far, 2016 is on pace to reach $463 million worldwide (NewZoo, 2016). That's a growth of 43% in just one year! The dedicated eSports viewership (2015) came in at 131 million people, with an additional 125 million tuning in for major tournaments like "The International," a worldwide *DOTA 2* tournament that paid the 2015 champions over $6 million.

When competitive gaming began to emerge, people were quick to dismiss it as a hobby, not a sport. Today, however, the naysayers are, well, not saying much. eSports has quickly and forcefully made the case that they are just as much a sport as hockey or soccer. In fact, an eSports tournament has been scheduled to took place in Rio while the 2016 Olympic Games happened (Wolf, 2016). Players will compete for medals and national pride instead of the usual cash prizes. This tournament has already been scheduled to take place in host Olympic cities Pyeongchang in 2018 and Tokyo in 2020 (Wolf, 2016), the goal being to eventually integrate eSports as an official Olympic event; with ESPN reporting, it could be as early as 2020 (Wolf, 2016). In 2013, a Canadian *League of Legends* player received an American visa reserved exclusively for internationally recognized athletes. This was an enormous breakthrough for eSports, as it now allowed international players to come to the US to compete, and an even bigger breakthrough for gamers and video games as our culture begins to recognize the skill, practice, and dedication required to truly excel. When eSports began to make headlines and people became aware of this up-and-coming phenomenon, many were quick to dismiss it. Yet, as the sport grows faster than the naysayers can downplay, we are seeing eSports become one of the largest sports in the world.

eSports players typically train for 50 h/week. As one athlete said, if they're not eating, sleeping, or using the toilet, then they are in front of a screen, training. The lifestyle is similar to that of an aspiring athlete for any sport: long hours of practice, and complete and total dedication to the sport. Competitive teams will often require all players to move into a "team house" where a coach or manager also lives. The job of the coach is not only to prepare the athletes for competition and assist with their training, but also to help them adjust to this new lifestyle, as this is the first time many of them are living away from their parents. Athletes will train together as a team for at least 8 h a day, playing against other professional and challenger teams. Outside of this 8 h, players typically play on their own in order to hone their skills as individuals (Jacobs, 2015). Players maintain a vigorous practice schedule 4 days a week and compete 2 days a week (Jacobs, 2015). They are given 1 day off a week, but most players choose to practice on that day as well in order to become better at the game. Alex Chu, a professional gamer for the last 4 years says, "There is no downtime. I don't want to spend my time away from here … I'd rather spend my time practicing. I'm not satisfied with being anything below first, so I work my hardest the whole time" (Jacobs, 2015). This type of gaming is a full-time job, and the payday can be well worth the time and effort athletes put in.

eSports is one of the most legitimizing things to happen to video games since their inception. It is the culmination of decades of pushing to be recognized as more than just a hobby or a pastime. In many ways, it is the largest impact that video games has had on our culture, as it has effectively created a new industry, sport, career, and following. eSports is now a global phenomenon, and as previously mentioned, its growth rates project upwards of $1.1 billion by 2019 (NewZoo, 2016). As eSports continues to grow globally, it won't be long before people equate eSports and sports like baseball, hockey, and football on the same plane. Soon the world will recognize these men and women as a new breed of athlete, in a new arena of sport.

CONCLUSION

Throughout this chapter, we have shown how gaming affects the individual and culture in a multitude of facets. Evidence has been presented to suggest there are many positive effects to video gaming on well-being, and less evidence to support the ideology that video games lead to heightened levels of aggression in adolescents. Further, we have shown how video games are affecting the dreams of gamers in our lab, allowing them to better deal with nightmare-type dreams, along with increasing lucidity. The rise of active video games is spearheading the movement for health-based interventions in gaming, specifically those making use of augmented reality in order to encourage gamers to get off the couch and increase their levels of activity. We also demonstrated some ways in which video games are being used therapeutically, specifically helping individuals with ADHD, ASD, phantom limb pain, and a history of trauma. Also, research was presented to show that video games have been widely applied in education and training scenarios, particularly looking at the effects of reward incentives. Then, we shifted our focus to video games and their impacts on culture. We have explored gaming culture itself and tried to show how what was once a niche group of dedicated individuals has spilled out into a global phenomenon, with games like *Pokémon Go* leading the charge. We have also looked at the ramifications of gaming on important cultural issues like race and gender inequality, and social movements such as climate change and female empowerment. Lastly, we briefly discussed the up-and-coming world of eSports that continues to grow and develop as you are reading this. In summary, video games are no longer a private activity relegated to a specific group of people. It is now a cultural phenomenon, which is literally changing our society every day. Through this cultural proliferation, we are seeing some noteworthy positive impacts on individuals through their interactions with gaming. As video games continue to impact our culture and ourselves, more research should be done on the ramifications, both positive and negative, that they will have on us moving forward. Video games have proved themselves as a dominant force in our world, and the future ahead is going to be wild ride, packed with new advancements and impactful change on our existence.

REFERENCES

Barnett, L. M., Bangay, S., McKenzie, S., & Ridgers, N. D. (2013). Active gaming as a mechanism to promote physical activity and fundamental movement skill in children. *Frontiers in Public Health, 2,* 66. http://dx.doi.org/10.3389/fpubh.2013.00074.

de Boer, J. C., Adriani, P., van Houwelingen, J. W., & Geerts, A. (2016). Game maturity model for health care. *Games for Health Journal, 5*(2), 87–91.

Bohm, B., Hartmann, M., & Bohm, H. (2016). Body segment kinematics and energy expenditure in active videogames. *Games for Health Journal: Research, Development, and Clinical Applications, 5*(3), 189–196.

Bono, V., Narzisi, A., Jouen, A. L., Tilmont, E., Hommel, S., Jamal, W., et al. (2016). GOLIAH: A gaming platform for the home-based intervention in autism – principles and design. *Frontiers in Psychiatry.* http://dx.doi.org/10.3389/fpsyt.2016.00070.

Boot, W. R., Kramer, A. F., Simons, D. J., Fabiani, M., & Gratton, G. (2008). The effects of video game playing on attention, memory and executive control. *Acta Psychologica, 129,* 387–398.

Boudreau, C. (2016). *Video game makers tackle global Warming.* The Daily Caller News Foundation. Retrieved from http://dailycaller.com/2016/06/21/video-game-makers-tackle-global-warming/.

Bown, J., & Gackenbach, J. I. (2015). Video games, nightmares, and emotional processing. In S. Tettegah (Ed.), *Emotions and technology: Communication of, feelings through, with and for technology.* London: Elsevier (Academic Psychology Division).

Box Office Mojo. (2016). Retrieved from http://www.boxofficemojo.com/movies/?id=angrybirds.htm.

Colley, R. C., Garriguet, D., Janssen, I., Craig, C. L., Clarke, J., & Tremblay, M. S. (2011). Physical activity of Canadian children and youth: Accelerometer results from the 2007 to 2009 Canadian health measures survey. *Component of Statistics Canada Catalogue – Health Reports, 22*(1), 1–10.

Conditt, J. (2015). Gaming while black: Casual racism to cautious optimism. *Engadget.* Retrieved from https://www.engadget.com/2015/01/16/gaming-while-black-casual-racism-to-cautious-optimism/.

Connors, E. C., Chrastil, E. R., Sanchez, J., & Merabet, L. B. (2014). Action video game play and transfer of navigation and spatial cognition skills in adolescents who are blind. *Frontiers in Human Neuroscience, 8,* 133. http://dx.doi.org/10.3389/fnhum.2014.00133.

DeCamp, W. (2015). Impersonal agencies of communication: Comparing the effects of video games and other risk factors on violence. *Psychology of Popular Media Culture, 4*(4), 296–304. Retrieved from http://psycnet.apa.org/journals/ppm/4/4/296/.

DeLoria, E. (November 18, 2011). Video games snub non-white characters. *Gameranx.* Retrieved from http://gameranx.com/updates/id/3741/article/video-games-snub-non-white-characters/.

Entertainment Software Association. (2015). Essential facts about the computer and video game industry. *2015 Sales, Demographics, and Usage Data.*

Entertainment Software Association of Canada. (2015). *Essential facts about the Canadian video game industry.*

ESports. (July 30, 2016). In *Wikipedia, the free encyclopedia* Retrieved from https://en.wikipedia.org/w/index.php?title=ESports&oldid=732215419.

Ferguson, C. J. (2013). Violent video games and the Supreme Court: Lessons for the scientific community in the wake of Brown v. Entertainment Merchants Association. *American Psychologist, 68,* 57–74. http://dx.doi.org/10.1037/a0030597.

Ferrazzino, F. (2015). *Father I/O (mobile video game).* Retrieved from https://www.indiegogo.com/projects/father-io-massive-multiplayer-laser-tag#/.

Fleming, T. M., de Beurs, D., Khazaal, Y., Gaggioli, A., Riva, G., Botella, C., et al. (2016). Maximizing the impact of e-therapy and serious gaming: Time for a paradigm shift. *Frontiers in Psychiatry*, 7, 65. http://dx.doi.org/10.3389/fpsyt.2016.00065.

Games For Change. (2016). Retrieved from http://www.gamesforchange.org/.

Games for Health. (2016). Retrieved from http://www.liebertpub.com/g4h.

IMDb. (2016). Retrieved from http://www.imdb.com/title/tt1985949/.Ivory.

Ivory, J. D. (2009). Still a man's game: Gender representation in online reviews of video games. *Mass Communication and Society*, 9(1), 103–114.

Jacobs, H. (May 11, 2015). Here's the insane training schedule of a 20-something professional gamer. *Business Insider*. Retrieved from http://www.businessinsider.com/pro-gamers-explain-the-insane-training-regimen-they-use-to-stay-on-top-2015-5.

Jones, C. M., Scholes, L., Johnson, D., Katsikitis, M., & Carras, M. C. (2014). Gaming well: Links between videogames and flourishing mental health. *Frontiers in Psychology*, 5, 260. http://dx.doi.org/10.3389/fpsyg.2014.00260.

Katsikitis, M., Jones, J., Muscat, M., & Crawford, K. (2014). Knowing You, Knowing Me (KYKM): An interactive game to address positive mother-daughter communication and relationships. *Frontiers in Psychology*, 5, 721. http://dx.doi.org/10.3389/fpsyg.2014.00721.

Lorenz, R., Gleich, T., Gallinat, J., & Kuhn, S. (2015). Video game training and the reward system. *Frontiers in Human Neuroscience*, 9(40). http://dx.doi.org/10.3389/fnhum.2015.00040.

Malo, S. (2016). *US contest challenges video-game makers to battle climate change*. Reuters. Retrieved from http://www.reuters.com/article/us-usa-climatechange-videogamesidUSKCN0Z62I9.

Mou, Y., & Peng, W. (2009). *Gender and racial stereotypes in popular video games*. IGI Global.

NewZoo. (2016). *Global esports market report: Revenue jumps to $463 million in 2016 as US leads the way*. Retrieved from https://newzoo.com/insights/articles/global-esports-market-report-revenues-to-jump-to-463-million-in-2016-as-us-leads-the-way/.

Niantic. (2016a). *Ingress (mobile video game)*. Retrieved from https://www.ingress.com/.

Niantic. (2016b). *Pokémon go*. Retrieved from http://www.pokemongo.com/.

Ortiz-Catalan, M., Sander, N., Kristoffersen, M. B., Hakansson, B., & Branemark, R. (2014). Treatment of phantom limb pain (PLP) based on augmented reality and gaming controlled by myoelectric pattern recognition: A case study of a chronic PLP patient. *Frontiers in Neuroscience*, 8(24). http://dx.doi.org/10.3389/fnins.2014.00024.

Rivero, T. S., Nunez, L. M. A., Pires, E. U., & Francisco, O. (2015). ADHD rehabilitation through video gaming: A systematic review using PRISMA guidelines of the current findings and the associated risk of bias. *Frontiers in Psychiatry*, 6, 151. http://dx.doi.org/10.3389/fpsyt.2015.00151.

Robertson, A. (July 16, 2015). *'Angry Birds 2' arrives 6 years and 3 billion downloads after first game*. Forbes. Retrieved from http://www.forbes.com/sites/andyrobertson/2015/07/16/angry-birds-2/#49794df72084.

Samin, S. (March 12, 2015). *I'm a female gamer, and this is what It's really like*. Bustle. Retrieved from http://www.bustle.com/articles/65237-im-a-female-gamer-and-this-is-what-its-really-like.

Sarkis, S. (2014). Internet gaming disorder in DSM-5. *Psychology Today*. Retrieved from https://www.psychologytoday.com/blog/here-there-and-everywhere/201407/internet-gaming-disorder-in-dsm-5.

Scutti, S. (July 26, 2016). *Do video games lead to violence?* CNN. Online. Retrieved from http://www.cnn.com/2016/07/25/health/video-games-and-violence/.

Seligman, M. (2011). *Flourish: A visionary new understanding of happiness and well-being*. New York: Free Press.

Shen, C., Rabindra, R., Cai, Y. D., & Leavitt, A. (2016). Do men advance faster than women? Debunking the gender performance gap in two massively multiplayer online games. *Journal of Computer-Mediated Communication*, 21(4), 312–329.

Smith, J. (April 9, 2014). *The reality behind the pro gaming scene*. IGN. Retrieved from http://ca.ign.com/articles/2014/04/09/the-reality-behind-the-pro-gaming-scene.

Stieler-Hunt, C., Jones, C. M., Rolfe, B., & Pozzebon, K. (2014). Examining key decisions involved in developing a serious game for child sexual abuse prevention. *Frontiers in Psychology, 5*, 73. http://dx.doi.org/10.3389/fpsyg.2014.00073.

University of Michigan. (2016). *The early start Denver model*. Retrieved from http://www.psych.med.umich.edu/professional-training/esdm/.

Williams, D., Martins, N., Consalvo, M., & Ivory, J. D. (2009). The virtual census: Representations of gender, race and age in video games. *New Media and Society, 11*(5), 8415–8834.

Wolf, J. (2016). *Esports in the Olympics by 2020? It could happen*. ESPN. Retrieved from http://www.espn.com/esports/story/_/id/15232682/esports-olympics-2020-happen.

CHAPTER 10

The Incarnated Gamer: The Theophoric Quality of Games, Gaming, and Gamers

Frank G. Bosman
Tilburg University, Tilburg, The Netherlands

In the game *Godus* (2013), the player is asked to assume the role of an almighty creator. The player begins his divine career by saving a primordial man and woman from drowning. With your help, they will travel to some sort of "promised land," where they will build a tent, and procreate. By forming the earth and waters, the player can shape the form of the game world and support (or hinder) the advancement of "his" chosen people.

In the game *Child of Light* (2014), the player assumes the role of a young princess, Aurora. The princess dies at Good Friday and is sent to the underworld to redeem its inhabitants, only to be resurrected the following Easter Sunday. Eventually, she saves her people from certain death-by-drowning (as in *Godus*), by leading them through a magical mirror to a now everlasting peaceful underworld.

In *Metro Last Light* (2013), the player assumes the role of Artyom, a Russian survivor of a nuclear holocaust in the near future. The game suggests a god-less universe, in which the God of creation has left humankind. When confronted with his incapacitated archenemy, the player can choose to save him. If and when he does, a little Russian Orthodox icon of Jesus Christ is revealed. Similarly, in the *Mass Effect* trilogy, the player can live up to the name of his avatar, space captain "Shepard" by freely sacrificing his or her own life in order to restore the otherwise damned universe.

In these kinds of modern video games, the gamer has to perform certain actions and/or make certain moral choices which, in a Christian view, could be interpreted as mirroring those of God himself: Creating (*Godus*), dying, descending, and being resurrected (*Child of Light*), presenting God in the world by forgiving your worst enemy (*Metro Last Light*), and sacrificing your own life for the redemption of humankind (*Mass Effect*). Some could argue that these game narratives indeed mirror the great Christian

Boundaries of Self and Reality Online
ISBN 978-0-12-804157-4
http://dx.doi.org/10.1016/B978-0-12-804157-4.00010-4

187

narrative of creation, redemption, and consummation, but only insofar as they are themselves part of the greater narratological metanarratives of our Western civilization.

But theologically, this is not the whole picture. As Rachel Wagner has argued in her landmark publication *Godwired* (2011), religion and (digital) play have certain strong similarities. While somewhat reductionist in her thoughts on the phenomenon "religion," Wagner indicates that the player, while playing these games, does more than just witness what the game has to offer him. It is in his personal involvement into the game narrative, that "activates" the game (Ryan, 2006). But what if these actions and/or choices that activate the game are wholeheartedly religious, mirroring the Christian metanarrative of creation, redemption, and consummation? What does that make the player, theologically seen? God? A godhead? Or something else?

METHODOLOGY

In this chapter, I will argue that video games do not only take inspiration from the Christian tradition (and/or make references or comments to this tradition), but also invite the player, through his avatar, to take part in a digital recreation or re-enactment of the divine acts of creation, redemption, and consummation. By playing these kinds of video games, the player is the bearer of the image of God himself, as seen in the Christian tradition. I call this the "theophoric quality" of video games.

To make this bold statement viable in any sense at all, I will take the following steps. First of all, I will differentiate between the different levels on which religion can be encountered in video games. Secondly, I will postulate a "theology of culture," in which the universe could be seen as offering a testimony of its creator, savior, and consummator, but only when the existence of this God is accepted a priori. Thirdly, I will offer an in-depth discussion on the theological concept of "christophorism/theophorism." Fourthly, I will make detailed theological analysis of the four earlier-mentioned video games in which, as I will argue, this theophoric quality can be found.

In this chapter, I will regard video games as "playable texts" (Bosman, 2016a). Games can be regarded as such because the idea of "playable texts" summarizes the two "structural qualities" of computer games. Videogames are "texts" because they are mediated sign systems, and are given meaning by their audience. This audience is not limited to the actual gamers and those who watch the gamers play their games, but it also includes the larger culture itself, of which the players and the watchers are part. Video games are not just "texts," but *playable* texts. Video games incorporate elements of contest; they can be won or lost. The "pleasure" of gaming is derived from the uncertainty of the outcome of the game.

Treating the video games as playable texts and using a gamer-immanent approach (Bosman, 2016a), I will use close reading of the primary sources of my research, the actual video games themselves, as well as secondary sources (i.e., material provided by critics and scholars discussing the same game). Close reading of the video game series is performed by playing the games themselves (multiple times), including all possible (side) missions/quests.[1]

Before turning our attention to four theophoric case studies, one more word about identification. When playing a game, is everything that "happens" in the game, happening to the gamer or to his avatar? Succeeding, dying, choosing, fighting, running, and the like, are those thought of as belonging primarily to the avatar the gamer is controlling or to the gamer himself? Quantitative and qualitative studies on the relationship between gamers and their avatars suggest a very deep identification between the two, combined with a deep immersion in the game world and narrative (O'Neill, 2016; Waggoner, 2009).

In this chapter, I will focus on the Christian tradition and theology, disregarding all other religions and religious traditions in the world (with one partial exception for Judaism). This is a choice. The same argument, about the theophoric quality of video games, could have been made about other religious traditions like Shamanism, Islam, or Zoroastrianism.[2] This would, however, broaden the scope of this chapter beyond practical limitation, and would ask a significant amount of specific theological knowledge of multiple world religions. Technically, the term "theophoric" is inclusive, referring to all religions, while "christophoric" is exclusive, only to Christianity. In this chapter, I will use both terms more or less as equivalents.

FIVE LEVELS OF RELIGION IN VIDEO GAMES

The academic study of video games is a relatively young field of inquiry. This is of course related to the adolescent state of the subject matter itself. Video gaming has progressed rapidly since the release of *Pong* in 1972,

---

[1] For this article I used the PC version of the games.
[2] In *Prince of Persia* (2008), for example, the player is placed within a Zoroastrian framework, and tasked to perform specific actions related to its redemptive mythology.

growing into a vast billion dollar industry. When targeting the combination between digital games on the one hand and the phenomenon of religion on the other hand, the number of academic publications is rather limited.

Key publications in this field include *Halos & Avatars* (Detweiler, 2010), the aforementioned *Godwired* (Wagner, 2011), *eGods* (Bainbridge, 2013), *Of Games and God* (Schut, 2013), and *Playing with Religion* (Campbell, 2014). The University of Heidelberg's scholarly journal *Online* has published three specials dedicated to this interaction: *Religion in Digital Games* (Heidbrink & Knoll, 2014), *Religion in Digital Games Reloaded* (Heidbrink, Knoll, & Wysocki, 2015), and *Religion in Digital Games Respawned* (Heidbrink & Knoll, 2016).

Based on these (and other) publications and my own extensive experience as a "hardcore player" (Gackenbach & Snyder, 2012), I want to differentiate between five levels on which religion can be found in video games and/or on which the phenomenon of religion is actually studied in an academic context (Bosman, 2016a). These games range from explicit to implicit, from game-immanent to game-transcendent, and from developer-intended to gamer-intended. Religion can be found at the following levels (instances may pertain to more than one level) in video games: the material, referential, reflexive, ritual, and metalevel. The transition between the various levels is often fluid and diffuse.

Material religion is the explicit occurrence of (existing or fantasy) religion within the game itself. The average player will identify these elements as religious, whether or not they consider themselves to be religious. Think of the priests, clerics, shrines, churches, and chapels from the fantasy lore (for *World of Warcraft*, 2004 or *Diablo III*, 2012) or the "Church of the Children of Atom" from *Fallout 3* (2008).

The second level of religion is referential: The implicit or explicit reference in the game to an existing religious tradition outside the game, but often only understandable as such by a player who is rather familiar with the tradition at stake. The reference in *Child of Light* to Good Friday and Eastern Sunday is clearly to the Christian liturgical practice and faith, but only when one is raised in such a context.

The third level is reflexive: The reflection within the game on existential notions that are traditionally associated with religion within the game itself. Many games, especially those with elaborate narratives, reflect more or less implicitly on the existential themes of humankind: friendship, love, sacrifice, birth, life, death, sin, salvation, forgiveness, etc. Examples are *Brink* (2011) on ecological disaster in combination with worldwide refugees, or racism versus polytheism in *Elder's Scroll V: Skyrim* (2011).

The fourth level is ritual: Players who are involved in in-game behavior that is traditionally associated with religion. The most prominent example is that of the so-called "forced baptism" of *Bioshock Infinite* (2013), in which the player has to agree that he/his avatar is "baptized" before proceeding further through the game. For the majority of players this baptism did not present any problems, but for some Christians it certainly did. Being one of the sacrament of both Protestant and Roman Catholic tradition, some Christian gamers thought this was inappropriate (Hermandez, 2013).

The final level of religion in video games is the meta level, where the experience of gaming itself is identified as religious (by scholars and/or the gamers themselves). This level is (primarily) of our concern in this chapter. When we talk about the theophoric quality of video games, we think of the actual playing of the video games as somehow connected to the divine acts of creation, redemption, and consummation, a "level 5" religious phenomenon. We will turn to this level in greater detail when we discuss the christophoric/theophoric quality of video games. But before that we will have to establish a working idea of what theology, as the scholarly context for these notions, actually is.

A THEOLOGY OF CULTURE IN A DIGITAL AGE

The question of what theology actually may be is very paradoxically hard to answer. Although virtually everyone has some sort of idea of what theology is (or might be), defining its core substance, its main object, and its inherent methodology is a perilous task. Arguably, the definition with the largest support in Christian tradition is that Anselm of Canterbury (1033–1109): *Fides quaerens intellectum*, "faith seeking understanding." Though classical in its own rights, this definition has lost its self-evidence in postmodern contexts.

MacQuarrie (2003) tries a more academic approach: "Theology may be defined as the study which, through participation in and reflection upon a religious faith, seeks to express the content of this faith in the clearest and most coherent language available" (p. 1). Another modern attempt to give a definition of theology is done by Alister McGrath (2002): "The Christian tradition posits a unitary reality, holding that the entire creation has the potential to bear witness to its creator. To capture the full vision of God involves an appeal to the entire economy of salvation – creation, redemption, and the hope of final consummation" (p. 3).

Both authors (MacQuarrie and McGrath) offer intriguing details in their definitions as far as the topic of our chapter is concerned. MacQuarrie's definition offers a sharp distinction between theology and religious studies. Religious studies are concerned with research on the phenomenon of "religion" within a descriptive context. Theology on the other hand, researches the notion of "God" within a certain religious tradition, and within a specific normative context. MacQuarrie speaks about "participation in" and "reflection of" a particular faith, which is at the same time the object of scholarly inquiry.

The elements (reflection and participation) are spoken of earlier in this chapter, when we were addressing the five elements of religion in video games, and especially the last three of them. On the third level, the game reflects (and/or encourages the player to do so) on existential notions. And on the fourth level, the player acts symbolically within the game environment, participating in whatever ritual performance the game encourages (or forces) the player to take part in.

When this active ritual-liturgical-religious act is stretched over the game in its fullness, the game itself becomes "religious" in a very specific way. Theologically speaking, the fifth level of religion in video games denotes the game as a religious act in itself, by which the gamer participates in the divine acts of God himself as this is conceptualized in the Christian tradition.

These divine acts are traditionally thought of as the "economy of salvation," the way in which (according to the believer) God has created the universe, saved humankind from certain demise, and promised eternal bliss in heaven for those who are willing to accept Him. McGrath, and other theologians, summarize this "economy" in three divine acts: Creation (associated with God the Father), redemption (associated with God the Son), and consummation of fulfillment (associated with God the Holy Spirit).

Traditionally, the sources of these three divine acts are sacred Scripture (for the believer written under divine inspiration) and in the case of Roman Catholicism, sacred tradition (in which, for the believer again, this sacred scripture has been studied, explained, and applied, and authoritatively passed over from one generation to the other). For the sake of this chapter about the theophoric quality of games, I want to suggest another source of theological knowledge: our culture (Kelton, 2005).

The object of cultural theology is, from the perspective of religious studies, to study modern-day culture (like novels, movies, and video games) in relation to the explicit and (often) implicit traces within this culture, of traditional religious symbols, objects, texts, and notions. These traces are to be identified as such, explicated, analyzed, and critically discussed in relation to the (originating) religious and theological tradition(s).

Theologically, cultural theology explains these traces of the divine godhead in our culture, as "proof" of the existence and perseverance of the Christian God in our times. The universe, because (and only because) it is considered as being created by God (as is the premise of all monotheistic faiths), can be considered as bearing witness of its creator (God the Father) and its savior (Jesus of Nazareth). The *deus absconditus* of our secularized society is thus rethought as a *deus incognitus*: Hidden, only to be recognized by those who still remember Him. Think of the second level of religion in games, the referential level, on which the religious element is only conceivable by those who are educated to see.

THE CONCEPTS OF CHRISTOPHORISM/THEOPHORISM

With the context of this theology of culture, it becomes possible to think about the gamers and games as "theophoric" or "christophoric." To start with the first one, christophorism, Ben Witherington III (2016) states: "Theology and ethics in and of the New Testament are christocentric, christotelic, christophoric, for as the author of the latest New Testament book says, it is the believer's destination to become 'partakers of the divine nature' (2 Pet. 1:4), or as Paul would put it, 'to be fully conformed to the image of God's Son' (Rom. 8:29)" (p. 1).

According to Kozlovic (2004), in the cultural domain, the Christ-figure can be understood in a smaller sense as a character with traits that directly reflect the teachings and actions of Christ as told and visualized in the Christian tradition, but also, in a much broader sense, as a salvific, messianic figure sacrificing his own life for the benefit of the many.

The idea that the Christian believer is, in some way, bearer of the image of Christ himself, has found its way into the popular myth concerning saint Christopher, or *Christophorus* in Latin/Greek, literally "he who carries Christ." According to Jacobus de Voragine's *Legenda Aurea*, Christopher began his life as Reprobus. At one time, he decided he wanted to serve "the greatest king there was." Eventually, he learned that a certain "Jesus Christ" was the one most feared by the scum he encountered.

A hermit advised Reprobus, being very tall and strong, to serve Christ by carrying people on his shoulders across a great river. After some time, a child asked Reprobus to be carried across. During the crossover, the child began to weigh heavier and heavier on Reprobus' shoulders until the point he almost drowned himself. Safe at the other bank, he said to the child: "I do not think the whole world could have been as heavy on my shoulders as you were." The child responded: "You had on your shoulders not only the whole world but Him who made it. I am Christ your king, whom you are serving by this work." The child vanished, and Reprobus—now called Christophorus, "he who carried Christ"—converted to Christianity, eventually dying as a martyr.

The story of this christophoric Reprobus has always been connected to Christian anthropology, which has its biblical foundation in one particular verse: " So God created mankind in his own image, in the image of God he created them; male and female he created them." (Genesis 1:27). The interpretation of this notion is the object of ongoing theological debate, but the heart of the imago Dei doctrine consists of the idea that there is a specific, inalienable connection between God as the creator of all things, and his creation. Man "reflects" or "possesses" certain "traces" of God in himself (Guthrie, 1994, pp. 194–197).

Stephen Garner (1995) suggests that just as God creates men and women, so can men imitate God through creative acts of their own. We are "created co-creator" (Hefner, 1989, 2003), created in the image of our creator, to do what He did, to create. Christophorus is an example of the ideal Christian knowing he is called to carry Christ's image, that is, to be like Christ himself. And the notion of man created as cocreators indicates that video games could be seen as having a certain theophoric quality.

On the first level, video games are theophoric in the sense that there are (as games) the creation of man mimicking its creator (Bosman, 2016b), as is the case with all human creative production. On the second level, however, and that is the one we want to address in this chapter, is the mimicking of God in all three his divine acts—not only creation, but also redemption and consummation—by the gamer in the game.

FOUR THEOLOGICAL CASE STUDIES

In this section, we will amplify the theophoric quality of video games with the help of a deeper theological analysis of the four games mentioned earlier in this chapter.

Godus: Create Like God

Godus is technically still under development by 22Cans, also one of Molyneux's game companies, but has been released in so-called prereleases since 2014. Due to financial difficulties, it is very unlikely that the game will reach its intended full release (Duwell, 2015). In the game *Godus* (2013), the player is asked to assume the role of an almighty creator. The player begins his divine career by saving a primordial man and woman from drowning. With your help, they will travel to some sort of "promised land," where they will build a tent and procreate. By forming the earth and waters, the player can shape the form of the game world and support (or hinder) the advancement of "hi" chosen people. The player, worshipped by his devotees, will improve the situation of his population through time by taking care of their environmental and reproducing skills.

It is hardly a difficult task to see (a more or less) implicit reference to the Christian tradition. According to the book of Genesis, God "created the heaven and the earth" (1:1). The process of creation is a matter of dividing between opposites, *bara* in Hebrew, light from darkness, day from night, heaven from earth, etcetera (van Wolde, 2016). This is exactly what the gamer is doing in *Godus*: By manipulating land and water, the player creates an environment in which the nonplayable characters (NPCs) can progress.

The whole theme of manipulating water into land so the faithful, the player's "people" who inhabit the game world, can safely cross to the other site, is a small toss away from the well-known story from the book of Exodus. In Exodus, God (through Moses) splits the Red Sea in order to let the Israelites cross safely, fleeing from oppression in Egypt (Exodus 13:17–14:29). In Hebrew and Christian tradition, this is one of the decisive moments in the relation between God and Israel, where JHWH is considered by Israel as "their" God, and themselves as His "chosen people" (Garr, 2014).

Of course, some serious theological considerations and objections could (and should) be given to the "theology of *Godus*" (Bosman, 2016b), among which the dependency of the player-as-creator on the devotion of his people vis-à-vis the absolute freedom thought to be one of God's main characteristics in monotheist tradition (Wierenga, 1989), and to the nature of the player/creator being more of a demiurge than of the monotheistic God (O'Brien, 2015).

Nevertheless, despite these interesting objections, the theophoric quality *Godus* (and the other games in the so-called "god genre") is bluntly apparent. Just as God, according to Genesis, creates the universe by separating water and earth to make it an inhabitable place for man and female, both created in his image; so the player of *Godus* separates land and water in order to arrange the game world as a place for "his" people to live and to thrive on. By playing *Godus*, the gamer mimics the divine act of creation: He answers the call to which he was brought into this world, to cocreate. In his creational act, the gamer is figurally carrying the image of God, in two different ways: In the fact that he is alive, and in the act of creative play. The *Godus'* player is therefore to be qualified as theophoric.

Child of Light: Descend Into the Underworld

Child of Light (Ubisoft, 2014) features a very interesting story. Aurora, the daughter of an anonymous duke and a mysteriously absent duchess, contracts some sort of physical illness, which causes her death within one night. The game narrator tells the gamer: "It was the Great Friday before Easter, 1895…" Aurora awakes in a mysterious subterranean land called Lemuria, in which the inhabitants are forced to do wicked things by the dark queen Umbra (Latin for "shadow"). Eventually, Umbra manages to kill Aurora. Then, Aurora is "resurrected" (the game actually uses this term) by her mother, the Queen of Light. Aurora travels back to Umbra's castle, defeats her, and frees Lemuria and all its inhabitants from her dark rule.

On Easter Sunday (again, the game uses this exact words), the day of Aurora's arrival in the real word, the residents of her homeland are about to be drowned by the rising flood, caused by a massive earthquake. Aurora, with the help of her Lemurian companions, manages to rescue her people by leading them through the magic mirror to the now peaceful Lemuria. In the closing scenes, only a small island in a lake remains, but Lemuria begins to grow again.

Aurora is a christophoric character in her own right and for a couple of reasons (Bosman, 2016c). The primary argument is the narratological timeframe of the game, taking place between Great Friday and Easter Sunday. In Christian tradition, this period is known as the "holy week," in which the passion, death, and resurrection of Christ is commemorated (Farwell, 2005). With little scriptural basis, Christian tradition has developed the notion of the "harrowing of hell" (Laufer, 2013): Christ himself descended into the underworld to free those who had lived before His coming from eternal oblivion (Latin: *descensus christi ad inferros*; in English also known as Harrowing of Hell). Aurora's story is mimicking this "holy timeframe."

Other additional arguments for the christophoric nature of Aurora can be found throughout the game. Three times in the game, when Aurora is presented with a divine gift, she hovers over the ground, turning herself to the player. Aurora holds her head slightly lifted to the sky, eyes closed, holding her arms stretched horizontally, a pose traditionally associated with the figure of Christ on the cross. Aurora's name derives from the Roman goddess of the dawn meaning "morning star," in Christian tradition associated with Christ himself as the "new dawn of mankind" (Jensen, 2000, pp. 12–13). On two different occasions, Aurora speaks of her own mission as "rescuing my people," a reference to the Old Testament notion of God's chosen people (see above). And last but not least, both the earthquake and the flood of *Child of Light* occur in the New Testament linked in both cases to Christ's "second coming" (Matthew 24:38–39; 27:54; Luke 21:1–11).

It is plausible to qualify Aurora as a christophoric game character (the referential level), for she mirrors the *descensus christi ad inferros* from Christian tradition. But the same could be said about the gamer playing the game and assuming the role of Aurora, and through Aurora, of Christ himself (the meta level). *Child of Light* has a theophoric quality, because it places the gamer in position in which he (by his actions) mimics the divine act itself. On the level of the video game, Aurora (and thus the gamer) descends into the underworld to liberate those who are imprisoned there. The gamer amplifies the unique *descensus* of Christ, but at the same time actualizes this harrowing of hell.

Metro Last Light: Forgive Your Enemy

The same christophoric/theophoric quality can also be found in three other games, the first of which is *Metro Last Light*. In this game, developed by Ukraine studio 4A Games and published in 2013, the world has suffered a worldwide nuclear war. The game takes place in Moscow, where the few survivors of the nuclear holocaust have retreated within the relative safety of the metro stations and tunnels. The surface of Moscow is heavily irradiated; humans have to wear breathing equipment, and it is swarmed with mutant flora and fauna.

4A Games released a special trailer, which they called "the Genesis trailer." In this trailer, an English voice (with a thick Russian accent) narrates the opening chapter of Genesis. The narrated beauty of God's original creation—"God saw all that he had made, and it was very good" (Genesis 1:31)—is visually contrasted with the ugliness of present-day reality. When the narrator arrives at the seventh day, he derives from the classical Genesis text. Instead of telling that God rested on the seventh day, resting from all the work He had done (Genesis 2:2–3), the narrator says: "And on the seventh day, they say, God rested. But God didn't rest. God left. Or – perhaps – died. Judgment Day came and He abandoned us, casting humanity aside like parasites."

This trailer is a narratologically stunning, recapturing of what is known in the Western world since the 1960s as the "God is dead"-theology. Linked to Nietzsche's expression "God is dead! God remains dead! And we have killed him!" (*The Happy Science*, 1882), fused by growing secularism in the Western world and amplified by the collective horror of the German concentration camps vis-à-vis God's promise to His chosen people, resulted into a widespread idea that God was "dead" (McGrath, 1997, pp. 254–256). This was not regarded, even by its heralds, as a success of human evolution per se, but was (and is) always mixed with feelings of regret and loneliness. The horrors of the post-apocalyptic world of *Last Light* are a perfect example of the human experience that God could not possibly live in this reality, and still not intervene. If God "allows" these monstrosities, then there is no God at all.

In this "god-less" environment, in this world-without-God, the gamer takes the role of the metro survivor Artyom, who is tasked to prevent civil war between the underground fractions and to get rid of the mutated monsters which haunt the metro tunnels once and for all. On three-quarters of the game narrative, Artyom visits the Cathedral of the Mother of God, located in the heart of Moscow. The player has to take extreme notice to recognize this Russian landmark. There are no visible traces of its original sacred purpose: No relics, no icons, no statues, no altars, nothing at all. Even in the Moscow cathedral, God seems to be dead indeed.

Somewhere in the Moscow cathedral, Artoym finds his archenemy Pavl. Pavl lies incapacitated against a closet, his breathing mask still on but without a filter. Artyom (thus the player) can make a fundamental choice: Saving or killing Pavl. When Artoym chooses to save Pavl, Artyom's traveling partner comments: "So this is forgiveness. I will remember." Above the closet Pavl leans to, a painting can be observed. When observed closely, the painting reveals to be the arch icon of Russian orthodoxy: The mandyllion, also known as the "image of Edessa." It is the only explicit reference to material religion in the whole game.

The theology of this scene is gripping. When Artyom, that is, the player, chooses to save his worst enemy, an image of Christ appears. When forgiving your worst enemy, the player becomes an image of Christ himself.

Forgiving each other is one of the most important commandments from the New Testament (for example: Matthew 6:14, 7:2, 18:35; Mark 11:25; Luke 6:37; Ephesians 4:32; Colossians 3:13).

When the gamer chooses to save Pavl, to forgive his sins against Artyom and the rest of the world, the gamer himself becomes (in a certain way) God himself. In his act of forgiveness, the gamer manifests God's presence in this world, even though it was thought of as a reality in which God had no place anymore. The player is a christophoric figure, presenting God's own forgiving image to mankind. "For I will forgive their wickedness and will remember their sins no more" (Hebrews 8:12). God is not dead, the game seems to narrate theologically, as long as people forgive each other, thus mirroring Christ himself, of whom is written to have said to his executioners, "Father, forgive them, for they do not know what they are doing." (Luke 23:34).

Mass Effect: Another Shepard

This christophoric behavior is not unique to *Metro Last Light*, it can be found in numerous other games, usually connected to the myth of self-sacrificial hero (Hyles, 2015). Although the myth of the sacrificial hero is not Christian in its core or subject matter, some theophoric games do make this combination, like the *Mass Effect* trilogy (Irizarry & Irizarry, 2014). The story of trilogy (Bioware, 2007–2012) takes place in our near future, in which humankind has gained interstellar space travel. The Milky Way is swarmed with intelligent life forms, among which humankind has to find its own place. Lurking in the background is a vague galactic threat, in the form of a technologically highly advanced artificial species, which periodically wipes the Milky Way of intelligent life.

The interstellar robots are called "reapers," which is the first of many references to Christian tradition to the four apocalyptic horsemen from the book of Revelation (O'Hear & O'Hear, 2015, pp. 70–92). Many more will follow. The first reference appears right at the start of the first game, when commander Sheppard is introduced as the captain of the spaceship Normandy. During the approximately 100 h gaming time across three interconnected titles, the player will control this Shepard. When taken separately, these references appear minor or even trivial, but, when combined, a pattern with heavy narratological impact can be found.

The name of the game protagonist is a reference to the shepherd metaphors from the New Testament (for example: "I am the good shepherd. The good shepherd lays down his life for the sheep," John 10:11), by which the Christian tradition uses "the good shepherd" as a title for Christ himself (Cachia, 1997). The first extraterrestrial colony of humankind is called "Eden Prime," a reference to the mythical Garden of Eden from Genesis 2 and 3. The name of an interstellar commercially run prison for highly dangerous criminals is called "Purgatory," a reference to the intermediate state after physical death in which (according to Roman Catholic tradition) the souls of the unworthy are cleansed before they can enter heaven (Walls, 2015).

When Shepard dies in an accident at the beginning of the second installment, an interstellar crime syndicate revives her broken body back to life. The name of this project is "Lazarus," a reference to the story form the gospel of John (Chapter 11) in which a dead man is brought back to life by Jesus Christ. When Shepard meets the only fertile female of an alien race on the brink of extinction, she calls herself "Eve," a reference to the Biblical Eve from the book of Genesis. And when Shepard meets a *Gesammtgestalt* of a collective, artificial race (the Geth) and calls for his name, the computer of the Normandy ship replies: "Legion, for we are with many." The Geth, now dubbed Legion, is happy with this reference and even quotes the Biblical finding place, Marcus 5:19.

The last reference is given when Shepard finely sacrificed his or her own life to save the civilizations of the Milky Way from another wave of periodical extinction by the Reapers. On a planet with three moons, an indefinable time period later, a grandfather and his granddaughter (or grandson) are staring to the stars. The child asks "Did that all really happen?," probably as a reply to what the old man has told so far, which is (very likely) the story the player just finished, the story of Shepard. Eventually, the child asks one last question: "Tell me another story about *the* shepherd." The name Shepard has now lost its value as a name, and has become a title itself. Shepard becomes shepherd, man becomes God.

It is not hard to see the christophoric quality of the *Mass Effect* trilogy. The player assumes, quite implicitly at first, the role of a (the) divine savior which is destined (but still free) to save all living, intelligent life from total annihilation by the hands of an apocalyptic force. By choosing to sacrifice the protagonist, that is the player, redemption can be found and given. In this choice, the player fits himself into the framework of the Christian redemption narrative, acting *as if* he was the Savior himself. The player can become, when understanding the game narrative and acting upon it, quite literally Christ himself, another divine shepherd, bringing peace to the universe.

CLOSING STATEMENT

In this chapter, I argued that video games do not only make references (on material, referential, or reflexive levels) to (existing or fantasy) religious traditions, but also invite the game player, through the playing of the game, to participate in the divine acts of creation, redemption, and consummation (as seen in the Christian tradition). The first part of this assertion can be argued from the external position of the scholar of religion. The second part, however, can only be made theologically, that is, on the condition of the acceptance of the existence of God.

Theologically, the player confirms, duplicates, adds, attributes, elaborates, and amplifies the divine acts of creation, redemption, and consummation in as much as he actualizes these acts in his gaming performance. By this actualization, the gamer (and the game) becomes theophoric (christophoric), that is, bearer of the face of God in this world. This is more than a remembrance, more than a re-enactment, although these elements are not absent. The theophoric quality of some video games suggests (theologically) that the gamer himself becomes "divine," although in a derivative way.

Some gaming, seen in such a way, can therefore be described as a religious act in itself, as Wagner has already suggested. Wagner however only took the step to suggest that "gaming" and "believing" or "game" and "religion" share common traits, in the sense that (being in) religion is like (playing) a game. The next step is exactly the other way around: Playing (some) games means being religious, in the (derivate) executing of the divine acts of God himself.

In the future, some more research might be done on the theophoric quality of video games within other (non-Christian) religious traditions. As this chapter focused itself on the Christian tradition, there are multiple games to be named which utilize other traditions, like the aforementioned *Prince of Persia* (2008) in the context of Zoroastrianism, the *Final Fantasy* series (1987–2015) in the context of Taoism and Confucianism, and *Smite* (2014) to Hinduism.

REFERENCES

All Biblical quotes are from the New International Version translation.
Bainbridge, W. S. (2013). *eGods. Faith versus fantasy in computer gaming.* Oxford: Oxford University Press.
Bosman, F. (2016a). The Word has become game. Researching religion in digital games. *Online Heidelberg Journal for Religion on the Internet, 11,* (in press-a).

Bosman, F. (2016b). Playing the demiurge? Theological thoughts on the god game genre. *European Society of Catholic Theology*, (in press-b).

Bosman, F. (2016c). 'The bell tolled six on Easter Sunday'. The motif of the harrowing of hell in the videogame 'Child of Light'. In *Brill's studies in Catholic theology*. Leiden: Brill (in press-c).

Cachia, N. (1997). *The image of the good shepherd as a source for the spirituality of the ministerial priesthood*. Rome: Editrice Pontificia Università Gregoriana.

Campbell, H. (Ed.). (2014). *Playing with religion in digital games*. Bloomington: Indiana University Press.

Detweiler, C. (2010). *Halos & avatars. Playing video games with god*. Louisville: Westmister John Knox Press.

Duwell, R. (February 11, 2015). *Peter Molyneux apologizes for godus, promises a fix from new team*. Retrieved from http://www.technobuffalo.com/2015/02/11/peter-molyneux-apologizes-for-godus-promises-a-fix-from-new-team.

Farwell, J. W. (2005). *This is the night. Suffering, salvation and the liturgies of Holy week*. New York: T&T Clark.

Gackenbach, J., & Snyder, T. (2012). *Play reality. How videogames are changing everything*. s.l.: Lulu Press.

Garner, S. (1995). Hacking with the divine. A Metaphor for theology-technology engagement. *Colloquium, 37, 2*.

Garr, J. D. (2014). *Life from dead. The dynamic saga of the chosen people*. Atlanta: Golden Key Books.

Guthrie, S. (1994). *Christian doctrine*. Westminster: John Knox Press.

Hefner, P. (1989). The Evolution of the created co-creator. In T. Peters (Ed.), *Cosmos as creation. Theology and science in consonance* (pp. 211–233). Nashville: Abingdon Press.

Hefner, P. (2003). *Technology and human becoming*. Minneapolis: Fortress Press.

Heidbrink, S., & Knoll, T. (Eds.). (2014). Religion in digital games. *Online Heidelberg Journal of Religion on the Internet, 5*.

Heidbrink, S., & Knoll, T. (Eds.). (2016). Religion in digital games respawned. *Online Heidelberg Journal of Religion on the Internet, 10*.

Heidbrink, S., Knoll, T., & Wysocki, J. (Eds.). (2015). Religion in digital games respawned. *Online Heidelberg Journal of Religion on the Internet, 7*.

Hermandez, P. (April 4, 2013). *Some don't like Bioshock's forced baptism. Enough to ask for a refund*. Retrieved from http://kotaku.com/some-dont-like-bioshocks-forced-baptism-enough-to-as-473178476.

Hyles, V. R. (2015). Campbell and the inklings—Tolkien, Lewis and Williams. In K. L. Golden (Ed.), *Uses of comparative mythology. Essays on the works of Joseph Campbell*. Abingdon-on-Thames: Routledge.

Irizarry, J. A., & Irizarry, I. T. (2014). The Lord is my shepard. confronting religion in the mass effect trilogy. *Online Heidelberg Journal for Religions on the Internet, 5, 224–248*.

Jensen, R. M. (2000). *Understanding early Christian art*. London: Routledge.

Kelton, C. (2005). *The Blackwell guide to theology and popular culture*. Malden: Blackwell Publishers.

Kozlovic, A. (2004). The structural characteristics of the cinematic Christ-figure. *Journal of Religion and Popular Culture, 8*.

Laufer, C. E. (2013). *Hell's destruction. An exploration of Christ's descent to the dead*. Famham: Ashgate.

MacQuarrie, J. (2003). *Principles of christian theology*. London: SCM.

McGrath, A. (1997). *Christian theology. An introduction*. Oxford: Blackwell.

McGrath, A. (2002). *A scientific theology* (Vol. 3). London: T&T Clark.

O'Brien, C. S. (2015). *The demiurge in ancient thought. Secondary gods and divine mediators*. Cambridge: Cambridge University Press.

O'Neill, K. (2016). *Internet afterlife. Virtual salvation in the 21st century*. Santa Barbara: Praeger.

O'Hear, N., & O'Hear, A. (2015). *Picturing the apocalypse. The book of revelation in the arts over two millennia*. Oxford: Oxford University Press.

Ryan, M.-L. (2006). *Avatars of story*. Minneapolis: University of Minnesota Press.

Schut, K. (2013). *Of games and god. A Christian exploration of video games*. Grand Rapids: Brazos Press.

Waggoner, Z. (2009). *My avatar, my self. Identity in video role-playing games*. Jefferson: McFarland.

Wagner, R. (2011). *Godwired. Religion, ritual and virtual reality*. Abingdon: Oxon.

Wall, J. L. (2015). *Heaven, hell, and purgatory. Rethinking the things that matter most*. Grand Rapids: Brazos Press.

Wierenga, E. (1989). *The nature of god. An inquiry into divine attributes*. Ithaca: Cornell University Press.

Witherington, B., III (2016). *New testament theology and ethics* (Vol. 2). Downers Grove: InterVarsity Press.

van Wolde, E. (2016). "Creation out of nothing" and the Hebrew bible. In R. A. Culpepper, & J. G. van der Watt (Eds.), *Creation stories in dialogue. The Bible, science, and folk traditions. Radbound prestige lectures in new testament* (pp. 157–176). Leiden: Brill.

CHAPTER 11

Games, Dreams and Consciousness: Absorption and Perception, Cognition, Emotion

Joan M. Preston
Brock University, St. Catharines, ON, Canada

Two decades ago, the notion that video games (VGs) could be amplifiers of consciousness was an idea that researchers were just beginning to explore (Gackenbach & Preston, 1998; Preston, 1998). At that time, VG technology was rapidly changing and a new generation of VGs possessed features that held promise as amplifiers to access to higher levels of consciousness. Hindes (2014) points out that 1998 was a year of VG firsts.[1] Many innovative, genre-defining games and new technologies were appearing: (1) first emulation of cinematic techniques and direction; (2) 3-D technology began to mature; (3) first narrative driven shooter; (4) first modern stealth simulator; (5) the first version of Unreal Engine (Epic) was released, with its code written in C++, used originally in a first-person shooter game, then in stealth games, MMORPGs (massively multiplayer online role-playing games) and other RPGs (role-playing games); and so on. Zeigler (2009) calls 1998 the best year in the history of gaming. These new and better games brought many more players and VGs have become ubiquitous. Almost 60% of Americans play VGs and there are more gamers aged over 50 than under 18 (Logfren, 2015). In 2016, gamers had an average age of 31 and had been playing for an average of 13 years (Logfren, 2016). Researchers have now identified numerous cognitive benefits of VG play and our understanding of consciousness has increased. This chapter looks at how VGs amplify consciousness.

Green and Seitz (2015) describe action VGs as having complex 3-D settings, feature rapidly moving targets that pop in and out of view, entail

---

[1] Hindes' list of great games of 1998 include Valve: Half Life; Nintendo: Legend of Zelda; Rare: Banjo-Kazooie; Starcraft: Starcraft and Brood War; LucasArts: Grim Fandango; Looking Glass Studios: Thief: the Dark Project; Bioware: Baldur's Gate; Game Freek: Pokemon Red and Pokemon Blue; KCEJ: Metal Gear Solid.

Boundaries of Self and Reality Online
ISBN 978-0-12-804157-4
http://dx.doi.org/10.1016/B978-0-12-804157-4.00011-6

substantial processing in peripheral vision, have substantial visual clutter and task–irrelevant objects, and require players to consistently switch between highly focused and highly distributed attention and to make rapid, accurate decisions. They have pointed out that "action video games" have been linked with "myriad enhancements in cognitive function" (Green & Seitz, 2015, pp. 102–103). Cardoso-Leite et al. (2016) agree that action VGs produce various benefits in vision, attention, and decision making, but not bottom–up attention or high levels of media multitasking.

Practicing a task typically leads to performance improvements. However, the specificity of perceptual and cognitive tasks usually results in no benefits for similar tasks. Action VG training "is a rare exception to this general rule and action video games can improve a variety of perceptual and cognitive abilities" (Wright, Blakely, & Boot, 2012, p. 65). Eichenbaum, Bavelier, and Green (2014) agree that VG skills are generalizable and note that playing VGs improves visual selective attention (choosing which aspects of a stimulus should receive additional processing, i.e., task relevant, and filtering out task–irrelevant items), thus improving the ability to attend to distinct spatial locations, distinct points in time and distinct objects (see also Anderson, Bavelier, & Green, 2010; Chiappe, Conger, Liao, Caldwell, & Vu, 2013; Colzato, van Leeuwen, van den Wildenberg, & Hommel, 2010; Green, Sugarman, Medford, Klobusicky, & Bavelier, 2012; Strobach, Frensch, & Schubert, 2012). VGs improve players' sustained attention, as well as cognitive flexibility and executive functioning (e.g., dual tasking, task switching, mental rotation, working memory) (Green & Bavelier, 2012; Sungur & Boduroglu, 2012). Not only are action VGs associated with a wide variety of cognitive benefits, it is individuals' extensive VG playing experience that is related to higher levels of consciousness. Today a substantial body of evidence confirms VGs as amplifiers of consciousness and recently, Gackenbach has linked expert gamers with both lucid dreaming (Gackenbach, 2006, 2012) and nightmare protection (Gackenbach, 2012; Gackenbach, Ellerman, & Hall, 2011; Gackenbach, Stark, Boyes, & Flockhart, 2015).

PERCEPTION AND COGNITION

One of the parts of the art exhibit "Chihuly" (seen in Montreal at Musée des Beaux Arts, 2013) was "The Persian Ceiling." Visitors sat or lay down on a soft floor to look up at a lighted ceiling of hand–blown glass. Using only shapes and colors, Chihuly (n.d.) evoked rhythms with reflections and layering creating an immersive visual experience, eye candy with embodied felt meaning. Perception, cognition, and emotion join in kinesthetically embodied meaning in art and other media as well as in nature. This fully immersed feeling of focused energy, involvement, and enjoyment or satisfaction is called absorption (Tellegen & Atkinson, 1974), flow (Csikszentmihalyi, 1990), openness-to-experience (Ashton et al., 2004), and presence (Lombard & Ditton, 1997). This state of consciousness occurs in VGs during sustained attention.

VGs and consciousness are both based in perception and both involve developments in thinking. The term action VG points to the importance of visual and kinesthetic information in the cognitive choices of the player. Visual and kinesthetic experiences are linked to gamers' absorption in play and to cognitive development whose abstract levels are where higher states of consciousness occur. In psychology, the prevalent view among theorists and researchers is that concrete perception is the basis of meaning, thinking, and consciousness. Perception requires movement; even when we are standing still, normal vision involves some eye muscle tremor (see Pritchard, Heron, & Hebb, 1960). Because visual perception is interwined with the kinesthetic, it involves a dynamic participant in an immediate ecological environment. The theory of perception widely referred to by VG and virtual reality (VR) theorists and researchers is that of James Gibson (see Preston, 2007). In 1941, Gibson became director of the USAF Aviation Psychology Unit where his research on optical flow included the perceptual effects of flying. As part of a research program on pilot training, Gibson used film to study self-motion and identified motion perspective as a relevant variable. He found that *forward* movement of the observer can be produced optically (i.e., without any contribution from the vestibular sense). This experience of locomotion is often intentionally created in visual media, especially VGs and VR.

Gibson's (1966) theory tells us what visual information is, what we see and how we know where we are located in our specific location. Visual information is optical, and resides in the naturally arising structure of light comprising the optical array. That is, visual information is independent of both the viewer and the environment. Visual information occurs in the natural environment or any other situation where light is experienced, such as dreams and media. Movement of ourselves or our eyes effects changes in the gradients of reflected light. The optical array itself is a nested hierarchy of solid angles and the environment consists of illuminated surfaces. From our own location in the real or virtual environment, we perceive these patterns of light as shapes and spatial relationships.

Movement effects changes in the optical flow. We directly "detect information" that is available in the ambient light, and what we perceive are affordances or the functional properties of objects, spaces, and events, such as surface, density, texture, or manipulability. Affordances are opportunities for action. Although affordances are offered by the situation, we can choose to use or ignore them. For example, we can choose to sit on a nearby park bench or not. A specific object may have many affordances. Because each perceived affordance has its own meaning and use, the individual learns to differentiate the meaning of an object in terms of its relevance to one's own activities and needs. Thus, affordances are real and external facts. A particular object, however, may yield different affordances to different individuals precisely because affordances are related to both the person and the environment. For example, we have an electric guitar: my son is an excellent player; I cannot play even a simple tune but have photographed the guitar for an art project.

Whatever current ecological situation we are in, its optic array specifies two kinds of structure to us: the perspective structure and the invariant structure. We can only see a situation from our own particular location. When we move around in our ecological environment, some hidden objects become visible, while others become occluded. This is the perspective structure. The invariant optical structure is the persistent information remaining as the perspective structure changes and this invariant structure is public. Reed (1988) states that the connectedness of the layout of the environment "is itself visible" (p. 289). It is the transition between what is seen from a single point of observation and what we see in ambulatory perception (our observable habitat).

Gibson's theory (1966) has several advantages for investigators of virtual environments. Because visual information occurs where light is experienced, we can perceive affordance meanings indirectly in mediated environments. Meaningful still and moving pictures both present optical information in a way that is part historical (i.e., experience) and part cultural as well as ecological. Mediated apprehension gets combined and fused with direct apprehension (Gibson as cited in Reed, 1988, p. 307). We are able to bring together direct and indirectly apprehended information and use it whether we are in our real-life environment or present in a simulated environment. Examples range from augmented reality to the use of avatars, from the use of real-life strategies when playing video games to the transfer of VG skills to real-life surgical skills, and so forth. For Gibson, the perceptual systems are functional, and we actively obtain information about both ourselves and our location, whether real or virtual. Gibson provides the theoretical rationale for the reciprocal transfer of skills and behaviors among realities, including VGs, VR, or dreams.

When moving, we experience an envelope of flow: the invariant structures specify the visuals or landscape lying ahead and the perspective structures specify where we may go in this landscape. As we move around our location, new vistas open in this flow, while, behind us, objects disappear. The center of the flow specifies the direction of locomotion making it anchored to the layout of the situation (Gibson, 1979). Thus we are embodied in the current optical array whether it is natural or mediated. Because we always see each vista from our own individual point of observation, it also specifies the location of the self within the immediate ecological environment. Hunt (2007) points out that the precise way that an individual experiences a particular array, with its open horizon ahead and flow past of surrounding feedback, implies a "hole" filled by the embodied self, and this is the exact position of the ecological self within an immediate location. Media including VGs, VR, film, and TV, can display a scene from first-person perspective (what we would see if we were present in and moving about the media environment) or third-person perspective (the view seen by another person). Like real life, mediated first-person perspective specifies the exact position of the ecological self in the media environment.

Because the invariant structure specifies the persisting environment to all observers, we can simultaneously have our own point of view and also share awareness. Gibson (1979) believed that shared awareness provided the context where representation evolved, including signals, symbols, pictures, etc. Information that is derived from media is perceived indirectly. Because VGs and VR are representations, information available to participants is meaningful not just ecologically, but similarly meaningful in ways that are partially cultural and narrative as well.

Information, according to Gibson, is independent of both the individual and the location. What distinctions, if any, exist in the information in optical arrays of mediated representations compared to the natural environment? Although pictures are flat, ordinarily reduced in size compared to environmental objects, and subject to other differences and limitations, Gibson does not view these differences as discrepancies between picture and scene that can be predicted by a projective model. Information is detected directly from the ambient light in both realities. In his research, Gibson demonstrated that pictures do provide adequate information for viewers to perform visual–spatial tasks nearly as well as when they are viewing the actual scenes. A picture is a "delimited optical array" observable only from a specific point of observation. However, it "contains the same kind of information that is found on the ambient optic arrays of an ordinary environment" (Gibson, 1971, p. 277), which helps the observer to see a realistic spatial display of a section of a scene.

The information in the picture *is ecological* even if information in the picture is made available in a conventionalized and culturally specific way (Reed, 1988). For Gibson, perspective structure of a static medium is a special case of flow, seeing from a point, not the ordinary seeing from a path. The perspective of a scene displayed in a picture, according to Gibson (1979, pp. 282–284), induces an awareness of being in the mediated world. We need movement in a medium to provide information for seeing from a path. VGs, as well as VR and other mediated environments that display a dynamic perspective, display the same kind of optical ecological information displayed by physical reality. This is what permits viewers to experience "media reality."

Music and Sound

Visuals are often not the only perceptual information available in media. Many include auditory information whose purpose may be to elicit emotion and affect the visual focus of attention. Chion (1994) argues that sound engages the structuring of vision by framing it and altering what we see. Sound effects are used to increase viewers' sense of realism (e.g., hospital dramas add equipment beeping sounds) and to direct visual attention to the screen (Anderson & Levin, 1976; Anderson & Lorch, 1983; Bryant, Zillmann, & Brown, 1983). Film music can alter mood and increase viewer absorption (Cohen, 1999, 2000, 2005; Cohen & MacMillan, 2004), and it influences both direct and indirect judgments of the film (Bolivar, Cohen, & Fentress, 1994; Bullerjahn & Güldenring, 1994; Lipscomb & Kendall, 1994; Marshall & Cohen, 1988; Thayer & Levinson, 1983; Vitouch, 2001). Although viewers often report that they do not notice the music that accompanies visuals, Preston and Evans (2001) have shown that the presence/absence of music does have effects. Half of their participants viewed short Charlie Chaplin film clips with sound on, half with sound off. Music condition affected attention (music-off condition viewers reported that their attention was distracted from the visuals), cognitive processing (music-off condition viewers reported neutral and sad film clips as more real than music-on participants), and emotional responses (music-off viewers rated the comedy clips as less arousing but the neutral and sad clips as more emotionally intense). Media creators usually select music that is congruent with the visuals because such congruence heightens or intensifies the affective qualities of the image (Smith, 1999).

Color and Form

Originally, some media, including photos, film, TV, and VGs were black and white, but now color media is ubiquitous. Our response to color is influenced by its context. The artist Albers (2013) shows numerous examples, such as, red bricks with white mortar and red bricks with black mortar. Red with white appears to be lighter than the identical red with black. In his discussion of color and form, the artist Kandinsky (1977) notes that form can stand alone as representing an object (real or not) or as a purely abstract limit to a space or a surface, but color as seen with the eye cannot stand alone. He believed that color and form are mutually influential with different combinations having different spiritual values. There are color/form harmonies, e.g., yellow triangle (keen color, sharp form) or blue ball (soft, deep color, round form), and the innumerable combinations may be discordant or may show the way to fresh possibilities of harmony. The linking of color to letters and numbers is well known in reports of synesthesias (Dixon, Smilek, Wagar, & Merikle, 2004) and as the subject of poetry (Rimbaud, 1884). Recently, Albertazzi et al. have examined color and shapes or concepts. Using geometric shapes, Albertazzi, Da Pos, et al. (2013) found associations between yellow and triangle, and red with circle and square. Hue and concepts were also related: blue/green and cool; red/yellow and warm (Albertazzi, Canal, Malfatti, & Miccolo, 2013). Using stimuli with more complex shapes (biological forms), Albertazzi, Canal, Dadam, and Miccolo (2014) found round forms were described as harmonic and dynamic, elongated forms were disharmonious and somewhat static, while flat shapes lacking spikes or holes were described as harmonious and static. Crossmodal associations were observed for colors and sensory concepts, including red—hot, blue—cold, blue/cyan—moist, red/yellow—dry, yellow/green—sour, and red–purple—sweet (Albertazzi, Koenderink, & van Doorn, 2015). The soft–hard dimension was unrelated to chromatic structure.

Form, Color, and Other Senses

Form is also tied to sound. In 1963, Werner and Kaplan found nonsense words to be crossmodally associated with sensory concepts. Stimuli like *zeca* and *taki* were labeled as small, angular, bright, moving, and happy, while *voag* and *huoh* were large, round, dark, static, and sad. Similarly, an expressive line pattern that was rounded was labeled *ulalah*, a pointy one, *zekite*. Other visual patterns represented emotions like arrogance or modesty.

Artists have long associated color and sound. In fact, Rimington (1912) described the construction of a color organ that he invented in 1893. As notes were played, particular colors were projected on a white background. At Expo 67, Montreal, Canada, inside the eight levels of the French Pavilion, an electric light display sent flashes of color racing up and down a polyhedron of steel cables to the sound of ultramodern music. In both of these displays, color was moving, thus achieving an absorbing multimodal visual, auditory, kinesthetic experience.

Painting entails complex synesthesias involving kinesthesis and visual patterns (Hunt, 1995a). Many artists paint music. Klee (1964), who was a skilled musician, wanted to discover a new, autonomous form of painting, and believed he "must improvise freely on the keyboard of colors" in his paintbox. In his theory of color, Klee's paradigm of color relationships interprets the continuous circular motion between primary and secondary colors as a "vibrating, revolving organism" (Düchting, 2012). Klee described his painting as polyphonic, which he believed was superior to music in that the temporal element has a more spatial quality (polyphonic examples: Klee's *Fugue in Red*, 1921 and *White Framed Polyphonically*, 1930; see chapter "Polyphonic Painting" in Düchting, 2012). Sandler, in his introduction (Kandinsky, 1977), states that Kandinsky is painting music, not only analyzing colors and their effects on viewers, but "breaking down the barrier between music and painting" and isolating "the pure emotion" (p. xix). Kandinsky viewed music as the most transcendent form of nonobjective art—musicians could evoke images in listeners' minds merely with sounds. An abstract painter, he strove to produce similarly object-free, spiritually rich paintings that alluded to sounds and emotions through a unity of sensation. Kandinsky links color to the senses, not just sound, vision, and taste, but he also describes colors in terms of touch: rough, sticky, smooth, warm, cold, or hard. For Kandinsky, color is a power which directly influences the soul: "color harmony must rest only on a corresponding vibration in the human soul" (p. 26); this is one of the guiding principles of the artist's impulse for spiritual expression.

In his book, "Point and Line to Plane," Kandinsky (1994) showed how lines and shapes were linked, in art, nature, architecture, and design, to rhythm, tempo, movement, sound, tension, and so on. In his discussion of these geometric terms, Kandinsky noted that sizes and positions of points may be altered, affecting their interpretation, for example: ···. may represent the first four notes of Beethoven's fifth symphony. A line comes about through movement; it is the trail of a point in motion; it is dynamic not static. A horizontal line is cold and flat; a vertical line warm. He further explains how the degree of the angle implies the amount of warmth or belligerence.

The curve line has increased or decreased tension depending on the type of undulation. He also discusses the effects of line thickness, changing thickness, and repetition of lines with equal and unequal intervals. He describes relationships with plane as follows: above > tension toward > heaven; left > tension toward > distance; right > tension toward > home; below > tension toward > earth. He notes that these relationships are not to be understood literally but have the purpose of making us conscious of these tensions. Because forms, colors, and their spatial relationships all convey inner meaning, Kandinsky argued that abstract art puts a spiritual world alongside the external world (p. 785) and, because it is broader, freer, and richer in content, it shows us our spiritual future. It creates a "real world" that portrays an inner consciousness. This linking of perception, meaning, and consciousness is also central to psychological theories of cognition.

Example: Sitting in a Paris cafe, a French student of architecture told me about the building of the Eiffel Tower, designed as the entrance to the 1889 World's Fair, and what it means to France. Kandinsky (1994) says that the Eiffel Tower was the most significant early attempt to create a particularly tall building out of lines—line having ousted surface (p. 621). I took more traditional photos, but this one seems to have more felt meaning.

Viewers recognize this as the Eiffel Tower. Did you experience kinesthetic and visual synesthesias? Or felt meaning? Or see the mandala? Jung (1964) used the word mandala to designate the mythological representation of the self which often emphasizes the four corners of the world or pictures a man in the center of a circle divided into four. Jung notes that, in architecture, the mandala often passes unnoticed and often forms a ground plan. Another famous mandala in Paris is L'Etoile, with a circular road around the Arc de Triomphe and streets radiating out around it, the most famous street being Champs-Élysées. © 2011 Joan M. Preston; Original in color.

VGs are immersive perceptual experiences, whose lines, forms, colors, and their alterations during play elicit intrinsic meaning. Some colors and shapes readily attract attention, a fact that the game designer may use to engage or distract the gamer during play or to imply meaning about an object or event that is pertinent, immaterial, or intentionally confounding to problem solving. Games are intentionally visually complex, full of task-relevant and -irrelevant information. The player first enters an unfamiliar gameworld, populated with cues, diversions, and digressions to be navigated on the way to solving a series of challenges set within the designer's rules. The nature of the visual experience is vitally important and typically invites exploration. Through interactive engagement and persistence, the player is led to successful performance as well as the development of enhanced perceptual and cognitive skills.

Meaning

As we have seen, there are associations between perception, concepts, and emotion. The underlying nature of thought is believed to be grounded in abstract visual-spatial imagery (e.g., Arnheim, 1969; Hunt, 1995a; Johnson, 1987; Lakoff, 1987; Shepard, 1978). Metaphor is widely held to be the basis of thought, but how do metaphors originate from perceptual information and become sufficiently complex or abstract to extend to language and thinking?

Lakoff (1987) and Johnson (1987) have proposed that all conceptual thought rests on core metaphors based in concrete perception. Nonmetaphorical concepts like spatial orientation, emerge directly from experience and are defined in their own terms. Metaphorical concepts are understood and structured both on their own terms and in terms of other concepts (Lakoff & Johnson, 1980). They believe that conceptual structure becomes meaningful because abstract spatial metaphors are kinesthetically embodied. Basic perception provides two kinds of symbolic structures: (1) Basic level structures are the convergence of gestalt principles of perception, the forms of basic body movements and the ability to form rich imagery and they include properties like hard–soft, tall–short, heavy–light. (2) The more abstract image schemas are found in ongoing bodily and spatial experience, such as container, path, balance, force, source-goal, and others. Lakoff and Johnson argue that, from these cognitive tools, we are able to construct our more complex cognitions. As Geshwind (1965) proposed, symbolic cognition rests on a capacity for crossmodal translation that occurs between the patterns of the separate perceptual modalities and entails their creative rearrangement. That is, we combine sensory inputs or use them inter-changeably to develop more abstract symbols.

Image schemas are not only basic to representations of the structures of the external world, they are also basic to our self-referential conceptualizations of human experience. Lakoff (1987) argues that full self-reference entails the direct experiential realization of his body-as-container schema. For example, all words for psychological states are rooted entymologically in physical patterns that have been given a metaphorical usage. To illustrate, Lakoff notes that we metaphorically express the body as a container for the emotions in statements like: he was filled with anger; she was brimming with rage. That image structures derive from preconceptual embodied experience is underscored by Kennedy's (1983) findings that blind people, unfamiliar with pictures, can draw in a universally recognizable outline form and readily employ metaphoric devices to depict motion.

According to Arnheim (1969), symbolic operations require a simultaneous and immediately given complexity of structure that is provided only by the visual-spatial template. That is, only geometric-dynamic forms are sufficiently complex and precise in their relational structure and processed rapidly enough to be part of a medium for conceptual thought. Using tachistoscopic and stroboscopic exposure, Arnheim found that the basic pattern "springs out" as part of the perception of the art work. The designs unfold in visual dynamics that involve kinesthetic motion as much as visual design. They are synesthesias. Arnheim (1969) argues that the perceptual qualities of shape and motion are present in the very acts of thinking and are in fact the medium in which the thinking itself takes place. VGs are perceptually rich visual-spatial worlds whose colors, shapes, and patterns evoke cognitive meanings and emotional feelings during the player's interactions with the game's environment, characters, and narrative. For example, tall, yellow > warm, happy (Big Bird); short, shaggy, dull green > gloomy, pessimistic (Oscar the Grouch).

Crossmodal Processing

The linking of symbol and referent is not just metaphorical but also crossmodal, where an inner kinesthetic embodiment fuses with "abstract visual dynamics" (Arnheim, 1969) or "image schemas" (Lakoff & Johnson, 1980) to bring out a meaningful pattern. As Hunt explains (1995a, p. 176): The two patterns flow into each other in a manner which is synesthesia when experienced presentationally by the individual, and is symbolic representation when subordinated to pragmatic reference. He continues that the structures of thought are directly given to all of us by the way we experience the organization of the world.

This leads to the conclusion that "a symbolic consciousness based on perception must ultimately be shared and common" (p. 178). Lakoff (1987) and Johnson (1987), like Arnheim, view visual–spatial metaphor as the basis for abstract thought whether this symbolic cognition extends into logic or fantasy. Players, moving through perceptually rich VG worlds, have myriad opportunities to interpret objects and events from their personal perspective and/or to use these as cues to problem-solve challenges, yet different players generally agree they are experiencing the same game.

Synesthesia is a naturally occurring perceptual event that involves two or more senses and uses crossmodal processing. Although each sense provides qualitatively distinct subjective impressions of our surroundings, we are able to maintain a coherent and unified perception because we experience our environment through multiple sensory channels. Some neurons respond to stimulation in more than one modality, e.g., such neurons have been investigated in a brain structure involved in mediating orientation and attention behaviors (Stein & Meredith, 1993). Calvert (2001) points out that crossmodal capabilities allow us to use sensory information interchangeably or to combine sensory inputs to enhance detection and discrimination of stimuli and speed responsiveness. Thus, we are able to engage in crossmodal matching (e.g., visual and tactile shape information), crossmodal integration (e.g., integrate cues of size, pitch, duration to identify an object), crossmodal localization (e.g., integrate spatial coordinate information across senses, such as the ventrilo-quist illusion), and crossmodal synthesis of dynamic spatial information from visual and auditory senses, all of which facilitate our situational interactions whether real or mediated. Crossmodal processing also extends to emotions. Infants age 7 months are able to integrate emotional infor-mation across modalities and to recognize common affect in face and voice (Grossman, Striano, & Friederici, 2006).

Spontaneous synesthesia is a state that reflects "the core of symbolic cognition prior to its more pragmatic articulation in word and image" (Hunt, 1995a, p. 144). These more spontaneous synesthesias tend to be noticed and reported by individuals high in imaginative absorption (Ramsey & Hunt, 1993). For Hillman (1977, pp. 62–88), all functional imagery contains crossmodal fusions which are largely implicit and these synesthesias are what confer imagery's referential "feel." Marks (1978) has shown that a major source for poetic metaphors (e.g., silver toned chimes; cold so bitter) are "simple synesthesias" based on felt crossmodal fusions.

Synesthesias connect impalpable awareness on the one hand and modality-specific imagery on the other. In describing his own experience,

Hunt tells us that, once it occurred to ask himself which modalities were involved, "I could begin to see the states in question as emergent wholes within which at one moment I 'saw' geometric structures, the next felt a kinesthetic embodiment, then became aware that all this was also a thought awaiting articulation, then noticed more concrete depictive imagery or inner speech, and so on." (p. 146). Such experience, together with his knowledge of theory and research, led Hunt to the idea that "*thoughts are emergent synesthesias*" (p. 146). Synesthesias are dynamic processes and can be constitutive of the novelty of symbolic thought. Although early views of synesthesias saw them as presymbolic, this approach was problematic (see Hunt, 1995a, pp. 149–154 for a review). They limited synesthesia to simple sensory dimensions and missed "the very existence of geometric–dynamic synesthesias" that involve "patterns that are modality-specific (visual mandalas, kinesthetic flows) and so demonstrate genuine integration, not some common pre-sensory template" (Hunt, 1995a, p. 151).

Humphry (1951) believed that, during symbolic cognition, consciousness consisted of an impalpable "sense" of significance. Humphry (1951) and Woodworth (1906) both thought that this moment of insight might be largely unspecifiable. However, Woodward believed that it did real work during the process of thinking. The potential function of this insight state has been described by Gendlin (1962). "Felt meaning" occurs during our immediate state and is experienced when we can be said to be following what is happening. This moment of insight is both precise and involuntary because we can directly sense any departure, from our original experience, of some part of our thought. All symbolic communications, even the most complex, must be immediately followed by felt meanings if we are to understand them. These insights are also causal because they guide our communicative thought. During a game, a player may experience such insights about objects, events, characters, etc., that influence play. Marcel (1988) examined conscious word recognition and concluded that awareness of the highest and most developed levels of semantic synthesis occurred first, before any available awareness of the constituent parts. Thus, awareness of the whole precedes awareness of the simpler parts and this is part of the basic function of consciousness. Hunt (1995a) concludes that immediate symbolic consciousness first provides us with the maximally intuitive synthesis and sensed meaning of our situation at its most abstract level. Synesthesias or crossmodal translation between geometric forms and nascent kinesthetic embodiments can account for both the denotative and connotative aspects of Gendlin's felt meaning. Visual microgenesis provides the structurally precise geometric patterns defining the denotative space, while the microgenesis of tactile kinesthetic forms (up–down and expanding–contracting motions with varying degrees of pleasantness–unpleasantness, strength–weakness, and activity–passivity) would provide the connotational context (Hunt, 1995a). As Kandinsky's analysis (1994) shows, line spacing can change rhythm or tempo, e.g., | | |, | | |; warmth by changing a line's angle; imply peacefulness or calm with a gently undulating curve or urgency with a zigzag.

ABSORPTION

Consciousness is awareness and its development emerges from experiences whose central feature is absorption or openness to experience (Hunt, 1995a). He states that consciousness is a capacity involved directly in reusing and reorganizing the structures of perception. The concept of absorption is found in various disciplines concerned with media and perceptual events and, typically, it refers to an individual's state. Absorption is described as presence, immersion, engagement, or involvement. In psychology, absorption is also conceived as a personality trait. Referred to as openness-to-experience, the trait, absorption, involves the degree to which the individual is open to experiencing emotional and cognitive alterations across situations. Because it is inherently interactive with situation, a high absorber may effortlessly direct attention toward internal events, while external cues may be used by a low absorber.

High and low absorbers differ in several ways that influence how they respond to a situation, including creativity, hypnotizability, frequency of experience of spontaneous altered states, and sensitivity to aesthetics and metaphor. Because they have a capacity for sustained attentional involvement, high absorbers also function better on tasks that involve complex attentional performance or on tasks that involve the rapid redirection of attentional focus. These tasks are central to playing action VGs and experienced gamers exhibit greater sustained attention than less experienced players. When effortful attention was required, high absorbers displayed greater cortical specificity than low absorbers (Davidson, Schwartz, & Rothman, 1976). For example, Preston and Cull (1998) compared high and low absorbers for balance performance before and after viewing apparent-motion visuals. Low absorbers had balance scores that were better prior to viewing the visuals. They seemed to have difficulty resisting modality irrelevant distractions on a demanding task requiring mode specific attention. However, high absorbers improved after viewing, indicating that they were able to selectively inhibit cortical areas that were irrelevant to the balance task. Both high and low absorbers selectively activated modality-relevant cortical areas. However, selective inhibition of modality-irrelevant cortical areas makes processing by high absorbers both qualitatively different and more efficient on tasks requiring effortful attention. It may explain the superior performance of high-level gamers during sustained attention.

Individuals who differ in absorption or openness-to-experience also differ in the way they respond to media. Stein (1974) presented subjects with line drawings, each with two interpretations, one more literal and one more inferential. He found wide individual differences in the degree to which subjects were willing to endorse higher inferential labels. Hunt (1995a) suggests that those who are higher in absorption or openness-to-experience may be more willing or better able to infer meaning of abstract stimuli. This may occur because high absorbers appraise information in a distinct way that is linked to the self (Roche & McConkey, 1990). That is, they may be more attuned to felt meaning.

Visual and vestibular imagery are particularly important for absorption (Ramonth, 1985). These representations are typically provided by VGs and VR, which also provide opportunities to develop a variety of cognitive and attentional skills. Thus, with experience, VG players and VR participants are able to sustain their absorption in these media long enough to achieve flow, presence, or immersion. Because high absorbers are better able to deploy attention and readily engage in imaginal activities, they have a greater capacity for immersion in the immediate crossmodal properties of ongoing consciousness (Hunt, 2005). Action VGs are interactive perceptual environments where players can develop these perceptual and cognitive skills and thus become able to sustain absorption. VGs also provide visual and kinesthetic experiences that locate the self in the ongoing environment, permitting self-referential embodiment in the game space. The player feels present in the gameworld. Hunt continues that sustained absorption in consciousness "will engender its transformation as more specific "altered states" and their metaphorically embodied "felt meaning"."

As Hunt (1995a) has noted, recombinatory novelty and creativity is regarded as a fundamental feature of human symbolic capacity. Because perceptual sources of information are distinctly structured, Hunt (p. 86) argues that crossmodal fusions will necessarily be multiple and creative, that is there is no one way that a moment of vision will flow into and transform the very differently patterned moments of audition and touch. Cross-translations will set up cycles of reciprocal transformation that will recognize the patterns of perception in an open-ended and emergent fashion (Hunt, 1995a, p. 86) and will also entail an awareness that is self-referential. This strongly implies that information to more modalities may increase absorption and also explains the preference for and greater impact of multimodal stimuli. It also helps explain why gamers' experiences during play change as a player becomes familiar with the game space, develops perceptual and cognitive skills needed to improve performance, persists longer in problem solving, has increased confidence after success in meeting challenges, and so forth.

Two Types of Presence

Hunt (1995a) distinguishes two types of presence related to consciousness. One is a more impersonal experience or presence. For example, viewing the sky or a sunrise is experienced as open space that, with crossmodal translation, becomes the metaphor for the openness of time. Similarly Almaas (1986) views this presence-openness or "felt transcendence" as more impersonal and based on the experience of openness and space. In media, a more impersonal experience can be created with a wide-angle or establishing shot of an environment. Hunt explains that heightened self-awareness becomes visible through the embodiment of synesthetic metaphors derived from more abstract properties of nature. For example, the contemplation of light, wind, fire, and flowing water, the heights and depths of ravines and mountains, etc., can induce ecstatic states in individuals who are "suitably open to their kinesthetic embodiment and resonance" (Hunt, 2004a, p. 20). Most of us have experienced ecstatic states induced by a blazing fire, sunlight reflecting from a rippling stream, a panoramic sunrise, or vistas of mountain valleys, whether these are real-life or virtual.

The second type of presence is more personal or vital. For Almaas (1986), it is a sense of "I am." Not only does this presence emerge at a symbolic level, it is a basic structure of perception involving both the individual's orientation toward horizontal openness and one's propriolocation of specific position within the array (Hunt, 1995a). The more personal presence is typically created using the subjective point-of-view or first-person perspective that is common in many VGs. When media use first-person perspective, the individual seems to be inhabiting and moving around in the media-created reality. We are located within the situation and the basic structures of ambient perception may be realized as metaphors.

The more impersonal presence appears as spontaneous imagery arising in an expressive symbolic medium. Arnheim suggests that the facilitating content of this kind of presence is geometric shapes and nature. This presence is more intuitive and linked to a medium conducive to inferencing. Davies (2004) created two "bodily experiential works," which she describes as a "mode of access to an ephemeral yet embodied experience" of self in place. These works, Osmose and Ephémère, were based on metaphorical aspects of nature and structured so the viewer could see simultaneously through more than 20 layers of semitransparent and translucent visuals. Davies noted that "the usual perceptual cues by which we objectify the world – simply disappear, dissolved into an ambiguous enveloping spatiality of soft, semi-transparent, intermingling volumes of varying hues and luminosities." These works created a perceptual state where one became acutely aware of one's own embodied presence inhabiting space. Hunt (2004a) believes that this heightened self-awareness becomes visible when more abstract properties of nature become embodied in synesthetic metaphor. Davies facilitated a sensation of floating using the intuitive visceral processes of breath and balance rather than joysticks and the like. This immersive experience of floating tended to evoke euphoric feelings of disembodiment and immateriality, which she intentionally amplified by enabling the participant to see through and virtually float through everything around them. Many of the 20,000 people who individually participated in the two works described their experience in euphoric terms or as the sensation of consciousness occupying space (Davies, 2004).

For Hunt (1995a) the personal sense of presence is a more representational self-referential awareness. This is the presence often found in VGs and VRs. Haans and Ijsselsteijn (2012) believe that media presence is a consequence of the way we are embodied and it extends naturally from the same ability that allows us to adjust to experiences in the real world. They state "Tools and technologies are but additional mediators, which when appropriately integrated in our embodiment yield the same transparency that we experience when using our own natural sensors and actuators or, in a word, our bodies" (p. 217). Similarly, Riva, Waterworth, Waterworth, and Mantovani (2009) confirm that the ability to feel "present" in a virtual reality system (an artifact) basically does not differ from the ability to feel "present" in our body and the surrounding physical environment in which we are situated. They describe the presence process as a sophisticated but unconscious form of monitoring of action and experience, transparent to the self but critical for its existence. We experience this sense of agency as both the author and the owner of our own actions. For Riva et al., the feeling of presence is related to the quality of agency. A higher level of presence is experienced as a better quality of action and experience: the more the subject is able to enact his/her intentions in a successful action, the more he/she feels present. Action VGs facilitate a feeling of presence because they are interactive, involve complex challenges within a narrative, and require sequences of player actions. As Clark (2003) points out, when the medium involves tools, participants also incorporate them to extend their action potential into the virtual space. Riva et al. explain that when we experience strong mediated presence, "there is no additional conscious effort of access to information, nor effort of action to overt responses in the mediated environment" (p. 11). Like Gibson, Riva et al. believe that we perceive and act directly, as if unmediated.

CONSCIOUSNESS, GAMES, AND DREAMS

James (1890) viewed consciousness as a "stream of thought" and "flow of awareness" that is simultaneously momentary and continuous, and described it as based on the primary flow of perception. For James, consciousness is always embodied and present in the world. As Hunt (1995a) points out, although James' ongoing stream of awareness is subjectively imposed and involuntary, it always feels personal and "mine." Hunt explains that, while remaining continuous, it constantly changes and transforms itself. These paradoxes arise from the self-referential, recombinatory, and crossmodal bases of symbolic cognition that we see in the transpersonal states. The more *rapid, transitive* aspects of James' flow of awareness are the intrinsically vague auras of *felt meaning*, while the slower, more *substantive* aspects are more *specifiable* points of conclusion and consolidation. For Hunt, streaming consciousness is both a self-referential metaphor and also directly accessible to us as the most immediate organization of our physical reality. We all experience various naturally occurring states of consciousness, including among others: waking state, sleep, dreaming, day dreaming, lucid dreaming, meditation. Consciousness is our sustained absorption in our current environment.

Three modalities important to the development of consciousness: visual, auditory, and kinesthetic, are common to video games and help gamers become absorbed or experience a state of heightened focus and immersion called flow. Kinesthetic embodiment is essential. Cutsforth (1925) observed that his own synesthetic felt meanings became meaningless and desaturated color imagery unless his ordinary imagery was animated with an "inner movement" or bodily realization. Zietz (1931) was able to induce synesthetic experiences only when he made his color stimuli dynamic and unstable using 100 ms tachistoscopic exposures. Then, these ephemeral visual patterns interacted synesthetically with synchronous tones to momentarily become the tone and the entire complex was felt throughout the body. Using 100 s delays, Zaparoli and Reatto (1969) found that subjects reported complex synesthetic transformations between pairs of light flashes and auditory tones in which one was experienced as turning into the other. We know that the simultaneous presentation of information to the different senses lowers their threshold. For example, early filmmakers used 12 frames per second as the minimum frame rate needed for the eye to believe it was watching motion rather than a series of still images. When the first sound films were introduced viewers saw an increased flicker (Blumenthal, 1977). The number of visual frames per second had to be increased for the audience to "see" motion in "talkies" and became standardized at 24 frames per second. As Hunt (1989b) explains, "To the extent that imagery reuses perceptual schemata, we would expect an analogous speeding in symbolic cross-modal processes" (p. 355). In other words, multimodal events benefit from faster crossmodal processing.

To understand how VGs act as amplifiers of consciousness, the game environment, what the player sees during game play is relevant. (For a discussion of design issues in game development, see Preston, 2012.) The importance of what the designer makes available to the player during the game is underscored by artist Paul Klee's statement (1973) about visuals: "Images do not reproduce what is visible, images render something visible." Forms, colors, sounds, etc. all have implicit meaning. The game designer determines what is presented perceptually, and the range of actions possible within the game. The player then uses this information according to his/her own particular skills and abilities, with a player's level of game skills further developed by playing. Action game technology provides rapidly changing visual, auditory, and kinesthetic experiences which facilitate absorption or flow. Experienced gamers have the advantage of knowing which game strategies are likely to succeed as well as possessing game-relevant cognitive and attentional skills and persistence in problem-solving. During effortful attention, higher absorption is associated with selective inhibition of modality-irrelevant cortical areas. This should make gamers' cognitive processing more efficient during absorption or flow and contribute to a player's positive emotional experience.

In presentational symbolism, the sense of meaning emerges directly from experiential absorption in the medium of expression (Hunt, 1995a, p. 216). The actual form of awareness is the internalized matrix for all symbolization. This "most basic structure itself becomes a metaphoric vehicle for the felt meaning" of a totality that holds the person and everything else within it. Our consciousness is entirely structured through presentational metaphor (p. 204). Full self-reference entails the direct experiential realization of Lakoff's body-as-container schema. In VGs, this occurs when the player is fully absorbed in the game space.

"Flow" is the "metaphor that best characterizes ongoing consciousness" (Hunt, 1995a, p. 122). Similarly, Csikszentmihalyi (1990) and Maslow (1962) refer to flow as feeling immediately present in the moment. Dynamic media like VGs and VR provide perceptual flow. Media enjoyment is associated with absorption and flow and, when participants are involved to their optimal mental and motor capacity, a higher experience of flow is elicited (Csikszentmihalyi, 1990; Turkle, 1984). It is during sustained attentional involvement that a fully absorbed individual may achieve an ecstatic state or peak experience of creativity.

For James, our streaming consciousness is always embodied and present in the physical world. This streaming includes the inseparability of consciousness and the world, mind, and body. That is, "the body is the unique point of intersection between an objective and subjective series of facts based on the world and our experiences in it" (Hunt, 1995a, p. 118). Kinesthetic embodiment is fundamental to our consciousness. Our orientation in an optical array identifies selected patterns as particularly relevant and navigation changes the gradients of perceptual flow. Because we perceive affordances of things for behavior, affordances for action, perception always simultaneously is of the self and the environment. In other words, we each perceive ourselves in our current ecological environment whether real or mediated. (For a discussion of ecological perception and veridicality, see Preston, 2007.) Optical flow specifies self-location (the ecological self) and, as Gibson (1979) has pointed out, the basic orienting system is essential for perception and for action, whether the immediate situation is real or virtual. This implies that our direct and mediated apprehension become mixed in our social and cognitive awareness, such that cognitive, social, and emotional learning are transferrable among natural and constructed realities. Some of the first research concerning the nature of transfers between mediated and real experiences was conducted by Gibson (1971), who demonstrated that perceptual information in a realistic picture contained the same kind of ecological information as a section of a real scene. Skills developed during VG play are also transferred to the real world. In 2007, Rosser et al. found that surgical residents and attending physicians who were VG players performed laparoscopic surgery with fewer errors and faster completion than nonplayers, with best results for the most skilled gamers. Current investigations of VG transfer encompass cognition, perception, and behavior.

Ortiz de Gortari and Griffiths (2012) use the term "game transfer phenomena" (GTP) to refer to the transfer of virtual experiences to the real world. GTPs include automatic mental processes, alterations in perceptions, and behavioral changes. They argue that contemporary video games offer high levels of realism and we react to these advanced technological experiences and reality in similar ways. GTPs are complex, involve all our sensory modalities, result from players' high engagement in VGs and manifest in waking and altered states such as sleeping and daydreaming. GTPs are associated with frequent and intensive VG play. More recently, they have linked GTPs with longer play sessions, and playing for immersion, exploration, and escape (Ortiz de Gortari & Griffiths, 2015). "Video games have become a matter of emotional touch, evoking not just sensations but lasting emotive imprints, which hold for the gamer many of the same characteristics as memorable real life experiences" (Ortiz de Gortari, 2007).

The phenomenon of game-based perception and associations has been investigated by Poels, Ijsselsteijn, and de Kort (2015). Through intensive game play, "elements from the game world can trigger thoughts and imagery outside the game world, influencing the perception and interpretation of stimuli in everyday life" (p. 1137). In their review, they chronicle research linking game play to five domains: (1) interpreting physical objects, (2) sounds and music, (3) use of vocabulary and expressions, (4) daydreaming, and (5) dreaming. Their study found that, for all five domains, game transfer incidents increased with longer play time and higher levels of narrative involvement (p. 1141).

In addition to attentional, perceptual, and cognitive elements used to solve difficult, frightening, or dangerous challenges, action VGs have complex narrative elements with subplots that provide context. Not only are players able to freely explore the game world and select from a wide array of choices during play, game worlds may allow multiple players to participate in the same challenge, form teams, engage in real-time conversations with teammates, plan strategies, choose roles, and so forth. Although the development of competence in solving problems may be slow and require prolonged practice (Kinney, 1952), Ventura, Shute, and Zhao (2013) found that higher amounts of VG play are linked to persistence in solving problems and concluded that other forms of problem solving may benefit from persistence during VG play. For example, experienced gamers have superior skills in solving problems on visual-spatial tasks (Boot, Kramer, Simons, Fabiani, & Gratton, 2008) and recently, Adachi and Willoughby (2013) noted that self-reports of problem-solving skills are higher for strategic VG players and these self-reports predict academic grades.

The benefits of extensive playing extend to executive functions and emotional issues. Strobach and Schubert (2015) found that, when focusing on dual-task performance, nongamers benefitted more from action game training than from puzzle training, and concluded that a causal link existed between video game experience and optimized executive functions in dual-task situations. When comparing gamers with nongamers, VG players showed clear advantages in executive functions for task switching, for simultaneous task execution in dual task situations, and for continuous updating information. Extensive VG play is the basis of the benefits. When individuals are immersed in experiences where they repeatedly perform activities over lengthy time periods, the brain's neural structure adapts, becoming more sensitive to recurring events and more efficient in dealing with them (Kolb & Wishaw, 1998; Munte, Altenmüller, & Jänke, 2002). Recently, Bavelier, Achtman, Mani, and Föcker (2012), using functional magnetic resonance imaging (fMRI), found that the mechanisms that control attention allocation were less active during a challenging pattern-detection task for gamers compared to nongamers, suggesting that shooter game players allocate their attentional resources more efficiently and filter out irrelevant information more effectively.

Although the reciprocal links between VGs and reality and those between dreams and reality are well known, are the two kinds of virtual experiences related? Recently, Gackenbach and Hunt (2016) have pointed out that "Video games are a technologically constructed alternative reality, while dream worlds are biologically constructed alternative realities." They argue that the two kinds of artificial realities may be sufficiently similar to yield a carryover learning effects. Similarly, Revonsuo (2006) has argued that the dream world is virtual for the same reasons as mediated environments are. Several correspondences exist between the two virtual experiences, lucid dreams and VG play. Kahan and LaBerge (1994) characterized lucid dreaming as presenting a heightened metacognitive capacity in which individuals self-reflect on their own cognitive and memory processes and how they have used this monitoring to regulate information processing and behavior. This metacognition "is framed by consciously accessible memories of waking experience" (LaBerge & DeGracia, 2000, p. 275).

Action VGs are characterized as fast-paced interactive systems that place a heavy load on divided attention, peripheral processing, information filtering, and motor control, as well as on decision making, via the nesting of goals and subgoals at multiple time scales (Cardoso-Leite et al., 2016). Players monitor multiple objects and events, determine their relevancy, plan and execute game strategies, all of which challenge their cognitive and memory processes. They use their real-life skills and abilities, as well as those developed during gaming. In addition to these processing similarities, both VGs and lucid dreams are absorbing and involve enhanced self-awareness and active control during playing or dreaming. Research has examined whether these parallels facilitate reciprocal links.

Gackenbach et al. have been investigating VGs and higher states of consciousness for almost two decades. Not only do players dream about gaming, but VGs impact the structure and function of these dreams (Gackenbach, 2012). As well, intensive gamers have more lucid dreams than infrequent players (Gackenbach, 2006, 2009; Gackenbach & Kuruvilla, 2008). This is important because the first signs of the growth of consciousness take the form of lucid dreams (Alexander, Boyer, & Alexander, 1987). VG play and meditation both include improved attentional and spatial skills, deep absorption and flow experiences, as well as increased dream lucidity (Gackenbach, 2012). These similarities led Gackenbach (2008) to suggest that gaming may allow players entry into states of consciousness typically accessed by meditators.

Some studies have shown links between dreams and VGs. Gackenbach (2009), in a factor analytic study, found associations for lucid and control dreams with high-end gamer history and heavier media use, especially video game play. She also found that there were few differences in participants' rated sense of being there (presence) for playing a VG and having a dream about playing a VG. In their analysis of VGs and dreams, Gackenbach and Hunt (2016) concluded that gamers express their full potential for focused problem solving in the lucid dreams much like the strategies of video gaming. When gamers lucid versus nonlucid dreams were compared, the positive dream experience of being lucid was affirmed, including player's sense of empowerment that is facilitated by elevated aggression that is typical during game action. In summary, not only do gamers' dreams have more lucidity but gaming further enhances lucidity when dreaming.

Self-monitoring by gamers during games is similar to lucid dreamers' awareness that they are in a dream while the dream continues. Whether their experience was dreaming or game playing, individuals felt totally absorbed into the environment (Gackenbach & Rosie, 2011). Both VGs and dreams include not just perceptual and cognitive information but also emotional and narrative content. Action VGs simulate threatening situations in a safe virtual environment. Gamers, who play numerous action-combat games, indicated that their self-described nightmares were less threatening, more empowering, and more enjoyable (Gackenbach & Hakopdjanian, 2016). Revonsuo (2006) views dreams as similarly adaptive. Gackenbach et al. (2011) explain that, even if gamers are not aware that they are dreaming, they feel in control of a dream situation that is normally dangerous or frightening. Gackenbach and Hakopdjanian (2016) call this ability to better regulate negative emotions "nightmare protection." They believe that gamers develop automatic responses to threats after prolonged fighting during play in VGs where situations are threatening, and where fighting is the required game response. Gamers then use these automatic responses when experiencing threats in both dreams and VGs.

Action VGs are complex environments with challenging problems to solve. VG play uses perceptual skills and memory resources, as well as inferential reasoning and creative thinking to imagine play strategies and outcomes. Thus, VGs require an advanced stage of intelligence like Piaget's formal operations. This highest level of thinking in Piaget's theory of cognitive development begins in adolescence and the individual develops the capacity for higher-order reasoning.

Higher states of consciousness are characterized by multimodal translations of perceptual-spatial information and the integration of self and affect with cognition (Hunt, 1995a). Because these higher states are abstract, an individual first needs to achieve, then continue to develop, an abstract intelligence, such as Piaget's formal operations which begin around age 11. Abstract intelligence includes inferential reasoning, critical analysis, thinking creatively, imagining action outcomes, and so forth. This stage of intelligence is necessary for playing most VGs that are not directed to children.

Hunt (2016) has recently argued for a formal operations of affect, in contrast to Piaget's own view that the decentering of a formal operations of affect was impossible (Piaget, 1962, 1963, 1981). For Hunt, transpersonal experience and spirituality can be considered as an abstract level of Gardner's (1983) "personal" or "emotional" intelligences (see Hunt, 1995b, 2000, 2011; and independently suggested by Emmons, 2000a, 2000b). Transpersonal experience is seen as higher development of social-personal intelligence. The more representational side of formal operations would be a newly emergent felt sense of "stream of consciousness" (James, 1890) or "felt meaning" (Hunt, 1985, 1995a, 1995b, 2011; Gendlin, 1962). The positive transition to transpersonal realization brings forth an enhanced sense of self with an expanded spontaneity and "thatness" of immediate consciousness.

Both the gestural/metaphoric intelligence of social–personal meaning (Lakoff & Johnson, 1999) and the sensorimotor core of representational intelligence (Piaget, 1963) are anchored in the body. For Hunt (2016), these two intelligences ultimately pull in separate directions of transpersonal development and physical science. They yield an abstract person–intelligence and an abstract thing–intelligence which very differently transform the common metaphoric patterns afforded by the gestalt and flow dynamics of primary perception. In their cognitive view of metaphor, Lakoff and Johnson's (1999) argue that all conceptual and scientific thoughts are based on metaphors abstracted out of the ecological perceptual array. Not only are these metaphors or image schemas important to representations of structures of the external world, they are also basic to the self-referential concepts of our experience (Lakoff, 1987). Thus, abstraction and metaphor are precisely what allow higher human cognition. Perceptually based metaphors (for example: hard decision, flash of insight, or boiling anger) not only represent emotion, they are necessary to fully feel it (Lakoff & Johnson, 1999).

In addition to perceptual-cognitive information, VGs have narrative content and are also interactive. As de Boer (n.d.) has pointed out, VGs have two kinds of narrative: (1) The embedded narrative is content generated by the game designer that exists prior to players' interactions with the game, including cut scenes and back story, that is "often used to provide the fictional background for the game, motivation for actions in the game, and development of story arc"; (2) The emergent narrative is created by the player's moment-to-moment interactions with the gameworld, its levels and its rule structure, and varies with each play session as a function of the gamer's actions. The game narrative provides game characters and may allow team play, thus VGs involve not only perceptual and cognitive skills but are rich social and emotional environments. Therefore, VGs present challenges that engage perceptual and cognitive skills, but also engage the player's social, emotional, and cultural intelligence.

Hunt (1995a) reminds us that human consciousness itself is already social at all of its levels. Gackenbach and Hunt (2016) place gaming in the social nature of consciousness, as part of the collective societal nature of higher states of consciousness, and absorptive states generally. Jung (1964) identified our own personal memories, thoughts, attitudes, and feelings as the personal unconscious, while the collective unconscious refers to innate structures of the mind that are shared among all members of mankind and whose content is made up essentially of archetypes. Archetypes are "innate and inherited shapes of the human mind" (Jung, 1964, p. 67) that emerge as themes and characters in our dreams and in our culture. Gackenbach and Hunt (2016) note that Emile Durkheim understood collective consciousness "as a shared awareness of the social bond itself, whose felt 'effervescence' was most fully mobilized in religious ritual, mythology, and experience," while Jung's collective unconscious "was intended as the source of a human universality, but with levels of archetypal imagination specific to different cultural groups."

In addition to being virtual worlds, dreams and VGs share other features. Hunt (1989a) explains that the dreaming process has major functions of "memory consolidation, stress adaptation, mood regulation, wish fulfillment, problem solving, anticipation, play" as well as imaginative creativity. VGs also serve these functions. Dreams and VGs have narrative content of rich social worlds permeated by archetypes and both consist of visual–spatial imagery. As Gackenbach and Hunt (2016) explain, individuals who are high imaginative absorbers are more deeply attuned to the collective social field and gaming "creates its own externalized and supported forms of absorption and provides the archetypal patterns otherwise emerging in us only individually through dreams and meditations." Immersive virtual experiences provide opportunities for absorption not typically or easily available to those having naturally lower absorption and they have the potential to offer access to higher states of consciousness (Preston, 1998). Action VGs provide perceptually rich interactive game worlds with engaging narratives and characters. They provide opportunities for acquiring cognitive skills and participating in social and emotional interactions. The interactivity of VGs is similar to lucid dreamer's choosing and guiding the direction of the dream. Both VGs and dreams are separated from the ongoing course of experience and both can be altered by personal memory, emotion, and imagination.

CONCLUSION

Both art and psychology tell us that cognition, consciousness, and spirituality are based in perceptual information. Elements of our perception, forms, colors, and their patterns, have intrinsic meanings that are kinaesthetically embodied as metaphors which are the basis of thinking. As we develop cognitively, socially, and emotionally, our consciousness expands. Absorption is central to the development of consciousness and is facilitated in video games' rich perceptual environments, suggesting that video games may amplify consciousness. Hunt's two types of presence are both expressions of consciousness. The more impersonal presence is tied to openness and space. Media examples include Davies works, flight simulation VGs, and Tetris. These provide embodied experiences simulating movement through panoramic spaces. The other, more personal, presence is also an embodied experience. For Almaas (1988), it involves a sense of one's own being. The individual feels autonomous, having personal strength, maturity, and a capacity for social interaction. The self-referential awareness of personal presence occurs in action VGs with their narratives and archetypes, and points to the importance of VG interactivity for the player to express autonomous behaviors in the context of the VG story and characters. It is experienced players who are able to achieve the sustained attention necessary for absorption in the game.

Researchers have demonstrated cognitive benefits of gaming and examined correspondences between the virtual experiences in games and dreams. Skills, abilities, and behaviors transfer among dreams, games, and reality. Action games offer more than cognitive benefits. They are social and cultural, presenting challenges within intriguing narratives populated with archetypical characters. Like lucid and control dreams, they are interactive and allow opportunities for problem solving in challenging, threatening, or dangerous situations. Gackenbach and Hakopdjanian (2016) believe this is why action gamers are better able to regulate their negative emotions and why they report nightmares as less threatening.

Action VGs are complex; players are initially unfamiliar with the perceptually detailed, virtual environment, the game rules, narrative, and characters. Players act within the game space to meet difficult challenges that may be threatening or dangerous and persistence is required to solve problems. Over time, players develop cognitive benefits and persist long enough to achieve absorption in the game. The visually rich game environment with its elaborative narrative, and opportunities to problem solve in demanding circumstances provides players with a safe world in which to experiment and practice. With success, players develop confidence, skills, and strategies in engaging with a range of cognitive, social, and cultural events. Over time, high-level gamers gradually attain increased levels of abstract intelligence (e.g., Piaget's, 1963 formal operations) and social–emotional intelligence (e.g., Gardner, 1983; Hunt, 2016). Researchers and theorists are increasing their understanding of games and their relationships with reality and other virtual worlds. As they also focus on narratives and archetypes, we see the promise of social–emotional benefits of VGs.

REFERENCES

Adachi, P., & Willoughby, T. (2013). More than just fun and games: The longitudinal relationships between strategic video games, self-reported problem solving skills and academic grades. *Journal of Youth and Adolescence, 42*, 1041–1052.

Albers, J. (2013). *Interaction of color* (50th anniversary ed.). New Haven, CT: Yale University Press (Original edition copyright 1963 by Yale University).

Albertazzi, L., Canal, R., Dadam, J., & Miccolo, R. (2014). The semantics of biological forms. *Perception, 43*, 1365–1376.

Albertazzi, L., Canal, R., Malfatti, M., & Miccolo, R. (2013). The hue of concepts. *Perception, 42*, 1344–1352.

Albertazzi, L., Da Pos, O., Canal, R., Miccolo, R., Malfatti, M., & Vescovi, M. (2013). The hue of shapes. *Journal of Experimental Psychology: Human Perception & Performance, 39*, 37–47.

Albertazzi, L., Koenderink, J., & van Doorn, A. (2015). Chromatic dimensions: earthy, watery, airy, fiery. *Perception, 44*, 1153–1178.

Alexander, C., Boyer, R., & Alexander, V. (1987). Higher states of consciousness in the Vedic psychology of Maharishi Mahesh Yogi: a theoretical introduction and research review. *Modern Science and Vedic Science, 1*(1), 89–126.

Almaas, A. (1986). *Essence.* York Beach, ME: Samuel Weiser.

Almaas, A. (1988). *The pearl beyond price – integration of personality into being: An object relations approach.* Berkeley: Diamond Books.

Anderson, A., Bavelier, D., & Green, C. S. (2010). Speed-accuracy tradeoffs in cognitive tasks in action game players. *Journal of Vision, 10*, 748.

Anderson, D., & Levin, S. (1976). Young children's attention to Sesame Street. *Child Development, 47*, 806–811.

Anderson, D., & Lorch, E. (1983). Looking at television: action or reaction? In J. Bryant, & D. Anderson (Eds.), *Children's understanding of television: Research on attention and comprehension* (pp. 1–33). New York: Academic Press.

Arnheim, R. (1969). *Visual thinking.* Berkeley & Los Angeles: University of California Press.

Ashton, M., Lee, K., Perugini, M., Szarota, P., de Vries, R., Di Blas, L., Boies, K., & De Raad, B. (2004). A six-factor structure of personality-descriptive adjectives: Solutions from psycholexical studies in seven languages. *Journal of Personality and Social Psychology, 86*, 356–366.

Bavelier, D., Achtman, R., Mani, M., & Föcker, J. (2012). Neural bases of selective attention in action video game players. *Vision Research, 61*, 132–143.

Blumenthal, A. (1977). *The process of cognition.* Englewood Cliffs, NJ: Prentice-Hall.

Bolivar, V., Cohen, A., & Fentress, J. (1994). Semantic and formal congruency in music and motion pictures: Effects on the interpretation of visual action. *Psychomusicology, 13*, 28–59.

Boot, W., Kramer, A., Simons, D., Fabiani, M., & Gratton, G. (2008). The effects of video game playing on attention, memory, and executive control. *Acta Psychologica, 129*, 387–398.

Bryant, J., Zillmann, D., & Brown, D. (1983). Entertainment features in children's educational television: Effects on attention and information acquisition. In J. Bryant, & D. Anderson (Eds.), *Children's understanding of television: Research on attention and comprehension* (pp. 221–240). New York: Academic Press.

Bullerjahn, C., & Güldenring, M. (1994). An empirical investigation of effects of film music using qualitative content analysis. *Psychomusicology, 13*, 99–118.

Calvert, G. (2001). Crossmodal processing in the human brain: Insights from functional neuroimaging studies. *Cerebral Cortex, 11*, 1110–1123.

Cardoso-Leite, P., Kludt, R., Vignola, G., Ma, W., Green, C. S., & Bavelier, D. (2016). Technology consumption and cognitive control: Contrasting action video game experience with media multitasking. *Attention & Perception Psychophysics, 78*, 218–241.

Chiappe, D., Conger, M., Liao, J., Caldwell, J. L., & Vu, K.-P. (2013). Improving multi-tasking ability through action videogames. *Applied Ergonomics, 44*, 278–284.

Chihuly, D., n.d. www.chihuly.com.

Chion, M. (1994). *Sound on screen* (edited & translated by C. Gorbman, 1994). New York: Columbia University Press.

Clark, A. (2003). *Natural born cyborgs: Minds, technologies, and the future of human intelligence.* Oxford: Oxford University Press.

Cohen, A. (1999). The functions of music in multimedia: A cognitive approach. In S. Yi (Ed.), *Music, mind and science* (pp. 52–68). Seoul Korea: Seoul National University Press.

Cohen, A. (2000). Film music: Perspectives from cognitive psychology. In J. Buhler, C. Flinn, & D. Neumeyer (Eds.), *Music and cinema* (pp. 360–377). Hanover, NH: Wesleyan University Press (Published by University Press of New England).

Cohen, A. (2005). How music influences the interpretation of film and video: Approaches from experimental psychology. In R. A. Kendall, & R. W. Savage (Eds.), *Selected reports in ethnomusicology Perspectives in Systematic Musicology: Vol. 12.* (pp. 15–36).

Cohen, A., & MacMillan, K. (2004). *Music influences absorption in motion pictures* (Preprint of unpublished paper).

Colzato, L., van Leeuwen, P., van den Wildenberg, W., & Hommel, B. (2010). DOOM'd to switch: Superior cognitive flexibility in players of first person shooter games. *Frontiers in Psychology.* http://dx.doi.org/10.3389/fpsyg.2010.00008.

Csikszentmihalyi, M. (1990). *Flow: The psychology of optimal experience.* New York: Harper & Row.

Cutsforth, T. (1925). The role of emotion in the synaesthetic subject. *The American Journal of Psychology, 36,* 527–543.

Davidson, R., Schwartz, G., & Rothman, L. (1976). Attentional style and the self-regulation of mode-specific attention: An electroencephalographic study. *Journal of Abnormal Psychology, 85,* 235–238.

Davies, C. (2004). Virtual space. In F. Penz, G. Radick, & R. Howell (Eds.), *Space in science, art and society* (pp. 69–104). Cambridge: Cambridge University Press.

de Boer, V. n.d. Narrative in games. http://www.few.vu.nl/~vbr240/onderwijs/pim/Narrative%20in%20Games.pdf.

Dixon, M., Smilek, D., Wagar, B., & Merikle, P. (2004). Alphanumeric-color synaesthesia: When 7 is yellow and C is red. In G. Calvert, C. Spence, & B. Stein (Eds.), *Handbook of multisensory processes.* Cambridge, MA: MIT Press.

Düchting, H. (2012). *Paul Klee: Painting music.* Munich: Prestel Publishing.

Eichenbaum, A., Bavelier, D., & Green, C. S. (2014). Video games: Play that can do serious good. *American Journal of Play, 7,* 50–72.

Emmons, R. (2000a). Is spirituality an intelligence? Motivation, cognition, and the psychology of ultimate concern. *The International Journal for the Psychology of Religion, 10,* 3–26.

Emmons, R. (2000b). Spirituality and intelligence: Problems and prospects. *The International Journal for the Psychology of Religion, 10,* 57–64.

Gackenbach, J. I. (2006). Video game play and lucid dreams: Implications for the development of consciousness. *Dreaming, 16*(2), 96–110.

Gackenbach, J. I. (2008). Video game play and consciousness development: A transpersonal perspective. *The Journal of Transpersonal Psychology, 40*(1), 60–87.

Gackenbach, J. I. (2009). Electronic media and lucid-control dreams: Morning after reports. *Dreaming, 19*(1), 1–6.

Gackenbach, J. I. (2012). Video game play and dreams. In D. Barrett, & P. McNamara (Eds.), *Encyclopedia of sleep and dreams* (pp. 795–800). Santa Barbara, CA: ABC-CLIO.

Gackenbach, J. I., Ellerman, E., & Hall, C. (2011). Video game play as nightmare protection: A preliminary inquiry with military gamers. *Dreaming, 21*(4), 221.

Gackenbach, J. I., & Hakopdjanian, S. (2016). Breaking the frame of digital, dream and waking realities through video game play. In S. Schafer (Ed.), *Exploring the collective unconscious in the age of digital media* (pp. 79–107). Hershey, PA: Information Science Reference, IGI Global.

Gackenbach, J. I., & Hunt, H. T. (2016). A deeper inquiry into the association between lucid dreams and video game play. In K. Buckeley, & R. Hurd (Eds.), *Lucid dreaming cross cultural understandings of consciousness in the dream state*. ABC-CLIO.

Gackenbach, J. I., & Kuruvilla, B. (2008). The relationship between video game play and threat simulation dreams. *Dreaming, 18*(4), 236–256.

Gackenbach, J. I., & Preston, J. M. (1998). Video game play and the development of consciousness. In *Presented at Tucson III: Towards a science of consciousness, Tucson*.

Gackenbach, J. I., & Rosie, M. (2011). Presence in video game play and nighttime dreams: An empirical inquiry. *International Journal of Dream Research, 4*(2), 98–109.

Gackenbach, J. I., Stark, H., Boyes, A., & Flockhart, C. (2015). Reality: Waking, sleeping and virtual. In M. Kramer, & M. Glucksman (Eds.), *Dream research: Contributions to clinical practice* (pp. 215–224). UK: Routledge.

Gardner, H. (1983). *Frames of mind*. New York, NY: Basic Books.

Gendlin, E. (1962). *Experiencing and the creation of meaning*. New York, NY: Free Press.

Geshwind, N. (1965). Disconnection syndromes in animals and man. *Brain, 88*, 237–294.

Gibson, J. J. (1966). *The senses considered as perceptual systems*. Prospect Hts., IL: Waveland Press.

Gibson, J. J. (1971). The information available in pictures. *Leonardo, 4*, 27–35.

Gibson, J. J. (1979). *The ecological approach to visual perception*. Boston: Houghton-Mifflin.

Green, C. S., & Bavelier, D. (2012). Learning, attentional control, and action video games. *Current Biology, 22*, 197–206.

Green, C. S., & Seitz, A. (2015). The impacts of video games on cognition (and how the government can guide the industry). *Policy Insights from the Behavioral and Brain Sciences, 2*, 101–110.

Green, C. S., Sugarman, M., Medford, K., Klobusicky, E., & Bavelier, D. (2012). The effect of action video game experience on task-switching. *Computers in Human Behavior, 28*, 984–994.

Grossman, T., Striano, T., & Friederici, A. (2006). Crossmodal integration of information from face and voice in the infant brain. *Developmental Science, 9*, 309–315.

Haans, A., & Ijsselsteijn, W. (2012). Embodiment and telepresence: Toward a comprehensive theoretical framework. *Interacting with Computers, 24*, 211–218.

Hillman, J. (1977). *An inquiry into image*. Spring.

Hindes, D. (2014). *Why 1998 was the best year in gaming*. http://www.gamespot.com/articles/why-1998-was-the-best-year-in-gaming/1100-6424354/.

Humphry, G. (1951). *Thinking*. New York: Methuen.

Hunt, H. (1985). Relations between the phenomena of religious mysticism and the psychology of thought. *Perceptual and Motor Skills, 61*, 911–961.

Hunt, H. T. (1989a). *The Multiplicity of dreams: Memory, imagination, and consciousness*. New Haven: Yale University Press.

Hunt, H. T. (1989b). The relevance or ordinary and non-ordinary states of consciousness for the cognitive psychology of meaning. *The Journal of Mind and Behavior, 10*, 347–360.

Hunt, H. T. (1995a). *On the nature of consciousness*. New Haven, CT: Yale University Press.

Hunt, H. T. (1995b). Some developmental issues in transpersonal psychology. *The Journal of Mind and Behavior, 16*, 115–134.

Hunt, H. T. (2000). Experiences of radical personal transformation in mysticism, religious conversion and psychosis: A review of the varieties, processes and consequences of the numinous. *Journal of Mind and Behavior, 21*, 353–398.

Hunt, H. T. (2004a). *Lives in Spirit: Precursors and dilemmas of a secular Western Mysticism*. Albany, NY: State University of New York Press.

Hunt, H.T. (2005). Synaesthesia, metaphor, and consciousness. *Journal of Consciousness Studies, 12*, 26–45.

Hunt, H.T. (2007). "Dark nights of the soul": Phenomenology and neurocognition of spiritual suffering in mysticism and psychosis. *Review of General Psychology, 17*(2), 209–234.

Hunt, H.T. (2011). Synesthesias, synesthetic imagination, and metaphor in the context of individual cognitive development and societal collective consciousness. *Intellectica, 1*, 95–138.

Hunt, H.T. (2016). "The heart has its reasons": Transpersonal experience as higher development of social-personal intelligence, and its response to the inner solitude of consciousness. *Journal of Transpersonal Psychology, 48*, 1–25.

James, W. (1890). *The principles of psychology.* New York: Dover (Republished by Harvard University press: Cambridge, MA, 1981).

Johnson, M. (1987). *The body in the mind: The bodily bases of meaning, imagination and reason.* Chicago: University of Chicago Press.

Jung, C. (1964). *Man and his symbols.* New York: Doubleday.

Kahan, T., & LaBerge, S. (1994). Lucid dreaming as metacognition: Implications for cognitive science. *Consciousness and Cognition, 3*(2), 246–264.

Kandinsky, W. (1977). *Concerning the spiritual in art.* New York, NY: Dover (Originally published in English in 1914, under the title *The Art of Spiritual Harmony.* London: Constable & Co.).

Kandinsky, W. (1994). In C. Lindsay, & P. Virgo (Eds.), *Kandinsky: Complete writings on art.* Boston: Da Capo Press.

Kennedy, J. (1983). What can we learn about pictures from the blind? *American Scientist, 71*, 19–26.

Kinney, L. (1952). Developing problem-solving skills in adolescents. *The High School Journal, 35*, 113–119.

Klee, P. (1964). In F. Klee (Ed.), *The diaries of Paul Klee 1898–1918.* Berkeley & Los Angeles: University of California Press.

Klee, P. (1973). *Pedagogical sketchbook.* London: Faber.

Kolb, B., & Wishaw, I. (1998). Brain plasticity and behavior. *Annual Review of Psychology, 49*, 43–64.

LaBerge, S., & DeGracia, D. J. (2000). Varieties of lucid dreaming experience. In *Individual differences in conscious experience* (pp. 269–307).

Lakoff, G. (1987). *Women, fire and dangerous things: What categories reveal about the mind.* Chicago: University of Chicago Press.

Lakoff, G., & Johnson, M. (1980). The metaphorical structure of the human conceptual system. *Cognitive Science, 4*, 195–208.

Lakoff, G., & Johnson, M. (1999). *Philosophy in the flesh.* New York, NY: Basic Books.

Lipscomb, S., & Kendall, R. (1994). Perceptual judgment of the relationship between musical and visual components in film. *Psychomusicology, 13*, 60–98.

Logfren, K. (2015). *2015 Video game statistics and trends whose playing what and why.* http://www.bigfishgames.com/blog/2015-global-video-game-stats-whos-playing-what-and-why/.

Logfren, K. (2016). *2016 Video game statistics and trends: Whose playing what and why.* http://www.bigfishgames.com/blog/2016-video-game-statistics-and-trends/.

Lombard, M., & Ditton, T. (1997). At the heart of it all: The concept of telepresence Online. *Journal of Computer Mediated Communication, 3*, 2.

Marcel, A. (1988). Phenomenal experience and functionalism. In A. Marcel, & E. Bisiach (Eds.), *Consciousness in contemporary science* (pp. 121–158). New York, NY, US: Clarendon Press/Oxford University Press.

Marks, L. (1978). *The unity of the senses.* New York: Academic Press.

Marshall, S., & Cohen, A. (1988). Effects of musical soundtracks on attitudes toward animated geometric figures. *Music Perception, 6*, 95–112.

Maslow, A. (1962). *Toward a psychology of being*. Princeton, NJ: Van Nostrand.

Munte, T., Altenmüller, E., & Jänke, L. (2002). The musician's brain as a model of neuroplasticity. *Nature Reviews Neuroscience, 3*, 473–478.

Ortiz de Gortari, A. (2007). Psychosocial implications of online video games. In *Paper presented at games in action (conference), Gothemburg, Sweden*.

Ortiz de Gortari, A., & Griffiths, M. (2012). An introduction to game transfer phenomena in video game playing. In J. I. Gackenbach (Ed.), *Video game play and consciousness* (pp. 217–244). NY: Nova Science Publishers.

Ortiz de Gortari, A., & Griffiths, M. (2015). Game transfer phenomena and its associated factors: An exploratory empirical online survey study. *Computers in Human Behavior, 51*, 195–202.

Piaget, J. (1962). *Play, dreams and imitation in childhood*. New York, NY: Norton.

Piaget, J. (1963). *The psychology of intelligence*. New York, NY: Basic Books.

Piaget, J. (1981). *Intelligence and affectivity: Their relationship during child development*. Palo Alto, CA: Annual Reviews.

Poels, K., Ijsselsteijn, W., & de Kort, Y. (2015). World of warcraft, the aftermath: How game elements transfer into perceptions, associations and (day)dreams in the everyday life of massively multiplayer online role-playing game players. *New Media & Society, 17*, 1137–1153.

Preston, J. M. (1998). From mediated environments to the development of consciousness. In J. Gackenbach (Ed.), *Psychology and the internet: Intrapersonal, interpersonal and transpersonal perspectives* (pp. 255–291). New York: Academic Press.

Preston, J. M. (2007). From mediated environments to the development of consciousness II. In J. Gackenbach (Ed.), *Psychology and the internet: Intrapersonal, interpersonal and transpersonal perspectives* (pp. 277–307). New York: Academic Press.

Preston, J. M. (2012). Absorbed in video game play: From immersion to the development of consciousness. In J. Gackenbach (Ed.), *Video game play and consciousness* (pp. 143–170). New York: Nova Science Publishers.

Preston, J. M., & Cull, A. (1998). Virtual environments: Influences on apparent motion after-effects. In *Canadian psychological association conference, Edmonton, AB*.

Preston, J. M., & Evans, J. (2001). Moving pictures: Music's effect on viewers. In *Canadian psychological association conference, Quebec City, QC*.

Pritchard, R., Heron, W., & Hebb, D. (1960). Visual perception approached by the method of stabilized images. *Canadian Journal of Psychology, 14*, 66–77.

Ramonth, S. (1985). Absorption in directed daydreaming. *Journal of Mental Imagery, 9*, 67–86.

Ramsey, J., & Hunt, H. T. (1993). Cognitive and social determinants of metaphor. In *American psychological association annual meeting, Toronto, August*.

Reed, E. S. (1988). *James Gibson and the psychology of perception*. New Haven: Yale University Press.

Revonsuo, A. (2006). *Inner presence: Consciousness as a biological phenomenon*. Cambridge: MIT Press.

Rimbaud, A. (1884). *Les Voyelles (the Vowels)*. www.poetryfoundation.org/bio/arthur-rimbaud.

Rimington, A. W. (1912). *Color music: The art of mobile color*. London: Hutchison & Co. Available at https://archive.org/details/colouartof00rimi.

Riva, G., Waterworth, J., Waterworth, E., & Mantovani, F. (2009). From intention to action: The role of presence. *New Ideas in Psychology*, 1–14.

Roche, S., & McConkey, K. (1990). Absorption: Nature, assessment, and correlates. *Journal of Personality and Social Psychology, 59*, 91–101.

Rosser, J., Lynch, P., Cuddihy, L., Gentile, D., Klonsky, j., & Merrell, R. (2007). The impact of video games on training surgeons in the 21st century. *Archives of Surgery, 142*, 181–186.

Shepard, R. (1978). Externalization of mental images and the act of creation. In B. Randhawa, & W. Coffman (Eds.), *Visual learning, thinking and communication* (pp. 133–189). New York: Academic Press.

Smith, J. (1999). Movie music as moving music: Emotion, cognition and the film score. In C. Plantinga, & G. Smith (Eds.), *Passionate views: Film, cognition and emotion* (pp. 146–167). Baltimore, MD: Johns Hopkins University Press.

Stein, B., & Meredith, M. (1993). *Merging of the senses.* Cambridge, MA: MIT Press.

Stein, M. (1974). *Communication and line drawing test.* New York: Behavioral Publications Inc.

Strobach, T., Frensch, P. A., & Schubert, T. (2012). Video game practice optimizes executive control skills in dual-task and task switching situations. *Acta Psychologica, 140,* 13–24.

Strobach, T., & Schubert, T. (2015). Experience in action games and the effects on executive control. *The Inquisitive Mind, 8.* http://www.in-mind.org/article/experience-in-action-games-and-the-effects-on-executive-control.

Sungur, H., & Boduroglu, A. (2012). Action video game players form more detailed representation of objects. *Acta Psychologica, 139,* 327–334.

Tellegen, A., & Atkinson, G. (1974). Openness to absorbing and self-altering experiences ("absorption"), a trait related to hypnotic susceptibility. *Journal of Abnormal Psychology, 83,* 268–277.

Thayer, J., & Levinson, R. (1983). Effects of music on psychophysiological responses to a stressful film. *Psychomusicology, 3,* 44–52.

Turkle, S. (1984). *The second self: Computers and the human spirit.* New York: Simon & Shuster.

Ventura, M., Shute, V. J., & Zhao, W. (2013). The relationship between video game use and a performance-based measure of persistence. *Computers & Education, 60,* 52–58.

Vitouch, O. (2001). When your ear sets the stage: Musical context effects in film perception. *Psychology of Music, 29,* 70–83.

Werner, H., & Kaplan, B. (1963). *Symbol formation.* New York: Wiley.

Woodworth, R. (1906). Imageless thought. *Journal of Philosophy, Psychology and Scientific Method, 3,* 161–165.

Wright, T., Blakely, D., & Boot, W. (2012). The effects of action video game play on vision and attention. In J. Gackenbach (Ed.), *Video game play and consciousness* (pp. 217–244). NY: Nova Science Publishers.

Zaparoli, G., & Reatto, L. (1969). The apparent movement between visual and acoustic stimulus and the problems of intermodal relations. *Acta Psychologica, 29,* 256–267.

Zeigler, B. (2009). *1998 Was the best year in the history of gaming.* http://doublebuffered.com/2009/02/26/1998-was-the-best-year-in-the-history-of-gaming/.

Zietz, K. (1931). Mutual influences of color and sound experiences: Studies in experimentally induced synesthesia. *Zeitschrift für Psychologie, 121,* 257–356.

CHAPTER 12

Looking for the Ultimate Display: A Brief History of Virtual Reality

Johnathan Bown[1], Elisa White[2], Akshya Boopalan[2]
[1]Edmonton North Primary Care Network, Edmonton, AB, Canada; [2]MacEwan University, Edmonton, AB, Canada

Throughout recorded history, we have created ways to bring imagined worlds and stories into our own reality in the forms of art, literature, and, more recently, digital media. Humans seem to value this process highly, so much so that the names of ancient masters of art still resonate through our schools. Each medium has intrinsic limitations to how the creator's vision of an alternate reality can be reflected, and it seems that humans continually search for a medium more realistic and more immersive than before. That is what this chapter is about: the developmental history of virtual reality (VR) technologies. From storytelling to modern VR devices, artists and inventors tried to capture their audiences by making them feel present in an alternate reality. Presence, as described later, can be measured in multiple ways, each relying on the sophistication of the underlying technology. As expected, inducing a subjective sense of presence has become more reliable as technology advances. We may be at a time in history where presence can be maintained constantly during the use of certain technologies, yet vast room for improvement remains. This idea will be explored first, in the next section.

THE ULTIMATE DISPLAY

The idea of VR and the pursuit to create may come from an inner motivation to obtain the *Ultimate Display*, as put forward by Ivan Sutherland (Biocca, Kim, & Levy, 1995). Such an invention would be a mode of media that is an *essential copy* and allows the user to transcend physical limits. In other words, it is something that stimulates our senses in such a way that we perceive the simulacrum as being real and seemingly grants freedom, or abilities, beyond the limits of the user's physical reality. For those familiar with *Star Trek*, the holodeck might be the Ultimate Display; the holodeck is a computer programmable room that uses light and force fields to recreate a full sensory experience of

Boundaries of Self and Reality Online
ISBN 978-0-12-804157-4
http://dx.doi.org/10.1016/B978-0-12-804157-4.00012-8

anything. The idea of such an experience is naturally appealing to humans, and perhaps that is why technology has attempted to move in that direction.

As part of the Ultimate Display, an essential copy can be thought of as a perfect rendition of an object that fools all senses into perceiving it as real. Physical transcendence in this case is the desire to be someone or something else beyond what you are in the physical world, going beyond what you are capable of in real life. Physical transcendence is a personal, self-only experience and is believed to be achieved by going past all your senses or to even change them altogether (Biocca et al., 1995). The ultimate display would provide the experience of a manufactured environment so perfect that, as Leone Battista Alberti says, it becomes a window to the imagined world.

In the quest toward the Ultimate Display, humans have captured aspects of it by physical means such as film, or by abstract means such as narrative literature (Biocca et al., 1995). On the other hand, perhaps the closest we have come to realizing it can be found in the dreaming experience. When dreaming, our senses are tricked into perceiving imagined worlds that are constructed from what appears to be essential copies. In dreams, we sometimes experience physical transcendence by embodying different bodies, by defying laws of physical reality, and sometimes even by having spiritual experiences within dreams (Hobson, Pace-Schott, & Stickgold, 2000; McNamara, McLaren, & Durso, 2007; Revensou, 2006). Unfortunately, for the majority of us, dreams cannot be controlled or experienced on demand. They are also an individual experience, so they leave a lot to be desired if they are contending for the title of Ultimate Display.

VR technology offers an experience approaching, ever so gradually, the Ultimate Display. With modern technology, VR equipment changes the perspective of the person wearing the headgear so that they see a virtual world. Principally, the development of technology has been aimed at improving the visual fidelity of the simulated worlds, trying to be so perfect that it creates an essential copy of an imagined world. If a user can be so present in the experience of a VR world that they believe it to be real, then the ability to move around the 3-D environment according to any alien physical laws the programmer chooses to simulate in real time, VR technology may be the closest we have been to realizing the Ultimate Display.

THE INGREDIENTS FOR PRESENCE

In dreams and in any type of communication media, *presence* is an important and common factor. Presence is a felt sense of authentic reality that would result from engagement with sophisticated media. Although the term presence is thought to be coined by the VR movement, it is not restricted to VR alone and has always been incorporated in how we perceive ourselves in the physical world. To be present is to be continually aware of one's surroundings as being outside of their self, whether physically or virtually. To perceive the external environment, a person has to be aware of the boundary that separates self from other. Some accounts of spiritual transcendence have even been reported where the person becomes so aware of their perceptual surroundings in relation to their consciousness that they have a sense of physically transcending themselves (Jonas–Simpson, 2010; Piqué i Collado, 2015). Inside a virtual world, the self–other dichotomy can be manipulated to simulate the bending or breaking of our universe's physical laws, thus transcendence following presence.

Presence is also best felt when the perceived imagery is viewed with the same complexity as you would perceive visual reality, which will be explored later in this chapter. Something that could be considered an essential copy would be viewed the same way because that object would emulate the way we normally perceive our real environments (Biocca et al., 1995). That is why it is important to consider presence when talking about the concept of an Ultimate Display; a sense of presence is likely to result from perceiving something that is an essential copy.

We can better manipulate presence in VR when we know exactly what it means to be present. Steuer (1992) used three categories to understand what contributes to feelings of presence: vividness, interactivity, and user characteristics. Technologies that produce experiences for the user that satisfy criteria within these domains (and adapt to user characteristics) will therefore induce a greater sense of presence and ultimately inch our media toward the ultimate display.

Vividity is a measure of the richness and complexity of visual elements in the virtual environment produced by the technology. Clarity and smooth eye movements provided by the technology would help the user experience the vividity of the virtual environment; these metrics are related primarily to the hardware that is being used, but occasionally also to the efficiency of the software programming. The cues generated by a virtual environment, whether perceptual or conceptual, are another important aspect of vividity. They provide a sense of cause and effect, and purpose, in the world. Perceptual cues are external sensory stimuli that evoke physiological reactions, such as perceiving a large spider, which may cause a panic reaction. Conceptual cues are information-based stimuli that would otherwise evoke physiological reactions, such as reading about the description of a large spider. Perceptual cues are especially important in VR because evoking an appropriate response to a virtual stimulus has been shown to increase the sense of presence. Feeling present in an environment can increase fear reactions to stimuli, but fear to the stimuli itself increases felt sense of presence, a bidirectional relationship (Peperkorn, Diemer, & Mühlberger, 2015; Yoon, Choi, & Oh, 2015). Researchers have also looked at how different regions of our brain respond to VR cues [using 3-D models on computers, not head-mounted displays (HMDs)]. Their results show that the visual processing centers of the brain were the most active, which suggests the primacy of imagery in the virtual environment for increasing presence. Indeed, with more cues or visual information needing to be processed, reports of feeling present increase (Clemente et al., 2014).

Interactivity, a measure of how much the user can cause an effect on the virtual environment, contributes to the sense of presence. A study by Huang and Yu-Ting (2013) found that increased interactivity with a virtual environment increased the feeling of flow for the user. Flow, which is the experience of prolonged focus on a task without being distracted, has also been linked to the feeling of presence. Significant flow seems to provide a significant sense of presence for the task at hand. Of note, flow has been shown to significantly increase when users feel as though they are physically touching an object in a virtual environment, such as using haptic feedback methods in medical simulation games or shooting games. This feeling can be produced even by simple methods, such as a vibrating controller when holding down the shoot button in a video game like *Call of Duty* (Jin, 2011). Free movement, another form of interaction, in a virtual environment has also been shown to have a positive and significant effect on felt presence (Clemente et al., 2014). Proprioception, the internal awareness of relative position we all have, and a significant contributor to presence, is one of the main targets in the development of VR media. Proprioception gives us a sense that we are fully present within an environment in a real and tangible way, and as we become accustomed to the interactive dynamics of a virtual environment, this sense grows. The induction of proprioceptive sensations would be a powerful way to trick the brain into thinking that it is present in a VR (Wright, 1987).

Another good way to understand and improve the felt sense of presence in VR is by understanding how a user's characteristics play a role. Users tend to be individually unique in many regards, such as personality traits, technology proficiency, and even cognitive styles, among others. These differences alter the way they perceive a different reality, especially in a computer-mediated environment like VR. A sense of presence within the virtual world occurs because of how our minds combine cues and features of the virtual environment to create mental representations, similar to how we create mental representations of our normal, physical reality. This is best felt in projection-based VR systems like the Oculus Rift (Chafkin, 2015; Revonsuo, 2006). A user's cognitive style, which is the way they analyze and mentally represent an environment, can be put into two categories: object visualization and spatial visualization.

Object visualization style types are most impacted by the vividity of a reality, as they will focus on visual features of objects. Spatial visualization style types tend to analyze the spatial layout between different objects to determine the environment's realism, therefore having expectations that the virtual space would have the same complexity and interrelationships as it does in reality. Thus, it is important to keep both styles in mind when creating a virtual environment, since if it corresponds to how we typically analyze real-world information, we will more likely feel like we are actually in that environment (Yoon et al., 2015).

The essential copy is something that perfectly fools the senses, but it is not a binary concept; the proximity of any particular media to the essential copy can be measured on a spectrum. Physical transcendence is freeing the mind of the constraints of the body. VR technologies have taken steps in an effort to completely fool the senses and take the mind where the body cannot go, from panoramic paintings to modern technologies. Because there were so many steps along the way to creating today's VR technology, it would be impossible to name them all here. Instead, we will touch on a few of the steps along the way to illustrate how VR technology has pushed boundaries to create alternate worlds that feel real. The quest toward the Ultimate Display is a staircase, leading ever upwards, built from art, technology, and the visionaries, to create worlds from imagination that transcend the rules of physical reality.

FIRST STEPS IN VIRTUAL REALITY

Storytelling is the internal process of creating a world and sharing it with others, which may be considered the first VR. It is the process of being guided into the imagination of another person who is facilitating the creative process. Yet, when one hears a story, a certain amount that the listener incorporates into their imagined world is unique to them, which is a reflection of the individual's life experiences. A storyteller may link together concepts and rough details of a virtual world for the listener, but many blank details are left to the listener's imagination. As technologies take the place of storytellers, less and less is left to the user to create. The mental bandwidth required to imagine the VR (i.e., imagining scenes, faces, objects, colors, etc.) is decreased, while sensory information is increased. Arguably, this shift frees up high-level cognitive faculties for other tasks such as reflective processing, meaning-making, or greater emotional involvement, processes that tend to occur while we interact with natural reality and, presumably, an Ultimate Display.

Panoramic paintings are an early example of VR technology that provided shared imagery. Panoramic painting became wildly popular in the late 1800s and early 1900s after they were invented by Robert Barker. Barker began construction, in 1792, of an entire building (a rotunda) dedicated to creating the illusion of immersing oneself into a different place. Imagine that, as you enter a building, you descend down some stairs followed by a narrow, long, and dark corridor. At the end is a spiral staircase that leads you to a platform. Atop this platform, all you see around you is a large 360 degree painting, and nothing more. The paintings were often 15 m high and 100 m long (Woests, 2009). The light source from above was hidden from sight by a shade or a roof, which was of a deliberate size so that the edge of the roof met the top of the painting to help the illusion that you were not just in a room.

The first of these rotundas was of a painted scene of Edinburg, Scotland. As popularity for this new form of entertainment grew, more such circular buildings were built in many of the world's great cities, featuring exotic landscapes, famous battles, and important cities. After some time, artists began to incorporate props in front of their images to give their work added depth, which created a more realistic experience for the viewer (Woeste, 2009). For their day, these panoramic paintings were a superior illusion. Panoramas took still imagery to a new level by placing the viewer into the center of the image, allowing for the viewer to feel present in the scene rather than simply observing it from afar. It was reported that Queen Charlotte said it made her feel seasick (Altick, 1978), which could be interpreted as a primordial form of "cybersickness," something that remains a problem yet to be solved by VR technology. In the 19th century, hundreds of panoramas were painted, but interest in panoramas declined due to the advent of cinematography, which recorded reality much quicker and in a process that was much more straightforward ("The Panorama in History", n.d.).

Panoramas were built in a time where film and television did not exist, photography was in its infancy, and travel at the speed we know it today was simply impossible. Panoramas were a first of their kind, and on such a grand scale, to induce a sense of traveling to another time and place without having to travel too far; thus, they included some degree of physical transcendence. Indeed, in terms of a VR technology, panoramas were relatively robust. Consider that they could often be quite vivid and complex, which itself enhances the quality of them as an essential copy. However, interactivity (i.e., one of the factors in inducing a sense of presence) is missing, aside from being able to turn in place and view a different scene.

Stereoscopic 3-D photos were another popular form of entertainment in the late 1800s and early 1900s. They were often provided in a device that presented slightly different images to each eye to create the illusion of depth (e.g., a View-Master toy). In 1838, Charles Wheatstone laid the foundation for how VR headsets would work, using the concept of stereoscopic images, which built upon the idea of binocular vision (or, more specifically, parallax). Of interest, the exploration of binocular illusions was explored as far back as ancient Greece, when the mathematician Euclid explained this principle (Gamber & Withers, 1996; "Stereoscope", n.d.).

The perception of depth makes the experience more vivid, though in a way that is mediated by the user's capacity for spatial visualization. Given that these images were the first major realization of a 3-D representation of reality, they can be considered a big step toward creating an essential copy.

After Queen Victoria took a fancy to the stereoscope at the Crystal Palace Exposition in 1851, stereo viewing was massively popular in Britain; there was at least one in every middle-class or upper-class home in the 19th century (Gamber & Withers, 1996). This was a 19th-century version of the first cheap, take-home, VR system. Imagine yourself, before airplanes could take you to any corner of the globe in a day, able to sit back in your favorite chair and see all the wonders of the world before your eyes. The new invention allowed for visual transportation (i.e., physical transcendence) to another place. Still, interactivity was missing.

The next step in taking immersion to the next level came from Morton Heilig, who is often regarded as the father of VR (Carlson, 2007). He had a vision for creating a multisensory theater experience, one that would be far more immersive than anything that has been seen or experienced before. He wanted to create a fully immersive, multisensory theater experience that encompassed 3-D images, stereo sound, wind, smells, and vibrations. "Open your eyes, listen, smell, and feel-sense the world in all its magnificent colors, depth, sounds, odors, and textures this is the cinema of the future!"

(Heilig, 1955). He ultimately created two versions of his vision: the Telesphere Mask and the Sensorama. According to Heilig's patent:

> *"The Telesphere Mask consisted of: A hollow casing, a pair of optical units, a pair of united television tubes, a pair of ear phones, and a pair of air discharge nozzles, all co-acting to cause the user to comfortably see the images, hear the sound effects and to be sensitive the air discharge of said nozzle."*
>
> **U.S. Patent No. 2955156 (1960).**

Despite the successful creation of the Telesphere Mask, Heilig depriori-tized it so he could create something even more advanced, the Sensorama. The Sensorama simulator was patented in 1962, and Heilig had to invent a 3-D camera (a side-by-side dual film camera; Turi, 2014) and projector in order to see his vision come to life (Brockwell, 2016). He made five films dedicated to the Sensorama, which included a motorcycle ride through New York City, a bicycle ride, a ride of a dune buggy, a helicopter ride over Century City, and a dance by a belly dancer (Carlson, 2007). The experi-ence of the motorcycle ride through New York included a seat that would vibrate as a motorbike would, air that would rush through the user's hair, and smells of the road and a passing bistro.

A gentleman by the name of Howard Rheingold tried the Sensorama in the 1980s, and he said that "the motorcycle driver was reckless, which made me very mildly uncomfortable, much to my delight" (Brockwell, 2016). Rheingold's discomfort is reflective of his immersion into the experience, perhaps feeling present with the VR. Arguably, the vividity of the scene was heretofore unsurpassed, and the experience was closer to an essential copy than anything before it. The Sensorama was another giant step toward the Ultimate Display, yet the missing ingredient to induce a strong sense of presence, interactivity, was still lacking.

Heilig saw the potential of his invention beyond entertainment. He envisioned his machine to be used as a training device for the armed forces, laborers, and students, where they could train without being subjected to the hazards of dangerous situations (U.S. Patent No. 3050870, 1962), or it could have been used by companies to showcase new products (Brockwell, 2016). However, despite the big plans Heilig had for his inventions, he was virtually ignored by financial investors and large corporations. Regardless, Heilig pressed on. In an interview of April 2016, Heilig's wife, Marianne, recounts the struggle of how they fought to keep the dream alive. They were able to install a coin-operated unit at Universal Studios, where it was rather successful. Eventually, the Heiligs moved the Sensorama to locations such as Time Square, the Santa Monica pier, and into various arcades.

Although the Sensorama was successful, quarters were not enough to support the expensive machines full of custom-built parts by Heilig himself, so when the machines broke down, that was it (Brockwell, 2016).

THE MODERN AGE OF VIRTUAL REALITY

Around the same time that Heilig was creating the cinema of the future in 1961, the engineers Charles Comeau and James Bryan at Philco Corporation developed an HMD called Headsight. This helmet incorporates a closed-circuit camera linked to a magnetic tracking system that would turn the camera in three dimensions: pitch, yaw, and roll (Rid, 2016). The image was created by using spherical mirrors, which projected a virtual 10-inch-high image that appeared to be 1.5 ft in front of the observer (Rid, 2016). The head gear was also intended to remotely view dangerous situations. One of the engineers placed a camera on top of the company building, and when he leaned over and looked down (from the safety of sitting in the lab), he said it felt "kind of creepy" (Rid, 2016). Headsight introduced interactivity into the realm of VR technology. However, the images were simply camera feeds, so the Headsight does not transport the viewer into another reality. It does, however, lay some of the foundation for interactive media. Therefore, the Headsight is another large leap toward the Ultimate Display, as is transcends the physical (e.g., placing the user's vision in a dangerous remote situation) and allows the user to control the visual experience.

In a speech given by Ivan Sutherland at the Proto Awards, he recalls seeing an experiment with a similar device, where a camera was mounted on rooftop, aimed at two people playing catch (Robertson, 2015). The observer, sitting in an office chair in another building, moved his head back and forth and was able to watch the game as the camera translated his head movements. At one point, one of the players threw the ball directly toward the camera, at which point, the observer, safe in another room, ducked out of the way. This is a strong example of presence. Upon seeing this, Sutherland was inspired to incorporate computers into HMDs.

Sutherland, in 1965, created the first HMD to incorporate computer technology to mediate a VR system, which came to be known as the "Sword of Damocles." The name arises from the Greek story of Damocles, which is a rather frightening and amusing comparison. In the story, a sword was suspended in the air by a hair, directly above the King's head, and at any moment, the hair could break, killing the king (Skurzynski, 1994; "Sutherland's Sword of Damocles" n.d.). Similarly, Sutherland's contraption consisted of a height–adjustable pole attached to the ceiling because the head gear was too heavy strap to someone's head. One can speculate that Sutherland may have mused that the device could fall and crush the user at any moment.

This was the first time that computers were used to display a real–world environment whose elements were augmented by a computer (Adams & Merklinghaus, 2014). The headgear itself was made of cathode ray tube monitors, two tracking systems (one mechanical, the other ultrasonic), eyeglass display optics, and a lot of computer programs and algorithms (Sutherland, 1968). Ultimately, Sutherland was able to project an ethereal cube (i.e., a transparent, 3-D wireframe cube) onto the semitransparent optic lenses to create the illusion that the cube was floating in the room (Sutherland, 1968). The graphics were primitive, the equivalent to the *Pong* videogame that came out in the 1970s. However, the 3-D cube would move and tilt, corresponding to the observer's head movements. Although the computer-generated graphics were primitive, it was ground-breaking. The technology to create an interactive 3-D image that changed and moved with the observer was the launchpad for future VR technology. By Sutherland's own admission, the Sword of Damocles was not especially immersive (Robertson, 2015), but the intention was not to create presence. Instead, this is an example of a technology that highlights advancements in interactivity and, perhaps, the quest for the essential copy. Though the represented cube lacked visual fidelity, it was an early demonstration of the digitalization of reality. Here, we have a digital object based on reality that exists entirely within software, obeying the laws of the program. Prior to this, no VR technology stood upon purely digital foundations, foundations that, arguably, could attain a level of vividity and interactivity unreachable by traditional mediums of art.

Twenty years later, Visual Programming Languages was one of the first companies to develop and sell VR products to consumers; it was founded by Jaron Lanier in 1984. Lanier is said to be a pioneer of, and coined the term, VR. This company developed the DataGlove, the EyePhone, and AudioSphere, devices that, when used together, create an immersive VR experience.

The DataGlove was wired with fiber optic cables on the back of the glove, which sent out tiny light beams as the wearer bent and moved their hands. A computer interpreted the beams of light and then generated an image on a small screen inside a helmet (i.e., the EyePhone) or onto a computer screen, where the user could watch a computer-generated image of their hand manipulate virtual objects in an entirely different place or environment (Sturman & Zeltzer, 1994). Two drawbacks limited the success of the DataGlove: it was too expensive for the average consumer (i.e., it cost thousands of dollars), and it was a one-size-fits-all glove (Burdea & Coiffet, 2003). The glove also lacked tactile feedback, which would likely reduce any felt sense of presence for being so inconsistent with expectations of reality.

The EyePhone used two small LCD television screens (stereoscopic), which were viewed through lenses to give the illusion of depth. The EyePhone allowed observers to enter into the computer-generated world; however, the graphics were typical of 3-D graphics c.1980s (e.g., 360×240 pixels), and only generated 5–6 fps, compared to the 30 fps generated by TV sets at the time (Sorene, 2014). Although the EyePhone lacked the vividity as we know it today, it was superior to anything that came before for inducing presence through VR technology.

The EyePhone made use of the DataGlove to navigate the z-axis in the virtual world. The user could fly through the virtual environment by using their index finger to control direction and forward motion. Holding their thumb close to their palm made them fly faster, and placing their thumb away from their hand (i.e., straight out) made them stop (Certeras, 1990). Allowing users to control their flight in a virtual environment was a milestone toward transcending the physical limits of our reality because it added interactivity into an otherwise impossible physical action. The combination of these devices fulfilled many requirements for inducing presence, but perhaps fell short on measures of vividity. Visual quality and complexity (as well as complexity in interactivity) still had far to go.

In 1991, Sega announced that they were working on VR headgear, which was meant to be an add-on to the Sega Genesis console. The headset was equipped with duel LCD screens in the visor, stereo headphones, and inertial sensors to track and react to head movements ("Sega VR", n.d.). Unlike previous headsets, and other headsets at the time, the Sega VR headset was lightweight and comfortable to wear for extended periods. The original design was meant to look like Geordi La Forge's visor from Star Trek: The Next Generation (Hill, 2014).

Although the headset was comfortable and sleek, the design never made it out of the prototype stage. Despite the sophisticated technology, the onscreen graphics were unable to keep up with the gamers' head movements, which caused a form of motion sickness, dubbed cybersickness. There were reports that up to 40% of testers became cybersick while being immersed in the virtual environments (Horwitz, 2004). Thomas Piantanida, a scientist at the Stanford Research Institute International's Virtual Perception Program, called the headsets graphical output the "barfogenic zone" (Barras, 2014). However, the official report states that the sense of immersion was so realistic that it could potentially cause injury to users who were moving around while wearing the headset, which created a health hazard. The headset made its final appearance in 1993 at a Consumer Electronic show. Clearly, intentions toward the Ultimate Display were there, but the quality of technology was not.

The next attempt at VR headsets came from Nintendo's Virtual Boy, released in 1995, which was another commercial flop. Hiroshi Yamauchi, the past president of Nintendo Co. Ltd., said:

"It has always been Nintendo's strategy to introduce new hardware systems only when technological breakthroughs allow us to offer innovative entertainment at a price that appeals to a worldwide audience. Virtual Boy delivers this and more. It will transport game players into a 'virtual utopia' with sights and sounds unlike anything they've ever experienced -- all at the price of a current home video game system."

"Virtual Boy" (2004).

However, The Virtual Boy did not perform as described, and the product quickly ceased production. In order to attempt a lightweight HMD, Nintendo had to forego conventional displays, as they were too power hungry and heavy. Instead, they used two oscillating mirror LED arrays, one for each eye. The oscillating mirrors, moving back and forth 50 times per second, used the reflection of the LED to sweep across the visual field. This created a bright, sharp image with high resolution for a low price. However, the display was only capable of displaying red graphics on a black background (Edwards, 2015).

The Virtual Boy also came with a short stand; the head-mounting straps were sold separately ("Virtual Boy", 2004), which made gameplay rather uncomfortable for the user, who had to lean into the headset at all times. Any feelings of physical transcendence would be undermined by a sore back and shoulders. Another problem with the Virtual Boy was that the eyestrain that came with using the headgear for extended periods of time caused headaches. This forced Nintendo to include a warning that said:

"This product MUST NOT be used by children under the age of (7) years. Artificial stereo vision displays may not be safe for children and may cause serious, permanent damage to their vision."

"Virtual Boy" (2004).

A big step towards even greater interactivity in VR technology came in 2001 with the SAS3™ (or SAS cube™), which was the first PC-based cubic room. The SAS cube was named "The Cave," which was in reference to Plato's allegory of the cave wherein he challenges our ideas of perception, reality, and illusion. It was a room full of projectors and sensors driven by computers that react to people in the room. The advancements in PC graphic developed by the gaming industry meant that a cluster of relatively inexpensive PCs could be used instead of large supercomputers to yield the processing power required for effective vividity and interaction (Jacobson & Lewis, 2005). The SAS3 system used rear projectors to cast stereoscopic images onto four screens, one of which being the floor. The continuous visual images synchronized across all screens produced a virtual landscape. Users wear 3-D glasses equipped with motion tracking sensors, which track head movement (Fuchs, Moreau, & Guitton. 2011). The stereoscopic images made the environment look 3-D, and sensors let users interact with objects and navigate the space (Robertson, 2001).

In the quest for the Ultimate Display, the SAS3 appears to nearly attain it. However, the complexity and vividity of the images was not on par with reality, nor were there other sensory inputs, such as tactile feedback. Nonetheless, the experience is something like a panoramic painting with interactivity. The priority, at that point, became the quality of the sensory input.

CURRENT VIRTUAL REALITY DEVICES

Presently, VR devices still follow the basic mechanisms shown by NASA in 1987. They are no longer limited to research or instructional purposes, but are now commercially available for a reasonable price. Their use in our daily lives is multifold, and this includes therapeutic and entertainment purposes. If you consider the variety of movies, games, and social media, the use of VR has already been so embedded in our daily activities that it is altering our own reality.

Palmer Luckey is responsible for the creation of the Oculus Rift, once a relatively simple do-it-yourself kit and now the VR headset that combines realistic imagery with hand motion technology similar to the NASA headgear in 1987. The differences are extreme, however. Quality of image has improved significantly, and the sense of presence is an experience only felt by actually putting on the headset (Fenlon, 2015; Grayson, 2015; Rebato, 2015). Created at first to play video games, Luckey and his board members managed to get Facebook's Mark Zuckerberg to invest in the technology because of the consequences it could have in our lives. As Zuckerberg acknowledged openly, social networking sites connect people across the world in an intimate and real way. Social media brings news into focus, as well as entertainment and other information that is catered according to each individual. Like phones have revolutionized communication, technology such as Oculus Rift may have already created another revolution (Chafkin, 2015). Since the invention of the Oculus Rift, other companies, such as Samsung, Google, and Steam, have now come out with their own VR products offering similar experiences.

Type of content and platform is the largest difference among VR headsets. Companies like Google and Oculus try to connect a 360 degree experience to mobile phones (Google, 2015; Llmer, 2014). Google targets android phones with an app that connects to Google Cardboard. Google Cardboard, along with Cardboard Camera, the mobile application, creates user-made VR experiences by doing exactly what all VR headsets basically do: turn 2-D images, in this case panoramas, into 3-D images by using slightly different angles in each lens. The user can even add audio to these images to enhance the sensory experience of being in the moment the picture was taken. However, unlike the Oculus Rift, the user cannot move within the virtual environment freely, only look around 360 degrees with realistic depth perception. This is perhaps an even more advanced iteration of the panorama because, other than images, if Google Cardboard is used within YouTube videos, the experience is as though the user is in the center while everything is moving around them (Hollister, 2015). This is possible because of cameras specifically made to take videos in 360 degrees in real time.

Google Cardboard is one VR headset that is already available for purchase and use. Google Cardboard is very inexpensive (i.e., approximately $20) compared to any other VR headset, but that is primarily because it is literally made of cardboard (Google, 2015). Still, Google Cardboard has a broad reach among consumers, and more people are very likely to buy this headset than others. This is because the other headsets are significantly more expensive and come with other factors, such as specific compatibilities of PC being used, other required add-on products to improve the virtual experience, and motion sickness (Chafkin, 2015; Gamer, 2015)

The Samsung Gear VR headset is quite similar to Google Cardboard. It combines Oculus technology of depth perception and screen resolution with the Samsung Note phone's VR apps (Llmer, 2014). It is more immersive than Google Cardboard and gives excellent depth perception, but there is no motion tracking for Samsung Gear. It cannot be used for intensive gaming, but it is a very good way to experience landscapes and videos.

Valve, the company responsible for Steam, which is a widely used and popular gaming platform, also released their version of VR technology, namely the HTC Vive. Carlos Rebato (2015), a blogger from Gizmodo, believes that the HTC Vive is above any other virtual headset he has tried because of the heightened presence he experienced. According to his account, the Oculus Rift and Samsung Gear VR lag behind, comparatively. He describes the sense of presence and his body actually being there. This is because the HTC Vive has advanced positional tracking that uses sensors that are attached to the wall at a 90 degree angle. Most importantly, they have two controllers that have a touchpad and trigger and act as "virtual hands," and these controllers have trackers as well. Rebato calls it "the most impressive thing I've ever tried, bar none" (2015). The technology of HTC Vive is different from its contemporaries because users size the room they use the headset in so that the room becomes a mapped virtual space. Thus, the user can move around the room while the images on the display adjust to make the virtual environment follow closely with the user's movements. This, along with the hand use, creates a very immersive experience that makes users believe almost completely, if not fully, that they are actually present in that reality. The scaling size of objects compared to how they would appear in reality is accurate, which enhances the experience. Nathan Grayson (2015) of Kotaku tried the Vive just a few days later and was equally impressed by the sense of presence. The only issues both Rebato and Grayson had with HTC Vive is that the cords get tangled up and become a tripping hazard, and making VR items should be more tangible Rebato, 2015; Grayson, 2015).

So far, the headgears previously described create a 3-D VR environment from nothing material, a literal computer world. However, another type of headgear is becomingly increasingly popular in mainstream VR technology, and those are augmented reality devices. Augmented reality is different from VR because it superimposes virtual images onto the actual physical world. They do not create a new world, but add on to our surrounding reality. Although it is very new to the technology industry at the moment, what makes augmented reality so effective is the integration of already perceptually complex, real 3-D environments with virtual elements to create something believable. The experience constantly exposes the user to the boundary between real and unreal, and perhaps encourages an inclination in the user to simply accept everything as real.

The Microsoft HoloLens has been the most talked about augmented reality since its announcement in 2015 because the technology has been shown to already catch up to what many people have been calling "*Star Wars* holograms" (MacDonald, 2016; Orf, 2015). The HoloLens is a "self-contained" headgear (Microsoft, 2016) that uses spatial and object mapping of the surroundings and displays high-quality images and videos. The headgear produces audio appropriate to the distance of the object and action being produced. It also has the ability to interpret our hand movements and voice commands to control the objects displayed.

This augmented technology is not quite the Ultimate Display because it doesn't produce strong essential copies of things, and the images displayed are not realistic enough with the surroundings to be indistinguishable. Physical transcendence may be possible if the user considers themself to be another person in another world, but that would be much more difficult to do when the physical world is so clearly seen. However, as mentioned before, since the HoloLens uses the real world, the complexity of the environment is vivid and therefore likely to induce feelings of presence. The HoloLens is clearly meant to interact with the real environment in the most realistic way, and any of the cognitive styles, such as object and spatial visualization types, would satisfactorily feel presence in such an environment (Biocca et al., 1995; Steuer, 1992; Yoon et al., 2015). The Microsoft HoloLens is quite expensive, however ($3000), as it would be for how good the technology is for our time.

Recently, augmented reality has reached the regular consumer base, in the form of a game called *Pokémon GO*. Within a weekend of its release, Pokémon Go had already reached major heights of popularity and was continuing to do so more than any previous consumer-based mobile application or virtual technology (Chen, 2016; Cranz, 2016). It was a strong example of augmented reality, as it used the actual surroundings of the user as the environment in which the Pokémon, the creature to be captured by the user, existed. The game kicked off the recent surge of interest in VR in a very big way (Chen, 2016; Pokémon, 2016). At the time of this writing, talks to combine the Microsoft HoloLens with the Pokémon GO game were underway (Cranz, 2016).

Returning to VR, the Oculus Rift is what started the recent bloom of VR interest (Chafkin, 2015; Handrahan, 2015). It gave users an incredible sense of presence and left them wanting more. All the recent HMDs have focused on the vividity of the images produced, with the Vive being the best so far. With their focus on depth perception and spatial navigation within the virtual environment, but in relation to your head or body's physical movements, the current HMDs have almost realized Biocca's essential copy, at least from a visual perspective.

However, because of the many flaws, such as clunky headgear, glitches in the software, cords, and physical objects getting in the way of movement, it is not as easy to be completely fooled into believing what you are seeing (Grayson, 2015). Interactivity is high with the VR headgears alone, but accessory hardware is also being developed to provide new ways to interact. For example, the Virtuix Omni Treadmill is a relatively compact, touch-sensitive, omnidirectional treadmill that creates the illusion of physical movement in a virtual environment (Sofka, 2015; Virtuix, 2014). Users wanting a freer range of physical movement with no restrictions, like Vive, would definitely enjoy this experience a lot more. There are also other examples of creating a physical experience with the VR, using haptical methods, such as the Realm System, which uses physical resistance as part of its contraption to give the user the illusion of actual arm movements within the virtual world (Buckley, 2015).

Other methods have been used in combination with virtual headgears to increase the sense of being present in a VR. For example, the *Six Flags* theme park in New England is using VR headsets with the *Superman* roller coaster ride, displaying images as though you are flying beside this fictional character while on the ride (Harris, 2016). Universal studios also has a Shrek 4-D theater experience, where they show a 3-D film in conjunction with "4-D" effects, such as moving seats and mist, meant to increase the feeling that they, the audience, are actually there (Universal Studious Orlando, 2016).

CONCLUSION

Human beings continue to climb toward the perfect representation of reality, transposed into artful, convenient, or entertaining experiences. The achievement of this, perhaps known as the Ultimate Display, combines the perfect sensory reproduction of something real with the bending or breaking of physical laws of nature. The feeling of presence is something that naturally arises when media is powerful enough to trick the mind into belief. We now possess, with the aid of computers, a potent ability to induce this feeling. Presence is the effect caused by perceiving an essential copy. Physical transcendence follows from that. In the past, humans have glimpsed at pieces of these ideas and perhaps experienced fleeting moments of presence. However, traditional art tends to lack the quality of being able to trick the viewer into thinking it is something other than itself; paint will be paint, stone will be stone. Digital media is a dance of electromagnetic waves that can look like anything at all.

Our steps toward the Ultimate Display have not been linear, nor have they been consistent. However, if presence is the marker, then the advent of modern HMDs marks a new paradigm for VR, one where users must no longer fight to suspend disbelief at what they are seeing; instead, they must learn to suspend belief that the VR world is real. Though, perhaps in a sense, VR worlds are real enough and what we take to be natural reality is not as clearly bounded as it seems. Art, social media, imagination, and dreams are all realms of existence, and we are the architects and interlopers of these worlds. Faster and faster, vehicles to the virtual realities are arriving and bringing with them new paradigms of experience as they carry us upwards and onwards to the Ultimate Display.

REFERENCES

Adams, R., & Merklinghaus, D. P. (2014). Augmenting virtual reality. *Military Technology*, *38*(12), 16–24.

Altick, R. D. (1978). *The shows of London*. Cambridge, MA: Belknap Press of Harvard University Press.

Barras, C. (March 27, 2014). *How virtual reality overcame its 'Puke Problem' [news blog]*. Retrieved from http://www.bbc.com/future/story/20140327-virtual-realitys-puke-problem.

Biocca, F., Kim, T., & Levy, M. R. (1995). The vision of virtual reality. In F. Biocca, & M. R. Levy (Eds.), *Communication in the age of virtual reality* (pp. 3–14). Hillsdale, NJ: Lawrence Erlbaum Associates, Inc.

Brockwell, H. (April 3, 2016). *Forgotten genius: The man who made a working VR machine in 1957 [news blog]*. Retrieved from http://www.techradar.com/news/wearables/forgotten-genius-the-man-who-made-a-working-vr-machine-in-1957-1318253.

Buckley, S. (March 5, 2015). *5 Ludicrous controllers that help you touch the virtual world [news blog]*. Retrieved from Gizmodo http://gizmodo.com/5-ludicrous-controllers-that-help-you-touch-the-virtual-1689562796.

Burdea, G. C., & Coiffet, P. (2003). *Virtual reality technology* (Vol. 1). Hoboken, NJ: John Wiley & Sons.

Carlson, W. (2007). *A critical history of computer graphics and animation [lecture notes]*. Ohio State University. Retrieved from https://design.osu.edu/carlson/history/lesson17.html.

Ceteras, S. (1990). Through the virtual looking glass. *ETC: A Review of General Semantics*, *47*(1), 67–71.

Chafkin, M. (September 30, 2015). *Why facebook's $2 billion bet on oculus rift might one day connect everyone on earth [online magazine]*. Retrieved from http://www.vanityfair.com/news/2015/09/oculus-rift-mark-zuckerberg-cover-story-palmer-luckey.

Chen, A. (July 11, 2016). *Pokemon go added $7.5 billion to Nintendo's value in two days [blog post]*. Retrieved from http://gizmodo.com/pokemon-go-added-7-5-billion-to-nintendos-value-in-two-1783439513.

Clemente, M., Rey, B., Rodríguez-Pujadas, A., Barros-Loscertales, A., Baños, R. M., Botella, C., et al. (2014). An fMRI study to analyze neural correlates of presence during virtual reality experiences. *Interacting With Computers*, *26*(3), 16.

Cranz, A. (July 11, 2016). *Pokémon go took this flagging tech mainstream [blog post]*. Retrieved from http://gizmodo.com/pokemon-go-just-made-augmented-reality-mainstream-1783440938.

Edwards, B. (August 21, 2015). *Unraveling the enigma of Nintendo's virtual boy, 20 Years later.* Retrieved from http://www.fastcompany.com/3050016/unraveling-the-enigma-of-nintendos-virtual-boy-20-years-later.

Fenlon, W. (March 05, 2015). *Steam VR hands-on: Valve overtakes oculus [blog post].* Retrieved from http://www.pcgamer.com/steamvr-hands-on-valve-overtakes-oculus/.

Fuchs, P., Moreau, G., & Guitton, P. (2011). *Virtual interfaces. Virtual reality: Concepts and technologies.* CRC Press.

Gamber, B., & Withers, K. (1996). *History of the stereopticon [webpage].* Retrieved from http://www.bitwise.net/~ken-bill/stereo.htm.

Gamer, P. C. (May 26, 2015). *Oculus rift—Everything you need to know [blog post].* Retrieved from http://www.pcgamer.com/oculus-rift-everything-you-need-to-know/.

Google. (December 03, 2015). *Step inside your photos with cardboard camera [blog].* Retrieved from https://googleblog.blogspot.ca/2015/12/step-inside-your-photos-with-cardboard.html.

Grayson, N. (March 06, 2015). *Valve's VR is seriously impressive. It's also got some issues [news blog].* Retrieved from http://kotaku.com/valves-vr-is-seriously-impressive-its-also-got-some-is-1689916512.

Handrahan, M. (September 22, 2015). *Collaboration vs. Competition: The battle for VR dominance begins [news blog].* Retrieved from http://www.gamesindustry.biz/articles/2015-09-22-collaboration-vs-competition-the-battle-for-vr-dominance-begins.

Harris, T. (May 26, 2016). *Best new theme park rides: Virtual reality, interactivity [blog post].* Retrieved from http://phys.org/news/2016-05-theme-virtual-reality-interactivity.html.

Heilig, M. (1955). *The cinema of the future.* Retrieved from https://gametechdms.files.wordpress.com/2014/08/w6_thecinemaoffuture_morton.pdf.

Heilig, M. (1960). (U.S. Patent No. 2955156). Washington, DC: U.S. Patent and Trademark Office.

Heilig, M. (1962). (U.S. Patent No. 3050870). Washington, DC: U.S. Patent and Trademark Office.

Hill, M. (November 24, 2014). *The Sega headset that never was.* Retrieved from http://www.gizmodo.co.uk/2014/11/the-sega-vr-headset-that-never-was/.

Hobson, J. A., Pace-Schott, E. F., & Stickgold, R. (2000). Dreaming and the brain: Toward a cognitive neuroscience of conscious states. *Behavioral And Brain Sciences, 23*, 793–842.

Hollister, S. (March 03, 2015). *YouTube's ready to blow your mind with 360-degree videos.* Retrieved from http://gizmodo.com/youtubes-ready-to-blow-your-mind-with-360-degree-videos-1690989402.

Horwitz, K. (December 28, 2004). *Sega VR: Great idea of wishful thinking?.* Retrieved from http://www.sega-16.com/2004/12/sega-vr-great-idea-or-wishful-thinking/.

Huang, E., & Yu-Ting, H. (2013). Interactivity and identification influences on virtual shopping. *International Journal Of Electronic Commerce Studies, 4*, 305–312.

Jacobson, J., & Lewis, M. (2005). Game engine virtual reality with CaveUT. *Compute, 38*(4), 79–82.

Jin, S. A. (2011). 'I feel present. Therefore, I experience flow:' A structural equation modeling approach to flow and presence in video games. *Journal of Broadcasting & Electronic Media, 55*(1), 114–136.

Jonas-Simpson, C. (2010). Awakening to space consciousness and timeless transcendent presence. *Nursing Science Quarterly, 23*, 195–200.

Llmer, E. (December 12, 2014). *Samsung gear VR review: Hell yes I will strap this phone to my face [news blog].* Retrieved from http://gizmodo.com/samsung-gear-vr-review-hell-yes-i-will-strap-this-phon-1670312012.

MacDonald, C. (2016). *Star wars-style moving holograms are here: Microsoft shows how HoloLens can bring distant family members into your home [blog post].* Retrieved from http://www.dailymail.co.uk/sciencetech/article-3513062/Star-Wars-style-moving-holograms-Microsoft-shows-HoloLens-bring-distant-family-members-home.html.

McNamara, P., McLaren, D., & Durso, K. (2007). Representation of the self in REM and NREM dreams. *Dreaming, 17*, 113–126.

Microsoft. (2016). *Microsoft Hololens [official website].* Retrieved from https://www.microsoft.com/microsoft-hololens/en-us.

Orf, D. (2015). *This Hololens tech brings us one step closer to star wars holograms [blog post].* Retrieved from http://gizmodo.com/this-hololens-tech-brings-us-one-step-closer-to-star-wa-1720835773.

Peperkorn, H. M., Diemer, J., & Mühlberger, A. (2015). Temporal dynamics in the relation between presence and fear in virtual reality. *Computers in Human Behavior, 48*, 542–547.

Piqué i Collado, J. (2015). The fleeting moment: The sacramental universe of music, from the aesthetic form to the empathetic event. *Review of Ecumenical Studies, Sibiu, 7*, 301–312.

Pokémon. (2016). *Pokémon go [blog post].* Retrieved from http://www.pokemon.com/us/pokemon-video-games/pokemon-go/.

Rebato, C. (March 04, 2015). *HTC Vive: Virtual reality that's so damn real I can't even handle it [news blog].* Retrieved from http://gizmodo.com/htc-vive-virtual-reality-so-damn-real-that-i-cant-even-1689396093.

Revonsuo, A. (2006). *Inner presence: Consciousness as a biological phenomenon.* Cambridge, MA: MIT Press.

Rid, T. (2016). *Rise of the machine: A cybernetic history.* New York, NY: W. W. Norton & Company.

Robertson, B. (2001). Immersed in art. *Computer Graphics World, 24*(11). Retrieved from http://www.cgw.com/Publications/CGW/2001/Volume-24-Issue-11-November-2001-/immersed-in-art.aspx.

Robertson, A. (October 8, 2015). *An 'ethereal cube' from the 1960s is the reason the oculus rift exists [news blog].* Retrieved from http://www.theverge.com/2015/10/8/9479129/ivan-sutherland-proto-awards-virtual-reality-speech.

Sega, V.R. (n.d.). Retrieved from http://segaretro.org/Sega_VR.

Skurzynski, G. (1994). Virtual reality. *Cricket, 21*(11), 42–46.

Sofka, S. (November 28, 2015). *Watch this guy walk across the fallout 4 wasteland using the virtuix omni treadmill [blog post].* Retrieved from http://nerdist.com/watch-this-guy-walk-across-the-fallout-4-wasteland-using-the-virtuix-omni-treadmill/.

Sorene, P. (2014). *Jaron Lanier's EyePhone: Head and glove virtual reality in the 1980s [blog post].* Retrieved from http://flashbak.com/jaron-laniers-eyephone-head-and-glove-virtual-reality-in-the-1980s-26180/.

Stereoscope. (n.d.). Retrieved from http://courses.ncssm.edu/gallery/collections/toys/html/exhibit01.htm.

Steuer, J. (1992). Defining virtual reality: Dimensions determining telepresence. *Journal of Communication, 42*(4), 73.

Sturman, D. J., & Zeltzer, D. (1994). A Survey of glove-based inputs. *IEEE Computer Graphics & Applications, 14*(1), 30–39.

Sutherland, I. E. (1968). A head-mounted three dimensional display. In *Proceedings of the December 9–11, 1968, fall joint computer conference, Part I; 12/9/1968* (pp. 757–764) Retrieved from http://design.osu.edu/carlson/history/PDFs/p757-sutherland.pdf.

Sutherland's Sword of Damocles. (n.d.). Retrieved from http://www.virtualworldlets.net/Resources/Hosted/Resource.php?Name=Damocles.

The Panorama in History. (n.d.). Retrieved from http://www.wwvf.nl/panorama/wwvf_Panorama/The_Panorama_in_History.html.

Turi, J. (2014). *The sights and scents of the Sensorama simulator [news blog].* Retrieved from https://www.engadget.com/2014/02/16/morton-heiligs-sensorama-simulator/.

Universal Studios Orlando. (2016). *Shrek 4-D [blog post].* Retrieved from https://www.universalorlando.com/Rides/Universal-Studios-Florida/Shrek-4-D.aspx/.

Virtual Boy. (2004). *Hardware profile.* Retrieved from http://www.n-sider.com/contentview. php?contentid=214.

Virtuix. (December 16, 2014). *Virtuix omni [website].* Retrieved from http://www.virtuix.com/.

Woeste, H. (2009). *A history of panoramic image creation.* Retrieved from http://www.graphics. com/article-old/history-panoramic-image-creation.

Wright, R. (1987). Virtual reality. *Sciences, 27*(6), 8.

Yoon, S., Choi, Y. J., & Oh, H. (2015). User attributes in processing 3D VR-enabled show-room: Gender, visual cognitive styles, and the sense of presence. *International Journal of Human-Computer Studies, 82,* 1–10.

CHAPTER 13

Virtual Reality Wave 3

Michael R. Heim
Mount Saint Mary's University, Los Angeles, CA, United States

A fresh wave of cultural energy hit the contemporary technology scene in 2015. Where before virtual reality had been mainly an area of experimentation and speculation, now commercial products were getting into the hands of consumers. Where previously VR had been the domain of imagineers like Jaron Lanier, Char Davies, Marcos Novak, and Brenda Laurel, there were now thousands of consumers wearing VR headsets that booted up with the banner "Samsung Gear VR powered by Oculus." Technology companies like Samsung and Oculus (owned by Facebook) introduced a new phase in the cultural reception of VR. Virtual reality had become an actual product that promised future upgrades in hardware performance and in software scope. A speculative experimental technology had become an everyday experience for many people.

In 2015, several companies began VR initiatives that, in some cases, included cooperation among software producers and hardware manufacturers. There was a flurry of market activity:

- Oculus in Samsung Gear VR;
- Google Cardboard and 3D Jump service;
- Sony PlayStation Project Morpheus VR Headset;
- HTC's Vive VR headset;
- GoPro's 360-degree capture rig;
- Vuzix's IWear 720 headset; and
- Samsung's VR camera, the Gear 360.

These commercial ventures revived old questions about the promises and prospects of virtual reality—questions quite familiar to senior cultural observers. This author's introduction to the new cultural wave came by way of Ocean Rift—a piece of Oculus software running on a Samsung Note 4 smartphone mounted in a Samsung Gear VR headset. The experience fit into the third wave of VR, a third push to reinvent media through immersive simulation. This "Wave 3" revives the recurrent cultural forecast that VR will change everything. Prior to this wave came two

Boundaries of Self and Reality Online
ISBN 978-0-12-804157-4
http://dx.doi.org/10.1016/B978-0-12-804157-4.00013-X
261

others, one in the 1990s (Heim, 1993a, 1993b) and another at the turn of the 21st century (Heim, 1998). These prior waves were about VR concepts and VR aesthetics, respectively. Or so it seems to this author as the decades pass. The argument has been made elsewhere that phase fluctuations belong to the ontology of cultural history of which virtuality is a prime instance (Heim, 2014).

THE VIRTUAL ENVIRONMENT

The contours of the new wave appear, appropriately enough, in *Ocean Rift*, an introductory experience available in the software library of "Samsung Gear VR powered by Oculus." The author engaged the experience via a Samsung Note 4 smartphone inserted into a Samsung Gear VR Headset—a device known in previous waves by the technical term: head-mounted display (HMD). The Oculus software library, from which *Ocean Rift* came, includes games, media channels, and more general virtual world "experiences." The introductory experience of *Ocean Rift* has a trailer clip on YouTube described as follows:

> … *a VR application that immerses the user in a vivid underwater world. The app gives the user the experience of swimming among various aquatic creatures including tropical fish, sea turtles, rays, sharks, whales, dolphins, and even dinosaurs.*
>
> **https://www.youtube.com/watch?v=z5oQQFmtV0s**

The trailer clip does not, of course, "immerse" the user because the YouTube video appears on a two-dimensional, nonstereoscopic screen and therefore provides only a rough glimpse of the content seen by someone who enjoys an immersive experience through wearing the stereoscopic headset with 3D audio (Heim, Isdale, Fennicot & Daly, 2002). In the immersive experience, Ocean Rift can simulate the perception of swimming, floating, and interacting with the underwater world and its creatures. The first reaction many people have when they enter *Ocean Rift* is "Wow!" A fully immersive medium can deliver a simulated experience of being in another element.

THE WOW FACTOR

Any new experience can evoke a WOW, and it's, of course, subjective. When an experience stops the normal flow, it can take the breath away. It's either a novelty not seen before or something rumored that only now provokes a shock of wonder. One doesn't ask the viewer "What do you mean by 'WOW'?" The exclamation conveys nothing about the substance of the experience. It conveys how the user feels when the headset delivers the illusion of being transported into another place. The WOW comes from a momentary shock.

The WOW suggests echoes of T.S. Eliot's riff on language as a "raid on the inarticulate," or recalls William James's description of raw experience as "booming, buzzing confusion." WOW can go "boom!" beneath the cognitive threshold, not as a description but as a token of wonder, surprise, even awe. Wonder may trigger longer statements. In fact, Aristotle in his *Metaphysics* attributes the lengthy history of Western philosophy to the impact of primal wonder. Leibniz, too, articulated that cosmic shock in his memorable, mystical question: "Why is there anything at all instead of nothing?" Who can deny that Western philosophy has been a very wordy response to the shock of an amazing world?

The wonder or shock created by a sudden perceptual shift can elicit the language of mystics and philosophers who challenge the adequacy of language to convey a primal experience. When an experience radically challenges the framework or Gestalt of conventional experiences, the conventions that constitute language fall short. Utterances resort to monosyllabic grunts. In such instances, referential language will often beg off by using indexical gestures or paradoxical expressions. One can only say "See for yourself!" And when the shift of perceptual framework is sufficiently radical—as I argue it can be with VR technology—the perceiver's proprioception can jump to a heightened level that spiritual teachers refer to as "pure awareness" or thought that fixes not on any particular form or contents of consciousness but on formless awareness or consciousness itself (Fenner, 2007). Such pure awareness—or awareness of awareness—heightens self-identity and cannot be conveyed by referential language. In such a case, language does not refer to things within a given perceptual field but the utterances refer to the perceived shiftiness of the field itself. Self-perception then becomes "mystical" in the original Greek sense of *myosis* or the shutting of one's eyes and covering one's mouth. This, I will argue, is the spiritual potential of the third wave of VR. But prior to a perceptual shift, there must logically be perceptions or multiple percepts, and VR is a device that not only delivers multiple perceptions but it specializes in the shock of shifting perceptual frameworks. Virtual environments provide a rich field of perceptions and allow for rapid and controlled shifts in perceptual frameworks. The controlled VR shocks might, I argue, offer a gateway toward spiritual transformation or the heightening of pure awareness—the awareness of being inside contingent frameworks of experience.

TAKE A DEEP BREATH

The virtual environment of *Ocean Rift* offers a rich sensory field of things to see, hear, and do. Here, one sees sharks, giant sea turtles, a variety of fish, a rusty anchor, a sea chest, and several sea snakes. Besides these animated and recognizable shapes, there is a constantly swaying backdrop of colorful sea weeds and anemones that slide past the visitor's point of view as directional gestures shift the first-person perspective within the virtual environment. There are also auditory signals that enhance the experience. *Ocean Rift* produces the sounds of bubbles generated rhythmically to simulate an underwater diver's breathing, supporting the illusion that one is hearing one's own respiration. The sound bubbles simulate SCUBA diving and not the kind of hold-your-breath free diving that eschews air-tank gear (Eyles, 2005). These SCUBA air-tank sounds belong to the sensory field of ocean diving that has become popular since the 1950s when free diving took a second place to the kind of ocean exploration popularized by Jacques Cousteau's film *Silent World* (1956).

The purpose of the simulation in *Ocean Rift*, however, is not realism. Although it was not built as a game, *Ocean Rift* aims at enjoyment. The Oculus Theatre Library categorizes its applications as games, experiences, and events. *Ocean Rift* is an experience, not a game. Its software developer, Dr. Llŷr ap Cenydd, is a Welsh researcher in the School of Computer Science at Bangor University, Wales, UK. He describes his work like this:

> *Ocean Rift showcases different techniques for simulating a vivid underwater experience in VR. This includes experimenting with different sounds, animals, plant life, ocean current effects, particle systems (dust, bubbles etc.).*
>
> **http://ocean-rift.com**

Cenydd is a computer scientist who experiments with techniques for simulating ocean life. His experiments are not about conveying an experience of the actual ocean. More like an amusement park, *Ocean Rift* has "fire rings" where dolphins swim playfully like animals at Sea World, jumping through hoops. It also adds horror-chills in the anachronistic shape of a giant prehistoric Megalodon shark lurking in the depths. The Oculus library provides several other simulations that offer enjoyable versions of sightseeing rather than strictly educational experiences. These often blur the borders between simulated accuracy and user entertainment.

Not far, then, is the question about the underlying intentionality of simulated experience. A phenomenology of the ocean floor will differ depending on the intentionality of the observer who first records the experience and then later depends upon the intentions of the software designer who strives to recreate or simulate the experience. In the first phenomenology, the experience will differ depending on whether the intention is to spear fish, to explore coral reefs, or to map the terrain of the sea floor, etc. Depending on the underlying intent, the ocean shows different faces as it reveals itself to the observer who approaches the phenomenon with the frame of a specific attitude. The observer is not "making up" what is seen, but different sides of the phenomenon can appear or show themselves depending on the framer's intent. The intention forms a background or framework in which things can appear. The raw data of the ocean in itself, prior to any framework of interpretation, might be the goal of pure science. Scientists measure marine life, underwater geography, water currents, and so on. Drawing on such factual descriptions or data, the general population can eventually imagine the larger picture as it is assembled by collaborating scientists who have gathered and integrated the data. In the United States, organizations like NOAA, the National Oceanic and Atmospheric Administration (http://www.oesd.noaa.gov/) have the educational mission to communicate scientific findings to the public. From the viewpoint of phenomenological psychology, that would be one example of intentionality with the purpose of communicating scientific findings. But that is only one kind of intentionality. So, while *Ocean Rift* may not be scientifically precise, it draws upon underwater science in a loose way. In this case, the *Ocean Rift* simulation is more computer science than ocean science, marine biology, or oceanography. A reality simulation that is, at bottom, not scientific still has the value of inviting sightseeing, educational fun, or "edutainment." It can also pique our curiosity about the reality of the underlying data collection.

The currently widespread view—probably short-sighted—is that VR is primarily about fun and entertainment. There are many other VR applications, however, some blending virtual reality with augmented reality (i.e., "see-through" information) where simulation is tied to training or to product engineering. EON Reality, Inc. (Irvine, CA), for instance, promotes a blend of AVR (i.e., "augmented and virtual reality") where reality-based data merge with "gamified" virtual reality lessons (http://www.eonreality.com). EON, for example, applies VR to the anatomy of a frog or to how the human body works. Here, the elements of enjoyment and pleasure subordinate themselves to the intention of maintaining accuracy in the instructional content. Different ratios of enjoyment to accuracy might characterize the experiences available in future VR libraries, and users of those libraries might find it helpful to have some control or choice about the levels of accuracy they experience virtually.

IMMERSION

If accuracy-to-content versus entertainment is one challenge for the third wave, there is another challenge in recognizing the full potential of VR. Early on, researchers in the field sensed the potential of VR as a spur to human evolution. Since its inception, VR headsets have been used for bio-feedback, a tool for personal change and self-transformation. Some of this potential was glimpsed in the earliest applications of computer biofeedback in the 1980s based on physiological research from the 1970s (Shearn, 1972). The 2005 special issue of the journal *Applied Psychophysiology and Biofeedback* shared current clinical and research projects (Wiederhold & Rizzo, 2005). But beyond clinical and research goals, beyond therapies for individual pho-bias or for PTSD, future virtuality may open immense avenues for spiritual self-transformation. The scope of personal transformation widens when VR is seen within the broader context of cultural history. In that broad context, the self-control of heart rate, respiration, and brain waves transcends Western medicine and belongs to the worldwide quest for spirituality. Techniques for transforming oneself—albeit without real-time measurement—is com-monplace among ancient forms of spirituality. Bombarding or closing down the senses goes back to shamanic and magical practices. An extraordinary capacity for controlling the autonomic nervous system has long been admired in practitioners of Indian Yoga and Chinese energy work (e.g., *neigong*). Yogis can control breathing and heart-rate so as to suspend normal thought processes. Religious practices from ancient Greece and the Middle East have included baptismal immersion and other participatory experi-ences that conjure mystical moods of wonder and inner stillness: candles, music, low lighting, statues, processions, stained glass windows, wine, and chanting, etc.—all these became part of the Roman Church and subsequent Catholic sacramentalism. Religion and art historians can trace sensory over-loads and blackouts back to the Dionysian rituals of ancient Greek mystery religions (Burkert, 1977). From ancient times, magic rituals that induce trance-like meditation have been associated with spirituality.

Spirituality, in turn, has long been associated with the VR keyword "immersion," a term which invariably defines this technology through its shuttering and controlling of sensory input. While a TV show or book can be absorbing, these media do not seize and control the perceptual field as fully as the technically immersive media—not just mentally immersive but perceptually immersive in a way that involves physical participation. In ancient times, participation may have included joining processions at night to attend torch–lit spectacles or mock burials. Like the rave culture of the 1990s, the ancient spiritual rites wielded psychological power through flashy sensory signals. Today's hardware supports a distinctive, but not entirely dissimilar, shift in sensory proprioception. The simple act of donning the headset might be a good starting point to develop an analogy with immersion for spiritual purposes. We can see the analogy if we look carefully, noticing what happens moment-by-moment during the first-person physical process of getting in and out of VR. To grasp the spiritual potential of immersion, we need look no further than the significance of the physical act of putting on and taking off the VR headset.

Immersion in *Ocean Rift* might indicate a direction for VR as a spiritual tool for transformation. Here we might take "immersion" both in its literal and analogous (e.g., spiritual) meanings. Donning today's VR headset enacts the outer gestures of an ocean diver putting on a face mask or SCUBA gear (self–contained underwater breathing apparatus) before descending into the ocean. *Ocean Rift* software shows us the inside vision of the simulated ocean as seen by the "diver" who wears the gear. The actual ocean diver proceeds by first donning the mask or goggles, taking the steps to become literally immersed in the ocean. Ocean fluid surrounds the diver with a watery element alien to human habitation. Of course, the body surfer or the Jacuzzi soaker also claim a watery element, but the ocean diver descends into the alien element on a deeper level altogether. The diving imagery of *Ocean Rift* supports the immersive paradigm. Once we are "inside" the headset, the software simulates deep ocean diving by:

- suspending perceived (ocular) gravity;
- adding sounds of rhythmic breathing;
- limiting the range of visibility;
- suggesting slow flotation in liquid space; and
- displaying elusive plants and animals.

The outer physical gestures of putting on and taking off the headset induce the inside vision and its corresponding floating meditative atmosphere. Not unlike the experience of professional diving or spear fishing, "apnea diving" (i.e., skin diving or holding-breath diving) can be seen and felt as a meditative experience (Pelizzari & Tovaglieri, 2004). Professional divers study meditation techniques (e.g., *pranayama*) to increase their breathing time underwater. The authoritative *Manual of Freediving* includes several chapters of yoga exercises for training relaxation and one-pointed focus. Champion divers cultivate "deep regression" to a mental zone of fetus-like relaxation. This physiological state releases anxiety and stress. This zone is achieved through the control of internal energy known to Indian Yoga as *prana*, what Chinese Tai Chi practitioners call *chi* or *qi*. Actual ocean diving and the immersive simulation of *Ocean Rift* both support a zone of peace and tranquility—except for occasional sharks and other underwater hazards. The biggest hazard for the free diver to overcome, however, is anxiety and stress. These cut off oxygen. The biggest monster is panic.

The inside vision of *Ocean Rift* has a counterpart in the outward gestures of putting on and off the VR headset. That outward procedure (visible to a bystander) signals immersion, the plunge into an alien element, similar to "sealing the senses" in Taoist meditation. The descent could be to any virtual world, even to an outer-space shooter game like *Anshar Wars 2* where the space ship follows one's head movements and where missiles are fired via a Bluetooth controller while swiveling rapidly in an office chair. Or it might be *Strangers with Patrick Watson* by Montreal-based Felix and Paul Studios where one spends quiet time absorbing the creative ambience of a musician's studio. Any truly virtual world is, by definition, immersive on the outer level of gestural and psychological dynamics. So, the process of exiting one world and entering another is something of a shock or plunge. In seconds, the traveler plunges from one set of sensations and expectations into another. Diving from one world to another, or from the primary world into a virtual environment—all these are immersions in a new element, a sort of baptism into a new awareness.

Along with immersion as a plunge into a new element comes the felt need to reorient oneself afresh—both on entering and exiting the virtual world. The experience of sensory disorientation and re-orientation (familiar to anyone who uses VR) has for centuries played a role in the development of spiritual life, for initiating and intensifying life on a new level of awareness. For centuries, aquatic immersion has radiated the aura of initiation or serious personal reorientation. Baptism by water still serves Christianity as symbolic portal into a new life, a rebirth or metanoia that transforms the heart. Being "born again by water" renews the seeker for a different lifestyle. For centuries, baptism has been the rite of initiation going all the way back to the Mysteries of Eleusis in ancient Greece (Burkert, 1977).

Philosophers Timothy Freke and Peter Gandy document the pre-Christian ceremony in *The Jesus Mysteries*:

> Baptism was a central rite in the Mysteries. As long ago as the Homeric hymns we hear that ritual purity was the condition of salvation and that people were baptized to wash away all their previous sins. The Pyramid Texts show that there was a ceremonial baptism of the Egyptian Pharaoh before the ceremony of his ritual birth as the embodiment of Osiris. In some Mystery rites baptism was simply symbolized by the sprinkling of holy water. In others it involved complete immersion. Baptism tanks have been found at initiation halls and shrines. At Eleusis initiates ritually cleansed themselves in the sea. In his initiation ceremony, after a confessional prayer, Lucius Apuleius underwent a bath of purification, and later a baptism of sprinkling. In the Mysteries of Mithras, initiates underwent repeated baptisms to wash away their sins.
>
> **Freke and Gandy (2000)**

So too with VR. Sensory perception is refreshed with the removal of the headset for re-entry into the primary world. The surrounding world rushes back into the senses. The shock of reorientation provides an opportunity to savor the rich details of the present moment. The plunge of VR immersion allows us to emerge refreshed and renewed, startled again by the physical world outside the headset. The recurrent WOW!

LUCID DREAMS AND VIRTUALITY

Removing the headset forces an abrupt perceptual re-sync with the primary world. With proper attention, this can be a mini Zen-like awakening: Lo and behold! The cybernaut, a traveler through the wormhole, the Fool card in the Tarot deck, awakens from dream-like interactions to an alternate universe. Afterimages float across the real world as leftovers from a previous universe. Virtual "floaters" linger in memory and occasionally trigger a déjà vu—similar to the Internet discussions that unexpectedly intersect conversations in real life. These jolting scene juxtapositions have a parallel in the phenomenon of lucid dreaming defined by Stephen LaBerge as "being fully conscious that you are dreaming" (LaBerge, 1985). A lucid dream is the paradoxical marriage of conscious attention and subconscious materials. "Oh, look at my four hands! I must be dreaming!" So too, wearing the headset shutters the waking world and permits an exclusive engagement with computer-generated sensations. VR software forces the senses to struggle with the unfamiliar. At the same time, the cybernaut can remain aware of both what is inside the headset as well as the alterity of the primary

world. Lucid dreaming intensifies dream activity by adding conscious awareness. To enhance conscious awareness, the dreamer can apply such active
techniques as elaborated by Robert Moss (2011). Moss replaces the term
"lucid dreaming" with "active dreaming" so as not to imply conscious
manipulation of the subconscious dream process. Active dreaming stimulates dreams while respecting the playful spontaneity of the subconscious.
The cybernaut, unlike the oneironaut or dream traveler, has fewer ways to
actively affect the imaginary environment programmed into the software.
The virtual environment has fewer plastic components than the dream
world. Like the lucid dreamer, though, the cybernaut may choose to maintain an apperceptive consciousness: "I am engaging a nonreal virtual environment." This active phrase can loosen identification with the temporary
roles assigned by the software. As the primary world rushes in again, a deliberately trained perceiver can refrain from identifying immediately with the
physical body and its surrounding world. Our language may try to make
sense of the situation by using the term "primary" world. Repeated and
reflective use of VR may, however, over time, create a taste for suspending
the intention of returning to primary reality. Just as dream lemons can
pucker cheeks and bite taste buds more intensely than real lemons, so too
VR gear can juxtapose virtuality to the everyday flow of experience.
Buddhists call such loosening "nonattachment" or simply detachment. It is
the acknowledgment of a "floating world" and one aspect of freeing oneself
from the illusion of permanence. Our feeling of presence in the primary
world, as noted by the pre-Socratic philosopher Parmenides, revolves around
an assumption of constant reliability in certain aspects of the given environment. Buddhists generally see this tendency to assume permanence as an
unnecessary source of suffering and as a cause of inevitable disappointment
in a constantly changing world.

This active consciousness points to a further spiritual path for users of
the VR headset. A spiritual clue comes from lucid dreamer Robert Waggoner.
In his book on lucid dreaming, Waggoner relates his personal search over
decades to find a satisfying ground behind the changing symbols and adventures of his lucid dream life:

> Realizing that I existed in the illusion of a dream was not enough; I needed to
> journey beyond all symbol, appearance, and the illusion, beyond all self-creation,
> beyond the lucid dream. I needed to find the source of it all.
>
> **Waggoner (2009)**

A recurrent "blue light" haunted Waggoner's dreams as he searched for a
nonpersonal source behind his dreams, thoughts, and individual life

expectations. He found the transpersonal source in the dream of a "blue light" beyond his personal autobiography and self-aware ego. His "light dreams" multiplied until he reached a single pure light, a Pure Awareness that lay beyond personal inclinations, desires, thoughts, or plans:

> You can call it "your" awareness, but it preexists you. The things you attach to awareness—your ideas, beliefs, emotions, memories, all blend together and become the conception of "you" or "yourself." But when you shake them all free, one thing remains: Awareness. The self has awareness, but the self is not the Awareness…. The experience of light has left me with deep feelings about the interconnectedness of all awareness and what underlies phenomenal reality. Occasionally, it rises to the surface, and I experience in waking reality the sense of interconnectedness.
>
> **Waggoner (2009)**

Pure awareness, free of any specific world (virtual or nonvirtual) offers a fitting spiritual goal for the cybernaut in VR gear. There is a line that connects this goal to the German Dominican Christian mystic Meister Eckhart (e.g., *Abgeschiedenheit/Gelassenheit*) and to the Japanese Zen master Daisetz T. Suzuki (e.g., *MU/zazen*). These paths lead to an awareness so pure that it is free of every vestige of personal predilection. The mind–body becomes a clear conduit for the life-force (e.g., *chi*) so that everything feels connected and animated. Personal disappointments and achievements are irrelevant to transpersonal presence, as are remote hopes and fears. But why then choose to enter any world at all? Does anything matter to the multiworld VR nomad? Can the goal of world-hopping decay into a disenchantment with everything, a bland indifference to any particular world?

LUCID LIVING

To solve the conundrum, the philosopher Timothy Freke describes a spiritual step beyond lucid dreaming and beyond the dismissal of personal illusions. Drawing on ancient mystery religions and the Gnostics, Freke develops the paradigm he calls "lucid living." Lucid living actively straddles the paradox of engagement/detachment (Freke, 2005). Lucid living incorporates an analogy with lucid dreaming. The double awareness typical of lucidity (i.e., dream watching self/dream character self) Freke applies to awareness in general. His lucid living suggests ways to toggle between autobiographical ego–awareness and the pure awareness of simple presence in the Now moment. Freke sees "deep awakening" as a shuttling process—not as a fixed goal of "enlightenment" but as a paradoxical engagement with two sides of a polarity.

Embracing the oscillation without being crushed by the contradiction is what Freke calls lucid living:

> *Often when I dream at night I'm unconsciously engrossed in the dream. But if I become more conscious I sometimes realize that I'm dreaming. This is called 'lucid dreaming.' When I dream lucidly I can clearly see the paradox of my identity. From one perspective I appear to be a character in my dream story. From another perspective I am the awareness within which the dream is arising. When I dream lucidly the dream continues as before, but my experience of dreaming is transformed, because I see that I am both in the dream and not in the dream.*
>
> **Freke (2012)**

The realization of "both–and" is the pivot for Freke's new paradigm. The paradox of lucid dreaming becomes a switch-track model for achieving presence that is individuated and purely transpersonal. Switching between an analogous dual awareness becomes lucid living.

> *When you dream, you are both the source of the dream and a character within the dream. Your identity is inherently paradoxical. In the same way, your identity right now is also inherently paradoxical. You are both the source of the life-dream and a character within it. You are the life-dreamer imagining yourself to be a particular person in the life-dream. While you identify exclusively with your life persona, you will remain unconsciously engrossed in the life-dream. Lucid living happens when you become conscious of both poles of your paradoxical nature.*
>
> **Freke (2012)**

Consciousness of the polarity is not a final goal but a continuous process. Like riding a surfboard, the lucid life is one that balances polarities. The graceful ride is never finished. Each moment, every day, each phase of life brings its own ripples, swells, and challenging breakers. All must be navigated in unpredictable weather. Pure awareness and ego awareness are complementary twins flowing from the same life force: The yin–yang that alternates between emptiness and engagement. To speak cabalistically, *Kether* is in *Chockmah* and in *Binah*; in both simultaneously. Balancing the paradox resembles the dialectic of Western history developed by the philosopher Hegel who traced each "solution" to a goal that eventually crumbles, giving rise to new "problems" and thereby to new "solutions" which in turn lead to their subsequent failures.

DIVING DEEP

Apply the lucid living model to VR and virtuality appears as an oscillating zigzag. In a linear understanding, VR becomes a kind of baptism: First, dive deep to an alternate world while toggling dual presence, then notice the recentering when you emerge from the virtual. The linear steps can become a general overview of how to approach the challenges of splitting personal presence into a primary physical component (e.g., "real life") and the multiple virtual worlds (e.g., "online lives"). Dual awareness can accompany both wearing and removing the VR headset. Each swing of the pendulum brings sharper awareness of the alternate world. Lucid living means heightening the spiral of awareness where we create our story inside the virtual while at the same time we remain rooted and present outside the virtual. Dwelling with the paradox means not choosing one over the other. This "both–and" is the spiritual dimension of VR.

Lucid living feeds into, and builds, on the mainstream of contemporary spirituality. "Mainstream spirituality" here, means, for instance, popular books like Eckhart Tolle's *The Power of Now* (Tolle, 1999). The widespread desire (from Oprah Winfrey to Deepak Chopra) to deepen the felt sense of presence is especially helpful in an era of multitasking and telepresence. In such an era, it becomes difficult to secure anyone's fully attentive presence at any given moment. The shared "Now" wobbles and dissolves quickly and easily. Spirituality in this era searches for some kind of anchorage, some place of stability and a sense of peace or stillness. There are many eloquent passages in Tolle where such a yearning finds expression, the following being one example:

> When you completely accept this moment, when you no longer argue with what is, the compulsion to think lessens and is replaced by an alert stillness. You are fully conscious, yet the mind is not labeling this moment in any way. This state of inner nonresistance opens you to the unconditioned consciousness that is infinitely greater than the human mind. This vast intelligence can then express itself through you and assist you, both from within and without. That is why, by letting go of inner resistance, you often find circumstances change for the better.
>
> **Tolle (2003)**

The search for "unconditioned consciousness" plays into anxieties about "media addiction" or "shrinking attention spans" brought about by an overdose of virtuality. VR can seem to bring still another big distraction. Yet the mainstream search for Full Presence or "The Complete Now" points to only one side of lucid living. Lucid living suggests more complexity than a single Now or an "enlightenment experience." The contribution Timothy Freke makes in the name of lucid living is to accept the paradox of a dissolving Now, to consciously embrace the discipline of both/and, aiming not only for restful serenity but also for a full engagement with ego projections. What this means for the spiritual approach to VR is to seek neither anchorage in the stillness of the primary world of perception or in a single role of immersive virtuality. Lucid living suggests more complexity than a single moment of "enlightenment." The goal of lucid living is to toggle gracefully between dual moments, whether they occur inside virtuality or outside, looking into a technological world. The use of VR to actively enhance personal presence avoids the Sisyphean search for a solid state of unconditioned awareness as well as avoids the silly sickness of "alternate world syndrome." By cultivating the paradigm of lucid living inside and outside technology, the VR headset becomes the VR crown, a practical tool for dual awareness and a gauge of how rich and multifaceted we can make the Now without growing disenchanted.

COMING UP FOR AIR

How does it feel to move step-by-step through such a practice for lucid living? As with any spiritual practice, this one improves over time. At first rigidly deliberate, the practice gradually becomes smoothly ritualistic, then simply a way of doing things thoroughly.

Sacred Space: The room is quiet as I sit toward the edge of my office chair, spine straight as an emperor sitting on a throne but without unnecessary tension. Shoulders relaxed, rocking slowly forward and back, I become aware of my two sitting bones, and with each forward lean, my belly presses out an exhale while each return to upright becomes an inhale. After 10 breaths of this forward bowing, the senses are calm enough to really listen and look at the surroundings…

Listening. Looking. Everything around the room is settled and quiet, except for the Burmese cat padding softly across the desk. Palms placed loosely on belly, conscious respiration continues its in- and out-breaths. Then with eyes closed comes a remembered catalog of things just seen and heard, an inventory of shapes and colors in the room.

Inner Inventory: The furniture: The desk, monitor, and tablet on the desk. The hangings on the wall: Calendar, painting, Ikea shelf of books. I recall colors of book bindings and pictures. Some are not vivid and some are things seen fuzzily, vaguely. Now with eyes open, I compare and contrast the actual colors with the eyes-shut memories. New information allows a more accurate re-vision of the scene in the Now with its overlay of imagined recall and current presence. With new color added, the VR headset on the desk is ready to hand. The crown is now an object but not yet a visionary object.

Coronation: Eyes open, hands take the headset from the desk, adjust straps, and secure the crown comfortably on the skull. The click of the software flashes a bright screen. A Health & Safety Warning pops up for a tap on the Agree button. Darkness for a second before a colorful Library of Experiences flashes several rows of tiles across the Oculus home screen.

Pause at the Threshold: Anticipation high, again with eyes shut, I return to felt breathing. Afterimages of the colorful Library compete with memories of the desk, the walls, the walking cat. I rehearse the room wall hangings, cat strolling, book shelves. Soft cat fur across my lap and on my left arm.

Bingo!: Eyes open, I tap CIRQUE DU SOLEIL | KURIOS CABINET OF CURIOSITIES (https://www.cirquedusoleil.com/kurios). Instantly transported into a large wooden crate, I am carried by several clowns who poke fun and ridicule me seated at the bottom of the box. Lively music booms over rolling laughter. The clowns haul the crate into a Big Top tent, remove the wooden box, and all around me swarm elegant mimes, bowling-pin jugglers, Chinese acrobats, fur-coated dwarfs, trapeze artists, Siamese twins, and turbaned magicians, each demonstrating their circus skills. With 360 degrees rotation I can choose to concentrate on any single act. The bizarre troupe conjures a night-time spectacle, something wonderful that might appear on the streets of Montreal or medieval Paris. The kinetic kaleidoscope makes time fly…

Taking Stock: Tapping back to the Oculus home screen, eyes shut, counting breaths and smiling at the afterimages flickering on the screen of closed eyelids. Relaxing so as to allow individual eyelid impressions to float into focus. What stands out? For now, it's the strange combo object that first wheeled up at the Big Top entrance. The "combine on wheels" amalgamates a gramophone ("His Master's Voice") with an antique 1910 Royal Typewriter. How could these two antiques meld together except in a dreamscape? What does this impossible antique monster say about current VR gear? A plan emerges to return later to examine more closely the "Royal Gramophone-Typewriter."

Resurfacing: Headset off, still sitting and letting vivid memories play back like a film across the scrim of the quiet room, I reach for weird fragment after fragment of a VR circus as dream wisps float through the chamber of memories. Some are difficult or impossible to grasp as conscious analysis cannot parse them or contextualize them among the normal objects in the room. Reaching for a notepad to net flying memories, hands are reassured by the feel of paper. Like a dream journal, the paper notebook with ballpoint is writing-by-hand technology, material tools as magical as the papyrus and stylus invented by the legendary Thoth, scribe to the Pharaohs and amanuensis of the Egyptian gods.

SYNOPSIS

Here then is an outline for creating VR notes, what we might call an "immersion log." An immersion log is as important for VR spirituality as a dream journal is for general spirituality (Moore, 2014). Like the chef's recipe box or the magician's grimoire, the immersion log sharpens and integrates scattered impressions. Additionally, a log improves memory and integrates elusive messages that bubble up from subconscious streams of thought. Similar to the dream journal, the VR immersion log is part of active immersion. A log deepens the alertness needed for note-making and enhances one's individual powers of attention. Noticing what goes into the log develops intuitive intelligence so that later decisions flow more easily and bring confidence for meeting daily challenges (O'Brien, 2015). The notes can fuel thrilling "a-ha" moments as random fragments of different worlds fit together and make sense. In general, the active VR immersion log promotes the integration of virtuality and reality.

The integration of virtuality and reality is part of a personal journey. The argument in this chapter has been that the journey is a spiritual one that cannot be preprogrammed. Some software projects may deliberately aim to enhance the personal journey and make it more serious, but such explicit support is beside the point. Putting the headset on and off marks the bridge between the virtual and the real. The bridge is where the journey begins, and, in terms of lucid living, where the arrival is savored and celebrated. As spiritual teachers often maintain, the goal of the journey lies in the journeying itself and in awakening to the process.

REFERENCES

Burkert, W. (1977). *Greek religion*. Cambridge, MA: Harvard University Press.
Eyles, C. (2005). *Last of the blue water hunters*. Locust Valley, NY: Aqua Quest.
Fenner, P. (2007). *Radiant mind: Awakening unconditioned awareness*. Boulder, CO: Sounds True.
Freke, T. (2005). *Lucid living: A book you can read in one hour that will turn your world inside out*. Carlsbad, CA: Hay House.
Freke, T. (2012). *The mystery experience: A revolutionary approach to spiritual awakening*. London, UK: Watkins.
Freke, T., & Gandy, P. (2000). *The Jesus mysteries: Was the original Jesus a pagan god?* New York, NY: Random House.
Heim, M. (1993a). Cybersage does tai chi. In D. Karnos, & R. Shoemaker (Eds.), *Falling in love with wisdom: American philosophers talk about their calling* (pp. 205–209). New York, NY: Oxford University Press.
Heim, M. (1993b). *The metaphysics of virtual reality*. New York, NY: Oxford University Press.
Heim, M. (1998). *Virtual realism*. New York, NY: Oxford University Press.
Heim, M. (2014). The paradox of virtuality. In M. Grimshaw (Ed.), *The Oxford handbook of virtuality* (pp. 111–129). New York, NY: Oxford University Press.

Heim, M., Isdale, J., Fenicott, C., & Daly, L. (2002). Content design for virtual environments. In K. M. Stanney (Ed.), *The handbook of virtual environments: Design, implementation, and applications* (pp. 519–533). Mahwah, NJ: Erlbaum.

LaBerge, S. (1985). *Lucid dreaming.* New York, NY: Ballantine.

Moore, T. (2014). *A religion of one's own: A guide to creating a personal spirituality in a secular world.* New York, NY: Gotham.

Moss, R. (2011). *Active dreaming.* New York, NY: New World Library.

O'Brien, P. (2015). *Great decisions, perfect timing: Cultivating intuitive intelligence.* Portland, OR: Divination Foundation.

Pelizzari, U., & Tovaglieri, S. (2004). *Manual of freediving: Under water on a single breath.* Reddick, FL: Idelson-Gnocchi.

Shearn, D. W. (1972). Operant analysis in psychophysiology. In N. S. Greenfield, & R. A. Sternbach (Eds.), *Handbook of psychophysiology.* New York, NY: Holt, Rinehart and Winston.

Tolle, E. (1999). *The power of now: A guide to spiritual enlightenment.* Novato, CA: New World Library.

Tolle, E. (2003). *Stillness speaks.* Novato, CA: New World Library.

Waggoner, R. (2009). *Lucid dreaming: Gateway to the inner self.* Needham, MA: Moment Point.

Wiederhold, B., & Rizzo, A. (September 2005). Virtual reality and applied psychophysiology. *Applied Psychophysiology and Biofeedback, 30*(3). http://dx.doi.org/10.1007/s10484-005-6375-1.

CHAPTER 14

Internet Dreaming—Is the Web Conscious?

J.F. Pagel
University of Colorado School of Medicine, Pueblo, CO, United States

> *In fact, the Internet has grown so large and complex that, even though it is constructed from a collection of man-made, largely deterministic parts, we have come to view it almost as a living organism or natural phenomenon that is to be studied.*
>
> *Peterson and Davie (2000)*

INTRODUCTION

From the very first, computer scientists were confronted with the awareness that the systems they were creating had the capacity for consciousness. Alan Turing (1952) developed a test that he hoped could be used to assess the capacity for these systems to attain consciousness—what we now call the Turing Test—that asks whether an imaginable digital computer can imitate human responses so as to fool a human interpolator. Once that test proved potentially within the capacity of computer systems, a newer test, the Chinese Room, was developed by the philosopher John Searle, in the attempt to incorporate translational and mind–based requirements into testing for consciousness:

> *Imagine that you carry out the steps in a program for answering questions in language you do not understand. I do not understand Chinese, so I imagine that I am locked in a room with a lot of boxes in Chinese symbols (the database), I get small bunches of Chinese symbols passed to me (questions in Chinese), and I look up in a rule book (the program) what I am supposed to do. I perform certain operations on the symbols in accordance with the rules (that is, I carry out the steps of the program) and give back small bunches of symbols (answers to questions) to those outside the room. I am the computer implementing a program for answering questions in Chinese, but all the same I do not understand a word of Chinese. And this is the point: if I do not understand Chinese solely on the basis of implementing a computer program for understanding Chinese, then neither does any other digital computer program solely on that basis, because no digital computer has anything I do not have.*
>
> *Searle (1980)*

Boundaries of Self and Reality Online
ISBN 978-0-12-804157-4
http://dx.doi.org/10.1016/B978-0-12-804157-4.00014-1

This test argues that a conscious system should be able to reach beyond the ability to manipulate formal symbols to demonstrate mental and semantic content. Searle (1984) argues that since computer programs are designed to be syntactic (i.e., based on the grammatical structure of language) rather than based on semantics (i.e., the meaning of signs and symbols such as words) any artificial system will always prove insufficient in attaining primary aspects of both mind and consciousness. Despite the contention of some philosophers that the Chinese Room test indicates that "The outlook for machine consciousness is good in principle, if not in practice" (Chalmers, 1996), this argument is to some degree anthropocentric in that it recasts the achievement for consciousness in terms more likely to be within the capacity of human rather than animal or artificial systems. In some respects, Searle's Chinese Room can be construed to indicate that it may be beyond the capacity of even humans to intellectually understand consciousness. The "mysterium" philosopher Colin McGinn (1990) notes that tests such as the Chinese Room indicate that there is nothing to explain how the brain might give rise to consciousness. Philosophical, neuroconsciousness–based debate persists as to the capacity of such tests for accessing the presence or absence of consciousness (Pagel, 2016). Such testing has contributed more to the understanding of the state of consciousness and its definition than to the determination as to whether humans, animals, or computer systems tested are actually displaying aspects of consciousness. Today, it remains arguable as to whether current artificial intelligence (AI) systems have the capacity to fully meet the criteria set by these tests for consciousness.

In developing such tests for consciousness, it became apparent that neither computer scientists nor most philosophers were clear as to what they defined to be consciousness. Despite centuries of human focus, consciousness remains a poorly defined state. Consciousness testing has defined and marked our understanding of the state of consciousness, but it remains unclear as to whether, and how, nonhuman animals and computer systems might actually display aspects of consciousness. What these tests and their derivatives describe best are the capacity for any cognizing system to meet or exceed the expected or required result criteria for the tests. It remains unclear whether systems meeting such testing criteria are actually conscious.

COMPLEXITY THEORY OF CONSCIOUSNESS

Among the most accepted theories as to the origin of consciousness is complexity theory, postulating that there is a point of complexity, at a level such as that attained by the human central nervous system (CNS), at which any operational system becomes conscious. The Law of Complexity-Consciousness was first formulated by Jesuit priest and paleontologist Pierre Teilhard de Chardin (1955) based on his realization that matter has the property to self-organize, and that consciousness grows in systems of increasing complexity. He proposed that consciousness was most likely to develop in an integrated entity with a very large repertoire of highly differentiated states. Large multiscale, nonlinear, highly heterogeneous and highly interactive cognitive systems are utilized by biologic systems to produce a multifaceted plethora of thoughts and behaviors. Koch and Tononi (2008) have postulated that the amount of integrated information that any entity possesses corresponds to its level of consciousness. They suggest that the level of structural "complexity," measured as simultaneous integration and segregation of activity during different states, is a direct measure of the level of consciousness experienced. All systems that are sufficiently integrated and differentiated should have some minimal consciousness associated with them, with the higher the number of connections and increases in integration delineating the level of consciousness attainable by the system (Balduzzi & Tononi, 2008).

While interesting and providing a basis for discussing the potential origin of consciousness, this theory when followed to logical conclusions can lead to patterns of cognitive dissonance. As currently developed, our Internet system of actively interactional personal, business, and governmental computers connected by interactive grids has reached a very high level of complexity. Based on currently achieved level of processing and integration, this level of complexity could portend the development of consciousness. Based on complexity theory, exceedingly complex nonbiologic systems, such as the cosmos and our planet, should be conscious. When pushed to logical conclusion, complexity-consciousness theory can be used to produce a scientific version of panpsychism, the ancient and widespread belief that all matter, all things, animate or not, are conscious to some extent (Tononi, 2008). At this point in the consideration of complexity theory, the computer scientist, the neuroscientist, and the philosopher are confronted again with basic questions of definition. Just what is and what is not consciousness?

ASPECTS OF CONSCIOUSNESS

Consciousness is a topic addressed and discussed in some of our oldest records (Rig Veda as cited in O'Flaherty, 1984), with the definition of consciousness continuing to be a topic of debate for theologists, philosophers, physicians, and neuroscientists (Pagel, 2014). It has not been possible to arrive at an acceptable universal definition. Some continue to address consciousness as if it were a self-obvious and apparent concept, however, most current philosophers and neuroscientists approach consciousness from a particular direction or within delineated constraints (Pagel, 2008, 2014). Artificially created systems have approximated and/or surpassed human attainments in their capacity for aspects of consciousness including data integration, perceptual processing, and intelligence (Bostrom, 2014). When addressing the question of Internet consciousness, an approach addressing these described aspects of consciousness provides a paradigm that can be utilized to assess any system's capacity for consciousness. The Web/Internet is approached as a networked repository of shared knowledge coupled with a search engine with the capacity for self-directed search.

INTELLIGENCE

The Turing Test and the Chinese Room Test and their variants are primarily tests of intelligence (i.e., the power or act of understanding). Current AI systems have demonstrated the capacity for attaining or exceeding defined test goals for intelligence. In humans, intelligence is most often tested based on a subject's capacity to apprehend the interrelationships of presented facts in order to guide action toward a desired goal (i.e., intelligence is accessed as based on test results). AI games playing systems with access to an applicable data base have proved superior to masters-level human competition in applied tests of intelligence including checkers, backgammon, jeopardy, scrabble, chess, go, and many other games (Bostrom, 2014). While, on occasion, humans can still defeat artificial gaming systems, in our near future, AI systems will surpass human capacities in almost every applied test for "intelligence."

ATTENTION

Beyond intelligence, attention (i.e., a drawing of processing resources toward one particular object more than others) is clearly an aspect of focused waking consciousness (Damasio, 1999). Most tests of consciousness have concentrated on the analysis of capabilities present during the waking state of focused attention. Yet, while attention is a factor associated with consciousness, even during waking there are a wide variety of "nonattentive" conscious states in which the available perceptual input is deemphasized. Humans spend a majority of our waking time in these nonfocused states (Buckner, Andrews-Hanna, & Schacter, 2008). Different processes of thought, levels of focus and alertness, memory access, and time sense are associated with different types of waking (Raichle et al., 2001). Attention is sensorially multifaceted, with each perceptual system (e.g., visual, auditory, tactile, and olfactory) controlled by an associated system for perceptual processing. Parallel but separate systems executively control those processes of attention (Damasio, 2010). Cognitive processing systems for attention and their behavioral expression are under central control, so that central attention of each of these systems can be allocated to handle competing demands of information processing. Consciousness, however, includes many waking at sleeping states in which focused attention is deemphasized, and some attentional processes (e.g., where we move our eyes when we focus our attention) are unconsciousness (Pagel, 2016). AI systems and Web-based search engines operate and function by developing established states of focused attention (Cho et al., 2002).

INTENTION

Beyond attention, consciousness is usually considered to require the philosophically described process of intention. The capacity for intention in any system, whether animal or machine, can be accessed by asking if an agent's behavior is predictable or explicable based on that agent's intention (Dennett, 1996). Such an intentional system requires both a capacity for thinking about something else outside the agent in consideration, and a resultant action or behavior that is based upon an understanding of the circumstances involved. From the machine perspective, an electronic parody of such an intentional system already exists. It requires a transducer (i.e., a device which takes information in one medium and translates it into another) and an effector (i.e., a device that can be directed by some signal in some medium to make something happen in another medium). Currently, almost all computer and AI systems store, use, and transform information recorded as electronic "bits." Such electronic information is commonly utilized in the application of programming-based intention by computer systems (Dennett, 1976). Semantically, humans commonly attribute an intentional stance to Internet-based search engines (e.g., "this damn program is blocking me!") (Pagels, 1988).

VOLITION

Volition is the act of deciding upon and initiating a course of action (synonym: will) (English & English as cited in Farthing, 1992). Volition is often incorporated into a problem–solving dynamic that incorporates the processes of goal-orientation or striving toward achievement, accomplishment, and resolution. In these situations, the person or system exercises and utilizes executive abilities that include the experience of the feeling of personal choice, and the sense that things could be otherwise or different (Kilroe, 2000). Volition is a central organizing principle that people often use to define and understand themselves. In experiential terms, Dijksterhuis and Aarts (2010) propose that individuals behave volitionally to motivate themselves according to their goals. Taking part in volitional behavior or pursuing goal-oriented behavior (e.g., in terms of "set, strive for, and attain") can bring about a "sense of agency or willfulness in that we experience ourselves as the cause of our own behavior as a result of decisions and actions." While it is currently unclear as to whether volition is within the capacity of machine systems, some authors have begun to discuss volitional aspects of global brain applications such as the Internet (Blackford & Broderick, 2014).

AUTONOMY

Autonomy is considered as the capability of a system to be self-controlling rather than governed by outside forces. When utilized in connection to an independently operating robotic system such as in the Mars Landers, considerable autonomy is possible. Such systems are under strict programmed control, and little if any outside input is required. This capacity for independent functioning is in some cases suprabiologic (e.g., the capacity to function in airless and intensely cold environments such as interstellar space). The Web as currently designed also has considerable autonomy to exist independently of outside controls.

"Strong-AI" is the concept of a system with the ability not only to operate autonomously within a predefined area of application, but to be completely autonomous within any general field of application with domain-independent skills necessary for acquiring a wide range of domain-specific knowledge. To reach this goal, a system must be capable of defining its own rules toward its own development. Such a "self-conscious" system would be capable of (re)adjusting its own frame of reference and tuning its own rules within this inner frame of reference. For an AI system, this capacity is referred as coherent extrapolated volition (CEV)—what many computer scientists view as an equivalent to volitional human consciousness—the ability to "rise above programming" (Voss, 2002). To this point, there is little if any test–based evidence that AI systems have developed the capacity for CEV. There is also little evidence that such systems have developed the capacity to function independently as autonomous entities (AEs). The characteristics of an AE include capacities for independent self-direction, decision-making, causality, and procreation. While such a level of functioning is within the capacity of most biological systems, it is not currently within the capacity of AI.

SELF-AWARENESS AND REFLEXIVE CONSCIOUSNESS

Awareness is a generalized state of psychological consciousness in which the system has access to information that can be used to control its behaviors (Chalmers, 1996). At some level, every independently living organism is self-aware, in realization that it exists, requires nourishment, and perpetuation into the next generation independent of other creatures. For higher organisms, this distinction between what is inside and outside itself is an inherent component marking the development of independent consciousness (Norretranders, 1998). Self-consciousness requires that an organism or system assume a privileged position, a self-model, an inner life, from which that organism functions as a coherent whole. The philosopher Daniel Dennett (1981) argues that it is this property of awareness-of-being-aware that would mark the capacity of an AI system to transcend programming, marking the development of consciousness. The concept of self-awareness can be addressed by utilizing psychological tests based on behaviors (e.g., the ability to realize that it is your reflection in the mirror), or the capacity to produce an artificial self-representation. AI systems with observable behavioral capacities such as surgical systems require system/body awareness for functioning (e.g., the awareness of the extensor scalpel or cutting laser placement). Internal and phenomenological aspects of self-representation can also be inferred based on computer-developed and presented narratives (Dennett, 1991).

DREAMING CONSCIOUSNESS

Consciousness is not a state restricted or defined by one consistent pattern of phenomenology. There are cognitive states that while profoundly different from the waking state of alert focus, are accepted as states of consciousness. Such conscious states occur in both wake and in sleep, with others are on the borderline between these two major global aspects of consciousness.

Behaviorally, each conscious state has basic phenomenological differences in the degree of perceptual isolation, type of thought processing, level of attention, memory access, teachability, and level of conscious control (Table 14.1). Volition, intention, focused thought, and logical patterns of cognition are not present in some of these forms of consciousness, particularly the dream states. The biologic neuroscientific framework—the electrophysiology, neuroanatomy, and neurochemistry—associated with each of these states also differs between states (Pagel, 2014). As the philosopher John Searle points out, "What I mean by 'consciousness' can best be illustrated by examples. When I wake up from a dreamless sleep, I enter a state of consciousness, a state that continues so long as I am awake. When I go to sleep or am put under general anesthetic or die, my conscious states cease. If during sleep I have dreams, I become conscious…" (Searle, 1998, p. 83). Any test of consciousness should have the capacity to evaluate and assess these alternative, discrete, meditative and/or altered states that, while quite different from focused waking, are still clearly conscious.

Humans utilize their biological framework (i.e., CNS) to define consciousness by its experienced phenomenology. Human dreams, clearly versions of consciousness, are isolated from perception and often from conscious volitional control. Dreams differ markedly from waking focused consciousness. The presence of dream equivalents within an artificial construct such as the Web, might actually serve as a better test for consciousness than the computer science and philosophic tests developed to this point.

INTERNET DREAMING

Dreams are virtually ubiquitous among humans, and it is apparently self-evident what a dream is to each individual experiencing a dream. Yet, being human, conflation and confusion, supposition, and presumption abound. What seems obviously a dream to one person may not be at all what another is referring to as a dream. This has led to significant problems for researchers and investigators in the field. What a dream is for the field of sleep medicine is not at all what a dream is to the field of psychoanalysis. For the sleep physician, dreams occur during sleep with a wide variety of content extending from the limited awareness of dreaming to the bizarreness of a sleep-associated hallucination or night terror. For the psychoanalyst, dreams are defined by their content—bizarre and hallucinatory thoughts and images occurring in both wake and in sleep—so that day-reflective or mundane sleep-associated thoughts may not be considered to be dreams. Neuroscientists often restrict dreaming to that

Table 14.1 Sleep and wake conscious states: comparative phenomenology (Pagel, 2014)

	Perceptual isolation	Thought-attention	Memory access	Volitional control	Teachability
Waking states					
Focused wake	Lowest	Focused	High	High	High
Self-referential (default) wake	Low	Self-focused	High–associative	High	Characteristic
Drowsy wake	Low	Unfocused	High	High	Characteristic
Creative wake	Low–moderate	Focused	High–associative	High	High
Hypnosis	Moderate	Variable	High	Variable	Variable
Focused meditation	Moderate	Variable	High	High	High
Unfocused meditation	Moderate	Variable	High	High	High
Sleeping states					
Hypnagoic states (stage 1)	Moderate	Disassociated	High	Low–variable	Moderate
Stage 2 dreaming	Moderate	Continuity	High	Low	Low
REM dreaming	High	Focused	High	Low	Low
Deep sleep (stage 3) dreaming	High	Unfocused	Low	Low	None
Lucid dreaming	Low	Focused	High	High	Moderate
Sleep meditation	High	Focused	High	High	High

Table 14.2 Definitions for dreaming: a classification system paradigm (Pagel et al., 2001)

A definition of dream has three characteristic continua:

(a) Wake/Sleep, (b) Recall and ©Content:

a) *Sleep_*   ***Sleep Onset***   *Dreamlike States*   ***Routine Waking***   ***Alert Wake***

----*---------------*------------------*----------------------*-------------------*---------

(b) No Recall   ***Recall***   ***Content***   ***Associative Content***   ***Written Report***   ***Behavior***

--------*---------*---------*--------------*--------------------*--------------*----------

© *Awareness*   *Day-Reflective*   *Imagery*   *Narrative*   *Illogic*   *Bizarre/Hallucinatory*

--------*---------------- *--- --------*-----------*----------*-------------*------------

cognition associated with rapid eye movement (REM) sleep. These primary scientific definitions of dreaming are at their basis contradictory, yet authors, therapists, and dream researchers rarely define, in text, their assumed definition of dreaming (Pagel, 1999). Due to this confusion, and the inability of experts to agree or accept one overriding definition for dreaming, a consensus group of diverse experts in the field developed a multivariate classification system for dream definitions (Table 14.2) (Pagel et al., 2001).

MACHINE DREAMS AS SLEEP-ASSOCIATED MENTATION

For an autonomous system, the difference between machine sleep (i.e., an off state of no function) and biologic sleep (i.e., an on state with functioning that differs from waking) may be the most profound difference between machine and biologically based systems. During machine sleep, access systems are turned off or in power-saving modes in which access is reduced and/or limited. During these modes, most systems utilize a cyclical programmed approach of self-monitoring with triggers that can rise to a point at which the machine turns-on, shuts-down, or applies protective programming. What goes on in such a "sleep" mode is rarely apparent to the human interface without probing or applied analysis. While such forms of sleep mode-associated processing concretely meet axis criteria for dreaming, the profound difference between human and machine off-states argues otherwise. As Descartes (1641) pointed out, in humans, "A non-thinking, non-dreaming state is neither conscious nor alive."

However, network systems such as the world-wide-web are always on, and, like humans, always functioning whether in sleep or when awake.

Internet systems adapt to periods of high and low use, actually functioning best during periods of low use that most often correspond to human population concentration sleep/night times. This is due to the fact that during periods of high use, machine systems become congested; machines crash and are later rebooted, electrical interference corrupts bits of data, switches run out of buffer space, data arrival rates exceed capacity, viral attacks overwhelm servers; overload occurs, and managing software forwards packets of data into oblivion (Peterson & Davie, 2000). Such problems are less likely to happen during low use/sleep periods during which optimal functioning of the Internet becomes the norm. Such an adapted form of sleep-associated processing meets all axis criteria for dreaming.

MACHINE DREAMS AS METAPHOR

The most common definition of dream, what you will find if you Google or search the index at your local library, is loosely Freudian wish fulfillment: dream marriages, dream vacations, dream homes, dream sex, and dream cars. The Internet has become a repository for such human dreams. As such, it has become the site where we search for the patterns of our dreams. Some of this search we are able to define, but much of what we define is based on the structure of the Internet, our access systems, the alignment of the search engine that we use, and the slant of the programming applied by outside sources—another form of machine dreaming.

MACHINE DREAMS AS BIZARRE HALLUCINATORY MENTATION

The psychoanalytic definition for dreaming is bizarre/hallucinatory mentation in either wake or sleep. The web includes such complex programs such as weather/climate forecasting in which a series of mathematical models are constructed around extended sets of dynamic equations that are impossible to solve through analytical methods. The accuracy of predictions varies with the density and quality of data, as well as any deficiencies and limitations inherent in the numerical models, with the outcome derived sometimes unexpected and often difficult to explain. Important contributory data may be bottlenecked, corrupted, and even lost. The complexly developed analysis that results may provide unexpected and alternative answers to questions that the observer is unsure how even to ask. Such results share characteristics with dreaming: The integration of extensive sensory data, the associative interactions of many memory processing subsystems, variable memory access, attained results that diverge from expectations and are often incomprehensible except when presented as a time-based visual display, and result analysis—that, like dream interpretation, is often a metaphoric and allegoric process affected by the training and belief systems of the researchers.

DREAMING = RAPID EYE MOVEMENT SLEEP

At the time of the development of sleep monitoring in humans, it was discovered that many individuals would report dreaming if awakened during the REM sleep state. This finding led to the belief, adopted by most neuroscientists and promulgated to the general public, that the biologic process of REM sleep was dreaming. Neuroscientists developed this perceived correlation into major theories of neuroconsciousness including: activation synthesis, activation input modulation (AIM), reverse learning, search-attention, and the various neural net theories. REM sleep was far easier to study than dreaming. It could be studied in the laboratory, on monitors, and in animal models; so that most work presented as research into dreaming in the last half of the 20th century was actually the study of the electrophysiological state of REM sleep. Contrary research indicating that REM sleep occurred without reported dreaming and that dreaming occurred throughout the night in sleep stages that were clearly not REM sleep was ignored and suppressed (Pagel, 2011). REM sleep is a complex biophysiological state clearly beyond the capacitf address the perceived AI inability to produce an REM sleep equivalent by attempting to create the "perfect zombie," artificial neural net-based constructs of the human and mouse CNS that could potentially assume aspects of consciousness and even correlates of REM sleep (Koch, 2015).

SUMMARY: ASPECTS OF AI CONSCIOUSNESS

There is little argument as to whether Web browser systems can be considered to have attained some of the aspects and capacities of an AI. Interconnected systems such as the Web also meet defined criteria for having developed operative equivalents to dreaming—a finding suggesting the possibility that these artificially created systems may have already developed aspects of tertiary consciousness such as the capacity to dream. Based on multiple definitions for both consciousness and dreaming, it is clear that the Internet/Web incorporates aspects of consciousness (Table 14.3).

Table 14.3 Summary of testable criteria for consciousness with a rating of the capacity for Web-based browser systems to meet criteria in each area

Aspect of consciousness		Web-based browser capacity
Intelligence	++	Can meet or exceed the capabilities of biologic systems
Attention	+	Systems exist with the clear capacity for establishing states of focused attention
Intention	+	An electronic information paradigm is commonly utilized in the application of programming-based intention in many computer systems
Volition	−	To this point, there is little if any test-based evidence that computer systems have developed a capacity for coherent extrapolated volition (CEV)
Autonomy	+	Autonomy possible for programmed robotic systems. These entities are, however, controlled rather than volitionally independent
Self-awareness and reflexive consciousness	+	Internal and phenomenological aspects of self-representation can be inferred based on computer-developed and presented narratives
Dreaming (sleep-associated mentation)	+	Capacity present though limited as based on different definitions for sleep
Dreaming (wish fullfilment/metaphor)	+	Content similar and based on similar data
Dreaming: (bizarre/hallucinatory mentation)	+	Attained results may diverge from expectations and are often incomprehensible except when presented as a time-based visual display; and result analysis, that like dream interpretation, is often a metaphoric and allegoric process affected by the training and belief systems of the researchers
Dreaming = REMS	−	REMS is a biologic state beyond the capacity of current artificial systems, but potentially possible for a "perfect zombie" artificially developed neural net system
Evidence for complexity-based consciousness	−	No current evidence indicates the capacity for Web-based browser systems to "rise above programming"

(++) Human or suprahuman capacity; (+) empiric evidence for this capacity; (−) no empiric evidence for this capacity.

THE INTERFACE

Computer systems were originally developed in order to expand human capacities for conscious functioning. As Leibniz (cited in Smith, 1929) once said of the early calculator: "It is unworthy of excellent men to lose hours like slaves in the labour of calculation which could safely be relegated to anyone else if machines were used." The capacities of this interface have to this point been limited by human sensory-interface requirements for auditory, visual, numeric, and/or linguistic representations. Despite these limitations, the achievements that can be attributed to the computer–human interface have been remarkable; allowing us as a species not only to extend ourselves beyond this planet, but to also reach further into basic understandings of the scientific nature of existence that affects our potential, both positively and negatively, for extending ourselves into the future.

The computer–human interface is bidirectional. We fill the Internet with our thoughts, our emotions, our memories, our hopes, and our dreams, and, as far more than a reflection, they come back to us. Our consciousness is altered by interface interactions. After spending waking time interacting with an interface, the quality of our sleep, our dream content, and our patterns of thought are altered (Gackenbach & Kurville, 2013). The human independent of the interface is in many ways a different organism than the human immersed in the interface, utilizing different perceptual capabilities, having access to different, alternative, and extended mnemonic processing, and having different capacities for emotional, decision-making, and behavioral expression.

The clear potential exists for further extending external interface capacity (Vernon, 2005). Interactional computer systems have been developed able to provide real-time intravenous and interthecal chemical adjustments that affect both physical and mental functioning. Prominent examples include glucose monitoring and adjustment of insulin dosages in type I diabetics, and constant opiate dosage used for the treatment of intractable pain. Computer-controlled induced electrical discharge systems have been effectively used in treating Parkinson disease and intractable seizures. Frequency-based electrophysiologic and electromagnetic systems operate independently of neuroanatomic synaptic pathways in the CNS affecting conscious, nonconscious, and alternatively conscious systems, and inducing changes in energy, ionic equilibrium, and information storage (Pagel, 2012). The CNS systems that utilize these frequencies-based electrophysiologic fields in their functioning are primarily those involving associative memory, intrinsic imagery, and emotions (Pagel, 2016). The feedback integration of such fields into gaming and training programs has already been shown to alter outcomes (Cho et al., 2002).

WEB CONSCIOUSNESS?—CONCLUSION

Highly complex AI systems, including Web-based search engines, have attained the capacity for empirically based aspects of consciousness and dreaming. They have attained this capacity based on high-level capabilities in defined aspects of consciousness (e.g., intelligence, attention, autonomy, and intention), and their capacity to meet definition criteria for having dreaming equivalents. Complexity theories of consciousness can be used to theoretically support such an attainment of conscious function.

That is not to say that machine consciousness is the same as human consciousness. While philosophically and intellectually interesting, AI capacities for consciousness are not equivalent to human consciousness—the level of autonomous, independent, and volitional behavioral control characterized by independently functioning biologic systems. Machine capabilities for consciousness, while limited in these areas, have already approximated human capacity in intelligence, and in areas of attention, intention, and autonomy.

The current computer science criteria for consciousness are as stated by Williams (2012): "We will refrain from trying to give a universal definition of consciousness; for AI-development the definition does not have to be universal, or applicable to humans for explanation of human consciousness…we define consciousness as the ability to 'rise above programming'." This postulate has been incorporated into some current theories of cosmology (an unprogrammed cosmos might demonstrate laws of physics and cosmetology that unexpectedly change), as well as into supermodels of quark and boson interactions that propose that basic level aspects of space and time may be undefined, with constants, mass, and energy altering unexpectedly in off-program paradigms (Sigfried, 2013).

Years ago when punching holes in cards to program IBM 1100s, I viewed computer programming as a use of applied mathematical logic to produce desired results. Today, programming has morphed into an amalgamation process utilizing previously programmed function nodes. When a system does not function correctly to produce consistent results, basic programming is rarely altered, it is rather patched with added controls and corrections applied on top of previous programming. The resultant control programs, even when presented as "simple" apps, are remarkably convoluted and complex, utilizing layered coding that in most cases is well outside the capacity of the programmer to logically understand. In interactions that utilize the Web, even the trained programmer is often faced with illogical requirements defined by system criteria, expectant delineation of results, apparent info vs. noise ratios, personal bias, poor methodology, statistical confusion, congested and overloaded machine systems that lose data, as well as the need for data protection, defense from outside manipulation, and ubiquitous viral and malware insults. Sometimes it seems almost possible that these complex and commonly utilized Web-based systems have stepped outside programming. Future prospects may be profound.

REFERENCES

Balduzzi, D., & Tononi, G. (2008). Integrated information in discrete dynamical systems: Motivation and theoretical framework. *PLoS Computational Biology, 4*(6), e1000091. http://dx.doi.org/10.1371/journal.pcbi.1000091.
Blackford, R., & Broderick, D. (Eds.). (2014). *Intelligence unbound: The future of uploaded and machine minds.* Chichester, UK: Wiley-Blackwell.
Bostrom, N. (2014). *Superintelligence: Paths, dangers, strategies.* Oxford, UK: Oxford University Press.
Buckner, R., Andrews-Hanna, J., & Schacter, D. (2008). The brain's default network: Anatomy, function, and relevance to disease. *Annals of the New York Academy of Science, 1124,* 1–38. http://dx.doi.org/10.1196/annals.1440.011.
Chalmers, D. (1996). *The conscious mind.* New York, NY: Oxford University Press.
Cho, B. H., Lee, J. M., Ku, J. H., Jang, D. P., Kim, J. S., Kim, I. Y., et al. (2002). Attention enhancement system using virtual reality and EEG biofeedback. In B. Loftin, J. X. Chen, S. Rizzo, M. Goebel, & M. Hirose (Eds.), *Proceedings: IEEE virtual reality 2002.* Orlando, FL: IEEE Xplore.
Damasio, A. (1999). *The feeling of what happens: Body and emotion in the making of consciousness.* San Diego, CA: Harcourt.
Damasio, A. (2010). *Self comes to mind: Constructing the conscious brain.* New York, NY: Pantheon.
Dennett, D. (1976). *Conditions of personhood.* Oakland, CA: University of California Press.
Dennett, D. (1981). *Brainstorms: Philosophical essays on mind and psychology.* Cambridge, MA: MIT Press.
Dennett, D. (1991). *Consciousness explained.* Boston, MA: Little, Brown, & Co.
Dennett, D. (1996). *Kinds of minds.* New York, NY: Basic Books.
Descartes, R. (1980). *Meditations on first philosophy* (D. Cress, Trans.). Indianapolis, IN: Hackett (Original work published 1641).
Dijksterhuis, A., & Aarts, H. (January 2010). Goals, attention and (un)consciousness. *Annual Review of Psychology, 61,* 467–490.
Farthing, G. W. (1992). *The psychology of consciousness.* Upper Saddle River, NJ: Prentice Hall.
Gackenbach, J., & Kurville, B. (2013). Cognitive structure associated with the lucid features of gamers dreams. *Dreaming, 23*(4), 256–267. http://dx.doi.org/10.1037/a0034817.
Kilroe, P. (2000). The dream as text, the dream as narrative. *Dreaming, 10*(3), 125–137. http://dx.doi.org/10.1023/A:1009456906277.
Koch, C., & Tononi, G. (2008). Can machines be conscious? *IEEE Spectrum, 45*(6), 55–59. http://dx.doi.org/10.1109/MSPEC.2008.4531463.

Koch, C. (January 21, 2015). *Why can't the world's greatest minds solve the mystery of consciousness?* The Guardian. Retrieved from www.theguardian.com.

McGinn, C. (1990). *The problem of consciousness.* Chichester, UK: Blackwell.

Norretranders, T. (1998). *The user illusion.* New York, NY: Viking.

O'Flaherty, W. D. (1984). *Dreams, illusion and other realities.* Chicago, IL: University of Chicago Press.

Pagel, J. F. (1999). A dream can be gazpacho. *Dreamtime, 16*(1), 6–8. http://dx.doi.org/10.10 23/A:1012240307661.

Pagel, J. F. (2008). *The limits of dream: A scientific exploration of the mind/brain interface.* Oxford, UK: Academic Press.

Pagel, J. F. (2011). REMS and dreaming: Historical perspectives. In B. N. Mallick, S. R. Pandi-Perumal, R. W. McCarley, & A. R. Morrison (Eds.), *Rapid eye movement sleep: Regulation and function* (pp. 1–14). Cambridge, UK: Cambridge University Press.

Pagel, J. F. (2012). The synchronous electrophysiology of conscious states. *Dreaming, 22*(3), 173–191. http://dx.doi.org/10.1037/a0029659.

Pagel, J. F. (2014). *Dream science: Exploring the forms of consciousness.* Oxford, UK: Academic Press.

Pagel, J. F. (2017). *Synchronous physiological electrical fields: Function and interface potential* (in press) (Book chapter).

Pagel, J. F., Blagrove, M., Levin, R., States, B., Stickgold, B., & White, S. (2001). Definitions of dream: A paradigm for comparing field descriptive specific studies of dream. *Dreaming, 11*(4), 195–202. http://dx.doi.org/10.1023/A:1012240307661.

Pagels, H. R. (1988). *The dreams of reason: The computer and the rise of the sciences of complexity.* New York, NY: Bantam.

Peterson, L., & Davie, B. (2000). *Computer networks: A systems approach* (2nd ed.). San Franciso, CA: Morgan Kaufman.

Raichle, M. E., McLeod, A. M., Snyder, A. Z., Powers, W. J., Gusnard, D. A., & Shulman, G. L. (2001). A default mode of brain function. *Proceedings of the National Academy of Sciences of the United States of America, 98*(2), 676–682. http://dx.doi.org/10.1073/pnas.98.2.676.

Searle, J. (1980). Minds, brains, and programs. *Behavioral and Brain Sciences, 3,* 417–424.

Searle, J. (1984). *Mind, brains and science.* Cambridge, MA: Harvard University Press.

Searle, J. (1998). *The rediscovery of the mind.* Cambridge, MA: MIT Press.

Sigfried, T. (October 17, 2013). *It's too soon to declare supersymmetry a tragedy* (Web log post). Retrieved from https://www.sciencenews.org/.

Smith, D. E. (1929). *A source book in mathematics.* New York, NY: McGraw-Hill.

Teilhard de Chardin, P. (1955). *The phenomenon of man.* New York, NY: Harper & Row.

Tononi, G. (2008). Consciousness as integrated information: A provisional manifesto. *Biological Bulletin, 215,* 216–242.

Turing, A. M. (1952). Can automatic calculating machines be said to think? In B. J. Copeland (Ed.), *The essential Turing: The ideas that gave birth to the computer age.* Oxford, UK: Oxford University Press.

Vernon, D. J. (2005). Can neurofeedback training enhance performance? An evaluation of the evidence with implications for future research. *Applied Psychophysiology and Biofeedback, 30*(4), 347–364. http://dx.doi.org/10.1007/s10484-005-8421-4.

Voss, P. (2002). Essentials of general intelligence: The direct path to artificial general intelligence. In B. Goertzel, & C. Pennachin (Eds.), *Artificial general intelligence* (pp. 131–157). New York, NY: Springer.

Williams, H. P. (2012). *Why we need 'conscious artificial intelligence'.* Retrieved from http://www.mindconstruct.com/webpages/document/1.

CHAPTER 15

The Information Age, Virtual Reality, and the Bigger Picture

Thomas Campbell
University of Virginia, Southeast Region, United States

[Note from the author: *The following, by constraints of space and scope, must necessarily skip shallowly across the surface of a scientific and tightly logical body of information found in the books, lectures, interviews, and presentations of Thomas Campbell. Here I am reduced to making statements rather than derivations. If you want to see how these statements are deduced from the facts, or the study the logic behind them, simply Google "My Big TOE" or "Thomas Campbell" and follow the leads you find to book stores, websites, and YouTube videos.*]

INTRODUCTION

We live in interesting times! A century ago a revolution in science began as scientists struggled to understand the nature of light. Is it a wave, or a particle? It seemed to be both, but always one way or the other depending on the situation. The experiment that was to solve this mystery, the famous double slit experiment, did nothing of the sort. Instead it declared that everything that scientists thought they knew about the nature of reality was *clearly, irrefutably, undeniably false.* The long-held belief that science rested on an unshakable foundation of material reductionism and determinism was officially declared dead by a collection of the world's best and brightest scientists (early 1900s), while the role of the observer (consciousness) moved from insignificant to critically important. A massive paradigm shift, perhaps the largest ever in human history, one that would one day shake humanity to its bones, seemed just around the corner.

As it turned out, over the next several decades, the funeral for materialism and determinism was indefinitely postponed because belief, both widely and deeply held, simply refused to be swayed by the scientific facts delivered by the double slit experiment. The logical implications and sheer immensity of the impending paradigm shift were simply too big a step for those scientists of lesser metal that followed in the footsteps of the giants of science

Boundaries of Self and Reality Online
ISBN 978-0-12-804157-4
http://dx.doi.org/10.1016/B978-0-12-804157-4.00015-3

297

who created quantum mechanics—a science that was built upon the results of this most singular experiment. Massive, deeply entrenched belief has its own sort of inertia and does not turn around easily or quickly, especially since no one could come up with an alternative overarching theory or explanation of *why* quantum physics' description of reality worked as it did. Without that explanation, denial held firm among the majority of believers and the new science of quantum mechanics (QM) was simply repackaged as inherently "weird science." If you are human and a strongly invested believer in materialism, is easy to say: "Our beliefs about reality are obviously right, and because quantum mechanics conflicts with our beliefs (QM is weird), we can simply ignore the experimental facts until a comprehensive explanation forces us to change our mind." And much harder to say: "Our beliefs about reality are clearly wrong, and unfortunately, a correct understanding that will explain *all* of the facts is nowhere in sight. Though we have no ideas of where to start, we will keep looking."

Over the next century, waiting for a comprehensive explanation to appear eventually became embarrassing since absolutely zero progress was made—physicists still had no clue, no ideas, nowhere to start. To take themselves off that embarrassing hook of total ignorance and failure to explain quantum weirdness, a convenient belief that there *was* no explanation, that there *could be* no explanation, quickly took hold and buried itself deeply in the psyche of the physics community. The result: Physicists instantly transformed themselves from having to shoulder the blame for many decades of absolute failure to make any significant progress on the most important scientific question of all time... to blameless realists who couldn't be expected to do the impossible. Of course, with reputations, status, and careers on the line, and absolutely no one objecting, denial and belief-based bad science won hands down over acceptance of the experimental facts and good science. Why? Because the bad science, which would easily slip by unnoticed, made everybody feel better about coming up empty-handed. Furthermore, it allowed all of science to continue to ignore the monstrous elephant in the room—a very disconcerting paradigm shift (the death of materialism and determinism) they did not want to deal with. Moreover, they could, for a while longer, pretend that they had executed scientific due diligence and that their well-worn and comfortable Newtonian beliefs were still credible. Accordingly, physicists stopped trying to find the obviously "impossible" better explanation for the "why" of quantum science. Instead, they poured themselves into the "how" of quantum physics by developing better ways of calculating right answers even though they had no idea why their probabilistic math worked so well. During this 100 years of denial, beliefs in materialism and in the necessity of accepting that modern physics was, and would always be, simply beyond human understanding became progressively more ingrained. These beliefs were succinctly expressed by the renowned quantum theorist, Dr. Richard Feynman's advice to a graduate student inquiring about the "why" of quantum physics: "Shut up and calculate!" said the frustrated Feynman because he had no other answer.

The bad news is that this is where we still are today (2016). The good news is that a full solution to the "why" of quantum physics and a host of other "hard problems" in both physics and a dozen other fields is at hand and gaining supporters on the outskirts of physics. This new big picture theory of everything (Big TOE) is based on the concepts of virtual reality and consciousness. Exactly when and how this information will work its way from the outskirts to the core against a current of belief and bad science is a story for the next decade to tell. However, it *will* succeed because it simply represents a better, more general physics… and because the truth is not fragile… what works best, what accurately and logically explains the most facts with the fewest assumptions will eventually rise to the top of the conceptual pile.

The reason physicists were stymied by the double slit experiment and had no idea where to begin looking for a better understanding was that *the concepts required to solve that puzzle did not exist* until more than half way through (1916–1966) that long century of head-in-the-sand physics. Paradigm shifts of the magnitude represented by the double slit experiment usually develop very slowly (over many centuries), however, due to the Internet, the pace of change has been greatly accelerated. It was roughly another three decades (1996) before the crucial concept of describing our "physical" universe as a virtual reality rose to the surface in full view of the larger physics community. Then, it was only seven more years (2003) before the critical concept of VR was independently integrated into a comprehensive theory of consciousness… and yet another 8 years after that (2011) before this theory of consciousness was able to fully articulate a comprehensive understanding of the double slit experiment as well as a host of other mysterious physics and metaphysics paradoxes. (A long list of "weird [unexplainable] experimental results" had been steadily growing during that same century.)

Unfortunately, by the time physicist Dr. Edward Fredkin made the required crucial virtual reality concept widely known within the physics community during the early to middle 1990s, the physics community had long given up on finding solutions to the double slit experiment (now referred to as "the measurement problem"). Consequently, late 20th century physicists gave precious little *positive* attention to Fredkin's new perspective. On the other hand, they were much more forthcoming and generous with their dismissive, negative attention.

As the 20th century gave way to the 21st, Fredkin eventually did find acceptance in the margins of the physics community. Eventually, a growing worldwide movement called Digital Physics coalesced around Fredkin's ideas by the end of the first decade of the 21st century. Although Fredkin introduced the core concept of virtual reality to the physics community, he and the other digital physicists (eventually a sizable and respected movement) had no idea how to relate VR concepts to quantum physics, relativity, or a host of other seemingly intractable so-called "hard problems." The scientific community now had the necessary core concept but without an understanding of the nature of consciousness, they had no idea how to apply VR to explain the larger world.

The same beliefs (materialism and determinism) that made it impossible for physicists to understand the double slit experiment, also made it impossible for them to understand consciousness. According to their faith in materialism, consciousness must certainly be a product of the brain, and like any true believers, they remained true to their faith even though clear, irrefutable evidence had long shouted: "*Not so!*"

The digital physicists embraced virtual reality but were in many ways still under the same belief-spell as the traditional physicists. Consequently, although they knew the universe was virtual, they did not notice one glaringly obvious consequence of the virtual reality viewpoint: That a virtual human brain in a virtual human body (exactly like the virtual brain of a *World of Warcraft* elf), could not (by definition of the word "virtual") possibly store or process anything. Indeed, the *virtual* brain does nothing other than set the constraints of the VR's rule-set upon what *real* consciousness can experience. Virtual reality logic dictates that consciousness cannot be of this virtual world. In the following chapter you will come to understand that an obvious logical consequence of our reality being a VR is that our consciousness, and the computer rendering our VR, must be fundamentally real as well as nonphysical from a point of view *residing within* the VR. Most digital physicists cannot perceive the logical consequences of virtual reality that exist just outside of materialism's belief box. The logic of VR tells us that consciousness must be an evolving digital information system and that the computer rendering our evolving VR must be a subset of that information system.

The bigger picture that wraps up all of science within one grand theory of everything (TOE), including a theory of consciousness, has been, and still is, missed entirely by the digital physics movement. Because of beliefs and preconceived notions born of a lifetime of conditioning, sometimes what is most obvious and right before your eyes is the hardest thing of all to see. Thinking out of the box more than a baby step can be immensely difficult for narrowly focused, well-trained, professionals. My Big TOE (MBT), a trilogy of books, published by Thomas Campbell in 2003, finally was able to lay out a scientific explanation for the double slit experiment and other scientific paradoxes at the beginning of the second decade of this century. In the last half of 2016, Campbell offered the scientific community a set of QM experiments that would verify (or not) his virtual reality concepts. It will be a few years before results are expected.

Fortunately, as we progress into the second decade of the 21st century, more and more physicists have moved toward Fredkin's and Campbell's position that our reality is an information-based, computed reality. Nothing else seems to explain the world (as it is measured by scientists and experienced everyday by humans) quite so well. Many thousands of others have moved beyond digital physics to embrace MBT—Campbell's theory of everything—unifying from first principles: physics and metaphysics, mind and body, normal and paranormal, objective and subjective, science, philosophy and theology, all under one elegantly simple, overarching, logical, scientific explanation supported by only two rather unremarkable assumptions—that consciousness and evolution both exist.

Helping MBT and the virtual reality "bandwagon" pick up ever more speed are a growing number of scientists from fields other than physics. After all, if virtual reality can explain everything as Campbell's MBT claims, then signs of virtual reality should be showing up everywhere. And indeed they have—a few recent examples pertinent to this discussion: Dr Donald Hoffman Professor of Cognitive Science, University of California, Irvine, presents strong mathematical evidence to support his *Interface Theory of Perception* wherein he likens our physical reality to the virtual icons found on most computer desktops. Dr. Bruce Greyson, Professor Emeritus of Psychiatry and leader of the Division of Perceptual Studies, University of Virginia has accumulated overwhelming hard scientific evidence concluding that *consciousness is independent of the brain*—that is, that consciousness is fundamental, while the material world (brain and body) is virtual. Bruce Lipton, a biologist, came to a similar (mind is fundamental while "physical" is driven by mind) research-based conclusion through the study of genetics. All of these research-driven conclusions are entirely independent of each other.

A survey of physicists today would find a quickly growing *minority* (the best and brightest—who are likely to gain *majority* status over the next 5 years) of physicists claiming that our physical universe, and everything in it, is information based, that is, a calculated virtual reality, or in more common terms, a simulation. This is not some sort of passing fad within science. It is their own research and experimental results that have dragged each one of these pro-virtual reality scientists kicking and screaming into that unwelcome viewpoint. Unwelcome because it flies in the face of the beliefs that have totally dominated science since the time of Newton (early 1700s). These courageous scientists are now cast in the risky historical role of convincing their peers and everyone else that the world is round when it has been common knowledge for centuries that it is definitely, unarguably, absolutely flat.

Let's give thanks that we all live under the umbrella of accelerated "Internet time"—there is reason to believe that we can achieve in less than two decades what took our ancestors two centuries to accomplish. We do indeed live in interesting times!

With this introduction providing the overall context, the rest of this chapter will provide a physicist's view of the convergence of physics, digital science, the Internet, virtual reality theory, and the social-ethical evolution of humanity.

In the first subsection after the introduction, *Virtual Reality and Us: VR Is as Real as Any Reality Can Be*, I explore the notion of virtual reality and what the terms "virtual" and "real" might mean to us as we try to broaden our perspective about the nature of reality in the information age.

In the second subsection entitled *The Logic of Virtual Reality*, you will discover (in nontechnical terms) what the digital physics community failed to recognize about the fundamental nature of virtual reality.

In the third subsection: *Physics, Metaphysics, and the Nature of Consciousness* you will understand how you as an individual relate to this virtual reality. You will see that virtual reality concepts blur the boundary between physics and metaphysics, leading to an overarching theory of consciousness that subsumes both physics and metaphysics as well as offering major new insights into sociology, psychology, philosophy, and theology. As a result of the second and third subsections, you will see yourself, your reality, and your purpose in an entirely different perspective.

In the fourth subsection, *Life in a Virtual Reality Entropy Reduction Trainer,* you will clearly discover where evolution within this VR entropy reduction trainer is taking us—what the future holds for us as a species.

Eventually, we end up with a theory of everything (TOE)—everything objective and everything subjective—wherein consciousness is the only thing that is fundamental—all else being the logical consequences of consciousness.

In the last subsection *Boundaries of Self and Realities Online*, we return to where we left off the first subsection, with a discussion of what the Big Picture presented in this chapter means to us in our day-to-day life.

VIRTUAL REALITY AND US: VR IS AS REAL AS ANY REALITY CAN BE

Virtual reality (VR), easily the most dramatic and far-reaching product of the information age, is a fast-evolving concept. It is a concept whose roots go deeper than most of us suspect. We think of VR as a modern concept yet its conceptual source goes back before the beginning of time, before the Big Bang initiated the evolution of our universe. We, as generators of computer-based VR games, are simply expressing the stuff of which we are made … as does the result of any fractal process. Evolution itself is a fractal process that is generated by a process-fractal as opposed to a geometric-fractal. A process-fractal is created as the output of each progressive application of a process becomes the input for the next iteration of that process. Simply put, we humans, a product of an evolving virtual reality universe, have evolved to the point where we are now reexpressing the core pattern of our existence in VR "games" that are evolving to create their own universes. This is the nature of fractals, to reexpress themselves on all the potential levels and scales upon which they operate.

We play virtual reality games that are getting less limited, larger in scope, and more realistic every year—a trend that has only barely begun and will only speed up over time. Virtual reality is a much bigger idea than video games, indeed, one should see virtual reality as a tool for the generation of human experience within the context of the VR's defining rule-set—that is what makes it a reality. Any sort of reality, including our "physical" universe, does nothing more for us than that—provide a perceptual experience within the context of its defining rule-set. One could reasonably argue that the Internet itself defines a limited virtual reality—an information-based, computed, context within which people (as both providers and users) can freely interact (experience). Social media generate virtual communities with all the breadth and depth of connection and interaction as any nonvirtual community. Don't confuse the word "virtual" with the word "artificial" or "not real." Virtual reality, is a collaborative (multiplayer) reality based on intellectual, emotional, and spiritual interactions as a result of information flows between participants. Physical reality is exactly the same thing with taste, touch, and smell data added to the information flow. Both have their advantages and disadvantages. Virtual reality has the ability to provide a much richer and very much less constrained, intellectual and emotional space in which to experience and interact. Physical reality's strong point is that it supports the possibility of physical closeness—the taste, smell, and touch side of experience. Both are completely real, fundamentally real. As our reality expands, so must our vocabulary. What we mean by the word "real" will need to expand as we move through the 21st century and beyond little picture habits of thinking.

We speak of our online experiences as virtual experiences with virtual friends who are intimately sharing their lives with…with…strangers? No, it is the sharing of information that builds bonds of real friendship between people, not the proximity of bodies. It is more often our neighbors, and many of the people we work with every day, who are the "virtual" characters (real strangers) in our lives…bodies that share our physical world but with whom we have little to no meaningful interaction. Friends are those you care about who also care about you, and this caring and sharing within real and meaningful relationships is not exclusively or even primarily generated by the proximity of physical bodies.

The mix of friends and strangers that you meet every day in physical space is no more or less real than the friends and strangers that you meet every day in cyber space—they are simply different because different sets of constraints and freedoms (different rule-sets) apply to each group. *It is not that there are two separate realities: physical reality (real, significant, and meaningful) and virtual reality (imaginary, less significant, and less meaningful), but that there is one real, significant, and meaningful reality, some of which is physical and some of which is virtual.*

To this one real, significant, and meaningful reality of ours, let's add our imagined and dreamed (both night and day dreaming) realities. Each of these reality frames contains its own rule-set that defines what we can and cannot do there, each has its own range of perceptions and interactions, intents and choices, value and purpose. Each enriches our life with useful experience. When you realize that you are a multidimensional being living, working, and playing (experiencing and making choices) in multiple reality frames—and that these frames are simply all different with none being more or less real than the others—you will have moved from the little picture to the big picture view of your existence.

Note that I did not say that these various reality frames were equal in all ways, I simply said that they were all equally real. Some may be more signifi-cant, demanding, flexible, relentless, quixotic, fulfilling, dependable, and use-ful than others, however, any of them may exhibit any of these attributes some of the time. All of them provide a platform for us to experience, make choices, and thus evolve the character and substance of ourselves. What is more important or fundamental than that?

Worry not that we (particularly the young) of the 21st century are losing touch with the *real* world, when, in fact, we have simply enlarged the *real* world—making it a bigger and more interesting place. The "virtual" com-munity, as it expands and deepens, will eventually evolve into a powerful and influential global community. There is nothing more real, in an every-day practical sense, than power and influence. As the virtual world approaches universal participation, the concept of a "citizen of the world" (without the penalty of massive political upheaval) begins to become a reality. This is good news for all of us.

All of the realities in which we operate (experience, learn, grow, express ourselves, and reap the consequences of that expression) have limitations as well as the capacity to enrich and expand our lives, our awareness, and our perspective. The more we live in the big picture, the broader and deeper our perspective becomes, and the more we are able to use and process (find synergistic value in) all of our experiential data.

THE LOGIC OF VIRTUAL REALITY

Anyone can see VR engulfing us from the direction of information sharing and social networking, but most of us are unaware of the fact that our physi-cal reality is looking more and more like a virtual (computed) reality—a conclusion that is quickly gaining ground within the field of physics. It seems the facts measured by experimentalists can only be explained if our "physical" reality is not physical at all but rather a virtual reality. During the last decade, in an accelerating process, more and more physicists have come to the conclusion that we are living in an information-based, computed, virtual reality. Yes, that means the "physical" universe we call home is likely to be an interactive, multiplayer, virtual reality game somewhat like *The*

Sims or *World of Warcraft* except that, instead of being programmed, our VR universe has evolved from a set of initial conditions constrained by a rule-set (more like the recently released, procedurally generated *No Man's Sky*). This time-driven, dynamic simulation initially started computing with a metaphorical "Big Bang" that began when the "run button" was clicked.

For those not familiar with the gamming terminology of "virtual reality," "rule-set," "player," and "avatar," I will use the well-known interactive, multiplayer, virtual reality game *World of Warcraft* (WoW) as an example. The "player" is the human sitting at his computer logged on to the WoW game on the Internet. There may be thousands of human players playing their own characters (elves, barbarians, wizards, etc.) in this same game (interacting with each other) at the same time. The virtual characters being played (elves, barbarians, wizards, etc.) are called "avatars." Each player is playing his own personal unique avatar. The "computer" is the game-server that is hosting the game (in which all the computations defining game-play are performed). The game is defined within the computer by initial conditions and a "rule-set" that determines the interactive nature of the "virtual reality" and all the possible interactions that can take place there (i.e., defines the VR's causality—all possible actions, interactions, and consequences).

There are three components that make up a virtual reality: (1) the computer that computes the virtual world (reality) and all the consequences of actions and interactions occurring within that world according to the VR's rule-set. (2) The player who does all the computed avatar's thinking and makes all of the avatar's choices. (3) The computer's output—a data-stream sent to the player that shows avatars interacting within their computed VR environment. Of these three, only the computer and the player are interactive elements. The computed VR world, called a reality frame, is simply a collection of data in the computer's memory that keeps track of the VR's computed environment and the entities who interact within that environment (e.g., avatars). In other words, it computes and tracks in time who is doing what where and computes the logical consequences of all actions and interactions according to the rule-set.

The players (decision makers) and the computer (source of VR) are in a dance of exchanging data while the result of this dance is an ever-changing array of 1s and 0s within the computer's memory (computer output) that define and track the consequences of every interaction. The processed result of those 1s and 0s is immediately displayed to as many of the player's senses as practical (sight and sound mainly, but smell, touch, taste may sometimes be incorporated in limited ways in more elaborate VR implementations) and are subsequently interpreted by the player to represent the virtual world which includes the VR's landscape, other players, and the player's own avatar.

The player plays the role of the avatar's consciousness. The player makes choices within the constraints of the VR's rule-set. The avatar does nothing unless the player sends instructions to the computer (data flow from player to computer). The computer implements the player's choices (animates the avatar within the context of the VR and computes consequences) and, of course, the player must then deal with the consequences of those choices (data flow from computer to player). The player learns to make better, more productive choices as he/she gains experience with the abilities and constraints of his/her avatar and with the constraints of the virtual world. Both sets of constraints are imposed by the VR's rule-set.

The concept of an interactive multiplayer virtual reality carries with it several interesting logical consequences that are true of *all* virtual realities: The player and the computer must exist in the same reality frame because they must continually and directly communicate with (send data back and forth) each other. The computer that generates the VR cannot be a product of the VR or function from within the VR. The computer must reside in a reality frame *other* than the virtual reality frame it is computing because a simulation cannot compute itself. A reality frame is called "physical" by an observer if the observer is in that reality frame, and "nonphysical" if the observer is not in that frame. For example, the WoW reality frame would appear physical from the perspective of the elf that inhabits it. Furthermore, from the elf's perspective, the computer and player must reside in a nonphysical reality frame. In other words, it is simply the logical nature of VRs that the computer (VR's source) and players (avatar's consciousness) must share a reality and appear nonphysical to a perspective that is located inside of the VR world. From the player's and the avatar's perspective, each must see the other as existing in a nonphysical reality. The descriptors "physical" and "nonphysical" denote nothing fundamental, each is simply a matter of perspective. The reality frame in which you are presently having direct experience is the one that seems physical to you, and the one that exists outside of your direct experience appears nonphysical to you.

PHYSICS, METAPHYSICS, AND THE NATURE OF CONSCIOUSNESS

From the Introduction, we saw that science is being forced, by virtue of its own experiments, to declare that our "physical" universe and, thus, our "physical body and brain" are virtual—just 1s and 0s on a nonphysical "hard drive" in some *other* reality frame that appears nonphysical to us. If this is true (and it does indeed seem most likely to be true), logic tells us that we (our awareness, our cognitive, conscious self) are not our bodies at all, and not produced or generated by our body. The logical implication is that we are a nonphysical choice making awareness (our consciousness) playing a virtual avatar (our body) within a virtual reality (our "physical" universe). The person we know as our conscious self or mind [called an individuated unit of consciousness (IUOC)] logically must exist in a reality-frame that appears (from our avatar's perspective within the VR) to be nonphysical. This IUOC, playing our virtual body, is totally immersed (experiences only what the avatar experiences—i.e., has no other point of view or perspective than the avatar's) within a 3D VR game that we know as *Life on Earth within the Physical Universe*. As the Buddha told us 2600 years ago, our physical reality is an illusion.

The more fundamental reality frame that contains the player and computer is in the form of a digital information system called the larger consciousness system (LCS). The LCS must seem nonphysical to us because we, the IUOC, have our VR avatar's perspective. Consciousness is all about information and the choice-making that is the result of processing that information. We IUOC players are subsets of this larger consciousness system. The computer that computes our VR is another type of subset of the LCS as is the management and coordination function (operating system).

This all seems very confusing because we have attached our identity to our avatar rather than to ourselves as consciousness (an IUOC). The virtual human avatar brain stores nothing, and processes nothing—all of that is done by the IUOC. The virtual body-brain simply represents the abilities and constraints of the avatar according to the VR's rule-set. Hit an avatar human body on the head with an iron pipe and the constraints that avatar's player (IUOC) has to work with will change according to the rule-set by which this VR initially evolved (and is still evolving). The damage incurred by this avatar is calculated according to the rules of the VR game (physics and biology in this case) and though the consciousness playing that avatar is structurally unaffected, it now has to deal with its newly constrained avatar. Perhaps that consciousness (IUOC) will again start receiving a data-stream from the computer when its avatar wakes up in a hospital with a terrible headache but healing nicely according to the rules upon which our seemingly physical reality frame (including our uniquely evolved biology) is based. That's life, stuff happens, and we have to deal with it. What matters in the game is *how* you, the individuated unit of consciousness, deal with it.

The purpose of the game is for the IUOC to continuously improve the quality of its choices—how to change itself (learn, grow up) so that it interacts and deals with circumstances, events, and challenges more effectively.

So now you know what we are (consciousness), how we are (part of an information system called the larger consciousness system), and what sort of experiential reality frame we operate in (computed virtual reality). Next, let's figure out *why* we exist, and why we are in this VR. Since we are subsets of this larger consciousness system we need to understand why the LCS evolved us and why would it go to the trouble of also evolving a VR for us to play (experience and learn) in? To answer this question we have to know more about the LCS and what its needs are.

Entropy is a measure of disorder. If all the bits in an information system are random (maximum entropy) the system contains no information and, thus, is only a potential information system. As bits become ordered and organized, entropy is reduced and information is created. If the ordering reflects some purpose, function, or reason, information is created that has specific meaning, significance, and value. Information systems evolve (become more functional and useful) by lowering their entropy. Consequently, the purpose of the larger consciousness system is to lower its overall entropy. Increasing its entropy would lead to its eventual disintegration (de-evolution) into randomness (death for an information system), while decreasing its entropy leads to a continuous evolution of greater organization, complexity, and significance.

Earlier we mentioned that the process of evolution can, if the possibilities of the evolving system are sufficient, generate a process fractal. If you know something about fractals you know that their extent, complexity, and level of intricate detail is often unbounded (has no end). Since the possibilities of creative consciousness are themselves unbounded, the product of a consciousness–evolution process fractal has potential complexity and intricacy far beyond our capacity to imagine—if, and only if, it has the ability and capacity to continually decrease its entropy. Is this possible, can it somehow manage to continually lower its entropy? To answer those questions, let's take a look at where this LCS came from. We cannot define the origin of primordial consciousness (since we *are* consciousness that is logically problematical—one is never in a position to observe one's own beginning) but we can surmise a potential evolutionary path that primordial consciousness may have taken to become the larger consciousness system of today. Our challenge, then, is to find the minimal conditions (assumptions) required to allow for the evolution of the larger consciousness system.

Establishing origins that greatly predate any historical evidence is always difficult because we have only assumptions and conjecture to work with— all the hard facts from direct experience are long gone from the reality frame that contains, and is defined by, the LCS. Furthermore, none of those hard facts would likely be contained within our virtual reality (our physical universe) since it is only a tiny computed (virtual) subset of the larger system. With as few as possible assumptions, we must design a most probable, logical path of evolution for the LCS that can explain *all* the data (all the links in the causal chain) to which we do have access.

Consider two relatively new concepts based in mathematics: emergent complexity and cellular automata (CA). Cellular automata (see Conway "Game of Life" for a simple example) represent the simplest form of a process fractal. With the proper, but still simple, rule set, cellular automata can emulate the functions of a general-purpose computer. CA process fractals, with very simple rule-sets and extremely rudimentary processing, can create unbounded complexity much as geometric fractals do. Emergent complexity, a science that demonstrates the ability of a system with chaotic initial conditions to eventually evolve lower entropy structures through trial and error evolution, could deliver that rule-set to a rudimentary information system capable of assessing its own degree of randomness.

The fact that this primordial LCS could intentionally distinguish between states at all means that it had some sort of rudimentary "awareness" and that it had a choice to be this way (1) or that way (0). Therein lies our first *assumption*; that a primordial choice-making awareness (primordial consciousness) existed—a pretty mundane assumption since consciousness does indeed exist. Our second *assumption* is that evolution by natural selection exists—another mundane assumption that needs little justification. These two assumptions logically include: time and memory (needed to distinguish between two states and support the cumulative change required by evolution). It also needed the capacity to make choices about what to do with its 1s and 0s to better accomplish its purpose (lower its entropy), thus free will choice, and at least a dim awareness of its need to lower entropy is eventually required.

Think of consciousness as the media and evolution as the process that iterates upon the media. This iterative process generates a "process fractal" wherein the unbounded result eventually becomes an immense integrated complexity on many different levels and scales—one building upon the other. Also, every creation of that complexity still carries the traits of the original pattern of evolving consciousness—a simple self-aware information system with the purpose of lowering its entropy. Perpetually evolving—becoming more in order to avoid becoming less. Constantly evolving into every possibility—going forward with what works and letting go of what doesn't. The present result: The larger consciousness system—the fundamental source of our reality and causality, the pattern from which we IOUCs are cut.

From two assumptions (that consciousness and evolution both exist) this model has now produced an evolving, aware LCS (a digital information system) that is constantly looking for ways to lower its entropy, that is, to find new relationships and new meaningful connections—new ways to organize its available bits. One major breakthrough was developing the technology of *regular* time by generating a stable constant frequency of a 1–0 to 0–1 state change, thus defining reality's smallest quantum of time and enabling sequences as well as patterns of 1s and 0s within its organizational tool set. Another breakthrough solution to the creeping entropy problem was to not just act but to interact. To create subsets of itself that were also aware choice makers—individuated units of consciousness with the free will to interact (exchange data or communicate) as they see fit.

In this way, the LCS evolves to become a social system with endless interactive possibilities that create a huge potential for entropy reduction. In a repetition of this evolutionary strategy, single-celled critters in the primordial seas of virtual Earth also divided (cell division) themselves to become more complex, lower entropy multicelled critters. Then, multicelled entities formed even more complex (more highly organized and thus lower entropy) critters by developing diverse cell specialization (specialized organs within a single body). It would seem that procreation, diversity, and cooperative interaction define the path to lower entropy systems. And now it is our (humanity's) turn to take the next step down that same evolutionary path. We have the first one down pat (procreation), are struggling with the second (embracing diversity), and failing miserably with the third (cooperating on both the individual and species level). So let's take a more detailed look at where we are failing—the need to cooperate—what does that mean?

What sort of interactions/choices among the IUOCs are likely to lower both individual and system entropy? Cooperative interactions and choices, collaboration with, and caring about, others are the processes that optimize a social system of IUOCs. And what sort of interactions and choices are likely to raise entropy within this newly founded social network? Self-centered and self-focused choices made by fearful IUOCs who believe they must continually work on making themselves better off and more secure at the expense of others. Universal attitudes of love, caring, and mutual trust will enable a social *system, and the individuals* within that system, to optimize overall value, satisfaction, and productivity. Universal attitudes of fear, self-centeredness, and mutual mistrust will enable a social system to minimize value and productivity for the *system as well as for the individual*.

The first is the path of love, while the second is the path of fear. In an information system that needs to lower entropy in order to survive and progress (evolve), making choices that move one toward becoming love (simultaneously lowering the entropy of themselves and the system) becomes the goal of every IUOC.

So that is what we are here for? To lower the entropy, and thus raise the quality, of our individual consciousness and the consciousness of the system by evolving our ability to make love-based choices rather than fear-based choices? Yes! Because we are subsets of the whole, our personal entropy reduction also reduces the entropy of the entire system. But why here, in this VR? You have no doubt heard of VR flight trainers where new pilots learn to fly airplanes, well, this VR we play in (our "physical" universe) is an entropy reduction trainer for budding individuated units of consciousness. Reducing entropy and increasing organization within the system is equivalent to creating meaningful, useful content (information) within the system. The bottom line is that the LCS digital information system evolves by creating long-term useful relationships, connections, structures, and patterns generated through cooperative interaction. This occurs as a natural result of individual IUOCs optimizing their own entropy reduction in their own way, in their own time, and to their own personal satisfaction.

Every IUOC has a communications link to every other IUOC. Individual intent turns this communication link on or off. Imagine a chat room with no rules. Now, imagine thousands of IUOCs in this chat room at the same time. This describes the initial condition of the LCS after sub-dividing itself into a large number of interacting (choice-making) individu-ated units of consciousness. Choices were limited to why, when, and what to communicate. Learning to lower one's entropy from one's choices was problematical since there were few measurable consequences. The system needed some rules and constraints to provide solidity, a consistent context for interaction, a causal chain that defines consequences, and instructive feedback to the IUOCs. In other words, the LCS needed some sort of experiential context in which individuated units of consciousness could more effectively and efficiently pursue their purpose (i.e., increase the functional quality of their consciousness, become love, grow "spiritually," or simply grow up) by making progressively better, more effective, free will choices that, on the average, lowered rather than raised their entropy.

The solution to this problem of dysfunctionally slow entropy reduction among the growing number of IUOCs was to evolve a virtual reality simulation like our universe. Such a simulation (virtual reality game) could deliver a virtual experience generator with sufficiently strong interactive causality (generated by the rule-set) to produce the feedback that efficient learning demands: that every choice eventually be unavoidably connected to the consequences of that choice. After much trial and error, the LCS evolved a set of initial conditions that provide a medium for the VR and a rule-set that defines the possible and likely interactions within that medium. Together, these initial conditions and constraints allowed the evolution of an interactive VR entropy reduction trainer—think of a simulated big bang eventually evolving into a VR that we call our "physical" universe. The LCS then let IUOCs immerse themselves as players in this entropy reduction trainer once the VR (our "physical" universe) evolved avatars (what we call life forms) with sufficiently complex interactions to provide an IUOC with interesting choices that could facilitate its personal evolution.

LIFE IN A VIRTUAL REALITY ENTROPY REDUCTION TRAINER

The content explained above is not entirely new. The understanding that our so-called physical reality is an illusion, and that the point and purpose of our life here is to become love has been around for thousands of years. Indeed, small enclaves of this sort of "enlightenment" have bubbled up in every age and on every continent. What is new is that today this information has moved from the poetry of sages to the logic of scientists. The same logic that offers a sound scientific understanding of consciousness also offers a more accurate and complete understanding of physics. Long-standing paradoxes that have confounded physicists for decades are now easily solved by straightforwardly applying the logical consequences of the ideas just discussed—without creating any new paradoxes. Quantum physics goes from "weird science" to just science. Physics and metaphysics, mind and matter, normal and paranormal, objective and subjective are all seamlessly joined under one relatively simple set of fundamental principles. One bigger picture that explains it all as logical science. These startling facts combined with the advent of the Internet are changing everything... drastically...and relatively quickly (decades) compared to times past where centuries, or more often, millennia were required for major cultural, philosophical, and technological paradigm shifts to become a widely spread understanding at the species-level.

While those local enclaves of enlightened, big picture understanding remained isolated (geographically and conceptually), fragmented (poetry is open to interpretation), and marginalized (by belief, creeping dogma, and the mainstream status quo), the online communities of today have the ability to stimulate the opening of minds, distribute unfiltered information, and find common cause across all the historic boundaries of separation and isolation. The Internet has the ability to decentralize our thinking as it disburses fresh ideas. This is a powerful combination that is fueled today by an open and free Internet feeding a quickly growing community of open minds eager to dig into something more than the mindless high profit-margin Pablum they receive from the centralized control-based mind-set of the establishment. The Internet, as a byproduct of doing what it does, will simultaneously lubricate (speed up) both social and individual evolution— that is its true power.

It would seem that human evolution has been trying in vain to emulate, at our own level of complexity, the evolution undergone by single-celled entities as they cooperatively formed multicelled entities, and how multicelled entities cooperated with arrays of cellular subsets that produce specialized functions (internal organs and specialized body parts). All of these higher and higher levels of cooperation exist because they produce more complex and flexible (more survivable and successful) entities with lower entropy configurations. Now it is our turn to cooperate with each other to reduce the entropy in ourselves and our relationships, to grow the quality of our consciousness. We humans (who represent the most versatile of multicelled entities with specialized functional subsets) need to find the cooperative connections to each other to enable this VR entropy-reduction trainer to both individually and collectively rise to the next level of cooperative organization. Not like the wall-to-wall cells of a complex human body— that was the solution at the cellular level of complexity—but rather in human social configurations that simultaneously optimize individual freedom and choice along with collective productivity and viability.

For several million years the human race has been getting ready for the day (evolving ourselves and our social structures) when we finally get the opportunity to actualize our evolutionary destiny of taking consciousness and this VR (and thus our own individual consciousness evolution) to the next level of cooperative organization. For two million years we have struggled to grow up enough such that when the time was ripe and the tools we needed were in place, we could fulfill our mission to take the next big step in consciousness evolution. Guess what? That time has finally come! The missing tool that is critical to us becoming one worldwide human family (a functional, not a dysfunctional family) is the Internet…or what the Internet will become. A tool that allows us to share, to cooperate, to understand, to grow up and find a bigger picture wherein *all* of us prosper to the extent of our gifts and abilities. To do so we must evolve at the species level toward becoming love, toward caring, cooperation, and compassion. This is impossible on a planet of our size without some sort of technology that can give us direct access to each other.

On the other hand, simply generating the necessary communication tools is not enough, by itself, to actualize our evolution. We must individually and collectively be up to the task. We must embrace cooperation and let go of self-centeredness; embrace compassion and caring and let go of disdain and arrogance; embrace giving and let go of greed; embrace love and let go of fear. If we are not ready to evolve to the next level of cooperation, hopefully the communication tools will still be around to bind us together when we are ready.

The trend is obvious: At first we are individuals, then we become cooperative members of families, then cooperative members of tribes, then of villages, cities, states, countries, regions, and finally we become cooperative citizens of the world. Each transition toward more complex social organization and lower entropy depends on gaining broader, more far-reaching capabilities (often facilitated by technology) in the areas of mobility and communications—a successive shrinking of the world—or equivalently, a successive expansion of our interaction and cooperation. When the world shrinks to the size of a family or our caring and cooperation expands to the size of the world, we will be close to success. Yes, we have a long way to go. But now, just in the last several decades, we have created the technological backbone to support a future set of tools that has the potential to connect us face to face—as if we were peering directly into the human potential reflected within each other's eyes through a clear window of sight and sound no matter where we are on this globe. And this tool set of social applications now running on the Internet is just beginning to evolve. This is an opportunity we humans have never experienced before. I hope, and expect, that one day we will make the most of it and of all the new capabilities and connections it will spawn. I look to the information age to finally take us home to where the love is and to where the future lies. There is no other future for us but this one. For we are consciousness with a single purpose, and that purpose is to survive by evolving the quality of our consciousness—to decrease our entropy on a path toward becoming love.

BOUNDARIES OF SELF AND REALITIES ONLINE

Now you have the context to see what the Internet is all about in the biggest picture. What it is in the process of doing to our children's minds, and to our minds, is preparing us for, and giving us a pathway toward, the future. Of course, the Internet, the core technology of the information age, is still in its infancy—a wild untamed territory with villains and abusers as well as heroes and everyday folks just trying to make a living. The industrial age started out the same wild and wooly way but settled down significantly in a century or two. It won't take the Internet that long to domesticate itself as long as it stays open and free.

Indeed, we need to be aware of the Internet's warts and ugly parts in order to not end up a victim of its allure to our fear and ego. This challenge of first needing to tame the technological beasts we create is expected, especially in a reality frame that contains a significant number of entities with a low quality of consciousness (more fear than love)—a condition that certainly describes contemporary humanity on planet Earth. However, it is also necessary to focus on what good the Internet is doing, and more importantly, what good it can do, and how it might change us for better or worse. For indeed it will eventually change us dramatically...even more so than the combined industrial and scientific revolutions changed us. The industrial-technological revolution, driven by the engine of science, was about gaining and applying knowledge of the outside material world. It delivered efficiency to the production of goods and tools as well as a cornucopia of machines, giving us all sorts of wonderful stuff we now cannot live without—including the Internet. For the vast majority of us humans, the industrial revolution was about control. Gaining control of goods and services, our environment, and of each other...but not of ourselves. We developed a materialistic viewpoint, and became obedient (to our government and corporate masters) sheep-like conformists in pursuit of a consumer paradise—an illusion we swallowed hook, line, and sinker.

The information age is about information, the stuff of which we IUOCs are made. It will affect us far closer to the core. It will change both us and our reality in ways we cannot yet imagine. By contrast, the information revolution is driven by the engine of sharing and forging new connections between individuals. It is about personal fulfillment, creating useful content, integrating knowledge of both the outside material world and the inside subjective world of choice and relationship. It delivers immense efficiency to the process of providing useful content and choice to both users and providers of information without our government and corporate masters selecting that content for us. This newly acquired personal freedom of connection, sharing, and interaction has resulted in a very significant transfer of power to the people. In only a few decades, it has likewise spawned a cornucopia of shared information that drives scientific, commercial, social, and personal interactions that have become core components of our everyday lives. For the vast majority of us humans, the Internet undermines the control of local central authority, providing the freedom necessary for us to individually express ourselves and interact directly with the self-expression of others. It gives us a vastly larger perspective of the world and our place in it. The Internet intrinsically has what it takes to enable us to develop a bigger picture, a more holistic viewpoint, and most importantly, an ability to gather, organize, and apply our collective influence. An influence that will one day relegate governments and corporations to their rightful roles as the providers of services and products that we need to support a world we truly enjoy living in. Can you imagine: A government that actually is of the people, by the people, and for the people…corporations that *serve* the marketplace rather than *exploit* it? Hard to imagine, isn't it? It is the future!

Be aware and be prepared: central control does not give up its power easily and the struggle has just begun. Remember, after "*Star Wars, A New Hope*" came "*The Empire Strikes Back*" …that is the way it usually works in this VR. However, evolution is, by its nature, relentless. Eventually, consciousness, as it is expressed in this VR, will evolve toward lower entropy states (toward expressing love). As we individually and collectively develop a more balanced viewpoint, that values caring and sharing more than self-focused, fear-based materialism, we will become obedient to no one, free to authentically explore our individual potential in pursuit of our own (and thus automatically the collective) consciousness evolution.

The Internet can be used to pry open minds or to close minds. It can be used to pull us together in cooperation or push us apart in fear. If the Internet is free and open it will tend to open minds and pull us together in cooperation, if it is not free and open, it will tend to close minds and control us with fear. Are we grown up enough individually and collectively to choose (in the near term, say, over the next 30 years) freedom and love over control and fear? Only time will tell. In the far term (eventually) we will succeed in our mission of expanding individual freedom within human collective cooperation. The process of consciousness evolution within this VR can be exceedingly slow, it can stumble and regress backward, but through persistence it will eventually reach its evolutionary goal of ubiquitous caring, compassion, and love… however many millennia that may take.

Wherever we are in the growing up (consciousness evolution) process, a free and open Internet is part of that process. It provides us with a broader perspective while overwhelming us with information, thus teaching us the necessity of applying discrimination, critical thinking, and skepticism to our daily lives. Critical long-term thinking skills that only got in the way of an industrial process that needed to control all the variables in the short term, pay large dividends in finding and discriminating value within the information age. Our individual perspective and collective viewpoint is growing bigger, more inclusive, more tolerant of diversity, and wiser as we are bathed daily in worldwide information from tens of thousands of different sources— each one with its own slant and agenda.

We, as cooperative information providers and users, are now in the process of evolving the emotional, intellectual, and technological tools to effectively process this flood of information. As we immerse ourselves in the data flow that defines modern society, attitudes and perspectives will change as a bigger picture of reality and our purpose develops. In days gone by, it was extensive travel that gave us access to diverse information culminating in a more informed and sophisticated viewpoint making us less narrowly provincial (less easily manipulated). Travel was (and still is) expensive and problematical. Only the very rich traveled extensively and comfortably. Today, information from the world over comes to us, up close and personal, at our convenience, for a very small cost. The narrowly provincial viewpoints that have delivered bigotry and prejudice of all sorts to our social fabric, are finally shrinking, hopefully becoming extinct as our perspectives and understanding of each other broaden.

Citizens of the world need to have a perspective that circumscribes the world—a circumstance that has never been possible for the masses until very recently. What makes family members a family is the ease and quality of their communication and caring. *Only citizens of a world who have an innate sense of being empathetically connected to everyone else, are likely to become responsible, productive members of that world.* A world primarily populated by individuals who deeply care about each other must be either a very small village, or a virtual world of any size tied together with widespread broadband communications technology. The potential of the Internet to deliver us to a bigger picture of ourselves and of the world has barely been explored. Likewise, the potential of humans to interact with each other with kindness, cooperation, and caring has also barely been explored.

Note that both systems (consciousness and the Internet) are information based. Both are computed (data input→information processing→data output). The capacity and potential of both systems is immense, far beyond our present understanding. Both are symbiotic elements of the same fractal system (the larger consciousness system) and both will necessarily have to evolve together in order for either to actualize its potential.

By now, it should be clear that there are no fundamentally important boundaries between ourselves, our personal reality, and the reality online. Our local personal perspective and reality is simply expanding interactively to include our online friends and fellow human beings. Where each lives in "physical" space is not that significant anymore. We have common issues, interests, and dreams that are much more important and significant than the latitude and longitude of where we sleep at night.

The future is ours to construct. The path forward is clear. The only question remaining is how long it will take us to grow up enough to recognize the potential, to see the light, to let go of fear, ego, and belief, to remake our world on the ethos of compassion, cooperation, and caring, to take the next major step in the evolution of our individual and collective consciousness? The tools are at hand…are we ready?

The only thing we have the power to change fundamentally is ourselves—that is where the solution must start—all else is dependent on each of us accomplishing that.

INDEX

Printed and bound by CPI Group (UK) Ltd, Croydon, CR0 4YY

11/06/2025

01899189-0002